Runrön

Runologiska bidrag utgivna av

Institutionen för nordiska språk vid Uppsala universitet

22

The printing of this book is made possible by a gift to the
University of Cambridge in memory of Dorothea Coke,
Skjæret, 1951, and through a gift by
Charles and Myrna Smith.

Runrön

Runologiska bidrag utgivna av
Institutionen för nordiska språk vid Uppsala universitet

22

Michael P. Barnes

THE RUNIC INSCRIPTIONS OF THE ISLE OF MAN

Based on a manuscript by R. I. Page,
and with contributions by James E. Knirk,
K. Jonas Nordby, Henrik Williams and Sir David Wilson

Institutionen för nordiska språk, Uppsala universitet
Viking Society for Northern Research, University College London
2019

Abstract

Barnes, Michael P. 2019. The Runic Inscriptions of the Isle of Man. Based on a manuscript by R.I. Page, and with contributions by James E. Knirk, K. Jonas Nordby, Henrik Williams and Sir David Wilson. *Runrön. Runologiska bidrag utgivna av Institutionen för nordiska språk vid Uppsala universitet* 22. 359 pp. Uppsala. ISSN 1100-1690, ISBN 978-0903521-97-0.

This volume provides a comprehensive edition of the runic inscriptions of the Isle of Man. All but two of these are written with Scandinavian runes in forms of Scandinavian language, and the edition thus fills a major gap in coverage of Scandinavian runic activity in the British Isles. The Shetlandic, Orcadian, Scottish and English corpora have already been edited in *The Scandinavian Runic Inscriptions of Britain* (2006) and *The Runic Inscriptions of Maeshowe, Orkney* (1994), while the runic artefacts from Ireland – the title notwithstanding – are examined in *The Runic Inscriptions of Viking Age Dublin* (1997). The Manx inscriptions form a discrete group in that they are all carved in stone (chiefly on stone crosses), are mainly of commemorative type, and appear for the most part to belong within a rather narrow time frame: c. 925–1020.

Each inscription is given detailed treatment, which includes transrunification (a conventionalised rendering of the runic graphs), transliteration into roman characters, a description of the runes and an interpretation of the content. The history and background of the runic artefacts are also investigated, and the work of earlier scholars in the field evaluated. There is copious illustration in the form of photographs and drawings (both recent and historical). Seven introductory chapters precede the detailed analysis of the corpus. These deal with general matters such as the genesis of the edition, the character of the corpus, the form and decoration of the stones, the history of Manx runic studies, dating, rune forms and runic orthography, and the language of the inscriptions. An appendix provides a handy key to the different ways of referring to the stones and their inscriptions that have over time been generated.

All of the inscriptions included in the present work have been described and discussed previously, but few of the earlier treatments fulfil the requirements of a modern scholarly edition. With the publication of this volume a resource for further and wider investigation of the Manx runic corpus has been established.

Key words: runes, runology, runic inscriptions, Old Norse, Anglo-Saxon, Scandinavian language history, orthography, transliteration, language contact, art history, archaeology, Isle of Man.

Michael P. Barnes, Department of Scandinavian Studies, University College London, Gower Street, London WC1E 6BT, England.

© Michael P. Barnes 2019

Reprinted: 2023

Typesetting: Rätt Satt Hård & Lagman HB
Typeface: Century Expanded

ISSN 1100-1690
ISBN 978-0903521-97-0

Printed by Short Run Press Limited, Exeter

Contents

Preface 15

Maps

Map 1. The Isle of Man in the Irish Sea region 21
Map 2. Distribution of runic inscriptions in the Isle of Man 22

Introductory chapters

1. Modus operandi 25
2. The Manx runic corpus 31
3. The form and decoration of the stones, by David M. Wilson 38
4. Some early drawings and discussions of Manx runic inscriptions 48
5. The dating of the Scandinavian runic inscriptions of Man 57
6. Rune forms and orthography 64
7. Language 79

The corpus

MM 99 Andreas I 89
MM 131 Andreas IIa–b 96
MM 128 Andreas III 100
MM 113 Andreas IV 104
MM 111 Andreas V 107
MM 121 Andreas VI 111
MM 193 Andreas VII 113
Andreas VIII † (recorded in an early drawing) 114
MM 106 Ballaugh 118
MM 159 Balleigh † 125
MM 112 Braddan I 127
MM 138 Braddan II 130
MM 136 Braddan III 135
MM 135 Braddan IV 139
MM 176 Braddan V 142

MM 200 Braddan VI	145
MM 118 Bride	146
MM 107 German I (St John's) *a–b*	151
MM 140 German II (Peel)	156
MM 127 Jurby	160
MM 102 Kirk Michael I	166
MM 101 Kirk Michael II	169
MM 130 Kirk Michael III	174
MM 126 Kirk Michael IV	182
MM 132 Kirk Michael V*a–b*	185
MM 129 Kirk Michael VI	192
MM 110 Kirk Michael VII	195
MM 123 Kirk Michael VIII	197
MM 139 Marown	200
MM 145 Maughold I	203
MM 144 Maughold II	207
MM 133 Maughold III	211
MM 142 Maughold IV*a–f*	213
MM 175 Maughold V	222
MM 141 Onchan *a–g*	227
MM 42 Maughold AS I	238
MM 43 Maughold AS II	240
Appendix. Cross-references to the principal naming and numbering systems applied to the Manx runic corpus	244
Abbreviations	247
Bibliography	249

Plates and figures

Acknowledgements	261

Plates

Plate 1. MM 99, Kermode's face A	263
Plate 2. MM 99 Andreas I	263
Plate 3. MM 99 Andreas I, rr. 1–20	264

Plate 4. MM 99 Andreas I, rr. 18–39 264
Plate 5. MM 99 Andreas I, rr. 37–50 265
Plate 6. MM 99 Andreas I, rr. 1–8 in detail 265
Plate 7. MM 131, Kermode's face A 266
Plate 8. MM 131 Andreas II*a* 266
Plate 9. MM 131 Andreas II*a*, rr. 1–19 267
Plate 10. MM 131 Andreas II*a*, rr. 17–35 267
Plate 11. MM 131 Andreas II*a*, rr. 35–54 268
Plate 12. MM 131 Andreas II*b* 269
Plate 13. MM 131 Andreas II*b*, in detail 269
Plate 14. MM 128, Kermode's face A 270
Plate 15. MM 128, Kermode's face B 271
Plate 16. MM 128 Andreas III 272
Plate 17. MM 128 Andreas III, before the lengthwise split 272
Plate 18. MM 113, Kermode's face B 273
Plate 19. MM 113 Andreas IV 273
Plate 20. MM 111 Andreas V, Kermode's face B with the inscription 274
Plate 21. MM 111 Andreas V, before the breakage 275
Plate 22. MM 111 Andreas V, showing the broken end 276
Plate 23. MM 121, Kermode's face A 277
Plate 24. MM 121 Andreas VI 278
Plate 25. MM 193 Andreas VII, decorated face and inscription 278
Plate 26. MM 193 Andreas VII, with the assumed original orientation
    of the runes 278
Plate 27. MM 106, Kermode's face A 279
Plate 28. MM 106 Ballaugh, Kermode's face B with the inscription 280
Plate 29. MM 106 Ballaugh, rr. 1–41 281
Plate 30. MM 106 Ballaugh, rr. 16–40 281
Plate 31. MM 106 Ballaugh, rr. 41–7 282
Plate 32. MM 159 Balleigh † 282
Plate 33. MM 112 Braddan I, MM 136 Braddan III, and MM 135
    Braddan IV, situated on a mound on the south side of Braddan Old
    Kirk churchyard 283
Plate 34. MM 112 Braddan I, Kermode's face B with the inscription 284
Plate 35. MM 112 Braddan I, rr. 1–15 284
Plate 36. MM 112 Braddan I, rr. 13–27 285
Plate 37. MM 112 Braddan I, rr. 26–33 285
Plate 38. MM 112 Braddan I, rr. 33–40 285
Plate 39. MM 138, Kermode's face A, oriented as the stone must
    originally have stood 286

Plate 40. MM 138 Braddan II, Kermode's face B with the inscription,
   oriented as the stone must originally have stood 287
Plate 41. MM 136, Kermode's face A 288
Plate 42. MM 136, Kermode's face B 288
Plate 43. MM 136 Braddan III 289
Plate 44. Museum of Scotland cast IC7 of MM 136 Braddan III,
   showing rr. 1–47 289
Plate 45. MM 135, Kermode's face B 290
Plate 46. MM 135 Braddan IV 290
Plate 47. MM 135 Braddan IV, rr. 1–19 291
Plate 48. MM 135 Braddan IV, rr. 17–38 291
Plate 49. MM 135 Braddan IV, rr. 37–52 and putative IHSVS 292
Plate 50. MM 176 Braddan V 293
Plate 51. MM 200 Braddan VI 293
Plate 52. MM 118, Kermode's face A 294
Plate 53. MM 118, Kermode's face B 294
Plate 54. MM 118 Bride 295
Plate 55. MM 118 Bride, rr. 1–22 295
Plate 56. MM 118 Bride, rr. 21–45 295
Plate 57. MM 107, decorated face 296
Plate 58. MM 107 German I (St John's) *a* 296
Plate 59. MM 107 German I (St John's) *a*, rr. 1–10 297
Plate 60. MM 107 German I (St John's) *a*, rr. 10–22 297
Plate 61. MM 107 German I (St John's) *a*, rr. 18–28 298
Plate 62. MM 107 German I (St John's) *b* 298
Plate 63. MM 140 German II (Peel) 299
Plate 64. MM 140 German II (Peel), rr. 1–18 299
Plate 65. MM 140 German II (Peel), rr. 13–30 300
Plate 66. MM 140 German II (Peel), rr. 27–41 300
Plate 67. MM 140 German II (Peel), rr. 35–41 in detail 301
Plate 68. MM 127, Kermode's face A 302
Plate 69. MM 127 Jurby, Kermode's face B with the inscription 303
Plate 70. MM 127 Jurby, Kermode's face B with the more fully
   preserved inscription in Robert Paterson's photograph of 1862 304
Plate 71. MM 127 Jurby 305
Plate 72. MM 102, Kermode's face A 306
Plate 73. MM 102 Kirk Michael I, Kermode's face B with the
   inscription 306
Plate 74. MM 102 Kirk Michael I 307
Plate 75. MM 101, Kermode's face A 308

Plate 76. MM 101 Kirk Michael II, Kermode's face B with rr. 65–84
visible at the top 308
Plate 77. MM 101 Kirk Michael II, rr. 1–18 309
Plate 78. MM 101 Kirk Michael II, rr. 15–41 309
Plate 79. MM 101 Kirk Michael II, rr. 40–64 310
Plate 80. MM 101 Kirk Michael II, rr. 65–76 310
Plate 81. MM 101 Kirk Michael II, rr. 77–84 310
Plate 82. MM 130, Kermode's face A 311
Plate 83. MM 130 set into the top of the churchyard wall and showing
Kermode's face A 311
Plate 84. MM 130 Kirk Michael III set against the churchyard wall
and showing Kermode's face B with the inscription 312
Plate 85. MM 130 Kirk Michael III, rr. 1–17 313
Plate 86. MM 130 Kirk Michael III, rr. 13–30 313
Plate 87. MM 130 Kirk Michael III, rr. 24–47 314
Plate 88. MM 130 Kirk Michael III, rr. 36–61 314
Plate 89. MM 130 Kirk Michael III, rr. 51–71 315
Plate 90. MM 130 Kirk Michael III, rr. 72–96 315
Plate 91. MM 130 Kirk Michael III, rr. 85–103 316
Plate 92. MM 130, the ogam inscription on the runic face 316
Plate 93. MM 126, Kermode's face A 317
Plate 94. MM 126, Kermode's face B 317
Plate 95. MM 126 Kirk Michael IV 318
Plate 96. MM 126 Kirk Michael IV, rr. 1–13 318
Plate 97. MM 126 Kirk Michael IV, rr. 12–22 318
Plate 98. MM 132, Kermode's face A 319
Plate 99. MM 132, Kermode's face B 319
Plate 100. MM 132 set on a horse block and showing Kermode's face B;
right: Kirk Michael V from the same photograph 320
Plate 101. MM 132 Kirk Michael V*a*, rr. 1–14; preceding and below
rr. 1–8, Kirk Michael V*b* is visible 321
Plate 102. MM 132 Kirk Michael V*a*, rr. 12–30 321
Plate 103. MM 132 Kirk Michael V*a*, rr. 25–43 322
Plate 104. MM 132 Kirk Michael V*a*, rr. 43–57 322
Plate 105. MM 132 Kirk Michael V*a*, rr. 52–7 and male figure above 323
Plate 106. MM 132 Kirk Michael V*b*, rr. 1–13 324
Plate 107. MM 132 Kirk Michael V*b*, rr. 12–26 324
Plate 108. MM 129, Kermode's face A 325
Plate 109. MM 129, Kermode's face B 326
Plate 110. MM 129 Kirk Michael VI 327

Plate 111. MM 110, Kermode's face A 328
Plate 112. MM 110, Kermode's face B 329
Plate 113. MM 110 Kirk Michael VII, rr. 1–7 330
Plate 114. MM 110 Kirk Michael VII, rr. 5–11 330
Plate 115. MM 123, the surviving face 331
Plate 116. MM 123 Kirk Michael VIII 331
Plate 117. MM 123 Kirk Michael VIII, rr. 1–7 in detail 332
Plate 118. MM 123 Kirk Michael VIII, rr. 11–15 in detail 332
Plate 119. MM 139 Marown, visible face with the inscription 333
Plate 120. MM 139 Marown 333
Plate 121. MM 145 Maughold I and the ogam inscription 334
Plate 122. MM 145 Maughold I 335
Plate 123. MM 145 Maughold I, rr. 30–36 in detail 335
Plate 124. MM 144 Maughold II, visible face with the inscription 336
Plate 125. MM 144 Maughold II, rr. 1–10 337
Plate 126. MM 144 Maughold II, rr. 9–21 337
Plate 127. MM 144 Maughold II, rr. 19–26 337
Plate 128. MM 144 Maughold II, rr. 27–38 338
Plate 129. MM 144 Maughold II, rr. 35–48 338
Plate 130. MM 144 Maughold II, rr. 44–55 338
Plate 131. MM 133, the surviving face 339
Plate 132. MM 133 Maughold III 339
Plate 133. MM 142 Maughold IV, "face A" with inscriptions IV*a* 1,
    IV*a* 2, and IV*e* visible 340
Plate 134. MM 142 Maughold IV*a* 1, rr. 1–18 341
Plate 135. MM 142 Maughold IV*a* 1, rr. 17–31 341
Plate 136. MM 142 Maughold IV*a* 2 341
Plate 137. MM 142 Maughold IV, "face B" with inscription IV*a* 3 and
    (faintly visible) IV*f* 342
Plate 138. MM 142 Maughold IV*a* 3, rr. 1–12 with inscription IV*f*,
    rr. 1–11, below 343
Plate 139. MM 142 Maughold IV*a* 3, rr. 7–19 with inscription IV*f*
    below 343
Plate 140. MM 142 Maughold IV*b* 343
Plate 141. MM 142 Maughold IV*c* and IV*d* with most of inscription
    IV*b* below 344
Plate 142. MM 142 Maughold IV*e* 345
Plate 143. MM 142 Maughold IV*f* 345
Plate 144. MM 175 Maughold V 346
Plate 145. MM 175 Maughold V, rr. 1–8 347

Plate 146. MM 175 Maughold V, rr. 8–17	347
Plate 147. MM 175 Maughold V, rr. 17–20	348
Plate 148. MM 175 Maughold V, rr. 21–5	348
Plate 149. MM 175 Maughold V, rr. 24–32	348
Plate 150. MM 175 Maughold V, rr. 29–37	349
Plate 151. MM 175 Maughold V, rr. 38–46	349
Plate 152. MM 141 Onchan, Kermode's face A with Onchan *a*, *b*, and *c*	350
Plate 153. MM 141 Onchan, Kermode's face B with Onchan *e*, *f*, and *g*	351
Plate 154. MM 141 Onchan, the photograph of Kermode's face B displayed in Kirk Onchan, showing Onchan *e*, *f*, and *g*	352
Plate 155. MM 141 Onchan *a*	353
Plate 156. MM 141 Onchan *b* (above) and *c* (below)	354
Plate 157. MM 141 Onchan *d*	354
Plate 158. MM 141 Onchan *e* on the photograph of Kermode's face B displayed in Kirk Onchan	355
Plate 159. MM 141 Onchan *f* (right) and *g* (left, inverted in relation to *f*) on the photograph of Kermode's face B displayed in Kirk Onchan; below: Onchan *g*, rotated 180°, from the same photograph	355
Plate 160. MM 42 Maughold AS I, the decorated face with design and inscription	356
Plate 161. MM 42 Maughold AS I, main design and inscription	357
Plate 162. MM 42 Maughold AS I	358
Plate 163. MM 43 Maughold AS II, the decorated face with design and inscription	359
Plate 164. MM 43 Maughold AS II	358

Figures (except where otherwise stated, the Figures enumerated below are the work of Jonas Nordby)

Fig. 1. MM 99 Andreas I	90
Fig. 2. MM 99 Andreas I, Cumming's 1857 drawings (1857: fig. 10)	91
Fig. 3. MM 131 Andreas II*a*	97
Fig. 4. MM 131 Andreas II*b*	99
Fig. 5. MM 128 Andreas III	101
Fig. 6. MM 113 Andreas IV	105
Fig. 7. MM 111 Andreas V	109
Fig. 8. MM 121 Andreas VI	112

Fig. 9. MM 193 Andreas VII 114
Fig. 10. Andreas VIII †, recorded in the third line of BL MS Add. 70484, Misc 17 (the first line depicts Kirk Michael V*a*, the second Andreas II*a*) 117
Fig. 11. MM 106 Ballaugh 121
Fig. 12. MM 159 Balleigh † 126
Fig. 13. MM 112 Braddan I 128
Fig. 14. MM 138 Braddan II 132
Fig. 15. MM 136 Braddan III 136
Fig. 16. MM 136 Braddan III, one of Cumming's *c.* 1855 rubbings (fol. 108r) 137
Fig. 17. MM 135 Braddan IV 140
Fig. 18. MM 176 Braddan V 143
Fig. 19. MM 200 Braddan VI 145
Fig. 20. MM 118 Bride 147
Fig. 21. MM 107 German I (St John's) *a* 152
Fig. 22. MM 107 German I (St John's) *b* 155
Fig. 23. MM 140 German II (Peel) 157
Fig. 24. MM 127 Jurby 162
Fig. 25. MM 127 Jurby, Cumming's *c.* 1855 drawings (fol. 29r) 163
Fig. 26. MM 127 Jurby, Cumming's 1857 drawings (1857: fig. 11) 165
Fig. 27. MM 102 Kirk Michael I 167
Fig. 28. MM 101 Kirk Michael II, rr. 1–64 170
Fig. 29. MM 101 Kirk Michael II, rr. 65–76 171
Fig. 30. MM 101 Kirk Michael II, rr. 77–84 171
Fig. 31. MM 130 Kirk Michael III 176
Fig. 32. MM 130 Kirk Michael III as portrayed in Gibson's 1722 revision of Camden's *Britannia* (pp. 1457–8) 178
Fig. 33. MM 130 Kirk Michael III, Cumming's 1857 drawings (1857: figs 28–9) 179
Fig. 34. MM 126 Kirk Michael IV 183
Fig. 35. MM 132 Kirk Michael V*a* 186
Fig. 36. MM 132 Kirk Michael V*a*, MM 135 Braddan IV, and MM 131 Andreas II*a* as portrayed in Gibson's 1722 revision of Camden's *Britannia* (pp. 1459–60) 188
Fig. 37. MM 132 Kirk Michael V*a*, MM 135 Braddan IV, MM 131 Andreas II*a*, and MM 130 Kirk Michael III as portrayed in Gough's 1789 revision of Camden's *Britannia* 189
Fig. 38. MM 132 Kirk Michael V*b* 192
Fig. 39. MM 129 Kirk Michael VI 193

Fig. 40. MM 110 Kirk Michael VII 196
Fig. 41. MM 123 Kirk Michael VIII 198
Fig. 42. MM 139 Marown 201
Fig. 43. MM 145 Maughold I 204
Fig. 44. MM 144 Maughold II 208
Fig. 45. MM 133 Maughold III 212
Fig. 46. MM 142 Maughold IV*a* 1 216
Fig. 47. MM 142 Maughold IV*a* 2 216
Fig. 48. MM 142 Maughold IV*a* 3 and IV*f* 216
Fig. 49. MM 142 Maughold IV*b* 216
Fig. 50. MM 142 Maughold IV*c* and IV*d* 217
Fig. 51. MM 142 Maughold IV*e* 217
Fig. 52. MM 175 Maughold V 223
Fig. 53. MM 141 Onchan *a* 231
Fig. 54. MM 141 Onchan *b* and *c* 231
Fig. 55. MM 141 Onchan *d* 231
Fig. 56. MM 141 Onchan *e* 233
Fig. 57. MM 141 Onchan *f* and *g* 233
Fig. 58. MM 42 Maughold AS I 239
Fig. 59. MM 43 Maughold AS II 241

Preface

The genesis of this volume is explained in ch. 1 'Modus operandi', while ch. 4 'Some early drawings and discussions of Manx runic inscriptions' offers a brief introduction to the history of Manx runic studies. The aim of the present work is to provide a modern scholarly edition of the runic inscriptions of the Isle of Man, thus filling a major gap in coverage of the Scandinavian runic inscriptions of the British Isles (see Barnes 1994; Barnes, Hagland and Page 1997; Barnes and Page 2006). Man also boasts two inscriptions in Anglo-Saxon runes, and these are included in the edition for their intrinsic interest as well as for completeness' sake.

The edition consists of (1) two maps, (2) seven introductory chapters dealing with particular aspects of the Manx rune-stones and their inscriptions, (3) individual entries on each inscription (following a set pattern, described in ch. 1, pp. 28–9), (4) an appendix cross-referencing the naming and numbering systems that have been applied to the Manx corpus, (5) a list of abbreviations, (6) a general bibliography, and (7) Plates illustrating stones and inscriptions. Additionally there are Figures accompanying the individual entries. These consist (a) of early drawings (and one rubbing), (b) drawings made specially for the edition. The latter are secondary to the descriptions and not intended as primary evidence. It is worth stressing, however, that each such drawing derives from one or more digital photographs and has been checked against the inscription itself by at least two runologists.

A broad view has been taken of the Manx runic material. While considerable weight is given to runological and linguistic questions, e.g. graph-types and their phonological implications, orthography, language contact and its possible consequences, attention is also directed to matters such as dating and the implications of what the inscriptions say for our (limited) understanding of Manx society at the time they were made. Emphasis is in addition placed on the nature of the discovery of the rune-stones, their subsequent history and their treatment by earlier scholars.

Throughout the work the terms "Viking Age" and "Middle Ages" are used. These are elastic concepts and there is little agreement about the beginning and end date of either period, let alone subdivisions within them. Here, "Viking Age" refers to the years AD 700–1050 (early VA 700–850; mid-VA

850–975; late VA 975–1050), and "Middle Ages" to the span 1050–1525 (early MA 1050–1200; high/mid-MA 1200–1300; late MA 1300–1525). All these dates are of course approximate.

The general bibliography (pp. 249–60) is a tool designed for use with the individual entries and introductory chapters. It makes no claim to exhaustiveness, but every contribution referred to in the work should have found a place there. For those seeking a wider selection of ancillary literature, there is always Marquardt's 1961 bibliography, though much has of course been written on the Manx inscriptions since the early 1960s.

Throughout the preparation of this edition, extensive help has been given by a wide range of institutions and individuals, and it is a pleasure to record here the obligations that have been incurred and to offer some token of thanks. None of the work could have been undertaken without the assistance of those who have the Manx rune-stones and runic fragments in their care: the Manx Museum, and the authorities and wardens of Kirk Andreas, Ballaugh Old Church, Braddan Old Kirk, Kirk Bride, German St John's, Kirk Patrick Jurby, Kirk Maughold, Kirk Michael, and Kirk Onchan. The compilers have been greatly assisted by various institutions, curators and archivists: the British Library, the Bodleian Library Oxford, the Dictionary of Old Norse Prose Copenhagen (in particular Þorbjörg Helgadóttir), the Manx Museum Library and Archives (in particular Sue Nicol), National Museums Scotland, Oslo Runic Archives, Universitetsbiblioteket Oslo, World Museum Liverpool. Where individual scholars have helped us, we trust we have given full acknowledgement within our text, but a number deserve to be singled out for special mention: Frances Coakley, for generously providing a copy of her electronic compendium *A Manx Note Book*, James Graham-Campbell for much sound advice on the art of the Manx rune-stones, Dave Quirk for readily sharing with us his expertise on the geology of Man, Paul Russell for painstaking and invaluable help with the identification of Irish personal names, Alison Sheridan and colleagues (National Museums Scotland) for providing excellent photographs of cast IC7 of MM 136 Braddan III, Edmund Southworth (Director, Manx National Heritage) for general assistance and encouragement, Ross Trench-Jellicoe for illustrations of MM 159 Balleigh and for important information on this stone and its discovery. To Andrew Johnson of Manx National Heritage go particular thanks. He facilitated several visits to examine the inscriptions, and on one of them gave up two whole days to act as chauffeur and guide. He also located a number of early photographs and organised their transmission to us, and in addition provided several elusive pieces of bibliographical information. Sir David Wilson, as well as writing a complete chapter for the edition, has throughout offered generous hospitality and willingly shared with us his encyclopaedic knowledge of the Manx stones and their art.

Without the blessing and enthusiastic participation of the research project *The Reading and Interpretation of Runic Inscriptions: the Theory and Method of Runology* (based at the Centre for Advanced Study at the Norwegian Academy of Science and Letters, Oslo, 2013–14), it is unlikely this edition would have been completed – certainly it would have been much the poorer. The crucial role played by the project, and in particular by James Knirk, its director, and Henrik Williams, are documented in ch. 1 (pp. 25–7), but other members of the group too gave great assistance: Martin Findell provided copious information on MM 42 Maughold AS I and MM 43 Maughold AS II, Judith Jesch took many excellent photographs of the stones and their inscriptions and readily gave permission for a large number of them to be included in this book, while Magnus Källström made drawings of and notes on all the inscriptions and kindly placed them at the edition's disposal. Jesch and Källström, furthermore, read the completed work and offered many valuable comments on points of detail. Jonas Nordby was not part of the Oslo project, but with his considerable runic expertise and technological skills, he devoted much time to the task of making computerised drawings of all the inscriptions to accompany the texts and Plates of the edition. Together with James Knirk, Nordby compiled an almost complete photographic record of the Manx runic stones, from which the majority of our Plates stem. Knirk, in addition, undertook the demanding and time-consuming task of Photo-Shopping the images, enhancing many of them, avoiding too great a degree of overlap, and ensuring reasonable consistency of lighting, size, etc. Indeed, so great was his input that he could justly be considered Plate editor of the volume.

Many individuals and institutions assisted Ray Page in his preliminary work on the Manx rune-stones, work which forms the foundation of this edition (see ch. 1). There is, however, difficulty in acknowledging all these separately since it is not always clear precisely who was involved and in what capacity. Rather than mention just some, we offer here a general thanks to all who in any way contributed to Page's labours.

Generous grants from The Royal Gustavus Adolphus Academy for Swedish Folk Culture helped several of the participating runologists to make visits to Man. For these contributions we offer our profound gratitude.

Maps

PART IV

Map 1. The Isle of Man in the Irish Sea region

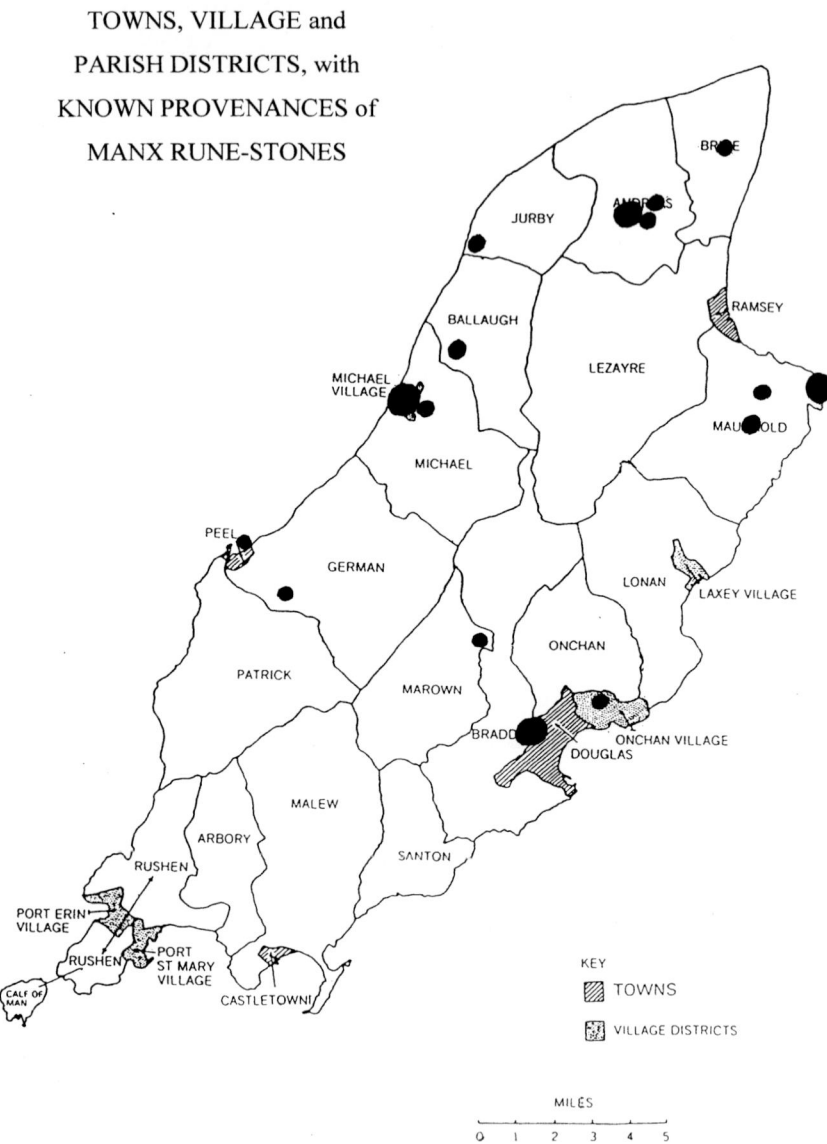

Map 2. Distribution of runic inscriptions in the Isle of Man

Introductory chapters

1. Modus operandi

This is a book that has been long in preparation. R.I. Page began working on the Manx Scandinavian runic corpus more than half a century ago – as early as the 1950s on the evidence of certain of his comments. Over the years he published several articles on the subject (most important are those from 1980, 1981 and 1983), but he never managed to complete the full corpus edition he had envisaged and had worked to bring to fruition. On his death in 2012, he left a number of preparatory drafts in the form of print-outs. These comprised accounts of each of the Scandinavian inscriptions from Man (based on repeated personal examination) and three general chapters with the titles 'On recording the Manx Scandinavian rune stones', 'The Manx corpus' (see ch. 2), and 'Some early drawings and discussions of Manx runic inscriptions' (see ch. 4). Among his papers there were also photocopies of early representations of certain of the Manx rune-stones and their inscriptions, personal drawings, copious notes, and a rudimentary bibliography.

In 2013 all Page's Manx material was passed by his widow Elin to Michael Barnes in the hope that it might be made ready for publication. In the academic year 2013–14 Barnes was a member of the research project *The Reading and Interpretation of Runic Inscriptions: the Theory and Method of Runology*, based at the Centre for Advanced Study at the Norwegian Academy of Science and Letters, Oslo. Seizing the opportunity he took Page's manuscripts and materials with him to Norway, and discussed the whole question of a corpus edition of the Manx runic inscriptions with other members of the project, in particular James Knirk, the leader, and Henrik Williams. It was decided that production of the edition should be incorporated into the Oslo project as a particularly apt example of field runology in practice. Barnes began by digitising all of Page's print-outs. This proved to be much more than a secretarial task, however, since it rapidly became clear that there were still large amounts of work to be done. Many of Page's accounts of individual inscriptions were far from complete, and most were decorated with marginal notes enjoining the author to check this and add that. His materials also threw up a great many questions, and it was felt that if Barnes and others were to take ultimate responsibility for the edition, they would have to re-examine each and every detail for themselves. An additional problem was the almost complete lack of illustrative material. And finally: Page had omitted the two Manx Anglo-Saxon runic inscriptions on the grounds that they represented a different tradition from the Scandinavian; Barnes, Knirk and Williams, however, were all agreed that these should be included for completeness' sake.

In the light of these various circumstances, it was determined that Barnes would circulate his amended electronic versions of Page's manuscripts to Knirk and Williams for comment. Having done so and considered their responses, Barnes prepared second drafts, which he submitted for further scrutiny and comment. Third drafts were then produced, and a field trip to Man organised to check the latest revised versions against the stones and inscriptions themselves. The trip took place over the period 23rd–30th March 2014; participating were Knirk, Williams, Magnus Källström and Jonas Nordby (Barnes himself was unable to travel for personal reasons). All the stones and inscriptions were subjected to detailed examination except MM 128 Andreas III (on loan to the *Vikings: Life and Legend* exhibition), and the face of MM 141 Onchan that bears inscriptions *e, f, g* (this is placed tight up against a wall of Kirk Onchan and the stone cannot not be taken down without risk of damage). In addition to checking Page's readings, and his and others' commentaries, members of the group took numerous photographs (a great many of which have found a place in this edition); considerable archival work was also done in the Manx Museum.

Armed with the material gathered on this trip Barnes produced revised versions of his third drafts, which were again scrutinised by Knirk and Williams. During the year in Oslo Barnes also compiled three additional introductory chapters: 'The dating of the Scandinavian runic inscriptions of Man' (ch. 5), 'Rune forms and orthography' (ch. 6), and 'Language' (ch. 7). In addition he revised Page's 'The Manx corpus', and 'Some early drawings and discussions of Manx runic inscriptions' and distributed the material in his 'On recording the Manx Scandinavian rune stones' across other chapters. These efforts, like the accounts of individual inscriptions, were submitted to Knirk and Williams and rewritten as appropriate in the light of their comments. On the basis chiefly of photographs taken during the April 2014 trip, Jonas Nordby compiled computerised drawings of each of the inscriptions.

In late 2014 Sir David Wilson agreed to contribute to the edition a chapter entitled 'The form and decoration of the stones' (ch. 3). This was submitted in early 2015, and reviewed by Barnes, Knirk and James Graham-Campbell, not least to ensure reasonable consistency with other parts of the volume.

Barnes and Knirk then spent the week 16th–23rd April 2015 in Man. They re-checked all readings, and compared Nordby's drawings with the inscriptions themselves, making various emendations. On this occasion it was possible to examine Andreas III, which had been returned to Man at the close of the Viking exhibition. The hidden face of Onchan, however (cf. above), remained inaccessible. Additional archival work was undertaken in the Manx Museum.

Over the summer of 2015 slightly amended drafts of all individual entries and introductory chapters were completed. Revised drawings were received from Nordby in October of that year and compared with the current reading and account of each inscription. During the course of 2015–16 a range of historical photographs was provided by the Manx Museum. In September 2016 the twenty-ninth symposium of field runologists took place in the Isle of Man, and this provided a further opportunity to check readings, take photographs and discuss problems. Resulting from work done at the symposium, Nordby made small adjustments to his drawings and the final versions were submitted in the autumn of 2018.

Close examination of the Manx rune-stones poses various problems (see p. 35 on their positioning within buildings). Some of them have hard surfaces that do not readily succumb to weathering. Others are more porous and granular, and it is these that cause most difficulties. We have frequently had to question how much can be read with certainty, how much with the eye of prejudgement, how much by guesswork. It is, for instance, hard and in some cases impossible to determine whether the opening or closing of a text is defined, and by what sort of symbol: a cross, a saltire, a faint vertical, or something other. Or is a rough patch in front of or after a text nothing more than that, an unworked section? A stone surface can be affected by casual pitting as well as wear or weathering. This may give the initial impression of word separation, but it may not be possible to define the separation symbols with any precision. How many are there? And are they dots, short vertical lines, or some form of cross? Direction of lighting can help, but can also confuse. It is striking how greatly inscriptions can appear to vary with light from different angles. This certainly applies to porous surfaces, and here we may expect divergent readings from individual runologists. Surprisingly, some of the lines carved on hard stone are also affected. A line which, from certain angles of lighting, appears clearly carved, may from others look like a chance chip or an accidental mark on the stone surface.

We have tried in our descriptions to be as dispassionate as possible: to record what we think to have seen. But we have not always agreed among ourselves, and the reader must allow for a margin of uncertainty. (On the sense of "we" and its implications, see the final paragraph of this chapter.)

In our accounts of the individual inscriptions (which also embrace informal sequences previously ignored or referred to in passing as "graffiti", cf. pp. 35–6) we follow a set pattern. Included in the heading is the Manx Museum number of the artefact and the name of the inscription, e.g. MM 99 Andreas I. In the matter of names we adopt those found on current Ordnance Survey maps (preferring in most cases place- to parish names), thus: Kirk Michael, Onchan, rather than the "Michael", "Conchan" of some previous investigators (on the classification of the Manx runic stones and their inscriptions, see pp. 31–2). Unless particularly germane to the discussion (as under MM 133 Maughold III, for example), National Grid References (NGRs) have been dispensed with: the original find-spots of several of the Manx rune-stones are uncertain, and we do not know for sure where any of the monuments were originally set up. Insofar as a stone is associated with and now kept in a particular church, the relevant NGR is easily ascertained from an Ordnance Survey map.

Following the heading is a section entitled LITERATURE. Here are listed what we judge the most significant contributions to the elucidation of the inscription under discussion. For readers who require fuller coverage, the list begins with a reference to the relevant entry in Marquardt (1961), although after the passage of 57 years, this once all-embracing bibliography is now somewhat out-of-date. The general bibliography that accompanies the present edition is intended to embrace every contribution to which reference is made.

Accounts begin with discussion of the circumstances in which stones and their inscriptions came to light and were recorded by early investigators. Thereafter the subsequent history of the object is detailed insofar as it is known. There follows a crude geological determination of the rock type, together with height, width and depth measurements. Many stones are fragmentary and irregular in their present state, so it can be hard to know how to measure and where from. In addition, they have often been set in concrete foundations in modern times, making it impossible to establish full height (in most cases P.M.C. Kermode's height measurements are also given since he appears to have had access to the stones while they were out of the ground; we round his inches up or down to the nearest whole centimetre). It would not surprise us if future field runologists were to arrive at slightly different measurements from our own. Last in this section comes a rudimentary description of the artefact: its ornamentation, if any, and the location on it of the runic inscription.

Our reading follows, given in the forms both of a transrunification (cf. pp. 67–8) and a transliteration in bold type (pp. 65–7). Thereafter is a description of individual graphs and separators, which will vary in complexity according to the state of preservation, carefulness of carving, and clarity of layout of each text. To assist the reader here, we have provided drawings of the inscriptions (cf. above), based on photographs, but checked during our 2015 and 2016 examinations of the originals. This section ends with a list of the diagnostic rune forms encountered in the inscription (cf. p. 71).

We then move on to the interpretation of the text, beginning, for consistency and ease of reference, with a version in normalised Old West Norse, immediately followed by a translation into English (some inscriptions are of course so fragmentary that no text can be established). Whereas in the descriptive passages we have tried to be as objective as possible, here we express our opinions about the material. We consider the views of earlier scholars on such matters as speech sounds and phonology (using both phonetic and phonemic notation, as appropriate), grammar, language affiliation, personal names, dating, sometimes agreeing with them and sometimes not; and we try to cast the investigative net a little wider than various of our predecessors. Because the language of the texts can on occasion deviate quite considerably from the Old West Norse ideal, the account ends with a transcription into a local, Manx variant that we hope reflects interesting features in the speech of the carver that can be obscured by the Old West Norse normalisation (cf. pp. 84–5). Celtic personal names are given in normalised Old Norse form in the edited West Norse texts, and in an approximation to the assumed Scandinavian pronunciation in the Manx transcriptions; in the English translations the Irish form is used, except where there exists a well-established anglicised form of the name (as, e.g., Patrick).

In a composite work of this kind, there is inevitably some overlap and repetition. One and the same phenomenon can be relevant in several contexts, and there is a limit to the number of cross-references that can be provided. Indeed, some repetition may aid general readability and help fix particular points more firmly in the reader's mind. Varied authorship also brings the danger of inconsistency, in matters like punctuation, compounding v hyphenation v separation ("runestone", "rune-stone", "rune stone"), and even in spelling. We have tried to eliminate this, but cannot be sure we have got rid of it altogether, and we ask our readers' understanding for any discrepancies that remain. We have also striven for consistency of notation in our composite bibliography, but have come up against occasional difficulties, not least in referring to certain Manx periodicals. These can undergo complex changes of title and numbering, and many years can elapse before the publication of a complete volume. We have sought to replicate titles as accurately as possible and (for the sake of the reader) to give dates close to the writing or first publication of a piece (rather than final publication of a volume). Information on the date of first publication in particular can be elusive. Indexes can vary in their attributions, and essential information can be lost as fascicules are bound together in a single volume and their covers consigned to the bin.

All this having been said, and bearing in mind the various reservations expressed, we believe the present edition of the runic inscriptions of the Isle of Man provides as reliable a guide to its subject matter as can reasonably be achieved in the current state of our knowledge.

A final note. As has been made clear, this edition is the product of work by several runologists. The use above and throughout the book of "we" and related first person plural pronouns forms is intended to reflect this. The readings presented and the arguments and views advanced have often resulted from discussions between Knirk, Williams and Barnes, while Page's preliminary studies form the starting-point of large parts of the edition. Nevertheless, ultimate editorial control has been exercised by Barnes, and such errors, inconsistencies and wrong-headed notions as may be found are his responsibility alone.

2. The Manx runic corpus

It is remarkable that, at any rate as far as today's finds go, the only runic inscriptions on Man are those carved in stone, most of them clearly memorial slabs. These rune-stones divide into two distinct groups, English and Scandinavian. The English group is small, comprising just two examples, from the same general find place, Maughold churchyard. Both give a personal name – seemingly the same one – and nothing more (pp. 238–43). By contrast, the Scandinavian corpus consists of well over 30 rune-stones or fragments thereof, some with quite extensive texts (and some with more than one). They are associated with a number of sites in the northern two-thirds or so of the island (Map 2). For a survey of their background and early record, see Page 1980 (also ch. 4 below).

Over the years there have been developed several different modes of referring to these stones. For general purposes the Manx Museum and National Trust has given each of them its number, prefixed by MM, and that is used in this edition, though as far as practicable it is applied to the monument as a whole rather than its inscription. For the inscriptions themselves we employ a slightly modified version of the naming system adopted by Magnus Olsen in his 1954 account. He divided the corpus into groups that reflected the parishes in which the stones were found (our system is for the most part based on the places – in effect the churches – with which they are associated, but in the majority of cases this makes no difference to an inscription's name; cf., however, p. 28). Odd man out in Olsen's scheme is MM 159 Balleigh, found in the parish of Lezayre and preserved, until its recent disappearance, in Lezayre church (cf. p. 125). Olsen's system was in turn based on the classification established by Brate (1907). Brate organises (and numbers) the inscriptions according to the "alfabetiska ordningsföljd" 'alphabetical order' of their names (1907: 22), such that the Andreas inscriptions come first, followed by Ballaugh, Braddan, and so on. What he does not explain fully is the order in which he places inscriptions grouped under the name of a particular parish (e.g. Andreas I, II, III, IV, etc.) There is a vague reference to "Kermode", which appears to be to his 1892 *Catalogue*, and to a large extent Brate's numbering follows the order there, but by no means entirely. The Brate-Olsen reference system is thus somewhat arbitrary, as is that applied by the Manx Museum and National Trust. Neither reflects the order of discovery of the rune-stones, nor do they necessarily concentrate in groups stones that come from the same site. Indeed, the Brate-Olsen method may put, under the same parish name, stones that derive from places quite far apart. Their German I was discovered at St John's (and is still there). Their German II is from Peel, some 4 km farther west (and is in the Manx Museum). Yet these systems are convenient to use if the reader takes care – the Brate-Olsen one continues, for example, in Sannes Johnsen (1968) and (in all essentials) Holman (1996) – and it seems unnecessary to invent a further pattern of numbering or naming for the present edition. Nor is it clear on what it might be based (though cf. the brief discussion under Andreas VII, p. 113). Thus the first entry in this edition is named Andreas I and numbered MM 99, the second is Andreas II, MM 131, and so on; and from Andreas we proceed alphabetically to Ballaugh, Balleigh, Bride, and arrive finally at Onchan. As noted, MM 99 and 131 refer first and foremost to the stones with their carvings, Andreas I and II to the runic inscriptions. The Manx Museum and Brate-Olsen reference systems are not the only ones. Kermode's *Manx Crosses* from 1907 still has, very properly, much prestige – and was republished in photographic facsimile in 1994. This work gives each cross a number, which may occasionally be quoted, as Kermode 73 (= MM 99 Andreas I). To assist the reader, an Appendix supplies cross-references for the three systems.

The two English inscriptions from Maughold have previously been numbered Maughold I and II (e.g. Page 1999: 143–4). This is impractical in the present work, dealing as it does with inscriptions in both the English and Scandinavian traditions, since Maughold I and II are designations also given to two Scandinavian examples from Maughold church or parish. As a distinguishing mark the letters AS (Anglo-Saxon) are added to the English inscriptions, making them Maughold AS I and Maughold AS II.

With declining attendance, there is a danger some Manx churches may close. What in such circumstances might be the fate of any archaeological artefacts they hold is unclear. The prospect does, however, raise the possibility that the designations currently given to runic and non-runic crosses may one day to a lesser extent than hitherto identify the places where they are housed.

The Manx Scandinavian runic inscriptions are markedly different from those found in nearby territories. The only comprehensive study of the inscriptions from Ireland (Barnes, Hagland and Page 1997) lists 16 items, 14 of them on portable objects, of wood, antler, bone, and metal (and since 1997 a further one in wood has been published, see Barnes and Hagland 2010). Just two are on stones, IR 2 Killaloe and IR 3 Beginish. Of these Killaloe alone is a carved standing cross, though its inscription (or possibly what is left of it) mentions the raiser only and does not formally record any one's memory. It also has an ogam text invoking a blessing, apparently on the raiser. From the mainland of England facing the Irish Sea the latest relevant runic corpus edition (Barnes and Page 2006) lists only the Bridekirk font (E 1), the Carlisle Cathedral graffiti (E 3, now augmented by the find of a further graffito in the building, cf. Barnes 2010), the Dearham slab (E 6, also sporting what seems to be a graffito), the Pennington tympanum (E 9), the lost (but recently rediscovered) Conishead stone, on which someone has inscribed a personal name (E 11), and the Penrith silver brooch (E 15), which is probably an import. None of these bear any obvious similarity to the runic inscriptions of Manx tradition. From nearby Scottish territory and the Western Isles, there is likewise little: the Kilbar cross (SC 8), the fragmentary Inchmarnock cross (SC 10) and Iona slab (SC 14), the Holy island graffiti (SC 3–7, 9, 12–13, fairly clearly made by visitors rather than inhabitants) and the elaborate Hunterston brooch (SC 2). Of these only Kilbar and Inchmarnock have possible connections with runic practices on Man (on the status of Kilbar, cf. Barnes and Page 2006: 227–32).

Not only is the Manx corpus different from those of surrounding areas, it is also, relatively speaking at least, much larger. At the current count thirty-six rune-bearing stone objects, complete or fragmentary, have been found on the island (thirty-four Scandinavian, two English). The total number of runic inscriptions is a little higher since some of the stones carry more than one discrete text (though some of these could be of later date than the bulk of the corpus). To the overall tally we can add a lengthy Scandinavian inscription recorded around 1700, which almost certainly does not survive (cf. pp. 114–18). Comparison of these figures with the approximately fifty runestones known from Viking-Age Norway and the scattering from the Irish Sea region makes clear that Man occupies a remarkable position in the history of runic writing. The island is only some 570 km^2 in area, insignificant when measured, for example, against Norway's roughly 324,000 km^2; and although thinly populated, Norway must have had vastly greater numbers of inhabitants than Man. Various reasons have been suggested for the vigorous tradition of rune-stone raising that developed in the island: the availability of easily worked local stone, the fusion of the Celtic habit of raising crosses with the Scandinavian one of putting up runic memorials, the encouragement of the Church, which is likely to have welcomed any method of recording for Christian purposes. Easily worked stone was of course also to be found in areas where Scandinavian settlers raised few or no runic monuments, England being a particularly striking example. There the Anglo-Saxons erected rune-stone memorials, apparently with the encouragement of the Church (Page 1999: 34–5); their newly-arrived Scandinavian neighbours, however, failed to follow suit. It is thus perhaps the intermingling of Celtic and Scandinavian culture in Man that provided the chief impetus. And once started, the idea of erecting rune-inscribed commemorative crosses may well have become a local fashion that persisted for two or three generations. From the distribution of runic finds, it would appear that the fashion, if such it was, spread only over the northern two-thirds of Man, for although Scandinavian sculptured crosses have been found in the south, none bears an inscription. Several are but fragments, however, and it is not impossible the missing portions once carried a runic legend.

No Manx rune-stone now stands (or is otherwise preserved) where it was originally set up, and attempts to identify the approximate location rely on often ambiguous information – leading to uncertain deduction. Most of the major churches on Man were built, or more accurately rebuilt, in the nineteenth century. Some replaced medieval churches, others buildings renewed in the eighteenth century. These earlier structures often preserved in their fabrics sculptured stones or fragments thereof which were to come to light during building operations (one explanation for the prevalence of runic crosses in the north of the island, attributed to P.M.C. Kermode, is that there was a greater number of church alterations there than in the south, cf. Brate 1907: 22; thus also Mayhew 1881: 54). Other runic stones were discovered in churchyards, sometimes reused as walling or stile stones; others again on neighbouring secular sites. Even when a group of stones was found in connection with a church (as at Maughold) we must not assume they belong to one and the same institution. A medieval church probably occupied an ancient ecclesiastical site, and its churchyard may once have held a number of smaller chapels (*keeills*, as they are called in Man), which is the case at Maughold. It could be to one or more of these that the stones belonged. Certainly the collections of runic inscriptions now to be found within or without the modern churches can come from different places in the general locality. To cite the case of Maughold again, MM 144 Maughold II was found, reused, in the Cornaa valley, while MM 133 Maughold III is from Ballagilley. Both places are within a few kilometres of Maughold church, but may well stand distinct from it, though there is a textual link between Maughold II and I, which would seem to be relevant here (the slab bearing the latter, MM 145, was reused as building stone in the church).

At times in the nineteenth century rune-stones were set up in the open air. In consequence they suffered the effects of weather, wear, casual use, and even of attack, and some have become less legible than they used to be. In certain cases the stones have incurred serious damage, losing parts of their inscriptions which remained extant until quite recently. This makes it important to examine early drawings, rubbings, casts, and photographs (cf. ch. 4), but also, and almost equally important, to study them critically (Page 2005: 216–20). In many cases the stones are now fixed in concrete settings, with the result that their bases are hidden and they cannot be seen complete. Moreover, they are often set up very close together and at difficult angles, and sometimes it is hard to study particular parts of an inscription; MM 110 Kirk Michael VII, placed tight up against a pew, was a case in point, but following recent refurbishment of the church access has dramatically improved. To discover the detail of a complete, or virtually complete, stone we have often to turn to early photographs, taken when it had been removed from its earlier situation. Fortunately a fair number of these survive, both in the Manx Museum and in nineteenth-century guide-books to the island.

There are two main arrangements of runes on a Manx stone. One has the inscription cut on a narrow edge of a slab each of whose broad faces bears a sculptured and decorative cross; usually the runes run from base to top (as, for example, on MM 132 Kirk Michael V*a*) but exceptionally from top to base (as on MM 128 Andreas III). The other arrangement also has a decorative cross on both faces, but with the runic text running up one of the faces, alongside its cross (as MM 106 Ballaugh). A few Manx stones fit neither of these patterns. It is difficult to deduce how, in detail, individual inscriptions were made. Sometimes traces of preliminary layout lines seem to remain; and there are indications of both top-to-base and base-to-top carving and of the widening and deepening of grooves. Attention is drawn to such features in the accounts of individual inscriptions.

As well as the principal, and presumably the original, inscription on a Manx rune-stone, there may also be additional text. Such additions can vary in type and age. Some are runic, some in ogam, yet others in roman, the last often consisting of initials and seemingly written in early modern times. It has been common practice to label all of these secondary texts "graffiti", and many investigators have ignored them: because they did not notice them, considered them unimportant – or because they were not yet on the stone at the time of the investigation. For we cannot be sure when any of them were added; nor yet, in the case of some of the secondary runic inscriptions, whether there might be a connection between them and the formal texts the stones carry. Secondary runic texts are found on MM 131 (Andreas II*b*), MM 107 (German I, St John's, *b*), MM 132 (Kirk Michael V*b*), and, in two less clear-cut cases, MM 142 (Maughold IV) and MM 141 (Onchan); secondary ogam texts occur on MM 130 Kirk Michael III and MM 145 Maughold I.

Additional runic material is presented and evaluated under the relevant entry; ogam is discussed insofar as it seems relevant to an understanding of MM 130 or MM 145 or their runic texts; however, no account is taken in this edition of what appear to be early modern graffiti in roman.

The Manx runic inscriptions contain a great many personal names, and these are discussed under the *Interpretation* section of the individual entries. Altogether some fifty occur (the exact number depending on whether holy names, names preserved only in drawings, and graffiti are included). Certain of them are recorded more than once, but only in the case of the ***uan+brist/iuan:brist** 'Jóan the priest' of MM 145 Maughold I and MM 144 Maughold II can we be reasonably sure one and the same individual is involved. It is, however, widely assumed that the **kautr/kaut** of MM 99 Andreas I and MM 101 Kirk Michael II refer to the same stone carver, notwithstanding the differences of runic form, spelling, accidence and layout that exist between the two inscriptions. Whether the **ufaik** of Andreas I, on the other hand, is to be identified with the **uf*ak** of MM 112 Braddan I, or the ***ufkals** of MM 118 Bride and **tufkals** of MM 130 Kirk Michael III are to be equated, is impossible to determine – to take a couple of examples. What can be said with reasonable assurance is that there are some forty distinct names representing somewhere between forty and fifty individuals. The majority of the names are Scandinavian, but about a quarter are Irish. Male names make up three-quarters or more of the total, but it is noteworthy that of the ten female names that occur, nine are of the person commemorated (six wives, two mothers/foster-mothers, one daughter), while the tenth belongs to a rune carver. By way of comparison just eight men are verifiably commemorated (two fathers, three sons, two with unclear relationship, one who commemorates himself). There thus seems to be a slight bias in favour of commemorated women (though had more inscriptions survived intact a different picture might emerge) – in stark contrast to other areas of the Scandinavian world in which memorial rune-stones were raised, where men predominate. As monument raisers or commissioners only men appear in the Manx corpus, whereas elsewhere women may sometimes fulfil this role (Sawyer 2000: 35–46, 168). Another feature worthy of note is the importance that seems to have been attached to the recording of paternal parentage; some eight or nine of the inscriptions add this information to the basic memorial formula.

The relatively large number of Irish names in a corpus written entirely in one or other form of Scandinavian gives rise to speculation about the language(s) spoken in the rune-stone raising families. Is an Irish name to be equated with an Irish language background, or did it become a fashion among the Manx Scandinavian population to take Irish names (which presupposes considerable language contact)? The Bride inscription is particularly striking in this respect, given that the raiser, his father and the commemorated wife all have Irish names, yet the memorial is written in Old Norse using Scandinavian runes. On the assumption that at least some of those bearing Irish names had Irish as their native language, there could be several reasons why they would be party to the raising of a Scandinavian language monument: intermarriage with Scandinavians; the dominance of Scandinavian at the time as a medium of public discourse; the lack of a solid native tradition of raising inscribed monuments to the dead (there are ogam inscriptions of this type, but they appear to belong to a much earlier age).

In general, the Manx rune-stones seem to have a fairly limited time range (excluding MM 145 and 144 Maughold I and II). For assessing their dates we are to a perilous degree dependent upon the work of art historians who have commented on the decoration of the stones. Their conclusions are not necessarily constant nor in close agreement with one another (cf. Holman 1998). Moreover there is always the danger of a circular argument. An art historian's date for a monument may be taken over by the runologist to help place the inscription in time, and the subsequent dating the runologist reaches can then be used by later art historians. This is a general problem in attempts to put dates to runic texts, but it is worth drawing attention to it here since on Man we have little if any archaeological evidence for such purposes (see further ch. 3).

3. The form and decoration of the stones
By David M. Wilson

The great corpuses of Scandinavian runic inscriptions were initiated by philologists, and have in general remained for use by "runologists, historical linguists and phonologists", and so deal "only in passing with matters of history, archaeology and art history" (Barnes and Page 2006: back cover). But such an approach – clearly limited by reasons of space – has the drawback that the compilers of the corpuses have generally tended not to take advantage of evidence incidental to their main interests which could provide a more holistic approach to runes. Consideration of the form of objects on which they occur and of their ornamentation, for example, can often refine interpretation of evidence derived from neighbouring disciplines such as archaeology and history. Many runic specialists, however, in work published outside the strait-jacket of the corpuses – for example Sven B.F. Jansson 1976, Erik Moltke 1985, various contributors to Stoklund *et al.* 2006 (in broad terms), and Judith Jesch 2001 and Anne-Sofie Gräslund 2002 (in more focused contexts) – have used evidence provided by Scandinavian runic inscriptions to illuminate social and historical aspects of the Viking Age.

The Scandinavian rune-stones of the Isle of Man provide a small, but geographically discrete, corpus carved within the fairly closely delimited period of the second quarter of the tenth century to the end of the first quarter of the eleventh. The art-historical evidence, taken together with archaeological testimony, allows us to date the majority of these stones, and thus their inscriptions, relatively closely – realistically to within half a century and possibly in some cases even less.

The basis on which the dates are determined is the chronological sequence of Scandinavian ornament derived from accurate dendrochronological determination of contexts in which objects decorated in individual styles have been found. Useful supporting evidence is provided by the rich coin hoards of the tenth century found in Scandinavia and Britain, some of which include objects of precious metal decorated in ornamental styles closely paralleled on the Manx crosses. One or two inscribed and ornamented stones which record the names of historical personages or political events – most importantly the great stone raised by Haraldr blacktooth at Jelling, Denmark (DR 42) – help to construct a vernier scale to which the art of the period can be related. The dating of the introduction of Scandinavian inscribed stones into Man is also helped by, and to some extent depends on, the less secure evidence for the date of the conversion of the Norse settlers to Christianity as indicated by a change in burial rite.

The Manx stones provide some of the earliest examples of Scandinavian memorials of standardised Christian character. Almost all of them are slabs with two main faces, each dominated by a substantial carved cross, decorated in low relief. The inscriptions (which survive on only about a third of the Viking-Age stones, cf. Wilson 2008: 60) often use Christian formulae, most commonly *reisti kross þenna* 'raised this cross', while three inscriptions mention Christ's name in one form or another. The ornament also includes Christian symbols other than the cross, including such images as the Crucifixion, angels, cocks (a symbol of the Resurrection) and a figure (presumed to be Christ) bearing a book and a cross, treading on snakes (presumably a symbol of conversion). Scenes of non-Christian origin (drawn from the Sigurðr cycle, for example; see below) are all dominated by the cross and were presumably exegetic in purpose. The date of the Scandinavian settlement of the island and of the conversion of the settlers, or at least of the earliest appearance of Christianity among them, is thus important in dating the inscriptions – though an end date which, in the absence of written annalistic record, depends on archaeological evidence and historical probability, is by its nature of course less reliable.

There is clear evidence of Manx contact, through trade, with markets around the Irish Sea in the Viking Age (Griffiths 2010: 110–18) – evidence now being considerably enhanced by metal-detector finds. Scandinavians were clearly a major element in this trading activity even before the tenth century through their bases in Ireland and the Scottish islands. There is, however, no incontrovertible archaeological evidence for the presence of Scandinavians as settlers in Man in the ninth century, although it is possible that in its dying years some Norse Vikings settled there, perhaps secondarily from the Scottish islands, or even from Cumbria or Dublin, to take advantage of the island's geographical situation as a centre of communication.

Early evidence for the presence of Scandinavian settlers in Man depends on graves and settlement-sites. The few such identifiable Viking-Age sites, however, are difficult to date with any degree of accuracy and are often situated on marginal land; the evidence provided by the furnished graves, therefore, is all that survives to indicate the rough date of the earliest Scandinavian settlers on Man – and their precise origin. Those burials identifiably belonging to Scandinavian settlers contain grave-goods, some of which confirm the pagan character of the graves or indicate the ethnic origin of the settlers.

The burials have been thoroughly discussed and the physical evidence they provide has been analysed in some detail (summarised in Wilson 2008: 25–56; 2014a: 117–22). The rite of accompanied burial is pagan and culturally Scandinavian, although some of the graves may be of Christians whose relatives were pagan or had residual respect for pagan practice.

All the graves so far recognised are inhumations, and the differences in burial ritual (in mounds, single graves and cemeteries) follow the normal Scandinavian customs of the settlers' homeland (Norway or the northern and western islands of the British Isles) – even when they occur in pre-existing Christian cemeteries. Such burials are often found in cists made of local mudstone, a type of interment common both before and after the Viking Age, and are frequently encountered in cemeteries which continued in use long after this period (in many cases in the graveyards of the later parish churches). Similar Scandinavian burial rites have been observed throughout northern England (although stone cists occur less frequently, Richards 2004: 189–212), particularly in Cumbria (Paterson *et al.* 2014: 157–77), which, on the basis of archaeological evidence, appears to have been settled by Vikings at roughly the same time as the Isle of Man. While the settlers in Cumbria and Man were mostly of Norwegian origin (having arrived either directly or by way of the Scottish isles), the grave-goods found in their more richly furnished burials, while including a number of objects of Norwegian provenance (chiefly swords and spearheads), also comprised a wide variety of material of insular or continental origin. It is, therefore, plausible to suggest that many of the settlers in both regions came from Ireland after the Scandinavians, under pressure, retreated temporarily from Dublin in 902 and settled in North Wales and north-west England.

From the fairly substantial evidence of the grave-goods found in Man it is clear that there were few, if any, Scandinavian settlers in the island before the very end of the ninth century, and that, when they did begin to settle, they lived on reasonably good terms with the indigenous inhabitants. This is shown by their respectful, if not universal, use of the existing Christian cemeteries, even though at least some of the settlers continued to practise the pagan rite of accompanied burial in these places – a practice tolerated, if not perhaps liked, by the indigenous inhabitants, who themselves continued to use the cemeteries. It is also possible that some settlers had already adopted Christianity before coming to the Island – in England, Wales, western Scotland or Dublin for instance.

It should be stressed that, save for monastic settlements, of which that at Maughold is the only one definitely identified (Wilson 2014b: 576–8), and possibly in the major Christian burial ground on St Patrick's Isle (Freke

2002: 58–82), there is unlikely to have been anything in the early years of the Scandinavian settlement which could be identified specifically as a church or chapel. The chief above-ground feature encountered by the settlers in the cemeteries would have been a series of standing Christian memorial stones, some of which would have been raised over graves as early as the sixth or seventh century – and possibly even earlier (Wilson 2009; 2014b: 576–9). Those who had travelled in Ireland or settled in Scotland or northern England would already have been familiar with such stones, which by this time either depicted a cross or were themselves cruciform. The settlers would also have found a similar form of memorial in Man, and such monuments were adapted to their own taste as they turned to Christianity.

The monuments produced by the settlers were on the whole remarkably uniform, though they varied a good deal in height. They were mostly carved in low relief on slabs of the local slate, a mudstone which splits easily and uniformly along its bedding. The quality of the stone varies throughout the island, but the carvers clearly selected easily workable pieces from a number of suitable quarries. The slabs vary in thickness between approximately 5 and 16 cm and were in most cases decorated on both faces. The runic inscriptions many of them bear are commonly, but not exclusively, incised along one of the narrow edges (where there is no inscription, edges are often decorated in relief). Thirty-four Scandinavian rune-inscribed slabs survive (including the occasional example possibly or clearly made after the first century or so of settlement – most notably MM 145 Maughold I and MM 144 Maughold II), about a third of the total of recognisably Scandinavian carved stones. Such a figure should, however, be treated with caution as many of these artefacts are damaged and some exist only as small fragments.

The important, and dominant, common carved element of the stones is a cross, which often fills the whole above-ground length. Many of the slabs are rectangular, but the head of the cross is occasionally carved at the broader end of a slab which tapers to its base; this allows for the arms to stand slightly proud of the side panels. The cross and the panels it creates around it are embellished with carvings – on the cross shaft this ornament is normally of an interlaced ribbon (the crucified Christ occurs on only two slabs, one of which – MM 126 Kirk Michael IV – has a runic inscription). In the panels on either side of the shafts are various motifs – some recognisably historiated or symbolic: human figures (both male and female), animals (some interlaced and some more naturalistic) and sundry forms of interlaced ribbon and tendrils. Two stones, both of which bear runic inscriptions (MM 136 Braddan III and MM 135 Braddan IV), are more elaborate in form and decoration, and can be dated reasonably closely (see below). They are substantial and pillar-like shafts of rectangular section. The head of Braddan IV survives, standing proud of its shaft (the upper portion of Braddan III, which would have included a similar cross head, is missing).

Some of the figures on the stones can be identified in Christian iconography, others are representative of Norse mythology, while the meaning and origin of yet others – warriors, women, and hunting scenes, for example – cannot generally be interpreted. The major ornamental features on the crosses have two, possibly three, sources. Most marked are those which are clearly derived directly from Scandinavia, presumably (as with the "short-twig" graph-types) directly from Norway. They include the Borre-style ring chain pattern and scenes from Norse heroic tales, taken particularly from the Sigurðr cycle preserved in the poetic *Edda* (though written down only much later; the cycle also features in the medieval prose *Edda* and *Vǫlsunga saga*). Women with long trailing skirts and simply knotted hair have sometimes been identified, possibly rather insecurely, as Valkyries, but are clearly of Scandinavian form and origin. A second group of motifs on the crosses, chiefly consisting of a foliate scroll and a series of simple ribbon-interlaces, are derived from northern England; while a third group, mainly hunting scenes and various animals and male figures, probably have their origin in Pictland or southern Scotland, or even possibly in Ireland. The treatment of certain motifs, particularly the interlace patterns of the cross heads, was most likely developed in the Isle of Man itself.

The ornamental treatment and form of various motifs on the stones, based on four distinct ornamental styles of Scandinavian origin, can be used to build up a clear chronology. These are:

1. The *Borre-style* 'ring chain', which appears, for example, on the shaft of the cross on MM 101 Kirk Michael II. This is the commonest motif found in the Island and appears in various modified guises.
2. The *Jellinge-style* animal, which occurs in its most typical form on the shaft of the (inscriptionless) cross fragment MM 120 from Malew.
3. The *Mammen style*, which appears, for example, on both faces of the crosses of MM 136 and MM 135 – Braddan III and IV.
4. The *Ringerike style*, which occurs, for instance, on MM 117 from Kirk Michael (which has no inscription) as a detail of the animal on the side panels of both faces and probably on the slightly damaged shaft of the cross on one side.

Since Klindt-Jensen and I proposed a series of dates for the styles in 1966 (dates used critically, for instance, by Palm 1992: 35–6, in his chronological consideration of the Scandinavian rune-stones), the schema has been much refined (summarised by Wilson 1995a; Graham-Campbell 2013). This is largely as a result of the dendrochronological examination of carefully selected samples of decorated wood found in Scandinavia and the study of metalwork from dated wooden contexts. Some of the ornamental elements of these styles were adapted sporadically into the mainstream art of England, the Scottish Isles and Ireland. In the Isle of Man, however, they appear more frequently in clearly recognisable versions of the Scandinavian originals (although some are purer than others). The approximate dates of the Scandinavian styles relevant to the Isle of Man are now generally accepted as: Borre: c. 860–c. 950; Jellinge: c. 900–c. 975; Mammen: c. 960s–1000+; Ringerike: c. 990–c. 1050.

If we apply these dates to Man, they reflect the evidence for the date of the earliest settlers provided by the pagan graves. These do not appear before the very end of the ninth, or beginning of the tenth, century. The first crosses, which may well overlap in date the end of the pagan rite of furnished graves (say c. 925), are often decorated with a single motif from the Borre style – the ring chain, which is most prevalent in Norway and in its Manx form must derive from that country. Interestingly, this general design appears on two crosses carved by Gautr (MM 101 Kirk Michael II and MM 99 Andreas I). On the latter we learn something of his background – that he was *sonr Bjarnar frá* **kuli** 'the son of Bjǫrn from ?Kollr'; while on the Michael cross he boasts that he 'made this one and all in Man' (*gerði þenna ok alla í Mǫn*), implying that he was the main sculptor in the Island at that time, unless it is the exaggeration of a clever advertiser (cf. Page 1983: 136). On Gautr's Andreas I cross the ring chain does not occur in its pure form and is replaced by a tight multi-strand interlace which can only loosely be related to any contemporary Scandinavian ornament. However, a modified version of a Borre-style ring chain comprises a series of closed circles interlacing regularly with an elongated looped element, and this is seen in the left-hand side panel on face A of the stone (Kermode 1907: pl. XXIX, fig. 73A; cf. Wilson and Klindt-Jensen 1966: pl. 27h; Plate 1 in this volume).

The Borre style also appears in Cumbria, interestingly in the inlay on a sword-guard from the Hesket-in-the-Forest mound-burial, which is surely a Norwegian import (Wilson 1995b: fig. 5; Paterson *et al.* 2014: fig. 125), but also in stone sculpture (Bailey and Cramp 1988: ills 296–8, 309 and 471), including the remarkable and iconographically complicated standing cross from Gosforth – sometimes in modified form (Bailey and Cramp 1988: 24). In this context it is worth noting that a fragmentary cross head from Gosforth bears a Borre ring chain as well as a piece of interlace not dissimilar to that on the shaft of Gautr's Andreas I cross (Bailey and Cramp 1988: ill. 309). It is thus probable that the style arrived in Man and Cumbria at roughly the same time, i.e. the early years of the tenth century. Bailey suggests a date after 920 (Bailey and Cramp 1988: 29), which seems a reasonable estimate. It is possible that at least some of the Manx interlace ornament came by way of Cumbria, where varieties or developments of the Borre-style interlace similar to those on the Manx stones are found. It is also possible, more likely perhaps, that the direction of influence is reversed and that the pure Borre ring chain, which appears on a number of Manx crosses, came, with the runes, directly from Norway: compare, for example, the ring chain on the rune-inscribed Bride stone (MM 118; Kermode 1907: pl. XLII, fig. 92B; Plate 53 in this volume) with that on the strap-end from Sundvor, Rogaland (Wilson and Klindt-Jensen 1966: fig. 49). All this evidence suggests a date of c. 925 for the beginning of the conversion of the earliest settlers in Man to Christianity and the erection of the first Scandinavian memorial stones.

The Borre ring chain, with slight variations, appears on the following eleven rune-inscribed stones: MM 99 Andreas I; MM 131 Andreas II; MM 106 Ballaugh; MM 112 Braddan I; MM 118 Bride; MM 107 German I (St John's); MM 102 Kirk Michael I; MM 101 Kirk Michael II; MM 130 Kirk Michael III (where, unusually, it forms a ring in the middle of the cross-head); MM 126 Kirk Michael IV; and MM 133 Maughold III. It is the first Scandinavian motif to be introduced in the island – possibly by Gautr. It was commonly used, developed and embellished there in a number of ways. The starting point of one of the developing patterns is the knotted Borre-style ornament on the head of MM 101 Kirk Michael II, which appears not only on crosses with the ring chain motif, but on others which are palpably later, as for example MM 132 Kirk Michael V (which has Mammen-style animals at the base of the cross) and the early eleventh-century MM 117 from Kirk Michael, with Ringerike-style animals. In its most extreme form – on the rune-inscribed stone MM 127 from Jurby – Borre-style elements are connected by elongated ribbons. Similar, less competent, examples of such treatment of this developed motif have been found in Yorkshire where, as pointed out by Bailey (1980: 219), it almost certainly derived from Man. Indeed, Shetelig (1954: 125–6) suggested that the ring chain motif was originally developed by Gautr, but this, while not impossible, is a case difficult to argue.

Such points should not be laboured here, but they tend to emphasise contacts around the northern Irish Sea in the tenth century. Most importantly, the route to Norway is illuminated by a small number of slabs in the Western Isles, which in form are not unlike those on Man. Of these the two most interesting in this context are the rune-inscribed fragment of a cross head from

Inchmarnock, Bute (SC 10, Barnes and Page 2006: pl. 54), and the cross slab from Kilbar, Barra (SC 8), which, runologically and in design, are related to Man. Of particular relevance is the ornament and layout of the non-runic face of SC 8 (Fisher 2001: 106–8; Barnes and Page 2006: pl. 53), which is clearly a simplified or degenerate form of that found in the Manx series and would seem to be derived thence (but see Barnes and Page 2006: 228–32).

The Manx style of cross does not appear to have travelled south from Man with any confidence. So far only one rune-inscribed stone has been found in Wales – Corwen 5, Merioneth, but the form and decoration on this cross is in no way related to the Manx series (and the runes, which are hard to identify, could as well be by an Anglo-Saxon as a Scandinavian writer, cf. Barnes and Page 2006: 26–7; Edwards 2013: 382 and fig. MR7.6). The Borre ring chain on Penmon 1, Anglesey (Edwards 2013: fig. AN51), the only definite example of Scandinavian ornament on a cross in Wales, is, however, clearly derived from Man.

The pure Jellinge style – as on the uninscribed Malew stone cited above – is rare in Man, but another animal of Jellinge type does appear, in a slightly ill-defined form, on the left-hand side of the head of the cross on one of the faces of MM 129 Kirk Michael VI.

The Mammen style in its pure form occurs on only four rune-inscribed stones – MM 136 and 135 Braddan III and IV, MM 121 Andreas VI (where the serpent Fáfnir from the Sigurðr cycle is depicted as a Mammen-style animal), and at the base of MM 132 Kirk Michael V. The style is also represented by the balanced, perhaps zoomorphic, interlace decorating one of the faces of MM 122 Maughold.

The Mammen style is uncommon in the Viking regions, usually appearing on objects indicative of elevated social status. It takes its name from a highly decorated axe found in a rich wooden chamber-grave from Bjerringhøj, Mammen, Denmark (Iversen 1991), built according to the dendrochronology of the corner-posts of the structure in 970/971 (Andersen 1991). The Manx beasts are classic examples of the style, and of the highest quality, so much so that at one time it was even proposed that Mammen style had its origin in Man, but it is now generally agreed that it first appeared in Denmark (although it need not have had its origin there) just before, or during, the early part of the reign of Haraldr blacktooth (c. 958–987), and that it flourished during the second half of the tenth century. The two Braddan crosses would clearly belong to the period in question (Fuglesang 1991: 103). That the Mammen style appeared elsewhere in a western British context is demonstrated by the fact that ornament of the same style, but in a different medium, occurs on the terminals of four of the silver penannular brooches in the Skaill, Orkney, hoard (Graham-Campbell 1995: nos. 24, 1, 5, 7 and 112; fig. 21). They form part of a large assemblage of silver which included coins; although some of them may have disappeared since the hoard was found in 1858, there is general agreement that the latest on record provide a *terminus ante quem* for the hoard's deposition of *c.* 970/80 (Fuglesang 1991: 103; Graham-Campbell 2011: 6, 18 note). The fact that the Manx and Orkney Mammen style appears in two different media makes exact comparison difficult, although it is clear that the animal on the Andreas VI cross is closer to those on the Skaill brooches than to the examples on the Braddan crosses.

The Ringerike style is represented by a detail – the form of the eyes (pear-shaped with the pointed element towards the snout) – of four animals on MM 117 from Kirk Michael and on the single animal on MM 116, also apparently from Kirk Michael (Kermode 1907: nos 89, 90). Interestingly, the Ringerike character of the ornament on the last-named stone was pointed out by Haakon Shetelig when he first defined the style in 1920 (Schetelig 1920: 320); although no Manx example was noticed by Fuglesang (1980) in her classic study. The arrangement of the interlaced animals on face B of MM 117 has an axiality, which, if it had a more foliate character, would relate to what becomes a major, if not defining, feature of the classic Ringerike style as defined by Fuglesang (1980: 14–15). The surviving traces of the Manx Borre style on this stone would suggest that it belongs to the very earliest phase of the Ringerike style; before say 1020.

Unfortunately, neither of the Manx stones bearing Ringerike decorative elements have surviving inscriptions. While the style had only minimal influence on Man, it flourished in Ireland (Wilson and Klindt-Jensen 1966: 143–5) and particularly in Dublin (O'Meadhra 1979: figs 106–30; Lang 1988: 58–67). It grew, almost experimentally, out of the Mammen style at the end of the tenth century in Scandinavia. In Ireland it was introduced probably at the beginning of the eleventh century (possibly from England). A Hiberno-Scandinavian version continued in use in Ireland into the second half of the eleventh century. The Ringerike elements on the Manx stones, however, need not concern us greatly in the context of this book since, as just noted, they have no inscriptions. They may nevertheless indicate the beginning of the end of the Scandinavian styles in stone sculpture, although a pure form of the succeeding Urnes style appears on a single piece of gold jewellery, possibly made in Man, from a presumed hoard in Greeba (Wilson 2004).

The only remaining Manx runic stone – other than those (a good few) with no datable decoration – is MM 142 Maughold IV, which is clearly out of series. This bears two long-shafted crosses, each with rope-like twisted borders and a linear design of interlocking five-sided boxes. The surviving parts of the head exhibit the remains of an undecorated straight-sided cross with rounded arm-pits. The main inscription is placed in one of the fields on either side of the cross shaft. On one of the other side panels, on which are carved a number of runic graffiti, is the scratched outline of a clinker-built ship with mast and stays supporting a yard with furled sail. Typologically the cross would seem to be later than the highly-ornamented main Manx series. The ship appears to have been carved in outline by the same hand that cut the cross and the principal runes; but it could be a later graffito, representing a badge of the Lords of the Isles, first mentioned as being used by Reginald, son of Somerled (died 1203). Lost seal-impressions of Harald, King of Man (1242–9), depicting a similar ship, appear in drawings made for Sir Christopher Hatton's *Book of Seals* of 1641 (Megaw 1959–60: pl. 241). Later it appears as a heraldic device of a number of late medieval Scottish chieftains (Goodall 2004), for example those of the MacKinnons whose Iona tombstones bear similar heraldic representations of ships (*RCAHMS* 1982: figs 207 and 208). It survives as a quartering in the 1701 arms of the Duke of Argyll (who could make some claim to be the descendant of the Lords of the Isles). The ornament of this cross cannot aid the dating of the main runic inscription; save that on general grounds it might be placed in the eleventh century (cf. pp. 221–2).

4. Some early drawings and discussions of Manx runic inscriptions

Many Manx rune-stones have spent long years out of doors, open to the elements and to attack and neglect. Therefore any student of their inscriptions needs to know something of the history of Manx runic studies, and in particular to take note of early drawings and descriptions both of the monuments themselves and of their place in the landscape. Yet it must be a critical interest. Not all of these early depictions are authoritative or first-hand. That is certainly the case with work from the mid- and late nineteenth century, when guide-books to the island and its antiquities abounded. Some of these are derivative, some inaccurate, and some misleading in their imprecise use of the word "runic". The present chapter is therefore deliberately selective, treating only such early representations as throw light on the whereabouts and condition of individual rune-stones: as give help in reading and interpreting their legends. Though a number of early reproductions are discussed, there will inevitably be others that our searches have missed. As far as is known, there is no complete catalogue of the pictures, casts, squeezes, etc. that might be relevant, and one can sometimes come upon examples by chance, while serendipping into the works of antiquaries and local historians. Meanwhile certain further details are in Wood (1924) and Page (1980; 2005); and can be followed up in the extensive (although now somewhat outdated) runic bibliography of Marquardt (1961: 55–82).

The earliest printed illustrations of Manx runic texts appear to be those in Edmund Gibson's revised and expanded version of William Camden's *Britannia* (1722: 1457–60). They accompany the description of the islands by Thomas Wilson, Bishop of Sodor and Man from 1697 to 1755, and probably derive ultimately from him. As reproduced in *Britannia* (see Figs 32, 36) the drawings are stylised yet useful copies of the runes of Andreas IIa (MM 131), Braddan IV (MM 135), and Kirk Michael III and Va (MM 130, 132). A further revision of Camden's great work, by Richard Gough (1789), claimed to give "exact representations" of the same stones (vol. 3, 704). In fact, his drawings, which show all four stones standing freely and independently out of doors (see Fig. 37), are in detail less precise than Gibson's, and may not be independent of them (Page 2005: 217–19).

Of roughly the same date as Gibson's reproductions are a group of sketches in one of Humfrey Wanley's papers (Wanley [*c.* 1700]; see Fig. 10). There is no statement there as to their origin or authority, but Wanley's diary and letters show that he knew Wilson, while Wilson certainly corresponded on antiquities with scholars at Oxford (where Wanley was a student and assistant in the Bodleian Library 1695–1700), so it is likely they derived from him again. This single sheet contains drawings of three inscriptions: a reasonably accurate reproduction of Kirk Michael V*a* (MM 132); a barbarised version of Andreas II*a* (MM 131); and one more from Andreas (similarly poor), which Page considered either an attempt at Andreas IV (MM 113), considerably more complete than it now is, or a depiction of another, subsequently lost, inscription (Page 1980: 187–9; 1983: 134, 145). The latter seems most likely to be the case (cf. pp. 106–7, 117–18). Each drawing is preceded by a simple account of the relevant stone and its decoration. As MM 132:

> At the West End of S^t. Michael's Church in the Isle of Man, near the Churchyard, stands an Old Cross; the shaft whereof is Flat, & about 9 Foot High, one foot & ½ Broad, and Five Inches Thick. On the Broad Sides are Engraven Two large Crosses, adorn'd with Stags, an Eagle & Child, a Man on Horse-back, a Dog Hunting a Stag, & other Animals. On the Top of the Edge, (which stands toward the North,) is the Figure of a Cock. And on the Top of the Edge, toward the South, is the Figure of a Man holding a Spear in his Right Hand, & a Shield in the Left; with a Cross Under and Between his Legs. Beneath the Cross is the Following Inscription, to be Read from the Bottom to the Top.

There follows a drawing of the runes, fairly accurate, though misrepresenting graphs that consist of vertical + branch; here often only the vertical is given (compare line 1 of Fig. 10 with Plates 101–5).

In 1789 the Icelandic scholar Grímur Jónsson Thorkelin visited Man, officially to prepare a report to the Danish king on the Scandinavian antiquities there. A slim diary and a number of drawings and notes survive (Thorkelin [1789]). Though his visit was short and his examination of the evidence pretty perfunctory (as noted by Townley 1791: 1, 156–8), yet the Icelander preserved in his journal a couple of interesting accounts of rune-stones, MM 135 (Braddan IV) and MM 132 (Kirk Michael V*a*). He seems to have been the first to try to draw, not only the inscriptions, but the decoration and shape of a cross too, though he does it in a very amateur way. Below a depiction of the Braddan IV runes he has a rough sketch of the cross, with its head undamaged and its shaft, unlike now, intact (for what that is worth, see p. 55 below). The picture is annotated, "on this side the inscript" and "intertwisted serpents", and, more ambitious and bilingual, "on three sides for & back, &

on the side backing the Inscription Slange Værk er ud hugged, Ligt det paa ?stenen i Scotland" 'a serpent composition is carved, like the one on ?the stone in Scotland'. In the case of Kirk Michael V*a* Thorkelin had two attempts at drawing the inscription "on a stone Cross in Kirk Michael on the outside of the Church yard", and then made rough sketches, with measurements, of the two faces of MM 132.

In 1822 the Society of Antiquaries of Scotland published a group of accounts of Manx runic and other inscriptions, a number of them by Henry Robert Oswald, a local surgeon who was an antiquary of some distinction. These included a selection of references, as well as depictions of the objects and inscriptions discussed (Anon 1822; Oswald 1822). Although the accounts are dated 1822, certain of the notes are earlier than that. Two accompanying plates, XVII and XVIII, are taken from drawings by George William Carrington, the originals of which are in the library of the Manx Museum, MSS MD 15017/18. These show MM 131 and its inscription Andreas II*a*, MM 132 and its inscription Kirk Michael V*a*, and the Braddan IV cross MM 135, this time with its top broken and its shaft fractured, damage which, apparently, it had suffered since 1789. Carrington's are much more serious representations of the crosses than previous attempts. MM 131 is depicted standing, presumably in Andreas churchyard. MM 132 is fixed in a two-stepped stone structure, probably to be identified with the horse-block outside Kirk Michael churchyard mentioned by Woods (1811: 162) and later writers (cf. Plate 100). MM 135 is set in a simple stone block.

The nineteenth century was a period when both knowledge and published record of Manx crosses increased dramatically (Page 1980: 181–2). Antiquaries identified, drew, described them, and of some stones casts were taken that would supply primary evidence, could we but trace them today. The monuments were even a source of poetic, or at any rate, verse inspiration (Laughton 1842: 98). Of all these developments only a sketch is appropriate in this chapter.

Two groups of drawings stand out. The Society of Antiquaries of London possesses a few elegant pictures of Manx crosses by one Capt. Edward Jones, infantry and militia officer (Jones [*c*. 1834–47]). Among them are several of the Braddan IV cross, MM 135. One, dated 1834 (p. 80), again shows the top and shaft damaged. A later drawing, from 1847 (p. 79), is taken from a cast, and curiously enough shows the cross and its inscription unblemished. The cast was presumably one of those made by William Bally of Manchester, noted in Train (1845: 2, 32–6, who dates Bally's work to 1839; cf. also Dryden 1887: 202–3, who gives the date as 1841) and interpreted there by John Just of Bury, Lancashire.

The second group is among the important material preserved in the Hibbert-Ware collection (Hibbert-Ware et al. [c. 1848]; it should be noted that 1848 is the approximate date of the final collocation rather than of the individual drawings, which are spread over at least two decades). The collection represents the interests of the Scots antiquary, Samuel Hibbert-Ware, but there is work here in various hands, by members of his family. It consists of twelve volumes in all, vol. 5 devoted to sculptured stones. Here there are rough, measured drawings of Andreas I (MM 99) and Andreas IIa (MM 131), and more detailed ones of MM 135 (in its broken state) and its inscription Braddan IV, and of MM 132 and its inscription Kirk Michael Va, as well as three lines of confused runic graphs marked as deriving from "Slate Stone Kirk Michael", presumably attempts at one of the severely damaged fragments from that church.

The first of the major illustrated published accounts of Manx memorial stones is Kinnebrook (1841). As far as can be judged, Kinnebrook took his material direct from the monuments themselves. From Kirk Michael he showed (in this order) MM 132 (Va) on its horse-block, MM 101 and 130 (II and III) upright on the churchyard wall, and the fragments MM 129, 126, 102 (VI, IV, I), the last without its inscription. He also illustrated: MM 106 Ballaugh (though not its runic face), in the churchyard; MM 99 Andreas I and MM 131 Andreas IIa, neither in easily identifiable surroundings (but described, p. 11, as "on the green, near the entrance to the Church-yard" and "in Andreas Church-yard, on the north side of the Church" respectively); MM 141 Onchan a–c, set up apparently in a garden (cf. p. 227); and MM 135 Braddan IV, upright in a stone setting that also accommodates another carved (but not runic) stone. He further portrayed MM 136 when it was still serving as a lintel in Braddan Old Kirk tower and before its runes (Braddan III) were discovered.

Following Kinnebrook, but criticising him for inaccuracy and lack of clarity, is J.G. Cumming, who was then Vice-Principal of King William's College, Castletown. In *The Runic and Other Monumental Remains of the Isle of Man* he used a more complex technique for recording the inscriptions (1857: v–vi).

> I employed an Italian to make me casts in plaster of Paris of the carved crosses [...] I found it far easier to make out the details of ornamentation from these casts than from the original stones, both from their colour and the facility of turning them about to any light. Having [...] made rubbings partly from the stones and partly from the casts, I filled up carefully the outlines, with the casts before me, and thus had rough drawings the full size of the originals. These were photographed to the size in which they now appear;

> and upon these photographs the lines were traced by my son [...] in anastatic ink and chalk, and then transferred to the zinc from which they are printed.

He adds an important note on his method:

> With respect to the Runic Inscriptions, these have been copied separately. I found it impossible for them to be drawn without a certain value being given to some very faint and uncertain lines – these therefore I myself traced with the readings which I believe to be the most correct. The doubtful parts, however, I have noticed in the body of this work.

Thus we are warned of the subjective element in some of his readings/illustrations. Cumming's rubbings are now in the Bodleian Library, Oxford (Cumming [c. 1855]), and they constitute primary, albeit prejudiced, evidence for certain runic sequences now unclear or even completely lost.

The use of casts is an important feature of the nineteenth-century study of the Manx rune-stones. An often ill-tempered exchange of letters printed in the periodical *The Academy* for January–June 1887 supplies some of our information on their confused history and uses. The chief controversialists are Isaac Taylor priest and philologist, the Icelandic scholar Gudbrand Vigfusson, the young P.M.C. Kermode, and the antiquary Sir Henry Dryden of Canons Ashby, Northamptonshire. Their point of departure is the brief study 'The Manx runic inscriptions re-read' (Vigfusson and Savage 1887). Sir Henry reported (Dryden 1887: 202) a group of casts that had been fashioned in 1841 "for a Mr. Jones; but I know no more about that gentleman nor the use that he made of them". It is a plausible guess that this was Capt. Edward Jones, but the comment here is rather abrupt and uninformative; in a later contribution to *The Academy* Dryden reveals that he bought the set in 1844 (1887: 290). Two of the casts were of whole stones, the others of inscriptions only. All were made available to Cumming (who "came here to examine my set", Dryden 1887: 203). But Cumming also had casts made in 1854/55, "a complete set of the whole stones of that day then known" (Dryden 1887: 203). These were kept in King William's College until Cumming left his mastership of the school and moved to Lichfield. They were then, according to Dryden (1887: 203), turned out and ultimately destroyed. An indignant letter written on the College's behalf by the Governor of the Isle of Man denied this, asserting the casts were "safely deposited in a suitable room at Castle Rushen" (*The Academy* 1887: 275, but note Dryden's rebuttal, 1887: 290). Kermode (1907: 8–9) gave his own account of the various casts, and an indication of all those still available (cf. also Kermode's letter of 12 iv 1887 to Dryden on this subject: Manx Museum MS 6020). Where, one may wonder, are any of these casts now? Some were once held in Liverpool Museum (now World Museum), but that collection seems to have been destroyed in World War II (during a raid in May 1941, which reduced the building to a shell; World Museum Antiquities Staff pers. com.). Those said formerly to have been at Castle Rushen, Castletown, remain hitherto undiscovered. So far only one of the significant casts has come to light, that of MM 136 Braddan III, which is now National Museum of Scotland, Edinburgh, cast IC7. This is an important example, for at some point in the later nineteenth century, after Cumming (apparently) but before Vigfusson and Savage's 1887 contribution (cf. Kermode 1887b: 151), part of the inscription was broken away. Cast IC7 testifies to what we have lost and seems to confirm Cumming's reading.

The whole *Academy* controversy developed from a critical letter by Taylor (1887: 113). He had studied squeezes of the Dryden casts, and doubted some of the readings in Vigfusson and Savage (1887). Vigfusson retorted stoutly that he read not from copies but from originals, which was a sounder technique (1887: 131–2). Taylor pointed to the advantages of using casts or squeezes for verification purposes, and detailed some of the errors in Vigfusson's versions ("The casts show forty-five runes which Dr. Vigfusson has either omitted, inserted, or misread", Taylor 1887: 152). Kermode intervened, attempting to judge between them, checking from the monuments themselves, and on the whole came down in favour of Taylor (Kermode 1887b). Vigfusson waxed more indignant, and the whole battle – *hólmganga* Taylor termed it (1887: 222) – ended with neither side retreating.

The importance of these casts and squeezes, however many of them there were and however different the techniques of production and evaluation, is that they must have recorded runic sequences as they existed *c*. 1850, before decades of weathering and damage had affected their legibility; as indeed National Museum of Scotland cast IC7 shows. Such casts served as sources for a number of interpretations by nineteenth-century scholars, a fact we should keep in mind when we judge their contributions to runic studies.

P.A. Munch seems to have been the first philologist/runologist to publish a discussion of the Manx inscriptions (1850). His readings, though, derive from rubbings taken from plaster casts in several different collections (particular mention is made of paper rubbings made by J.J.A. Worsaae from casts in the possession of Sir Henry Dryden). This must be borne in mind when considering the versions he presents of the inscriptions on nine stones, which appear in the following order: Kirk Michael II (MM 101), Andreas I (MM 99), Andreas IIa (MM 131), Kirk Michael Va (MM 132), Braddan IV (MM 135), Kirk Michael III (MM 130, the second line presented separately and wrongly ascribed to "Kirk Onchan"), Onchan *e*, *f*, *a*, *b* (MM 141), Braddan II

(MM 138), Kirk Michael VI (MM 129). Worsaae in turn acknowledged Kinnebrook's contribution to the runic material he assembled in his investigation into the Dano-Norwegian impact on the British Isles (1851: 351; see also p. 14 in his [c. 1850] notebook).

From all of this it is clear that there was considerable interaction between the works of various runic investigators of the mid- and later nineteenth century. Towards the end of that century new techniques of photography came to assist the distant scholar. The Manx corpus produced by Sophus Bugge (1899) relied on photographs and drawings made by his son Alexander under Kermode's direction. In contrast, Erik Brate made his study (1907) at first hand, on a visit to the island in 1905. For some texts, however, he still used casts: Braddan II (MM 138; the original was then, he claimed, in the Wallace Museum, Distington [Cumberland/Cumbria], which is odd, since that museum had been closed and the collection sold off in the late 1890s), Onchan e–g (MM 141, only the side bearing a–d being accessible), German I (St John's) a (MM 107), German II (Peel; MM 140), Marown (MM 139), Kirk Michael I (MM 102); while Kirk Michael VII (MM 110) was known to him only from the manuscript of Kermode's 1907 work.

Magnus Olsen's survey (1954) was based on a journey to the island made in 1911, from which he returned bearing "squeezes or tracings of practically all" of the inscriptions then known (1954: 158). Presumably his discussion derives from these, and from his notes made during examination of the stones themselves, though for some later finds, MM 159 Balleigh, MM 142 Maughold IV (a, d, e), MM 123 Kirk Michael VIII, he relied on second-hand information (without always stating this explicitly); as also, apparently, for the runes on the back of MM 141 Onchan (e–g). By 1911 most of the Manx rune-stones were under some sort of protection so we would not expect to find much deterioration since Olsen saw them. Today (2018) the only ones still in the open are MM 139 Marown and, in their relatively sheltered cross house, the various Maughold stones.

The importance of a critical study of photographs cannot be overestimated. There are valuable early examples in the Manx National Heritage archives, many of good quality (see, e.g., Plates 17, 21, 33, 83–4). Some show stones *in situ*, others the complete cross taken from the ground, so that the whole, including the very base, is visible. Illuminating are the various photographs recording rune-stones in their then habitats. These may be in popular guide-books to the island, which should not be entirely ignored, despite the generally indifferent quality of their information. An example is Paterson (1863: facing p. 38), which shows three Braddan stones, MM 112 (I), MM 135 (IV), MM 136 (III), set upright in a group in the churchyard there.

The value of older records and studies varies greatly. It is not always easy to tell what is reported from first-hand viewing, what copied from earlier writings. Elementary errors abound. Even Munch, as noted above, was able to record the second line of MM 130 Kirk Michael III as coming from Onchan (1850: 279; his no. 7). Woods (1811: 168) writes of Andreas II*a* (MM 131) as being in Bride churchyard. An example of a more complex aspect of the problem is posed by MM 135 Braddan IV, of which there are several drawings by Jones [*c.* 1834–47] (cf. above, p. 50); one (from 1834) shows the cross damaged, another (1847), copied from a cast, has it complete. In 1789 Thorkelin drew it complete, though with confusion of the central section of the inscription, perhaps implying damage: in 1822 Carrington's picture (in Oswald 1822, cf. above) shows the cross broken. Clearly in at least one part of this sequence a damaged stone was portrayed as though it were entire (Page 2005: 216–19). Another case is MM 128 Andreas III. Some of its runes are now hard to read, for the stone has laminated, producing a gash that runs lengthwise along the runic edge destroying the centres of a good many of its graphs. This damage is not shown on the earliest drawings (as Black 1889: 338, from a photograph; and cf. Plate 17), and it is not reported or signalled in, for instance, Kermode (1907: 192–3 and pl. LII), Olsen (1954: 185, but presumably deriving from his 1911 examination) or in Sanness Johnsen (1968: 223–4). Yet Page observes (in a draft of this chapter) that he recorded the damage in notes from the late 1950s. Sanness Johnsen gives no clear account of the source of her material, claiming only that she checked readings as far as possible (1968: 2, but note Liestøl's severely critical comment, 1969: 173–4). Oddly enough, her plate 80 (p. xix) shows Andreas III much as it is today with the gash taking out the middle part of many of its runes.

Clearly we must approach warily statements made by any one writer or drawings made by any one artist which are otherwise unconfirmed. This leads to an uncertainty whether or which early readings can be judged independent authorities, for not all writers bother to tell us. To take a pertinent example: can we determine whether the transrunifications of Kneale [*c.* 1860]: 61 are based on scrutiny of the originals or not? Kermode writes of them with apparent approbation (1907: 9), but is he right to do so? Kneale's runes are depicted schematically, with no attempt at individual characteristics, and he fails to divide texts into the distinct sections occasionally found on stones. His attempt at MM 106 Ballaugh (no. 13) reproduces errors found in Cumming (1857: 17 and fig. 2). The implication is that at any rate part of Kneale's work is secondary, derivative.

Throughout this book the works of predecessors in the field have been used, but their findings have been approached with due circumspection. We have tried, wherever possible, to judge their authority, to distinguish what they say from what we have observed. The bibliography attached to each entry is deliberately selective. There is no point in completeness in a field where there is copying from one writer to another, particularly as Marquardt (1961) is at hand to supply much of this need.

Side-by-side with the runic corpora go the publications of new finds made in the last hundred years or so. Such accounts and the illustrations that accompany them are often of high quality, as, for instance, the find report of MM 142 Maughold IV from excavations at Maughold (Kermode 1916: 56–62; Kermode 1925). Yet their value to us is less than that of some earlier reports, however defective, for these more recently discovered stones survive today largely undamaged.

A final reference draws attention to one scholar hitherto largely omitted from the survey: the most important of all students of the Manx rune-stones, P.M.C. Kermode. He published extensively and over many years on the subject, and his great book *Manx Crosses* (1907) must form a centre-point of any revision of the Manx runic corpus. It has been republished in facsimile, with a perceptive introduction by David Wilson, which is essential reading for anyone starting work in this field (Wilson 1994). Kermode was not a trained philologist or historical linguist, nor had he access to the immense thesaurus of Scandinavian runic material that later publication has given to the world. Inevitably there will be flaws and gaps in his treatment. But his descriptions and the accompanying drawings form a foundation for later scholars to build upon and they neglect them at their peril. Originals of many of his drawings survive for consultation in the Manx Museum.

From this short history of Manx runic studies it is, one hopes, evident that any account of the island's rune-stones must make clear what access the writer has had to the originals or to copies or drawings of them, and hence what is the authority for his/her descriptions. From this may be deduced something of the authority of the interpretations. For the present edition observations have of course been taken primarily from the stones themselves (cf. pp. 26–7), earlier representations and readings being consulted chiefly for sections of text that do not survive or are now unclear.

5. The dating of the Scandinavian runic inscriptions of Man

Art historians currently date the bulk of the Manx runic crosses to the period *c.* 925–1020 (Wilson in ch. 3 of this volume). The artwork of the crosses has been identified as representing in the main either Borre (*c.* 860–950) or Mammen style (*c.* 960s–1000+). There is, however, no reason to suppose Christian crosses were being raised by Scandinavian settlers in Man much before *c.* 925. In Scandinavia raised rune-stones go back at least as far as the fifth century, and probably somewhat farther than that, but it is important to draw a distinction between these sporadic early manifestations of the genre and the memorial rune-stone fashion of the Viking Age. The latter seems to begin in Denmark towards the middle of the tenth century from where it spreads into Sweden in the eleventh. Norway was never part of the trend, and cannot boast more than fifty or so Viking-Age memorial stones in all. These are for the most part dated in the period *c.* 950–1050, with an apparent concentration around the year 1000.

The art-historical dating of the Manx runic crosses suggests the tradition they represent pre-dates the eruption of the rune-stone fashion in Denmark. There are Viking-Age memorial stones in Denmark and Sweden, seemingly Norway too, that are older than 925, but not a great many. And while it may be argued that a number of the Manx crosses could stem from the latter part of the *c.* 925–1020 period (in particular those that now bear little or nothing in the way of decorative elements), it is not always easy to show that particular examples differ in respect of their graph-types, language or formula from what have been deemed on art-historical grounds the earliest representatives of the series. Graph-types, except in a few cases, do not vary significantly (see below), nor does the language (below), while the memorial formula 'NN put up this cross in memory of MM' is well-nigh ubiquitous.

This last fact has been taken as an indication "that the traditional date of *c.*930 [as it then was] for the beginnings of the Manx corpus may be too early" (Holman 1998: 47). The memorial formula, so this line of thinking goes, would appear to have been established before people started to put up inscribed crosses in the island (or at least before the making of those crosses that chance has preserved), and is therefore likely to have been imported ready-made. There are at any rate few indications of rival formulas as rune writers searched for the most suitable way of wording their memorial texts – as we find in Scandinavia. A handful of early Viking-Age runic monuments have inscriptions that begin: 'After NN stands this stone' (e.g. DR 192 Flemløse 1; N 209 Oddernes 1) or 'After NN stand these runes' (Ög 136 Rök). From ?ninth-century Denmark come texts that proclaim 'NN's stone' or 'NN's monument', followed by others, probably mostly or all from the following century, which use a variety of formulas to communicate the fact that a person or persons set up a monument in someone's memory, such as *gerði kumbl* 'made a monument', *hjó rúnar* 'hewed runes', *setti stein* 'placed a stone', as well as *reisti stein* 'put up a stone', which last becomes the most popular. The only indication of variation from anywhere near Man is on the ?tenth-century Kilbar cross from Barra (SC 8), which, if correctly read, says: *Eptir Þorgerði Steinars dóttur er kross sjá reistr* 'In memory of Þorgerðr Steinarr's daughter this cross is put up', a formula reminiscent of 'After NN stand(s) this stone/these runes'. Occasional variation can be found on Man itself, though it is doubtful that it has relevance for the present discussion. MM 142 Maughold IV*a* records *Heðinn setti kross þenna...* 'Heðinn placed this cross...', but the graph-types of this inscription, together with the design of the MM 142 monument as a whole, suggest that it comes late in the Manx series (see below and pp. 46–7). MM 175 Maughold V, of uncertain date but quite possibly late, has **kirþi+lik+tinn** 'made a ?' (see pp. 225–6); however this is not a sculptured cross, rather an unornamented, perhaps recumbent, graveslab. Finally, on MM 127 Jurby we find the verb form **raiti**, which, if not a mistake for **raisti**, appears to be a spelling of *rétti* 'raised up', an alternative to *reisti* particularly common in late Viking-Age Uppland, Sweden.

The graph-types used by the bulk of the Manx carvers are those commonly designated "short-twig". In Scandinavia this variant of the sixteen-character rune-row belongs to the period *c.* 800–1000, and is found chiefly in Sweden and Norway. To that extent there is no conflict between the dating of the Manx crosses and runic usage as documented in the Scandinavian homelands. One could surmise that runic script was brought from Norway to Man (directly or indirectly) some time before 925. However, not all the Manx carvers employ short-twig runes pure and simple. MM 140 German II (Peel) and MM 141 Onchan *e* include ᛁ, the dotted form of ᛁ. The MM 142 Maughold IV inscriptions are mainly, and MM 130 Kirk Michael III entirely, in "long-branch" runes, the variant associated before about the year 1000 chiefly with Denmark. In addition, Maughold IV*a* sports two examples of ᛏ while Kirk Michael III has six of ᛏ and two of ᚽ, the dotted form of ᚼ. According to current thinking the diacritic dotting of runes (p. 65) first manifests itself towards the end of the 900s, appearing on a small number of Danish rune-stones. It is thus unexpected to find the phenomenon in Man in a corpus dated in the main between 925 and 1020. It could be argued that dotting is somewhat older than the first Danish attestations, and further that the Manx stones on which dotting occurs are among the latest of the series. While the latter may well be true of MM 142 Maughold IV (cf. Wilson 1983: 185; pp. 46–7), the age of MM 140 German II and MM 141 Onchan (not least the Onchan e inscription) is quite uncertain, while MM 130 Kirk Michael III, because of the Borre style featured in its decoration (cf. pp. 44, 81), should be among the older of the Manx runic crosses. To solve the Kirk Michael III conundrum, we might adopt Shetelig's suggestion that runes were added to a pre-existing cross (1925: 270). Certainly, the design of this monument is unusual in that its texts are placed on a face which is otherwise blank. Possibly this side of the stone was never decorated; alternatively, earlier carvings might have been cut away to allow for the runes, although no traces are now visible of older artwork or writing.

Whatever the approximate dates of MM 140 German II (Peel), MM 141 Onchan, MM 142 Maughold IV and MM 130 Kirk Michael III, it has to be assumed that their dotted runes originate from Danish (or conceivably Swedish) tradition if the occurrence of these characters in Man is to fit in with what is otherwise held to be true of developments in runic writing. The evidence available suggests ᛁ came into use in Norway in perhaps the second quarter of the eleventh century and did not become a regular feature there until about 1050, while other dotted runes were even slower to catch on (Spurkland 1995: 12). Thus, while the short-twig runes may have come to Man from Norway, that can hardly be true of the dotted characters. In these circumstances, the use of long-branch graph-types in Maughold IV and Kirk Michael III may be thought to point towards Denmark (hardly Sweden if the *terminus ante quem* is c. 1020?), even though such forms also occur in tenth- and early eleventh-century Norway.

A purely orthographical feature found in two of the Manx inscriptions likewise points to a later rather than an earlier date. The use of ᚢ, ᚬ to denote /o(:)/ (as opposed to /ā(:)/) is not documented in Scandinavia until about 1020–1030, yet it occurs in MM 138 Braddan II (ᚱᚢᛋᚴᛁᛏᛁᛚ *Hrossketill*) and Kirk Michael III (e.g. ᛋᚢᚾ *son*). Either, then, the art historians are wrong, and these two inscriptions, at least, should be placed after the c. 925–1020 period, or the use of ᚢ, ᚬ for /o/ is somewhat earlier than has been supposed. The allegedly late Maughold IV, on the other hand, has only ᚢ for /o(:)/, notwithstanding it employs the dotted rune ᛁ (all the relevant examples are in Maughold IV*a* 1).

A development in Norwegian runic writing chronologically more or less parallel with that of ᚴ, ᚭ /ā(:)/ > /o(:)/ is the use of the sixteenth rune for /y(:)/. At the beginning of the Viking Age this rune, in the "long-branch" shape ᛦ or "short-twig" form ᛦ, stood for /R/, supposedly a palatal with sibilant quality. In Norway /R/ appears by 900 to have coalesced with /r/, rendering the sixteenth rune available to denote a different phoneme. Since its designation, in Norway at least, appears to have been *ýr*, application of the acrophonic principle (whereby the initial sound of a rune's designation indicated the phonetic value) resulted in its use for /y(:)/. There are no examples of the correlation ᛦ, ᛦ /y(:)/ in the Manx corpus, but there is one of ᛦ /R/, on MM 113 Andreas IV. If the use is Norwegian-inspired it suggests the inscription predates 900, which places it somewhat earlier than the *c.* 925–1020 time-frame. This solitary ᛦ might of course reflect East Scandinavian tradition, where /R/ and /r/ were distinguished (though not consistently) until well after the end of the Viking Age. Should that be so, the "short-twig" guise in which the rune appears would point towards Sweden: in Denmark "long-branch" ᛦ was the norm. A further possibility is that the carver of Andreas IV decided for one reason or another to employ an archaic Norwegian form in his inscription. The summoning into being of an archaising rune writer is certainly a way of accounting for the occurrence of features that belong to a bygone age. Innovations that appear earlier than expected, on the other hand, raise fundamental questions about dating.

A linguistic problem affecting the *c.* 925–1020 period assigned to the bulk of the Manx corpus is the common occurrence of the longer form of the preposition meaning 'after' 'in memory of': *eptir* as opposed to *ept*. In Scandinavia the longer form would not be expected to appear regularly before the end of the tenth century (Peterson 1996: 242–4), yet it is found in about half of the Manx inscriptions. Here too we must either reckon that the development began earlier than we have so far supposed, or deem (much of) the Manx corpus to be later than the art-historical dating implies. There is in fact a faint indication that the longer form of the preposition was already in use early in the tenth century. The Kilbar cross (SC 8) almost certainly opens with the word *eptir* (cf. above). The difficulty is to understand the relationship between Kilbar and the Manx corpus, about which differing views have been expressed. While Shetelig (1954: 125) considered Kilbar "the starting point of the remarkable series of Norse monuments in the Isle of Man", Wilson (1983: 183) notes that many have thought it influenced by Manx tradition (cf. also pp. 44–5). Barnes and Page (2006: 231–2) conclude that Kilbar is probably slightly older than the Manx crosses, but find a connection between the two hard to demonstrate with reference to specific features.

Whatever reasoning may be employed to account for the individual Manx runographical, orthographical and linguistic features discussed here, cumulatively they seem to conflict with the art-historical datings. We are thus faced with two possibilities. (1) The art-historians are for whatever reason wrong, and the time-span allotted to the Manx corpus should be moved forward by some decades. (2) The art-historical datings must be upheld, and our conception of certain developments in runic writing revised. Possibility (1) raises a problem that confronts all who rely on expertise from disciplines they do not command: unless art-historians can be found who can provide good reasons for challenging the consensus, the runologist can do little more than point to the conflict of evidence. S/he can hardly hope to overturn art-historical opinion on the basis of runological data alone. A plea might be made that art styles could have changed at a slower pace in the Norse colonies of the West than at home in Scandinavia (cf. Holman 1998: 51, with references), but evidence to back up this notion seems at best uncertain (Holman 1998: 52; cf. also ch. 3). With that in mind, possibility (2) perhaps offers a more hopeful way forward. If the making of runic crosses in Man to all intents and purposes ceased during the early eleventh century, the innovative runological features the crosses exhibit must belong to a period in which these features either were only just starting to appear in Scandinavia (dotting) or had as yet to appear (the use of ᚴ, ᛆ for /o(:)/). The conclusion to be drawn from those circumstances must be that the innovations we see in Man arose independently of Scandinavian tradition.

There are reasons for thinking that might be so, and a number have been advanced by runologists of the past (e.g. von Friesen 1933: 172; Olsen 1933: 89). The Scandinavian practice of dotting, it has been proposed, might have arisen in imitation of Anglo-Saxon ᚣ, a ᚢ into which a small ᛁ has been inserted to mark the value /y/ (the product of the *i*-mutation of *u*). In favour of this idea is the evidence of Anglo-Saxon runic activity in Man (though almost certainly belonging to a much earlier period than the Scandinavian crosses, cf. p. 240), supported by the fact that a clear ᚣ is found in IR 12 from Dublin, archaeologically dated to around 1000. It has further been suggested that the use of ᚴ, ᛆ with the value /o(:)/ could be due to Anglo-Saxon influence. In Anglo-Saxon runic writing the fourth rune, ᚩ, came by the seventh century to have the value /o(:)/, and a name, *os* 'mouth' (seemingly, and of less certain age), to match. If, as appears to have been the case, the designation of the fourth Scandinavian rune vacillated between the pronunciation /ā:s:/ and /ɔ̄:s:/, it could be that rune carvers exposed to English tradition made a connection with the designation and value of the fourth English rune and adopted both, giving *óss* /o(:)/ as an alternative to *ā́ss* ('god') /ā(:)/. Most recently, on the basis of early attestations of dotted runes in English manuscripts, it has been suggested that the practice of diacritic dotting may have been developed "in Scandinavian communities, perhaps in Danish-influenced areas, of the British Isles [...] and exported from there to Scandinavia" (Page and Hagland 1998: 68; for a rebuttal of this view, see Knirk 2010).

The acceptance of Man – or perhaps a wider area bordering the Irish Sea – as a centre of innovation may help explain a further oddity in the Manx runic corpus alluded to earlier: the fact that the crosses show a fully developed memorial formula as early as the tenth century. Some have toyed with the idea that the Manx carvers could have modelled their formula on Anglo-Saxon usage: that *arærde æfter* 'put up in memory of' might have given rise to *reisti eptir* (cf. Olsen 1933: 89). Palm goes further, attributing use in Scandinavia itself of what he terms the "raiser formula" to Anglo-Saxon influence (1992: 250). There is unfortunately no obvious way of substantiating these ideas. It does not seem implausible that a small area like Man in which Irish, Scandinavian and (even if only to a very limited extent) Old English were spoken and Latin known, and where three writing systems, roman, ogam and runes, were in use, could have been a place where fresh ideas about language and writing took shape. On the other hand, it is hard to imagine a series of innovations, encompassing writing system, orthography and language, spreading from Man or the Irish Sea region across the whole of Scandinavia. Runic writing practices might just have been carried back to Denmark, Norway and Sweden and emulated there, but it is harder to envisage the same in the case of the longer preposition form *eptir*. It seems questionable too, whether the Manx inscriptions, or practice in the British Isles more generally, could have exerted a stronger influence on rune-stone raisers in Scandinavia than that attributed to the greater Jelling stone, DR 41 Jelling 2 (see, e.g., Palm 1992: 251; Sawyer 2000: 147). To be sure, Jelling 2 does not have what became the ubiquitous formula *reisti stein* 'put up a/the stone' or *lét reisa stein* 'had a/the stone put up', but says rather: *bað gera kumbl þausi* 'commanded these monuments to be made'. Presumably, however, the specific wording of the "raiser" or "commissioner" formula was to a degree dependent on the actual circumstances: King Haraldr black-tooth was organising the building of substantial monuments, for which *reisa stein* would hardly have been appropriate. People inspired by Jelling 2 but simply putting up a stone to commemorate the dead will presumably have found *reisti stein* a more apt mode of expression.

The dating of the Manx Scandinavian runic inscriptions is a difficult matter to resolve. On balance we are inclined to agree with current art-historical opinion and place the bulk of the Manx corpus in the *c.* 925–1020 slot. A possible piece of supporting evidence is the occurrence, spread over three of the inscriptions, of four personal names with first element Irish *Máel-* (MM 101 Kirk Michael II, MM 130 Kirk Michael III, MM 175 Maughold V). According to O'Brien (1973: 229) this name element is "common up to A.D. 850, and [...] out of use by A.D. 950" (which, though, seems to mean "non-productive" rather than out of use altogether). We think it not impossible that the dotting of runes as a diacritic device and the use of ᚽ, ᚭ for /o(:)/ originated in the British Isles (where intermingling of scripts as well as languages is to be presumed) and spread from there to Scandinavia (unless these innovations are to be counted independent developments in the North, parallel to those in Britain). On the evidence of the Kilbar cross (SC 8), we find it plausible that use of *eptir*, the long form of the preposition meaning 'in memory of', goes back (in some areas, at least) to the early tenth century. The wellnigh ubiquitous Manx wording *reisti kross* we consider a native usage arising naturally from the circumstances being described, not the import from Scandinavia of a ready-made phrase. All of this is, of course, little more than informed surmise, and may ultimately be shown to be incorrect, but, with the evidence currently at our disposal, it is a way of reconciling the art-historical and runological datings.

An alternative approach would be to isolate those Manx runic monuments in which innovative runic writing practices appear: MM 138 Braddan II, MM 140 German II (Peel), MM 130 Kirk Michael III, MM 142 Maughold IV, MM 141 Onchan). It could be stressed that none of these save MM 130 can be firmly dated on the basis of their decorative style, and that the Kirk Michael III runic text may be an addition to a pre-existing monument (cf. p. 59 above). There is thus the possibility all the inscriptions concerned were made after the *c.* 925–1020 period assigned to the bulk of the Manx corpus. Such a proposal would, however, rely heavily on lack of positive dating evidence. There are certain indications that Kirk Michael III may be a secondary text, and that MM 142 Maughold IV could be a late monument relative to the main Manx series, but the only features positively indicating a late date for MM 138 Braddan II, MM 140 German II (Peel) and MM 141 Onchan are runological – and, as the preceding discussion has shown, this must be deemed an uncertain criterion. There is also the danger that the whole argument becomes circular.

6. Rune forms and orthography

(In this chapter phonetic notation is used more or less throughout, since the discussion often concerns precise denotation of sound.)

Rune-rows, writing systems, transliteration and transrunification

The original rune-row, known as the older *fuþark* (after its first six characters), consisted of 24 symbols. In Anglo-Saxon England, to take account of the advent of new phonemes in Old English, the number was gradually increased (to 28 and in some areas to as many as 31), resulting by the seventh century in what is known as the Anglo-Saxon or English *fuþorc* (also called the Anglo-Frisian *fuþorc* since Frisia shared in some of the runic developments that took place in England). New phonemes also arose in the Germanic spoken in Scandinavia, but there, oddly enough, the number of runes in the row was reduced from 24 to 16. This process, whenever it began, seems to have been complete by the early eighth century. Because of the limited number of runes available, the 16 character rune-row, known as the younger *fuþark*, was a rather crude tool for the representation of speech. Most of its members denoted more than one distinctive sound, and some could stand for several. While there may only have been 16 runes, they could appear in a number of variant forms. To simplify matters, a rough distinction has been drawn between a more complex set of characters, often called "long-branch" runes, and a simpler series, commonly known as "short-twig". Other younger-*fuþark* types have also been identified, but these distinctions (often quite fine) need not concern us here. By way of illustration, three model rune-rows are now presented: an Anglo-Saxon *fuþorc*, and a long-branch and short-twig younger *fuþark*. For greater clarification roman transliterations of each rune are given (on transliteration see below).

ᚠᚢᚦᚩᚱᚳᚷᚹᚻᚾᛁᛄᛇᛈᛉᛋᛏᛒᛖᛗᛚᛝᛞᛟᚪᚫᛠ
f u þ o r c g w h n i j ï p x s t b e m l ŋ d œ a æ y ea
1   5   10   15   20   25 28

(a) The Anglo-Saxon *fuþorc*

ᚠᚢᚦᚬᚱᚴᚼᚾᛁᛅᛋᛏᛒᛘᛚᛦ
f u þ ã r k h n i a s t b m l ʀ
1   5   10   15

(b) The long-branch younger *fuþark*

ᚠᚢᚦᚭᚱᚴᚽᚿᛁᛆᛌᛐᛒᛙᛚᛣ
f u þ ã r k h n i a s t b m l ʀ
1   5   10   15

(c) The short-twig younger *fuþark*

The two Manx inscriptions in Anglo-Saxon runes show no significant deviations from row (a) above, save that the branches on one example of what is taken to be ᛗ **m**, the twentieth rune, are placed quite low down, making the graph look a little like ᛞ **d**, the twenty-third. The carvers of the bulk of the Manx Scandinavian inscriptions seem to use the short-twig variant of the younger *fuþark*, though with ᛦ in place of ᛙ for the fourteenth rune, **m**. In several inscriptions, however, there are too few diagnostic forms (see p. 71 below) to enable the runologist confidently to identify a particular selection of characters, and in a few cases there are no diagnostic forms at all. MM 130 Kirk Michael III and MM 142 Maughold IV are clear exceptions to the general pattern: Kirk Michael III is carved throughout in long-branch runes, the bulk of the writing on MM 142 likewise, except that there the eleventh rune, **s**, is ᛌ rather than the ᛋ of Kirk Michael III. In addition these two stones, together with MM 140 German II (Peel) and MM 141 Onchan, exhibit one or more dotted runes. Dotting was a diacritic device introduced apparently towards the end of the tenth century, whereby certain runes could be furnished with a dot (sometimes a short line instead) to indicate a marked (though not precisely specified) phonetic value from among those the rune represented. Thus younger *fuþark* ᛁ, for example, could denote [i(:)], [e(:)], [æ(:)]; the application to it of a dot tended to limit its range to the lower vowels [e(:)], [æ(:)], though on occasion ᛁ could in addition be used to denote [j], seemingly also [ə], and sometimes even [i(:)]. A similar variation affects ᚢ. These two, ᛁ and ᚢ, are the only dotted runes found in the Manx corpus (pp. 69, 75–6).

In this edition, as in runological work in general, we transliterate runes into roman equivalents (as has already been done above). This is chiefly to help readers unfamiliar with runic writing, but the roman letters, given in bold type, also serve as abstract representations of the distinctive runes of a particular row. Distinctive in this sense means contrasting. Runic ᛁ, for example, contrasts with ᚾ in the Manx inscriptions, just as 'i' with 'u' in roman-alphabet writing. Thus ᛁᛁᛏ **sin** gives *sinn* 'his/her/their [reflexive possessive nom./acc. m. sg.]', while ᛁᚾᛏ **sun** renders *son* 'son [acc. sg.]'. Similarly, in English writing 'sin' denotes a different word from 'sun'. Younger-*fuþark* ᛁ and ᚽ, on the other hand, do not contrast in this way: either ᚴᚱᚾᛁ (as in, e.g., Andreas IIa) or ᚴᚱᚾᚽ can be written (or for that matter ᚴᚱᚾᛁ or the ᚴᚱᚾᚿ of Kirk Michael III) and the word remains *kross* 'cross'. Likewise, 'ink', 'Ink', '*ink*' all give the English word *ink*, and 'i', 'I' and '*i*' are variants of the ninth letter of the roman alphabet. In consequence, ᛁ and ᚾ are represented by different roman letters, **i** and **u**, in transliteration, whereas ᛁ, ᛁ, ᚿ and ᚽ are all rendered **s**, making **s** a good abstract representation of the rune of which ᛁ, ᛁ, ᚿ and ᚽ are graph-types.

It follows from this that a transliteration is first and foremost a rendering into roman of the distinctive runes of a particular system (the Anglo-Saxon or the younger-*fuþark* in the case of the Manx corpus). A transliteration does not necessarily indicate the shape of individual runes (and certainly not their precise shape). Nor is it much of a guide to sound value. For practical reasons, roman equivalents are normally chosen that will indicate the approximate sound or sounds denoted by the runes being transliterated, but it cannot be stressed too strongly that a transliterated runic text is not a phonetic transcription and is not intended as such. We may take by way of example ᚠ, ᛅ, the fourth rune of the younger *fuþark*. In this edition it is romanised as **ã** because its value in most of the Manx inscriptions (as commonly in the early and mid-Viking Age) is [ã(ː)]. However, in a few cases it denotes [o(ː)], and once even [w]. It is nevertheless consistently transliterated **ã** even though that results in forms such as **kãna** (*kona* 'wife'), **aiþsãara** (*eiðsvara* 'person to whom one is bound by oath'), which to a reader of standardised Old Norse will present a rather outlandish appearance. What **ã** shows the reader is that the character in question is the fourth rune of the younger *fuþark*. The accompanying transrunification (see below), as well as the discussion following the transliteration, will make clear which graph-type of **ã** is involved, and the interpretation will indicate the sound value it is considered most likely to denote.

While the basic principles of transliteration are fairly well established, transliteration practice can vary. Many runologists, for example, render the younger-*fuþark* fourth rune as **o**. That is the norm when dealing with medieval inscriptions, which can be considered to have a discrete system of runic writing and in which ᚠ, ᛅ regularly denote [o(ː)]. However, for the sake of consistency **o** is often employed to transliterate the fourth rune in Viking-Age inscriptions as well. Dotted runes have commonly been given different

30 objects with their *c.* 44 inscriptions the following runic inventory can be presented. Each distinctive rune is listed in transliterated form followed by the graph-types the Manx carvers used to represent it.

f	ᚠ
u	ᚢ
þ	ᚦ
ã	ᚫ / ᚭ / ᚯ
r	ᛦ / ᚱ
k	ᚴ
h	ᛏ / ✳
n	ᚼ / ᚾ
i	ᛁ
a	ᚭ / ᚫ / ᚼ / ᚬ
s	ᛁ / ' / ᚿ
t	1 / ᛏ
b	ᛒ
m	ᛘ
l	ᛚ
R	ı
ü	ᛆ
ï	ᛏ

The common Manx graph-type is given first. Of the others, ' occurs in five or more inscriptions (positive identification of the dot can sometimes be difficult), ᛏ in four or perhaps five, ᚫ in three, perhaps four, ᚼ in three, ᚭ ã in two, possibly three, ᚬ in one or conceivably two, while, ᚠ, ᚱ, ✳, ᚾ and ᚿ all appear in one inscription only. In addition to these various runic graphemes and graph-types, there is a suggested occurrence of medieval ᚫ æ on MM 141 Onchan (inscription *c*). At some point in the second half of the eleventh century rune carvers began to differentiate ᚭ and ᚫ, limiting ᚭ to the denotation of [a(:)] and using ᚫ for [æ(:)]. It is unclear, however, whether the shape read as ᚫ in Onchan *c* is a rune at all, and it is best omitted from the discussion.

The implications of the graph-types encountered in the Scandinavian runic inscriptions of Man are many and far-reaching, and are discussed in detail in ch. 5. The consistent use in the majority of the inscriptions of short-twig forms (and in some fragmentary texts the occurrence of such forms and absence of evidence for the use of long-branch variants) indicates a date for the bulk of the corpus not later than the tenth century. Given the replacement of short-twig ᛁ by long-branch ᛏ (cf. *NIyR*: 5, 240–41; Sanness Johnsen 1968: 22–31), the linguistic flavour of many of the Manx texts, and the layout of the majority (with the inscription running up the narrow edge of the stone), it is reasonable to suppose the short-twig rune forms represent a Norwegian import (rather than a Swedish, even though short-twig rune forms were also the norm in Sweden until the eleventh century). The occurrence of long-branch variants in MM 130 Kirk Michael III and MM 142 Maughold IV*a, e, f* (Maughold IV with ¹/¹ **s** throughout, however) need not disturb the image of Norwegian inspiration, for long-branch as well as short-twig runes occur in Norway in the tenth century. Alternatively it is possible that one or other, or both, of the inscriptions concerned are Danish-inspired (long-branch runes being almost ubiquitous in Viking-Age Denmark), and that has indeed been suggested for Kirk Michael III (e.g. Olsen 1954: 217; cf. pp. 80–81). At the same time, the use of dotted runes both in Kirk Michael III and Maughold IV*a*, and also in MM 140 German II (Peel) and MM 141 Onchan *e*, raises significant questions about the dating of the Manx inscriptions and our understanding of late tenth-century developments in runic writing (see ch. 5).

It is more difficult to attach significance to the occurrence of ᚽ, ᚭ, ᚿ. The first is an alternative to ᚭ **a** found in early (mainly Swedish) short-twig inscriptions (Sanness Johnsen 1968: 22–3). In Norway it is not documented certainly at all, but that does not of course mean it was unknown there. Its appearance twice in MM 101 Kirk Michael II, however, need not be as a relic of earlier Norwegian usage, but could, as suggested in the account of this inscription, stem from a desire on the part of the carver to highlight the names of the sponsor and sculptor of the monument; which he achieved by using an unusual graph-type he either happened to know or constructed for the purpose. That explanation can hardly cover MM 107 German I*a*'s ᚭ, however, which appears in the word **þsar** *þessar* 'these'. An extremely rare form (discussed on p. 154), its use in place of ᚭ **a** (which occurs twice elsewhere in the inscription) lacks obvious motivation. The final form of this trio, Ballaugh's ᚿ, seems best considered a graph-type of ᚼ **ã**. Its possible orthographical and runological significance is examined on pp. 123–4.

A warning against dating by graph-type comes from MM 145 Maughold I and MM 144 Maughold II. The carver of these two non-memorial stones, 'Jóan priest', stuck rigidly to the forms found on the majority of the Manx crosses, i.e. the "short-twig" variant of the younger *fuþark* without augmentation (but with ᛏ for ᛁ, cf. above). Yet his texts were clearly written much later than the bulk of the inscriptions, perhaps as late as the thirteenth century, and appear to reflect an antiquarian interest in scripts (cf. pp. 205–6).

Nowhere in the Manx Scandinavian memorial corpus is there a certain example of a bind-rune (= runic ligature; cf., however, the apparent ᛏ in Onchan *c* and the clear ᛕ in Onchan *d*, neither of them memorial texts). The complex and so-far undeciphered characters of MM 111 Andreas V have by many been described as bind-runes (e.g. Black 1889: 332–5; Brate 1907: 24), but if so they are certainly not binds of conventional type. Bugge also recognises "Kvistruner" 'twig-runes' in some of them (1899: 244), but there is no obvious pointer among the multifarious branches and bows of Andreas V to the cipher of which twig-runes are the most common manifestation. This cipher is based on a division of the rune-row into three groups: (1) **tbmlʀ**; (2) **hnias**; (3) **fuþārk**. Runes are identified by group and number within the group, and a popular way of presenting the relevant numbers was by arranging "twigs" on either side of a vertical, the total on the first side denoting the group, that on the other side position within it. Thus ᛦ, reading from left to right, gives group 3, position 2, and represents **u**. Those symbols on Andreas V that resemble twig-runes tend to have too many twigs to conform to the cipher, twigs on one side of the vertical only, or twigs combined with bows and/or other features.

At the end of the reading and accompanying account of each of the Manx Scandinavian inscriptions a list of "diagnostic rune forms" is given. By this is meant either forms that represent the short-twig or long-branch tradition (or particular graph-types within those traditions), or forms that are primarily diagnostic of age – in the Manx corpus almost exclusively dotted runes.

The runic orthography of the Manx corpus

Little can be said about the orthography of Maughold AS I and II. Page (1999: 137) describes Maughold AS I's **blagcmon** as "an unusual spelling" of the name *Blacmon*, by which he seems to be referring to the use of **gc** rather than simply **c**. He suggests this is a way of marking "a palatalised […] consonant" (for which there is some manuscript evidence), but it is not clear why the consonant in question should be palatalised, preceded as it seems to be by [a], which is what ᚠ normally denotes, and followed by [m] (cf. further p. 239).

The Scandinavian runic inscriptions of Man, as befits their number, and the length of some of them, present an altogether more complex orthographical picture. Language historians have over the years developed a reasonable understanding of the sounds and sound systems of Viking-Age Scandinavian, yet precise identification can in many cases be difficult, not least in an overseas settlement where speech is likely to have been influenced by contact between different forms of Scandinavian and with one or more indigenous languages. A general problem, noted above, is that the Viking-Age rune-row was not a very sophisticated medium for the denotation of speech sounds. We also have to take into account the fact that pronunciation can change, while spelling lags behind; and there will almost certainly have been different views among rune carvers about the appropriate rendering of particular segments or sequences of speech. For all these reasons the account offered here of the sounds denoted by the different runes must be treated with considerable caution. Subject to such necessary reservations, however, the relationship between spelling and sound in the Manx Scandinavian corpus may be presented as follows. (To be observed: [ɸ], [β] denote unvoiced and voiced bilabial spirant respectively, [χ], [ɣ] unvoiced and voiced velar spirant; [A], [I], [U] mark the three unstressed vowels of Old Norse.)

ᚠ   [ɸ], [β]

ᚢ   [u(:)], [o(:)], [y], [ø], [w], [U]; the value [w] is assumed both before vowels (unless the vowel denoted by ᚢ is long) and in the second element of the /au/ diphthong.

ᚦ   [θ], [ð], [t], [d] (see p. 77 below)

ᚭ ᚬ ᚯ   [ã(:)], [o(:)], [w], [U]; possibly [ɔ] or [ɔ̃]; on [w], see ᚢ above.

ᚱ ᛦ   [r]

ᚴ   [k(:)], [g(:)], [χ], [ɣ]

ᚼ ᚽ   [h]

ᚾ ᚿ   [n(:)]

ᛁ   [i(:)], [e], [j], [I]; possibly [e:], [æ], [y], [æj], and conceivably [je]; the value [j] is assumed both before vowels and in the second element of the /æi/ diphthong.

ᛆ ᛅ ᚬ ᚭ   [a(:)], [æ], [A]; in all probability [ã(:)]; possibly [ɔ], [ə], [æj].

ᛌ ᛍ ᛋ   [s(:)]

ᛐ ᛏ   [t(:)], [d(:)]

ᛒ   [p], [b], [β]

ᛘ   [m]

ᛚ   [l(ː)]

ᛁ   probably [r].

ᚭ   possibly [o], [ə].

ᛂ   [e]; possibly [æ], [ə].

Digraphic spellings occur of what are assumed to be monophthongs: ᛂᚢ in Ballaugh's **āulaibr** (*Óleifr*) most probably denotes [ɔ̃ː] (pp. 123–4); ᛂᚢ regularly stands for [ɔ] as well as [aw], as in Andreas I's **fauþur** (*fǫður*); ᛂᛁ can, in addition to [æj], sometimes represent [e], and perhaps [æ], as in Andreas IV's **þ(a)ina** [θen:A], Ballaugh's **ai(f)tir** ?[æftɪr], ?[eftɪr] while in Jurby's **raiti** it seems to mark [eː] (*rétti*). Conversely, ᛁ appears to denote [æj] in Braddan IV's **þurlibr** (*Þorleifr*), as also in **risti** (*reisti*), a spelling that occurs in the same inscription – and several others. In Braddan I's **uf∗ak** (*Ófeig*), ∗ᛂ (by some read **aa**) must be presumed to stand for [æj], while in Braddan II's **siin** (*sinn*) ᛁᛁ would seem to denote [i]; the reason or reasons for the occurrence of this one, or these two, doubled runes are unclear. The ᛂᛂ in Maughold V's **lik+tinn** (an uncertainly interpreted sequence) may be a way of marking [nː], in which case it is likely to be a medieval spelling. Runes were seldom doubled before Scandinavian vernacular writing in the roman alphabet became common (in which long consonants were marked by gemination); it may be noted that even the two [s]s at the morpheme boundary in Ballaugh's **liutulbsunr** (*Ljótólfssonr*) are denoted by a single ᛁ.

In the younger *fuþark* rounded vowels mostly appear as **u**. In accordance with this we find in the Manx inscriptions **sãnt:ulf** with [u] in the second syllable (*Sǫndulf*, Andreas IIa), **runar** with [uː] in the first (*rúnar*, e.g. German Ia), **sunr** with [o] (*sonr*, e.g. Kirk Michael II), **muþur** with [oː] in the first, [ʊ] in the second syllable (*móður*, Kirk Michael Va), **fur** with [y] (*fyr*, Kirk Michael II), **āsruþr** with [ø] in the second syllable (*Ásrøðr*, German Ia), **þurualtr** with the semi-vowel [w] (*Þorvaldr*, with [w] conventionally normalised 'v', Andreas III). Around 1020–1030, or even a little earlier, carvers began to use the fourth rune, ᚮ, ᚭ (etc.), for [o(ː)], [ɔ(ː)], and sometimes seemingly for [ɔ̃(ː)] (cf. pp: 59, 98). Examples from the Manx corpus are (in each case in the first syllable): **rãskitil** with [o] (*Hrossketill*, Braddan II), **tãtãr** with [oː] (*dóttur*, Kirk Michael III), **sãnt:ulf** with, perhaps, [ɔ] or [ɔ̃] (*Sǫndulf*, Andreas IIa; cf. p. 98). The forms **aiþsãara** (*eiðsvara*, Braddan II) and **tãtãr** (*dóttur*, Kirk Michael III, second syllable) exhibit unusual uses of **ã**. The semi-vowel [w] (normalised as 'v') and unstressed [ʊ] normally appear as **u** in runic writing. That [w] and [ʊ] can also be written **ã** has to do with identification: [w] is neither [u] nor [o], but may be identified with either (though by most medieval Scandinavian writers it seems to have been more closely associated with [u]); similarly, unstressed [ʊ] was probably unlike either [u] or [o], at least in many early forms of Scandinavian, and might be identified with the one or the other (in the earliest written Icelandic, for example, unstressed [ʊ] regularly appears as 'o' – and [ɪ] as 'e'). Originally, younger *fuþark* **ã** stood for [ã(:)], and that is how it seems to be used in the bulk of the Manx inscriptions, e.g. **þãnã**, presumably [θãn:ã] (Braddan III), **ãsruþr** [ã:srøðr] (< **ansu-*, German Ia). Occasionally historical [ã] is written **a**, as in the initial syllables of **þanã** (Kirk Michael II) and **asriþi** (German II). This may be because nasal vowels had been lost from the language of the relevant rune carver (as was presumably the case with those who used **ã** for [o(:)], [ɔ(:)], etc.), or because nasality was not always consistently marked. Inconsistency is to be expected at a time of linguistic change, and we find examples among the Manx inscriptions. The carver of Kirk Michael III, for example, writes [o(:)] now **u**, now **ã**, as **krus** (*kross*), **kuþan** (*góðan*), **sãn** (*son*), **tãtãr** (*dóttur*). The carver of Maughold II does the same, but he was probably working at a time long after the Viking Age (p. 210).

Like **u**, **i** and **a** can denote a range of vowel sounds. There seems to be a degree of overlap between **i** and the two other principal vowel runes, but the question is fraught with difficulty because of uncertainty in a number of cases about exact pronunciation. Chiefly, **i** stands for [i(:)], as in **sin** with [i] (*sinn*, e.g. Andreas I), **sina** with [i:] (*sína*, e.g. German II), but it can also denote [e] as presumably in **in** (*en*, e.g. Andreas I), **þina** (*þenna*, Bride; on the occurrence of forms of this pronoun with the root vowel denoted **ã** or **a**, cf. below); and further, unstressed [ɪ], as in **suarti** (*svarti*, Andreas IIa) – and also the semi-vowel [j], as in **liutulbsunr** (*Ljótólfssonr*, Ballaugh). Stressed [a(:)] and unstressed [ʌ] are the vowels mainly represented by **a**, as in **habrs** with [a] (*Hafrs*, Braddan IV), **salu** with [a:] (*sálu*, Kirk Michael II), **fustra** with [ʌ] (*fóstra*, Kirk Michael III). But there are a good number of words in the Manx corpus in which we have reason to suspect the presence of stressed [æ], the *i*-mutation product of [a], and here **a** (and perhaps **i**) may also be pressed into service. That is particularly the case with the preposition forms *aft* (< **aftr*), *eptir* (<**aftiri* – originally an adverb), which appear in various guises including **aft** (e.g. Braddan III), **ift** (e.g. Braddan I), **aftir** (e.g. Andreas IIa), **iftir** (Maughold V). The problem here is to know whether these are all attempts to spell [æft], [æftir], there being no dedicated rune for [æ], or whether there were varying pronunciations of the root vowel, ?[a], ?[æ], ?[e], as suggested in part by the dual origin of the forms, in part by the spellings.

Where **i** appears to overlap with **u**, as in Braddan II's **triku** (?*tryggu*) the matter is somewhat different. With no dedicated rune for [y(:)] most carvers rendered the sound **u**, but theoretically **i** is an equally plausible choice: [y] is a high front rounded vowel, [u] high rounded, but back, [i] high front, but unrounded; both [u] and [i] thus differ from [y] in respect of one feature, and **i** may just as well denote [y(:)] as **u**. In reality, however, rune carvers do not appear to have thought along such lines since, until ᛦ became established as the way of rendering [y(:)], they by and large stuck to **u** as the means of denoting this vowel, and virtually never employed **i**. An alternative possibility in the case of **triku**, which removes the suggestion of overlap, is that it represents a case of delabialisation [y] > [i], although that seems to be a largely East Scandinavian, in particular Swedish, phenomenon, where *inter alia* the personal name element *-tryggr* can be found with the root vowel spelt **i** (cf. Lagman 1990: 36–50, especially 36–9; *DR*: 710–11).

There also appears to be variation in the denotation of [ɔ], the *u*-mutation product of [a], but again uncertainty about pronunciation makes it hard to be sure. As noted above, [ɔ] is commonly written **au**. Sometimes, however, where [ɔ] is (perhaps) to be expected, we find **a** (though cf. pp. 138, 234), as in Braddan III's [**f**](**aþ**)[**ur**] (?*foðr*), Onchan *a*'s **murkialu** (?*Myrgjǫlu*). (On **sãnt:ulf** for possible *Sǫndulf*, Andreas IIa, see above.)

Certain of the differences observable in the denotation of the root vowel of *þenna* (acc. m. sg.) stem not from the uncertainties of runic orthography but without doubt from the existence of rival forms of the word. The demonstrative *sjá*, *þetta* 'this' develops from the basic pronoun *sá*, *sú*, *þat* 'that', which historically has both root vowel [a] and [e], cf. acc. m. sg. *þann*, nom./acc. n. sg. *þat*, gen. m./n. sg. *þess*, dat. m. sg./dat. pl. *þeim*. Although the Icelandic (and thus the standardised Old Norse) paradigms of both demonstratives have relatively fixed forms, they were clearly subject to considerable variation in spoken Viking-Age and medieval Scandinavian, and this is apparent not least from runic inscriptions. Bride's **þina** and Kirk Michael III's **pïna** can thus be assumed to denote [θen:a], or perhaps [θẽn:a], while the slightly more common **þãnã**, and less common **þãna** (Andreas IIa) and **þanã** (Kirk Michael II), reflect *þanna*, with [a]s presumably nasalised by [n:] and marked accordingly, or left unmarked, by the carver.

Given what is said above (p. 65) about the function of diacritic dotting, it is no surprise to find that ᛦ and ᛁ appear to denote a variety of vowel sounds in the Manx inscriptions. There are only two occurrences of ᛦ, both in Kirk Michael III, where the rune is used in the Irish personal names **mal:lümkun** and **mal:murü**. This makes its value hard to assess. Seemingly **mal:lümkun** is a Manx Norse spelling of *Máel Lomchon* ['mail 'lomχon/-ən] (see p. 180), which suggests that **ü** is here intended to represent a vowel in the region of [o]. Although the dotted form of **u** mostly denotes [y(:)] or [ø(:)], it can on occasion stand for [o]. That seems commonly to be its value in Greenland, and much closer to Man we have IR 12 Fishamble Street, Dublin, with the sequence **aüsaʀ**, interpreted as *á ós ár* 'at the river mouth' (with *ós* lacking its normal dative *-i* ending). The second name, **mal:murü**, appears to render Irish *Máel Muire* ['mail 'murjə] (p. 180), and it must thus be supposed that **ü** stands for the schwa following the palatalised [r], or for [jə], as the (presumed) Norse carver probably heard the ending of this word.

Another means of denoting schwa, or at least a weakened end vowel, may have been **ɨ**, although in none of the relevant examples can we rule out the possibility that [e] was intended (cf. p. 65). German II has **þïnsï** ?[θensə], ?[θense] and both German II and Kirk Michael III **ïftïr** ?[æftər], ?[efter], etc., all with historical unstressed [-ɪ(-)], while the Kirk Michael III and Onchan *e* carvers write **sinï** and **runï**∗ respectively for the usual Old Norse *sína* (though cf. pp. 180–81) and *rúnar* (contrast, e.g., **kuinu:sina**, Andreas II*a*, **runar**, German I*a*). An example which could be thought to point in the opposite direction is the (uncertainly read) **iual**∗**ir** of Kirk Michael V*a*. If what we have here is the personal name *Jóalfr*, as many have surmised, the final vowel must be epenthetic, and one might then have expected its sound to have been indeterminate and so a good candidate for denotation by **ï**. On the other hand, there is no indication the carver of Kirk Michael V*a* knew or used dotted runes. Nor, indeed, is the reading **iual**∗**ir** accepted by all, or the interpretation *Jóalfr* in any way assured.

In stressed syllables **ï** more clearly denotes [e], and perhaps [æ] as well: the root vowel in German II's **þïnsï** and Kirk Michael III's **þïna** must be presumed to have been [e] (cf. above), as also that in the verb form **ïs** (*es*, Kirk Michael III) and the personal name **hïþin** (*Heðinn*, Maughold IV*a* 1), whereas in **ïftïr** (cf. above), Kirk Michael III's **ïtra** (= *betra*), and Maughold IV*a* 1's **sïti** (*setti*) we are dealing with the *i*-mutation product of [a]. Historically this is [æ], but in many forms of Scandinavian [æ] and [e] coalesced, some generalising [æ], some [e]. We have only the runic inscriptions to tell us what the situation was in Man, and unfortunately their witness is ambiguous.

A striking orthographical feature of the Manx inscriptions is the use of **b** rather than **f** to denote [β]. This occurs in Ballaugh, where we find **ãulaibr:liutulbsunr** (*Óleifr Ljótólfssonr*), Braddan IV, which has **þurlibr**, **habrs** (*Þorleifr, Hafrs*, the latter gen.), and possibly in Andreas VIII † (see p. 117). It is noticeable that in Man the usage occurs only in personal names, but whether any significance should be attached to that is unclear. The employment of younger-*fuþark* **b** for [β] is documented sporadically between the ninth and fifteenth centuries in various parts of the Scandinavian speaking world, with a small concentration in Scotland (cf. SC 11 with two examples,

SC 12, 14). Phonetically **b** may represent [β] just as well as **f** since [β] shares two features with [b] (which **b** commonly represents): + bilabial, + voiced, and two with [ɸ] (regularly denoted by **f**): + bilabial, + spirant. However, the younger *fuþark* tends to mark the stop-spirant distinction rather than the voiced-unvoiced (thus **þ** stands for [θ] and [ð], for example, and contrasts with **t**, which denotes [t] and [d]), and that is presumably why the correlation **b** [β] is rare.

Somewhat in contradistinction to the point just made, **þ** in Maughold II is used to denote [d] as well as [ð], as in **baþrik** for *Pátraic* ['pa:drig], **kurnaþal** for *Kornadal* (< ?*Kvernárdal(i)*). It also represents the final consonant in **krisþ** *Krist*, where the distinction between [t] and [d] is neutralised following [s] and we have a /t/-/d/ archiphoneme. Like the examples of **b** for [β], all three instances of this phenomenon occur in names, but since most of Maughold II's text consists of names, that can hardly be a significant consideration. As pointed out under the interpretation of this inscription (pp. 210–11), **þ** for [d] is found sporadically in Scandinavia, not least in the Middle Ages; and in printed literature of the Reformation period **þ** is given as the runic equivalent of roman 'd' (cf., e.g., Barnes 2012: 133–5). Nevertheless, the feature is unexpected in Man; particularly striking is the relative consistency with which **þ** marks [d] or the /t/-/d/ archiphoneme in Maughold II (the only exception being **brist** for *prest*). There is good reason to think this inscription late in the Manx context, as also Maughold I, by the same 'Jóan priest' (cf. p. 206), and that might explain the choice of **þ** to mark dental stops – provided the carver had had contact with medieval Scandinavian rune writers (which is far from clear). However, there is also reason to think Jóan was trying to imitate earlier Manx runic writing, and there is little in the surviving Viking-Age Manx inscriptions that could have suggested to him that [d] or the /t/-/d/ archiphoneme should be written **þ**. Perhaps he was so far removed from both runic script and the Norse language (Page 1992a: 134–7) that he simply regarded **þ** as an exotic form of **t**.

In the schematic presentation of the relationship between spelling and sound given above, ᛧ **R**, which occurs only once (in Andreas IV), is said probably to denote [r]. The reason for thinking this is the belief that the voiced sibilant which **R** originally represented had by about 900 coalesced with [r] in western Scandinavia. Of course we have no way of knowing whether that was also true of speech in Man, not least because there are likely to have been groups of people from eastern Scandinavia on the island as well, and in the East /ʀ/ was retained much longer as a separate phoneme. However, apart from the single Andreas IV example, there is no sign anywhere in the Manx corpus that carvers recognised a distinction between [r] and [ʀ]. Too little remains of Andreas IV for us to determine whether it was made by a western or eastern Scandinavian rune carver, although the placement of the inscription on the narrow edge of the stone is suggestive of someone familiar with western tradition. With so much uncertainty the reason for this one occurrence of **ʀ** in Man is hard to fathom (cf. pp. 60, 106–7).

Several commonly occurring words in the Manx inscriptions lack one of the runes to be expected in them. We find *****rs**, **krs** for *kross* (Ballaugh, Bride), **sur** for *sonr* (Bride), **þna** for *þenna* or *þanna* (Kirk Michael I and IV), and **þsar** for *þessar* (German I*a*). These may be instances of deliberate abbreviation, since they all involve words it would be easy for the rune reader to recognise. Bride, moreover, has two words with missing runes (out of the ten in total that survive), implying perhaps a deliberate policy. However, it is also possible in one or more of these cases that the missing rune has been omitted in error. In Bride's **krs**, for example, it looks as though the **s** has been inserted between **kr** and the **þ** that begins the next word, and that suggests carelessness; but **sur** in the same inscription seems to have been carved all of a piece and is adequately spaced.

Finally, we must return to the orthography of Maughold II, and also bring Maughold I more firmly into the discussion. Apart from the use in the former of **þ** to denote [d] and the /t/-/d/ archiphoneme, discussed above, we encounter in it **aþanman**, a rendering of *Adamnán*, the name of the Irish saint. Given the likely Middle Irish pronunciation [ˈaðəµnaːn], the use of **þ** in the initial syllable is perhaps to be expected, but the spelling **nm** for expected **mn** suggests either metathesis in the spoken form of the name or confusion by the carver. In view of the many unusual orthographical and/or grammatical features encountered in Maughold I and II (cf. pp. 205–6, 210–11), confusion is perhaps more likely. Maughold I, most notably, contains the phrase **raisti+þasir+runur**. Taken at face value the wording here states that the carver 'put up these runes', which implies muddle between the verbs *rísta* (strong), or perhaps *rista* (weak), both meaning '[to] carve', and *reisa* '[to] put up', with past tense forms *reist*, *risti*, *reisti* respectively. And the form in which the object of the verb is cast, **þasir+runur** (for traditional *þessar rúnar/rúnir*), suggests either a mix-up or that the Manx dialect of Norse had by this time undergone quite drastic changes in parts of its inflectional morphology.

7. Language

With certain exceptions there is little difficulty in grasping the general sense of the Manx runic inscriptions. Most of them transmit the same basic text: 'NN put up this cross in memory of MM'. There may be supplementary information, but much of it is of a kind common on memorial rune-stones, as *Gautr gerði* … 'Gautr made …' (MM 99 Andreas I, MM 101 Kirk Michael II), *En Ásrøðr reist rúnar þessar* 'But Ásrøðr carved these runes' (MM 107 German I, St John's, *a*). Identification of personal names can be a lot trickier, and apart from the observation that about a third of them are Celtic (cf. pp. 36–7), little in the way of generalisation is possible. Each name is treated individually in the interpretation of the inscription in which it occurs.

Linguistic analysis of the Manx Scandinavian runic corpus is usefully concentrated on three matters: regional Scandinavian origin, age, and the influence of the indigenous Celtic tongue. The more reliable guides here are word forms and vocabulary, inflections and word-order. Subtle differences of pronunciation, to the extent such existed among those who carved the Manx crosses and other rune-stones, are much harder to capture. For one thing, we have no way of knowing how many types of Scandinavian were in use on Man in the tenth and eleventh centuries. The island occupied a central position in the Irish Sea, and settlers may have come directly from the Scandinavian homelands or indirectly via Ireland, England, the Hebrides, Orkney, or elsewhere, where they or an earlier generation could have picked up a variety of local speech patterns. Another problem is to understand how rune carvers moved from the spoken to the written word. Did they undertake rudimentary phonetic analysis? Or did they write as they had been taught, or as others did? Or was it a combination of all three strategies? Various examples illustrating the difficulty of using runic spelling to assess pronunciation will be found in the discussion of Manx runic orthography in ch. 6, pp. 71–8.

Olsen (1954: 153–4) appears to define the language of all the Manx runic inscriptions of Scandinavian type as Norwegian. At least, they are said to be "written with Old Norse runes in the Old Norse language" as distinct from the twelfth-century demotic Scandinavian inscriptions from north-west England, of which "scarcely any […] has a distinctively O. Norse stamp", and whose language is not "specifically Old Norse". There is also a clear delimitation vis-à-vis eastern Scandinavian, for the reader is informed in a footnote that the runic inscription on the Lincoln comb case "is regarded as Danish, not Norse" (and is thus published in *DR*).

It is true that many (but by no means all) of the rune-inscribed Manx crosses have a Norwegian (Viking-Age) layout, with the inscription running up one of the narrow edges of the stone. It is also true that the "short-twig" graph-types characteristic of the bulk of the corpus have counterparts in tenth-century Norway and Sweden, but scarcely in Denmark. Regarding the language in which the inscriptions are framed, however, there is little that must be Norwegian (though it is fair to say there is a great deal that could be). The common Manx acc. m. sg. demonstrative *þanna* 'this' (with or without the marking of nasalised *a*-vowels) is well attested in Viking-Age Norway, but hardly found in Denmark: it does, however, occur in Sweden, quite frequently in some provinces (notably Småland and, to a lesser extent, Östergötland). Much the same is true of the variant form *penna*: common in Norway, little evidenced in Denmark, and not uncommon in many parts of Sweden. The strong past tense *reist* 'carved' is the norm in Norway, at least until the thirteenth century, but it is also fairly well documented in Denmark and Sweden. It occurs in MM 107 German I (St John's) *a* and MM 141 Onchan *e*, but MM 142 Maughold IV*a* 3 and *f* have the weak form *risti*, more characteristic of eastern Scandinavia.

The falling diphthongs /æi/, /au/, /øy/ appear to have been monophthongised to /e:/, /ø:/, /ø:/ respectively during the tenth century in Denmark, and during the eleventh in Sweden. In Norway they were by and large retained. Apparent retention or loss of the relevant diphthongs does not, however, provide a safe criterion for the determination of linguistic affiliation in the Manx inscriptions. This is for two reasons. First, if the Manx corpus is, or could be, from the tenth century, it is possible diphthongal pronunciation was still current in at least parts of Denmark and almost certain it was maintained in Sweden. Second, the denotation of monophthongs and diphthongs in Man is haphazard, to say the least (for examples cf. p. 73).

As well as lacking linguistic features that would indisputably link them with Norwegian tradition, the Manx inscriptions exhibit a number of forms and usages which point, or may point, towards the East, or particular areas thereof. The acc. m. sg. demonstrative with deictic particle -*si*, as þïnsï 'this' (MM 140 German II, Peel), is very rare in Norway at any period, but common in Denmark and Sweden. The use of the verb *setja* 'place' (rather than *reisa* 'put up') to describe the establishing of a runic monument, as in MM 142 Maughold IV*a* 1, is well attested in south-western Sweden and northern Jutland, whereas only a couple of instances are documented from Norway. The verb *rétta* 'raise up' in the same sense, as apparently on MM 127 Jurby, is unknown in Norway and Denmark and south-western Sweden, but very common in Uppland. It has further been suggested that *þan* 'than' (as opposed to the more usual *en*) in MM 130 Kirk Michael III is Swedish (Bugge 1899: 243–4) or Danish (Olsen 1954: 216–17). Certainly, *þan* (as a form of the correlative clause-introducer) is documented in the Swedish and Danish runic corpora, and not apparently in the Norwegian, but, truth to tell, the need for the Old Norse equivalent of 'than' hardly arises in Norwegian inscriptions at all. There are yet other cases where the possibility of East Scandinavian involvement might be mooted: MM 136 Braddan III, which combines the monographic spelling **risti** 'put up' with unmutated **[f](aþ)[ur]** (possibly indicating the eastern forms /re:sti/, /faþur/ as opposed to western /ræisti/, /fɔþur/; cf. p. 138); MM 140 German II (Peel), which conceivably exhibits vowel balance (p. 160).

A problem with this kind of exercise is that the application of traditional criteria for distinguishing between West and East Scandinavian involvement often leads to conflicting results – not perhaps unexpected in the Isle of Man, which one imagines must have been something of a linguistic melting pot. MM 130 Kirk Michael III provides a useful example. On art-historical grounds it has been dated in the tenth century, possibly its first half (Wilson 1970–71: 7, 9 and pp. 42–4 in this edition; but cf. p. 59). Its carver uses "long-branch" graph-types throughout, typical of Denmark in the tenth century. Yet the historical diphthong /æi/ is apparently unmonophthongised, at least it is written **ai** in **raisti** 'put up' and **laifa** '[to] leave', and the acc. m. sg. of the demonstrative pronoun 'this' is **þïna**, a form scarcely to be found in Viking-Age Denmark. The carver also employs the dotted runes ᛁ and ᚴ, attested in Denmark towards the end of the tenth century but not in Norway until somewhat later, yet on occasion he uses the fourth rune ᚢ to denote /o(:)/, a feature that in Norway and Sweden seems to become established in the early eleventh century, but in Denmark only in its second half.

There is not much otherwise in the language of the Manx inscriptions indicative of age. The preposition *eptir* 'in memory of' occurs in a short (**aft**, **ift**) and a long form (**aftir**, **ïftïr**, etc.), the latter being slightly commoner than the former. According to Peterson (1996: 242–4) the short form is in regular use in Scandinavia until about the beginning of the eleventh century, whereafter it fades away, though persisting perhaps longer in Norway than in Denmark or Sweden. Peterson is less specific about the age of the long form, but it seems we should expect it to occur only sporadically in the latter half of the tenth century. If the evidence from Scandinavia is applicable to Man, this should mean a date range of perhaps thirty to fifty years either side of 1000. That conflicts with the art-historical dating of the Manx crosses to

c. 925–1020, though perhaps not wildly. However, if the bulk of the corpus is considered to be from the tenth century (as for example Wilson argues: 1994: xix-xx; ch. 3 in this edition), the regular occurrence of long forms like **aftir**, **ïftïr** is surprising. It is worth noting, however, that the Kilbar cross (SC 8) also has the long form, notwithstanding it seems to employ the early memorial formula *Eptir Þorgerði Steinars dóttur er kross sjá reistr* 'in memory of Þorgerðr Steinarr's daughter this cross is put up' (see further p. 60).

According to most estimates, initial /h-/ in the clusters /hl-/, /hn-/, /hr-/ is lost in Denmark about 900 or before, in Sweden and Norway around 1000 or shortly thereafter. In the Manx inscriptions we find the byname **nhaki** (*hnakki*) 'neck' (MM 135 Braddan IV) and the personal names **rãskitil** (*Hrossketill*, MM 138 Braddan II, though cf. p. 132) and **rumu...** (almost certainly the remains of *Hrómund*, acc., MM 126 Kirk Michael IV). These three examples, one with **nh-** rather than the usual **hn-** and two lacking **h-** altogether, suggest a date around 1000 (or a little later) if the inspiration is Norwegian or Swedish. Braddan IV's **nhaki** can hardly be Danish-inspired since that would place the inscription in the ninth century, and a Danish background is unlikely in Braddan II whose carver uses ᚠ for /o/. The question arises, however, whether it is justifiable to date Manx loss of initial /h-/ in the relevant clusters by reference to the estimated time of its disappearance in different parts of Scandinavia. Ultimately /h-/ was lost before /l/, /n/, /r/ in all areas where Scandinavian was spoken except Iceland, and the only evidence for when or how the development proceeded in Man comes from the three examples just quoted.

There seem to be a few cases in the Manx inscriptions of what is referred to by the blanket terms "reduction" or "weakening". MM 140 German II (Peel) has **þïnsï** 'this [acc. m. sg.]' with final **-ï** rather than **-i**; the writer of MM 130 Kirk Michael III uses the reflexive possessive form **sinï** where we might expect **sina** (acc. f. sg.?); and the Þuríðr who contributed to the inscriptions on the Onchan cross renders as **ï** the historical /A/ vowel of plural *rúnar* 'runes'. In Scandinavia such apparent weakening of unstressed vowels is by and large a medieval phenomenon, although sporadic examples exist from earlier periods. Various explanations can be and have been offered for individual instances (cf. in particular here the accounts of German II (Peel), Kirk Michael III and Onchan), but it appears impossible to date inscriptions on the basis of such seemingly weakened forms, not least in the Manx context.

There is much to suggest that the *Jóan prestr* who carved MM 145 Maughold I and MM 144 Maughold II was writing in the late twelfth or early thirteenth century (pp. 206, 210). The language of Maughold I corroborates other evidence that points in that direction. In the phrase **raisti+þasir+runur** there seems to be confusion between *reisti* 'put up' and *reist* or *risti* 'carved', which, together with the aberrant vocalic ending of **þasir** and the unusual *ōn*-stem form **runur** (ON *þessar rúnar* 'these runes [acc. f. pl.]') indicates a person with an uncertain grasp of Old Scandinavian (as we know it, at least; but cf. further pp. 205–6). The linguistic evidence in itself, however, cannot provide a clear indication of age, since there are several examples of missing or unexpected inflections in Manx inscriptions that otherwise appear to be from the tenth century.

Such departures from standard Old Scandinavian grammar (in the widest sense) have generally been seen as the result of prolonged and intimate contact with speakers of Irish (from which a separate Manx variety of *Q*-Celtic cannot be distinguished at this period) – grammatical simplification being a commonly observed outcome of language contact. Seip (1930) points to parallels in Norwegian manuscripts, but they are of considerably later date than the Manx examples, and extracted from a vastly more extensive material. What is striking about the Manx deviations from the grammatical norm is their number relative to the size of the corpus. No obvious runic parallels suggest themselves. Nominative -*r* is missing in the personal names **sãnt:ulf** (MM 131 Andreas IIa), **kaut** (MM 101 Kirk Michael II),]**rim** (a damaged **krim**, MM 126 Kirk Michael IV), and **þuriþ** (MM 141 Onchan *e*, though see the comment on this form pp. 235–6). Accusative -*i* is lacking in the personal name **lifilt** (MM 142 Maughold IV*e*, but cf. p. 219), and presumed genitive -*s* in **smiþ** 'smith' (MM 101 Kirk Michael II, though see p. 171). In MM 130 Kirk Michael III **fustra:sinï** '?his foster mother' and **kãna** 'wife' appear to stand in apposition to the personal name **mal:murü**, acc. f. sg., which would lead us to expect *fóstru sína* and *konu* (cf. the discussion on pp. 180–81). Finally, MM 175 Maughold V has **kuinasina** acc. for standard *kvinnu sína*. No clear patterns emerge from these examples, and the conclusion that they indicate incipient breakdown in the inflexional system after a period of intensive language contact seems warranted.

Language contact has also been suggested as the reason for what has been deemed an unusual word-order pattern in some of the Manx inscriptions, specifically 'son/daughter of MM/PP' rather than 'MM/PP's son/daughter', as MM 112 Braddan I **uf∗ak:sun:k(r)inais** 'Ófeigr son of K-'. While it is true that 'NN son of MM' is a regular formation in commemorative ogams (and standard patronymic usage in the insular Celtic languages), apparent parallels can be found in Scandinavian runic inscriptions, as **(s)un:nairbis** 'son of NærfiR' in DR 230 Tryggevælde, **(t)u(t)ur:kunars** 'daughter of Gunnarr' in N 225 Klepp I, and **muþiR:alriks:tutiR:urms** 'mother of AlrikR, daughter of OrmR' on Sö 101 Ramsund. As observed on p. 150–51, however, a distinction needs to be made between true patro-/metronymics and appositional phrases, the latter supplying additional information about a person rather than identifying them. Unfortunately the difference is by no means always obvious. The Scandinavian examples just given are most plausibly considered appositional phrases ('... [who was] the son/the daughter/the mother ...') judging from their respective contexts. With Irish in the background the Manx cases hover uncertainly between the two interpretations. MM 118 Bride offers the most persuasive instance of a patronymic. There is nothing in its opening – **truian:sur⁕ufkals:raistikrsþina:** 'Drúan son of Dubgall put up this cross' – to suggest background information is being offered about Drúan. According to Olsen (1954: 227), the deployment of separation marks in this inscription offers further evidence in favour of the patronymic interpretation, but that is hard to substantiate (see p. 150–51).

Cultural contact must underlie the custom of putting up crosses rather than plain memorial rune-stones – and thus the ubiquitous use on the Manx runic memorials of the term *kross*. The word itself comes ultimately of course from Latin *crux*, and in the Manx context probably via Irish rather than late Old English *cros*. Use of the term is not, however, restricted to the Isle of Man. It is attested in runic inscriptions from other parts of the British Isles where Irish traditions were strong – Ireland itself (IR 2 Killaloe), the Hebrides (SC 8 Kilbar, SC 10 Inchmarnock), and now also northern England (E 19 Sockburn Hall, cf. Rye 2017). It is seemingly also found once in Norway (N 417 Svanøy). Norway boasts three more stone crosses inscribed with runes: N 223 Njærheim I, N 237 Sele II, and N 252 Stavanger III (the first two known only from drawings), but they are all identified by the term 'stone' rather than 'cross'.

To take account of the linguistic peculiarities of the Manx Scandinavian inscriptions, this edition includes (where practicable) transcriptions intended to reflect the language encountered more closely than the standard Old West Norse normalisations that are also provided. Since we know so little for sure about the variety or varieties of Scandinavian in use on Man in the mid- and late Viking Age, the inclusion of such "local" or "Manx" transcriptions is a hazardous undertaking. What the reader is offered is inspired guesswork based partly on the language of the inscriptions themselves as seen through the lens of Viking-Age runic orthography, partly on our knowledge of Scandinavian language development in general. A few unusual conventions have been adopted, notably the use of *ã* to indicate assumed /ã:/, [ã], unless the orthography or any other feature of a particular inscription suggests that the writer had lost nasal vowels from his (or her) pronunciation. Nasalisation is not marked in other vowels, however, in accordance with orthographical practice in runic writing (an exception is Ballaugh's Ṓlæiƀr, where nasality is the point at issue, cf. pp. 123–4).

There is little of linguistic note in the two Anglo-Saxon inscriptions from the Isle of Man (MM 42, 43 Maughold AS I and II). Such commentary as is required on their language will be found under *Interpretation* in the relevant individual accounts.

The corpus

MM 99 Andreas I
Plates 1–6, Figs 1–2

LITERATURE. Marquardt 1961: 57–8. Kinnebrook 1841: 11 and fig. 8; Train 1845, 2: 34; Hibbert-Ware *et al.* [*c.* 1848]: 135; Munch 1850: 273–4, 276; Cumming 1857: 22 and fig. 10; Kneale [*c.* 1860]: 61, no. 16; Cumming 1868a: facing 23, no. 2, and 26; Kermode 1887b: 151; Taylor 1887: 185; Bugge 1899: 234–5; Kermode 1907: 146–9; Brate 1907: 23; Marstrander 1938; Olsen 1954: 183–4; Sanness Johnsen 1968: 221–2; Page 1983: 136, 140; Holman 1996: 100–103.

MM 99 is recorded by Kinnebrook at "Kirk Andreas, on the green, near the entrance to the Church-yard", and by Cumming (1857) more precisely "on the Green […] opposite the Church gates", a site now occupied by a War Memorial. Both Kinnebrook ("very much defaced") and Cumming ("in a sadly worn and dilapidated condition", 1857) reported its degraded state, though both suggest a slightly greater number of incisions than now survive, which could imply more recent damage to the stone. Paterson (1863: facing 18) showed it surmounting a low mound, and it is presumably there that the 1870 Ordnance Survey 6" map puts it (though there is insufficient detail to be entirely sure). If the cross had been long on this prominent site it is strange that it was not depicted earlier, considering the number of visitors who mentioned MM 131 Andreas II, near at hand. Gibson (1722), Anon. (1822), and Oswald (1822), for example, failed to note it, though it may be the runic cross recorded as "near the entrance gate" in the anonymous *Illustrated Guide and Visitor's Companion* (1836: 105). Train commented on the stone's vulnerability "in the middle of the green […] where the villagers sport", adding that it was also an object "against which the cows rub themselves". It was used to post bills on, and Kermode (1907) claimed that "for a long time children passing on their way to the village school made it a target for stones and other missiles", so it would not be surprising if earlier drawings preserved details that no longer survive. In November 1886, following the passing by Tynwald earlier in the year of a Museum and Ancient Monuments Act, MM 99, together with other Andreas crosses, was laid in the south porch of the church (Anon. 1886; Kermode 1907: 147). It has been under some sort of cover ever since, though for a long time that consisted of an open-sided shelter on the north side of the church. In 1957 MM 99 and the other crosses were moved into the church and ultimately displayed in the antechapel formed by the west end of the church nave (Manx Museum and National Trust 1958: 7; Moore 1959: [3]). There the stone now stands, set in the floor so its full height cannot be measured.

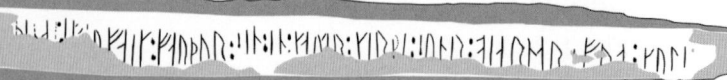

Fig. 1. MM 99 Andreas I (drawing: Jonas Nordby).

The Andreas I runes are carved on a substantial slab of laminated siltstone. According to Kermode (1907) the material is "tough blue clay-slate, possibly quarried from the hills about five miles to the south-west between Sulby and Ballaugh". Modern geological expertise defines it as "banded mudstone-siltstone-fine grained sandstone typical of Port Erin" (though with no suggestion it comes from that area). The slab measures *c.* 185.5 cm (visible height) × 45 × *c.* 15. Kermode (1907) gives the height as 97 inches (= 246 cm). The surface of the stone is much weathered. Both faces have a circle-headed cross, with interlace on the shaft, and further interlace or key pattern ornament to each side of it. The inscription runs upwards along one of the narrow edges, its opening graphs completely lost. The other edge of the slab is blank. The runes read:

](þ)i(n)a:if(:)ufaik:fauþur:sin:in:kautr:kir[þ]i: sunr:biarnar:fra:kuli(:)

The length of the surviving inscription is 96.5 cm. The runes form an irregular line, and there were apparently no framing lines. Kermode (1907: 148) concluded their appearance shows "that the edge was rough and undressed when they were cut". Parts of many runes are lost or uncertainly traceable: the lower halves of rr. 1–9, 34–6, and 45–6, for instance, are broken away (Holman despairs of the first sequence, remarking that "the words **þana aft** are now so heavily damaged as to be virtually illegible"). It is therefore not possible to give more than a general idea of rune height. Fairly well-preserved examples are rr. 14 (**u**), 42 (**a**); both are 45 mm. Because of the weathering of the surface even clearly identifiable runes no longer show subtleties of cutting. Indeed, if Kermode is correct, there may have been no subtleties. Andreas I has a text which shows up rather differently in different light conditions. That should be kept in mind in reading the following description.

Before r. 1 a large part of the surface has broken away and nothing can

Fig. 2. MM 99 Andreas I, Cumming's 1857 drawings (1857: fig. 10).

now be made out here (cf., however, below). Rune 1 consists of the remains of a vertical and the upper half of what is most probably a bow. Rune 2 consists of the upper half or more of a vertical; it shows no further distinguishing feature, at least none that is obvious. It has been read **i** (Olsen, Sanness Johnsen), but also **a** (Brate, Kermode); the former seems the plausible reading, given the length of what remains of the vertical and the difficulty in discerning any branch. Rune 3 is the top half of a vertical with what seems to be the remnant of a right descending branch by its current base, as of ᚺ; the context strongly suggests **n**. Olsen and Sanness Johnsen signal damage or uncertainty in this graph, as does the illustration (but not the text) in Kermode (1907: pl. XXIX). The base of r. 4 is lost, though the identification as ᚨ **a** is clear enough – the branch is well preserved. Following this graph is a series of nicks and indentations among which two carved elongated dots can be discerned: the usual form of the separator in this inscription. Of r. 5 there survives the upper half or more of a vertical with no further distinguishing feature (thus necessarily **i**), and of r. 6 a vertical and parts of two rising branches near the top, surely **f**. Between rr. 6 and 7 there is no easily recognisable graph or separator. There is, however, an area of damage here in which something might once have been carved, and we thought to see traces of an upper dot. Brate notes: "t är borta men måste ha funnits på grund af rummet" 't is lost, but must have been there as the spacing makes clear'; Sanness Johnsen agrees: "Rune 7 er helt forsvunnet i et brudd, men **t** er den eneste utfylling mulig her" '[Her] rune 7 has been completely lost in surface damage, but **t** is the only possible graph to be supplied here'. Kermode (1907) originally read AF or IF, but then accepted IFT on the basis of Brate's observation. Holman comments (1996: 101): "the only rune I can clearly distinguish before **ufaik** is an a-rune."

After r. 22 there was clearly a word separator: an upper point remains, and possible traces of a lower one, in a badly damaged passage of the surface. Rune 29 is a plain vertical. Page felt he could observe here a rising branch which either crossed the vertical (to form ┼) or met it (to give ┤, which he thought more likely in the context of other runes on the stone). We cannot confirm his observation. Brate had no difficulty in reading r. 29 as **a**: "ka i karþi: äro fullständiga" '**ka** in **karþi:** are complete'. Kermode comments on the vowel rune that it "has a flake or hollow mark, but one can trace the cut showing it to have been A". Olsen has ┤ in a tracing he reproduces, but his reading is a cautious "(**a**)". Sanness Johnsen indicates an uncertain **i** here, while Holman prefers a verbal form **kirþi**, in part, apparently, on the evidence of earlier accounts. Both **karþi** and **kirþi** are well attested in Scandinavia, though Man has otherwise only **kirþi** (on MM 200 Braddan VI, MM 101 Kirk Michael II, MM 175 Maughold V).

Rune 31 shows the shadow of a bow in a worn patch to the right of its vertical. Others have had no problem in recognising **þ** here, and of course the context confirms that as the most likely character. Rune 33 appears as an interrupted vertical, slightly shorter than those of the surrounding characters, with what seems to be a dot at its base. The branches of r. 37 sit unusually high on the vertical, but there is no doubt about the identity of this rune. Between rr. 43 and 44 is a wide gap in which there is the trace of a separation point at about mid-height. Brate, Kermode and Sanness Johnsen show a pair of dots in vertical line here; Olsen has one dot above and a tentative second below. Holman shows neither dots nor space. Runes 45–6 have lost their lower halves, but there is no problem of identification in either case. Following the final graph, r. 50, is a very damaged part of the surface where the upper of a pair of punctuation points or dashes can perhaps be dimly discerned. Brate gives a pair of points here; Kermode, Olsen, Sanness Johnsen and Holman none.

The appearance of the incisions as they remain indicates that the runes were firmly cut. Indeed, in some cases only the deepest v-shaped sections are left. There are occasional double or multiple overcuts at the tops of graphs (e.g. rr. 7, 9–11), suggesting the grooves were widened and deepened in an upward direction. Thin overcuts at the bases of a couple of graphs (rr. 10, 14) indicate perhaps that the initial direction of cutting was downwards.

Diagnostic rune forms are ᚾ **n**, ᚽ **a**, ᛁ **s**, ᛐ **t**, ᚼ **b**.

Earlier readings

From the mid-nineteenth century, that is before the cross was taken under shelter, there survive the depictions of Kinnebrook (1841), Hibbert-Ware [*c.* 1848], Cumming (1857; 1868a) and Kneale [*c.* 1860], and the readings in Train (1845: printed roman letters based on a cast or casts) and Munch (1850: printed runes based on casts). There are also the 1887 comments by Taylor and Kermode in the correspondence of *The Academy*. Some of these can be used, though with caution, to elucidate or supplement missing or imperfectly preserved parts of the inscription.

Kinnebrook records r. 1 as a complete **þ** with, before it, part of a vertical. Runes 2, 3 are verticals, the first with perhaps a slight hint of an ascending left branch at its centre. Rune 4 is **a**, and rr. 5, 6 a vertical and **f** respectively, followed by two points in vertical line. Two similar points follow r. 22. Rune 29 is a vertical, and r. 31 a clear **þ**. Rune 33 seems to be a full vertical, though the depiction here is murky. The final runes are not shown as damaged at their bases, but they are not clearly reproduced either. There are also occasional errors of identification of letters that are still visible on the stone, notably r. 37 read as **t** rather than **b**. The inscription ends with a single point, set midline.

The sketchy drawing in the Hibbert-Ware collection opens promisingly: **þina.if.ufaik fauþur:sin:in kautriirþi**, then declines in a second line of runes that look something like **sunr iiirnarsiu∗ k∗li**, a number of the graphs represented by rough verticals or anomalous forms. The draughtsman (not necessarily Hibbert-Ware himself) had trouble with his identifications here, for though he understood his line 1, not entirely unreasonably, to say *Thesaaf. Ufaic Fauthur sin in Gautr Urthi*, the second line had him baffled, and he attempted a roman-alphabet rendering of only parts of it, and then confusedly.

Munch's text derives from rubbings taken from casts. His printed runes show **þāna:af:ufaik:fauþur:sin:in:kautr:kirþi:sunr:biarnar:k...**, with ᚠ for **ā**.

The drawing in Cumming (1857; see Fig. 2) confirms some of Kinnebrook's readings. Runes 1–4 are **þana**, the first rune defective as now at its base, and this is preceded by three damaged graphs: a vertical, **u**, and another vertical. Runes 5–6 are **af**, followed by two points. Runes 29, 31 are **i**, **þ**, while r. 33 is the standard dotted **s** [1]. The final runes are recorded as **kub:kuli**, with no final stop. Cumming (1868a) is an obvious rethinking (or perhaps re-creation) of his 1857 reading, though he claims (p. 26) to be able to "make out distinctly": "CRUS : THANA : AF : UFAIG : FAUTHUR : SIN : IN : GAUTR : GIRTHI : SUNR : BIARNAR". His drawing shows **krus:þana:af:ufaik:fauþur:sin:in:kautr:kurþi:sunr:biarna**(r), followed by seven indistinct graphs which he later (p. 26) defines as "some runes which look like *Cub Culi*".

Kneale shows a set of suspiciously undamaged runes but leaves the text incomplete, perhaps unintentionally: **þana:af:ufaik:fauþur:sin:in:kautr:kirþi :sunr:biarnar**.

The quite detailed accounts by Kermode and Taylor in *The Academy* correspondence confirm the problems with the opening of this inscription. Taylor, responding to a confused reading by Vigfusson and Savage (and working from a cast) has "bracketing all defective letters [...] ... TH[A]NA : [A]F : UFAIC : FAUTHUR : SIN : [E]N : CAUTR : CIRTHI : SUNR : BIARNAR : FRO : CUL[I]".

Interpretation

The general sense of the inscription is clear enough though it is not possible to supply the lost opening words otherwise than by conjecture. There could be some 60 cm missing (depending on how far up the edge the text originally began), and that would be equivalent to about 30 graphs. This section presumably had the formula *NN reisti kross* (of which Cumming claimed to be able to identify the last word – perhaps a triumph of hope over observation), from where the preserved text continued, giving:

[*NN reisti kross*] *þenna eptir Ófeig fǫður sinn, en Gautr gerði, sonr Bjarnar frá ?Kolli.*

'[NN (personal name + perhaps byname or patronymic) put up] this [cross] in memory of Ófeigr his father, but Gautr made (it), son of Bjǫrn from ?Kollr.'

The interpretation throws up two problems. The preposition for 'in memory of' on Manx stones appears otherwise as forms of *ept* or *eptir* (**aftir, aftiʀ, aiftir, iftir, ïftïr, aft, ift**). MM 99 seems to have had **if** (although most have read **af**). Unless we believe, with Brate and Sanness Johnsen, that there is space for a now lost rune (cf. the discussion of the reading above), we must assume that the preposition's final **t** has been omitted.

A question that has exercised students of Andreas I hitherto involves the identity of the cross's maker, Gautr. The same name, without its usual nominative -*r*, occurs on MM 101 Kirk Michael II, and has been assumed to refer to the same man. On Andreas I we are told that he is the son of Bjǫrn and that his father (or perhaps he himself) is from **kuli** (dat. sg.). Scholars have pondered long on where this place might be. Kermode (1907: 149) pointed to Cooley "which may well be the farm in Michael still bearing that name" (*cooill* 'nook' 'corner' is in fact a common enough element in Manx placenames, cf. Broderick 1994–2005: indexes, *s.v.*; Manx *keyll*, Irish *caill*, *coill* 'wood' 'forest' might also be a possibility, as Kermode 1887b: 151 appears to envisage). Marstrander (1938: 381) asserted that **kuli** refers instead to the tiny Hebridean island of Coll but gave no evidence. This Olsen accepted, rejecting his own cogent linguistic argument against – that in referring to movement from an island one would expect the preposition *ór* 'out of' rather than *frá* 'from'. To overcome this difficulty he identified the island name Coll as a use of ON *kollr* 'head' 'hill-top', where, judging by usage with similar topographic names, the likely preposition is *frá*. There are occasional examples of *kollr* in place-names elsewhere in the West (Jakobsen 1936: *s.v. kollr*, also *kūla*; Stewart 1987: *s.v. kollr*; but note too Gaelic *coll* = Manx *coull* 'hazel', also a name element, cf. Broderick 1994–2005: indexes, *s.v.*). There is clearly neither likelihood of nor perhaps necessity for geographical precision here.

However, a runic link with the Western Isles could lead to interesting speculation about the politics of this region (see ch. 3 on the art-historical links). The Scottish islands are not noted for their runic monuments. There is a collection of graffiti at Holy Island, off Arran, but these are almost certainly all from the thirteenth century, and made by Norwegian passers-by (Barnes and Page 2006: 274–8). Otherwise there survive only the crosses of Kilbar and Inchmarnock (SC 8, SC 10), and the Iona graveslab (SC 14). Both Kilbar and Inchmarnock show use of the noun *kross* rather than *steinn*, and in this they agree with the generality of the Manx monuments as against usual (but not invariable) Scandinavian practice. So, too, however, does IR 2 the Killaloe cross from County Clare, Ireland, and the superfluity of raised stone crosses in Ireland, Man and elsewhere in the Gaelic West makes it clear that the phenomenon has a much wider reach than Man and the Hebrides. It has nevertheless been proposed that there is a special connection between the Kilbar cross and the Manx series (cf. Barnes and Page 2006: 226–32). The difficulty has been to elaborate the connection, some urging that the Kilbar tradition influenced practice on Man, others the exact opposite (cf. p. 60). (See further the discussion in Liestøl 1983; also Alfvegren 1959: 220–21.)

In the light of various points discussed above a transcription more in keeping with local pronunciation might be:

[NN ræisti kross] þennā æft Ófæig fǫður sinn, en Gautr gærði, sonr Bjarnār frā ?Kolli.

MM 131 Andreas IIa–b
Plates 7–13, Figs 3–4, 36–7

LITERATURE. Marquardt 1961: 58–9. Wanley [c. 1700]; Camden/Gibson 1722: 1459–60; Camden/Gough 1789: 3, 704; Anon. 1822: 494 and pl. XVI; Oswald 1822: 505–6 and pl. XVIII; Kinnebrook 1841: 11–12 and fig. 9; Hibbert-Ware et al. [c. 1848]: 134; Worsaae [c. 1850]: 11; Munch 1850: 277; Cumming 1857: 21–2 and fig. 9; Kneale [c. 1860]: 61, no. 14; Cumming 1868a: facing 23, no. 9, and 30; Vigfusson and Savage 1887: 15; Bugge 1899: 235; Kermode 1907: 194–5; Brate 1907: 23; Olsen 1954: 184; Sanness Johnsen 1968: 222–3; Page 1981: 132–3; Page 1983: 140; Holman 1996: 103–4.

Andreas IIa

This inscription makes its appearance in Camden/Gibson 1722, the earliest printed record of runes on Man. It is also the subject of the rather confused sketch in Wanley [c. 1700], which locates the stone bearing the inscription "in S^t. Andrews Church-Yard [...] near the Stile" (cf. line 2 of Fig. 10). On one of the faces of this monument is a graffito dated apparently 1608 or 1609, showing it was readily accessible as early as that (and not, say, built into the church or churchyard wall). The 1870 Ordnance Survey 6" map places the stone north of the church, where it seems to have remained until 1886. Thereafter it was moved into various forms of shelter together with the other Andreas monuments, before finally being set up inside the church (cf. the history of MM 99 Andreas I outlined on p. 89). Like MM 99, MM 131 is now fixed in the floor, which makes measurement of its full height impossible.

The Andreas II inscriptions are carved on a large slab of dark grey mudstone, measuring c. 151.5 cm (visible height) × 43 × 14. Kermode gives the height as 76 inches (= 193 cm). Both faces have a relief cross, with interlace on the shaft, and animal decoration on either side and above the cross arms.

Fig. 3. MM 131 Andreas IIa (drawing: Jonas Nordby).

Andreas II*a* runs upwards along one edge. The other edge is blank. The runes read:

ᛋᚬᚾᛏ:ᚢᛚᚠ:ᚼᛁᚾ:ᛋᚢᛅᚱᛏᛁ:ᚱᛅᛁᛋᛏᛁ:ᚴᚱᚢᛋ:ᚦᚬᚾᛅ:ᛅᚠᛏᛁᚱ:
ᛅᚱᛁᚾ:ᛒᛁᛅᚢ(:)ᚱᚴᛁᚾ:ᛋᛁᚾᛅ

s ã n t : u l f : h i n : s u a r t i : r a i s t i : k r u s : þ ã n a : a f t i r : a r i n : b i a u
1   5   10   15   20   25   30   35   40
r k : k u i n u : s i n a
45   50   54

The length of the inscription is 115 cm. Space at either end could have accommodated further runes, so this text is clearly complete. There is a lower incised line which the runes roughly follow, many verticals not quite reaching, others touching or even just overlapping it. No corresponding top line is found, and runes vary somewhat in height; representative figures are r. 10 (**n**) 60 mm, r. 18 (**a**) 62 mm, r. 37 (**r**) 74 mm (with light overcuts extending to a total height of 80 mm). The stone surface, though quite well preserved, has occasional chips out of it, which can make some details (in particular word separation points) hard to distinguish. Graphs are boldly, but not always neatly, cut – there are traces throughout of slips of the tool, and of over- double- or multiple-cutting as the grooves were widened and deepened. Rune 3 **n**, for example, has a shallow extension to its branch which crosses r. 4, while r. 13 **a** shows a thin, oblique line on either side of its base. There are gashes around rr. 28–31 (**ãna:a**) and damage to the lower branch of r. 28, but the readings are certain. Gibson's 1722 drawing (see Fig. 36) shows a number of these details, and it is clear the inscription's condition has not changed much over the centuries. Runes 33–5 and 52–4 are shorter than their fellows owing to pre-existing damage above (rr. 33–5) and below (rr. 52–4). No closing points are observable after r. 54. Neither Gibson nor Gough record any, nor do Oswald, Hibbert-Ware, Munch, Cumming (1857: fig. 9), Kneale or Holman. Kinnebrook has a single point here, Cumming (1857: 22) a double, while Cumming (1868a: no. 9) has a midline saltire cross. Kermode (1907) shows two clear points in vertical line in his drawing (pl. LIII), as does Anon. (1822: pl. XVI); Brate and Sanness Johnsen give the same in their transliterations. Olsen has the dots too, but within brackets, apparently indicating that they are "incompletely preserved but [...] certain" (cf. Olsen 1954: 233). The separation symbol after r. 45 consists of one obvious dot and the probable remains of a second (lower) one; pairs of dots in vertical line are the norm for this inscription.

Diagnostic rune forms are ᚬ ã, ᚼ h, ᚾ n, ᛅ a, ᛋ s, ᛏ t, ᛒ b.

Interpretation

The text presents virtually no problems of interpretation. We have:

Sǫndulfr hinn svarti reisti kross þenna eptir Arinbjǫrg kvinnu sína.

'Sǫndulfr the black put up this cross in memory of Arinbjǫrg his wife.'

The nominative -*r* is missing from the raiser's name. Endingless nominatives of personal names also occur on MM 101 Kirk Michael II (*Gaut*), MM 126 Kirk Michael IV (*Grím*), and MM 141 Onchan e (*Þúríð*). (See further pp. 83, 171, 236.)

The quality of the root vowel in what is normalised as *Sǫnd-* is uncertain. Forms exist indicating both /ɔ/ and /a/ (Lind 1905–15: *s.n.*). The usual way of denoting /ɔ/ in the Manx inscriptions is **au** (as in **arin:biaurk**), so one might suspect a pronunciation with some form of *a* here. On the other hand, the vowel is represented by ᚬ, which could almost certainly render /ɔ̃(:)/ as well as /ã(:)/. It is nevertheless worth noting that the island name *Mǫn* 'Man' is spelt **maun** in Kirk Michael II. The question cannot easily be resolved.

There has been some discussion of **kuinu**. It has commonly been taken as acc. sg. of ON *kvinna* 'wife', but Finnur Jónsson (1913–16: *s.v.*) signals the word as a late loan (from Danish?), no earlier than the fourteenth century. Bugge (1899) suggests it is "en Nydannelse efter Gen. pl. *kuinna, kuenna* og ikke en fra Urtiden bevaret form" 'a new formation based on gen. pl. *kuinna, kuenna* and not a form inherited from ancient times'. Marstrander (1915: 107), in his usual assertive spirit, prefers to interpret it as *kuenu* 'woman', otherwise unrecorded independently. But there is really no problem with the word (be it old or new), which recurs as **kuina** (acc. sg.) on MM 175 Maughold V; also as **kuino** (nom. sg.), **kuinu** (acc. sg.) on a couple of Swedish rune-stones (U 1039, U 148, cf. Peterson 2006: *s.v.*) in the sense "kvinna; hustru" 'woman' 'wife'.

In the light, *inter alia*, of these considerations, a transcription more in keeping with the local speech of the time might be:

Sãndulb̃ hinn svarti ræisti kross þānnā æftir Arinbjǫrg kvinnu sínā.

Andreas II*b*

On one of the broad faces of MM 131 is portrayed an elaborate series of beasts, their feet facing inward towards the cross shaft. One of the animals is a pig, and running down its belly is a set of fine grooves which form a short, very faint, runic text, clearly a graffito (upside down in relation to the pig). The runes are set between framing lines, bases outwards, and are divided by pairs of separation points in vertical line. The reading is:

$$\overset{1}{(\mathsf{l})}\mathsf{\cap I(\mathord{\mathsf{F}})} : \overset{5}{\mathsf{\dashv \cap}} * : \overset{10}{\mathsf{\dashv \mathsf{P} \mathsf{l}}} *$$

$$\underset{1}{(\mathsf{s})\mathsf{u i(n)}} : \underset{5}{\mathsf{a u}} * : \underset{10}{\tilde{\mathsf{a}} \mathsf{k s}} *$$

Rune 1 is the top part of a vertical only, most likely **s** – in the form ¹, judging from traces of an apparent dot and the appearance of r. 10; it is followed by a small gash at the same height. Rune 2 is clearly the upper part of **u**, while r. 3 is a full vertical without further distinguishing feature. Rune 4 has considerable damage at its centre; what is left are the remains of most of a vertical, with indications of a descending right branch at mid height. Rune 7 is a full vertical with a deep gash to the right of its upper part. Rune 8 is assumed to be a graph-type of **ã** since the inscription appears to be meaningful and a sequence **bks** would not conform to the phonotactic rules of any type of Germanic language, Latin or Irish. Rune 11 is the remains of a vertical; what is left is compatible with **i** or **ï**.

Diagnostic runes are ⊣ **ã**, ⊣ **a**, ¹ **s**.

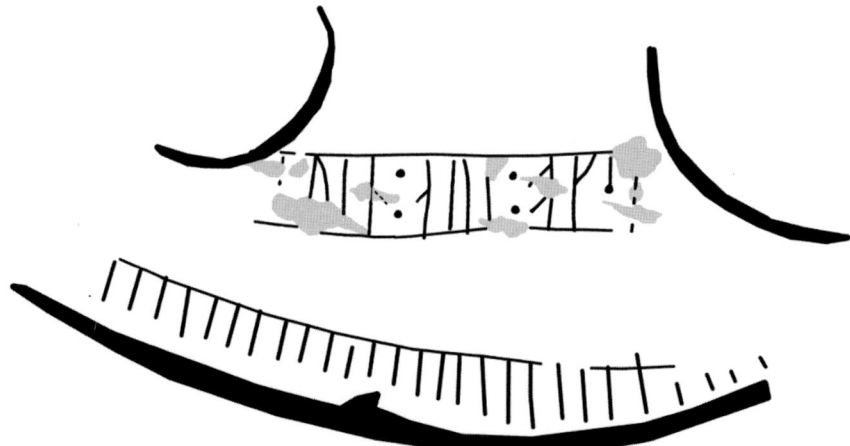

*Fig. 4. MM 131 Andreas II*b *(drawing: Jonas Nordby).*

Interpretation

Given that r. 1 is a probable **s**, r. 4 perhaps ᛀ **n**, that r. 7 could be **k**, and r. 11 |
i or ᛏ **ï**; further: that the inscription is placed on the image of a pig, and that
behind the pig comes an ox, it is not far-fetched to suggest the inscription
was intended to say:

> Svín ok oxi.

> 'Pig and ox.'

The form of the postulated conjunction, **auk**, belongs essentially in the Viking
Age, the correlation ᛆ /o/ towards the end of that period or in the Middle
Ages. In most of the Manx inscriptions ᛆ is a graph-type of **b** and ᛒ a graph-
type of **ã**, with the (possibly late) Maughold IV*a* 1 an exception, but there ᛆ
denotes [ã] rather than /o/. Andreas II*b* thus seems to reflect Scandinavian
language development and runic orthography as it might have been in Man
in the eleventh century, perhaps its first half. The graffito may well be from
that time.

A Manx transcription of the text could only differ materially from the
above normalisation in respect of the conjunction, though whether presumed
auk denotes /auk/ or /ɔk/ (cf. the common spelling **au** for /ɔ/ as in **arin:biaurk**
/arinbiɔrg/ in Andreas II*a*) cannot be known (see further Elmevik 1992).

MM 128 Andreas III

Plates 14–17, Fig. 5

LITERATURE. Marquardt 1961: 59–60. Vigfusson and Savage 1887: 15; Kermode
1887a: 26; Black 1889: 335–8; Kermode 1892: 37; Kermode 1907: 192–3; Brate 1907:
23; Olsen 1954: 185; Margeson 1983: 96 (on the iconography); Sanness Johnsen 1968:
223–4; Page 1983: 140; Holman 1996: 104–6.

There is some uncertainty about the find place of MM 128. The earliest published notice of the fragment appeared in the *Ramsey Courier*, 20 xi 1886, in
an anonymous report which furnished a detailed account of a lecture on the
Kirk Andreas runic crosses by P.M.C. Kermode. Nothing is said here of the
find circumstances, however. Black (1889: 335) quoted Kermode as authority
for the discovery of the stone "as far back as 1848, in pulling down the wall
north of the church [Andreas], after which it lay for many years in the rectory garden". Kermode's notebook XXIX in the Manx Museum (undated)
certainly records it there. Kermode (1907) recalled that it had long been at

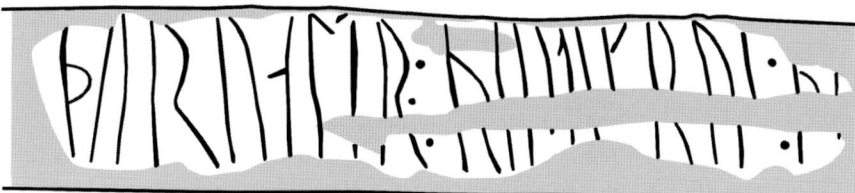

Fig. 5. MM128 Andreas III (drawing: Jonas Nordby).

the rectory. He had, however, failed to discover anything about its earlier history, though he deduced that "it had evidently been used as building material, probably in the old church". This was rebuilt in 1821 and again in 1864–9. In 1886 the stone was placed in the south porch of the church together with the other Andreas crosses, from where some twenty years later it was moved into an open-sided shelter, before finally being set up inside the church (cf. the history of MM 99 Andreas I outlined on p. 89). It is now set in a resin and metal frame.

Andreas III is carved on a fragment of dark grey siltstone, maximum measurements 35 cm × 19 × 6. Kermode (1907) gives the almost identical 14 inches × 7½ × 2¼ (= 36 cm × 19 × 6). Only a small part of the original slab survives, irregular in shape. Both faces have the remains of a relief cross. Part of the cross heads and the top of the shafts survive, the latter decorated with interlace and accompanied, at the side, by figure sculpture (cf. Margeson 1983: 96). On one face (Kermode 1907: pl. LII A) there is a human figure bearing a spear; a raven perches on his shoulder, while below a wolf tears at one of his legs (interpreted as Óðinn at Ragnarǫk attacked by the wolf Fenrir). On the other face (Kermode 1907: pl. LII B) we find Christian symbolism: a human figure bearing a cross and a book, and trampling on a serpent; a fish is by his side. The surviving edge of the stone holds the runes, which, unusually, run from top to bottom. They read:

þurualtr:r*(i)s**krus:þ*[

The runes begin well below the present (damaged) stone top, but it is unlikely there was anything preceding r. 1. At the present base the inscription is broken away, and there are no means of knowing how much has been lost. The total length of the surviving text that can now be seen (rr. 1–20) is 23.5 cm. The graphs are cut across almost the full width of the edge without framing lines, so often tops or bases are lost with the wear the stone has sustained, making rune height hard to measure. Average cases are r. 2 **u**, 49 mm, r. 6 **l**, 46 mm. The runes are clearly cut, though not very evenly, nor with a particularly sharp tool. Lines which should be vertical are often sloping, as rr. 2, 4, or are crooked, as rr. 1, 5. There is some double-cutting, as with the top of r. 1 and the bow and tail of r. 3. The vertical of r. 9 **r** protrudes above its bow top, and in overall appearance this graph is quite unlike its neighbour, r. 8. There is damage here near the top edge of the surface; possibly this existed prior to the carving of the inscription and was the cause of the aberrant form of r. 9. The separation symbol appears to be three points in vertical line (cf. the following and further below).

In general incisions are fairly well preserved, save where recent severe damage has afflicted the stone (cf. Moore 1959: [3]). The slab has split lengthwise producing an extensive gash which runs along the middle of the runic edge. As a result, the centres of rr. 7–11, 13–14, 16–17, 19–20, the whole of the lower part of r. 15, and much of the lower parts of rr. 12 and 18 are missing, which affects particularly the identification of rr. 10, 11, 14, 20; the middle point of the separation symbol after r. 18 is also gone (see below). Runes 12 and 18 are clearly both **s**, but little if anything of the dot in which they once terminated (see below) can now be made out. The branch that would convert r. 13 into **t** is perhaps to be identified with a light incision a little way below the top.

In the first publication of the text Vigfusson and Savage read "ÞURUALTR : RAISTI : CRUS : ÞO – –" without comment. However, Black's careful reproduction (from a photograph) a couple of years later shows plain verticals for rr. 10, 13, 20, though the text he gives is essentially that of the two earlier scholars. Kermode (1892) and Brate have the same reading as Vigfusson and Savage, except that Kermode supplies "N" after the final "O" while Brate indicates uncertainty over r. 13. Kermode (1907) agrees in all essentials with previous renderings (though his drawing seems to show two verticals following r. 19). Olsen appears to have read rr. 1–19 without difficulty, but thereafter he could only see a vertical "as r. 20 [...] was covered with cement". Sanness Johnsen compromised by admitting that "kvistene i **k a t l** [er] meget korte" 'the branches of [the runes] **k a t l** are very short'. Holman comments on the problems of identification arising from the fact that "the central part of the runes from r. 10 onwards have [...] disappeared".

Luckily there survive in the Manx Museum early photographs of this text (e.g. MNH PG/13721 - MC128C, reproduced as Plate 17), as well as an old cast. These record MM 128 and its inscription before the lengthwise split, and enable us to give a more complete reading. We can thus revise our text:

ᚦᚢᚱᚢᛅᛚᛏᚱ:ᚱ[ᛅᛁ](ᛏ)ᛁ]ᚴᚱᚢᛋ[ᛁ:]ᚦ∗∗[

þurualtr:r[ai]s[(t)i]krus:þ∗∗[

In the photographs r. 10 looks to be a plain vertical, but the cast shows what seems to be an ascending left branch that extends all the way from the bow of r. 9 **r**. Conversely, the cast indicates only a plain vertical for r. 13, while the photographs contain the hint of a branch as of ᛏ **t** (cf. above). Rune 20 is a vertical with possibly one or more branches, quite faint, to the right. Of r. 21 all that survives is a tiny length of a vertical. Runes 12 and 18 are both dotted. Separation symbols were clearly three points, set out in more or less vertical line.

Diagnostic rune forms are ᛅ **a**, [ᛁ] **s**, ᛏ **t**.

Interpretation

The text, as far as it can be followed, is clearly to be normalised and supplied as:

Þorvaldr reisti kross þenna…

'Þorvaldr put up this cross…'

The opening statement was presumably followed by *eptir* 'in memory of' + the name and perhaps title, patronymic or byname of the deceased, and almost certainly a statement about his or her relationship to Þorvaldr. As noted by Kermode (1907), "Thorwald is a rare Runic man's name". It is common enough in non-runic contexts, but Peterson (2007: *s.n.*) cites only the Andreas III example and the damaged **þoral…** on N 62, acc. sg. of the variant form *Þóraldr*.

On the basis of the fragment of r. 20 that survives, and of its appearance in early photographs, it is tempting to suggest the form **þāna** or **þãnã** for the demonstrative pronoun. Kermode (1907), Brate, Olsen and Sannes Johnsen all take r. 20 to be ᚠ (or at least some graph-type of the fourth rune), but how far their readings are based on actual observation is unclear. In Olsen's case it patently was not (cf. above).

Taking this last point into consideration, a transcription reflecting local pronunciation might be:

Þorvaldr ræisti kross ?þãnnã…

MM 113 Andreas IV

Plates 18–19, Fig. 6

LITERATURE. Marquardt 1961: 60. Kermode 1907: 164–5; Brate 1907: 23; Olsen 1954: 185; Sanness Johnsen 1968: 224–5; Page 1983: 140–41; Holman 1996: 106–8. For the possible identification of Andreas IV with the drawing in Wanley [*c*. 1700], see pp. 117–18.

Kermode was alerted to the cross fragment MM 113 in November 1886 when it was spotted "built as a lintel over a stable window at the Rectory, in which position it must have been for many years [...] the inscribed edge was exposed" (1907; cf. also Kermode notebook XXIX, Manx Museum, undated; Anon. 1886). The Glebe-house suffered in a great storm of 1839 and was thereafter fully rebuilt in the time of Archdeacon Hall (rector 1839–44), and the stable may date from that period. Nearly two hundred years earlier, however, an unknown hand recorded an Andreas rune-stone text, which may have been that of MM 113 in a more complete state than now (cf. Wanley [*c*. 1700], reproduced as Fig. 10: line 3), but which more probably represents an independent inscription (Andreas VIII ✝). The problems of reading and identifying that inscription are discussed on pp. 114–18. Together with the other Andreas crosses MM 113 was moved into different forms of shelter, before finally being placed inside the church (see the history of MM 99 Andreas I outlined on p. 89). Like two of its fellows, it is now set in a cement base which makes measurement of its full height impossible.

Andreas IV is carved on a fragment of dark grey mudstone, measuring *c*. 85.5 cm (visible height) × 19 × *c*. 8.5. Kermode records the height as 34 inches (= 86 cm), which – given the odd rounding up or down agrees (surprisingly) with our 85.5 cm. The fragment is much worn and damaged. About half the width of the original slab survives, the stone having possibly been cut in two at some point for use as building material. Both faces are badly worn, and on one the design has been chipped away, leaving very little to be seen. What survive are the outlines of relief crosses. Part of one of the narrow edges of the slab remains, and here are cut the runes, from the base upwards. The inscription has lost beginning and end, and is in general in poor condition. It reads:

]∗∗(')∗∗(:)∗ R ᚾ (ᛁ:) ᚦ (ᛁ) ᛁ ᚼ ᛁ (:) ᛁ ᚠ ᛏ ᛁ ᚱ [

]∗∗s∗∗:∗rus:þ(a)ina:aftiʀ[

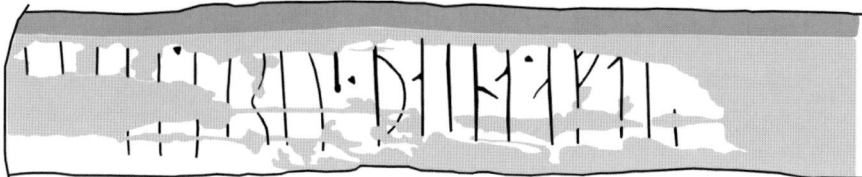

Fig. 6. MM 113 Andreas IV (drawing: Jonas Nordby).

The length of the surviving inscription is 31 cm. The tops of all runes have been lost, and a lamination has damaged the bases of many, so that accurate height measurement cannot be made: an approximate figure is 55–60 mm. As far as the incisions survive they show the runes to be clearly but lightly cut.

A gash running centrally through the entire length of the inscribed edge, widest at the lower end, has been repaired with cement. This badly obscures the forms of rr. 1–6, although an attempt has been made to refashion the missing elements of the inscription in the cement filling. Kermode (1907) claimed to be able to make out "distinctly" here the runes AISTI : K. Brate and Olsen also read **aisti:k**, Brate indicating that both **t** and **k** were badly damaged, Olsen that they were incompletely preserved though certain. Sanness Johnsen also has the **aisti:k** reading, but marks only **t** as damaged or unclear. Olsen and Sanness Johnsen agree that r. 3 is ¹ rather than ↓, but Kermode's murky drawing of the inscription (pl. XXXIX 87 C) appears to show ↓. For rr. 1–6 Page offers [**ai**]**s**[**t**]**i**[**k**], the brackets (seemingly) indicating readings taken from older reproductions. Holman prints a series of plain verticals here, of which one, r. 3, is shorter than the others and read by her as **s**; to the right of r. 6 she shows a tiny groove as of the beginning of a rising branch, and reads the whole as **k**. Page's account of Andreas IV drafted for his planned edition of the Manx runic inscriptions notes that the opening graphs were covered with a thin skin of cement when the stone was set in a new base, thus disguising the forms of rr. 1–3. He observes that early drawings he made of the inscription show here two verticals followed by ¹. The branch of r. 4, **t**, he comments, is very faint. After r. 5 he thought to see a point in the surface (there appears to be one placed quite high up), which he felt could be the remnant of a pair of separation dots; however, he conceded that the limited space between the verticals made this somewhat uncertain. "Of r. 6", he says, "only a vertical remains". It is hard to judge from these accounts how badly the initial part of Andreas IV has suffered over the past century or so, and at what point or points various features of its runes may have been lost. Kermode's drawing shows the runic edge of the stone unaffected by any gash, and his reading of rr. 1–6, as also those of Brate and Olsen (the latter made as early as 1911), implies that considerably more was visible then than is the case now. The fact that Page makes reference to early drawings (that he did perhaps in the 1950s or 1960s) suggests he was able to read more at that time than when he started writing up his commentary, though he clearly could not see all that Kermode, Brate and Olsen managed to make out. In contrast to Page's cautious reading and Holman's sequence of verticals stands Sanness Johnsen's confident **ais(t)i:k**, but some doubt exists about whether the Norwegian scholar examined personally all the inscriptions she describes in her work (Liestøl 1969: 173).

The remainder of Andreas IV is fortunately somewhat easier to read than rr. 1–6. Rune 9, **s**, appears to have a small dot at the base of its vertical. Olsen and Sanness Johnsen saw a clear ', but Holman gives ⌐. A single point is observable after r. 9; this may have been the upper one of a pair, its lower fellow lost through damage to the surface. There is uncertainty about rr. 11, 12, two verticals set close to r. 10 and to each other. Rune 11 has what appears to be a very short ascending branch on the left, which suggests **a**, though it is hard to be absolutely sure. This is how Olsen, Sanness Johnsen and Holman took it, but Brate saw **i** here (in a word **þiina**), while Kermode found the improbable form PAANA. No branch is observable in r. 12, and the likelihood is that rr. 11–12 are to be read **ai**. Following r. 14 **a** is a single point, placed high up; it is likely it was originally accompanied by a lower one – perhaps at the point where the gash opened up and there is now a cement filling. The middle section of r. 19 has been lost in the same gash and the area is now covered by cement, but the reading ׀ **R** seems convincing enough. Holman ponders whether this half-height (broken) line might be "the remains of a long-branch r-rune", since the inscription is damaged and **R** otherwise unattested in Man. There is, however, no trace of the branches of either ᚱ or ᚴ (whichever is meant) on what seems (the gash apart) to be a relatively undamaged area of the surface.

Diagnostic rune forms are ᚿ **n**, ᚭ **a**, ' and/or ᛆ **s**, ᛐ **t**, ׀ **R**.

Interpretation

It is evident that this stone preserves the remains of the common Manx memorial formula, to be normalised as:

[NN] *reisti kross þenna eptir* [MM].

'[NN] put up this cross in memory of [MM].'

How much is missing at the beginning and end cannot be properly estimated, though what remains of the cross and its design offers limited guidance (cf. Kermode 1907: 164–5). Before r. 1 there may have been, say, 10 cm of text (*c.* 6 runes), which would have given opportunity for a personal name only. After r. 19 there could perhaps have been up to 50 cm of further text – say 30 runes – though the inscription need not have been as extensive as that (on the implications of these estimates for the identity of the inscription in the Wanley drawing [*c.* 1700], see pp. 117–18).

A form **þaina** for the acc. m. sg. of the demonstrative pronoun is unparalleled both in the Manx and wider Scandinavian corpus, unless it be attested in the Wanley drawing, and provided, of course, this does not present a (more) complete version of Andreas IV. In establishing a reading, however, what can be seen must take precedence over the unexpectedness of any form that emerges, and on balance the runes look more like **þaina** than anything else. Underlying the digraphic spelling **ai** is almost certainly a pronunciation /e/ or /æ/, as evidenced by, for example, **ai(f)tir** on MM 106 Ballaugh (an identical form was perhaps once also to be found on MM 123 Kirk Michael VIII; cf. further **þainsi** DR 275, 278, **þaisi** DR 268, 276, Vg 113, acc. m. sg. 'this', and see Nielsen 1960: 6–19).

On Man the use of ı **R** is also unique (cf. Holman's reflections above). The occurrence of **R**, and of the graph-type ı, is discussed on pp. 60, 77-8.

In the light of the previous two points, the following "local" transcription of the text may be suggested:

[*NN*] *ræisti kross þennā æftir* [*MM*].

MM 111 Andreas V
Plates 20–22, Fig. 7

LITERATURE. Marquardt 1961: 60–61. Black 1889: 332–5; Kermode 1892: fig. 1, facing 1, and 36; Bugge 1899: 244; Kermode 1907: 161–2; Brate 1907: 24; Olsen 1954: 185–9; Holman 1996: 108–9; MacLeod 2000.

P.M.C. Kermode found MM 111 in November 1886 in the south-east corner of Andreas churchyard "at the head of a modern grave", and took it immediately into the church (1907: 161; cf. also Anon. 1886; Black 1889: 332). On its likely subsequent movements, cf. the account of MM 99 Andreas I, p. 89. It is now set in a cement base, which makes precise measurement of the full height impossible.

The Andreas V inscription is carved on a fragment of laminated mudstone, measuring 50 cm (visible height) × 26 × 8. Kermode (1907) gives the height as 22 inches (= 56 cm). The piece appears to represent the central section of a slab that once bore a relief cross on either face. The cross shafts have interlace patterns and there is further decoration at their side. The inscription is found on one of the faces, to the left of the shaft as the stone is currently oriented, and has generally been thought to run upward (which implies that the tops of the symbols point outwards). The cross's original orientation cannot in fact be determined on the basis of what remains, nor does it seem possible to show conclusively, whichever orientation is chosen, whether the symbols run up or down the face. The inscription is separated from the shaft by a raised border. Both its beginning and end appear to have been lost at the time it was discovered. Where the symbols approach the edge of the stone, they have in most cases suffered damage. Heights of two of the best preserved characters are 55 and 61 mm respectively. The visible length of the inscription (measured from the current base to the branches of the final rune-like character) is 39 cm, but an early photograph in the Manx Museum (MNH PG/13721 - MC111B, reproduced as Plate 21), as well as early drawings (cf., e.g., Black 1889: 333) show three additional symbols above/below. These have been thought to lie buried in the cement base, but a 1958 Manx Museum photograph (MNH PG/5211-2 – MC111B, reproduced as Plate 22) shows that the relevant end of the stone had by that stage been broken off and with it the three symbols. When these are taken into account the length of the inscription increases to 45–6 cm (cf. the total height discrepancy above between our 50 cm and Kermode's 22 inches).

As will be seen from Plates 20–22, the graphs of Andreas V (we count 25 in all including the three now broken off) are no ordinary runes, and despite various attempts, it has so far proved impossible to decipher them. No transliteration and interpretation can therefore be provided. Instead a brief account is given of what earlier scholars have made of the inscription.

Black presents a drawing of the runic face of MM 111, but in his representation the fragment is turned 180° so the characters are located to the right of the shaft. He comments on the inscription's "excessively complicated form" and its "apparent absence of vowels", but recognises "twenty-five compound letters or groups of letters" as well as "two dots in the form of a colon" after letters 15 and 18, which he takes to be separation marks. Black clearly considers the symbols of Andreas V to be bind-runes, as shown, for example, by his attempts to read "the first three groups [i.e. characters]", which lead to the suggested combinations "*mth, ky, kthth*, or *thm, yk, thkth, ththk*".

Fig. 7. MM 111 Andreas V (drawing: Jonas Nordby).

After having tried to combine all the symbols in similar ways, he concludes: "we must be content to regard the inscription as insoluble".

Kermode (1892) also provides a drawing of the runic face of MM 111 (with the stone oriented as now and the three additional symbols still in place at the base), but otherwise offers only the laconic comment: "Inscription in Bind Runes not yet deciphered".

Bugge, who saw in Andreas V a mixture of bind- and twig-runes, had to admit defeat as well. He did, though, throw up the suggestion that "de tre Binderuner, som staar mellem to Prikker, skulde kunne læses **krus þạna af**" 'the three bind-runes that stand between two dots might be read **krus þạna af** ['this cross ?in memory of']'.

Kermode (1907) counted twenty-eight characters including "the word-divisions or punctuation signs" (and the three symbols subsequently lost). He considered the inscription to be written in bind-runes, but despite providing a detailed account of each character, got no nearer an interpretation than he had in 1892. His final comment is testimony to his bafflement: "This reading gives us no vowels excepting the u five times, and that may have been designed with the express intention of making it [the inscription] more difficult to decipher."

Brate had little to add save the thoughts that Bugge's reading **krus þạna af** was probably based on the rather unclear depiction of the inscription in Kermode (1892), and was "svårt att förena med verkligheten" 'difficult to reconcile with reality'. In fact the problem with Bugge's reading does not stem from the Kermode drawing, which is accurate enough. Rather, it is undermined by the arbitrary way in which the Norwegian scholar chooses to interpret the sundry branches and bows attached to the three verticals in question.

In contrast to Brate, Olsen offers a lengthy and detailed account. He describes each individual symbol, in all essentials following Kermode, but supplementing the work of the earlier scholar with observations based on his own examination of the stone (which did not extend to the three characters now missing since they "were not accessible for examination in 1911"; Olsen 1954: 186). He agrees with Brate that Bugge's reading **krus þąna af** is unlikely, and goes on to draw attention to a certain outward similarity between the symbols of Andreas V and those of the twelfth-century Maeshowe inscription no. 15 (XXII in the numbering used by Olsen; cf. Barnes 1994: 118–23). As early as 1903 (pp. 1–16) Olsen had made a persuasive suggestion about how most of Maeshowe no. 15 might be read. As with Andreas V, its "runes" have many apparently extraneous branches and bows, but he had noticed that symbols 6–20 of the inscription were distributed in a way compatible with a reading **ræistrunarþesar** 'carved these runes', and since that is the commonest phrase in the Maeshowe corpus, he reasoned that must be what the writer had intended. Symbols 1–5 would then give the writer's name (which has proved less easy to identify). Unfortunately, application of Olsen's method does not seem to offer a solution to Andreas V. Very few, if any, of its symbols recur in precisely identical form; even allowing for a small amount of free variation in the detail, no obvious pattern emerges. Clearly, Olsen saw nothing suggestive: beyond airing the possibility that Maeshowe no. 15 and Andreas V "are to be assigned to one and the same groping after new, bizarre forms of expression" he had little to add to the general understanding of the inscription.

Holman, rather than attempting an interpretation of Andreas V, draws attention to the "decorative as well as cryptic purpose" of its runes (for runes, like earlier scholars, she considers the symbols to be). Maeshowe no. 15 is brought in by way of comparison, and one or two other inscriptions besides, including those on the medieval Kingittorsuaq stone from Greenland (GR 1) and Norum baptismal font from Bohuslän (Bo NIYR;3). Holman's conclusion is that the Andreas runes "seem to be an early example of a type that became more common at a later period".

MacLeod, after consideration of the inscription itself, of the various attempts to get to grips with it, and of other inscriptions with unusual and complex symbols that defy transliteration and interpretation, concurs with Holman's suggestion that the "runes" of Andreas V have a decorative function. MacLeod, though, sees them solely as decoration. She writes (2000: 213) of "the complicated runic artistry of the Andreas stone", which she describes as "ornate, mysterious, rune-like but probably not genuinely runic".

To these deliberations of over one hundred years just a couple of thoughts may be appended. There is no indication in Andreas V of use of the 6:5:5 cipher, so its symbols are not "twig-runes" in the sense that their position in the *fuþark*, and thus value, can be determined by counting their branches and bows (cf. pp. 70–71). Nor are they bind-runes in the common sense of the term. Black's "*mth, ky, kthth,* or *thm, yk, thkth, ththk*" (cf. above) shows that clearly enough, as do essays of a similar nature by other scholars. It would indeed be surprising to find a Manx inscription written throughout in bind-runes since there is otherwise only one clear and one uncertain example of a runic ligature in the whole of the Manx corpus (and those both in graffito inscriptions, cf. Onchan *c* and *d*, pp. 229, 232).

MM 121 Andreas VI
Plates 23–4, Fig. 8

LITERATURE. Kermode 1907: 177–8; Page 1981: 133; Page 1998: 8–9.

Kermode spotted the fragmentary MM 121 in 1885, "serving for a headstone to a modern grave about ten yards from the north entrance to Andreas churchyard". Scholars to whom he sent photographs of the stone quickly recognised its depiction of scenes from the story of Sigurðr the dragon-slayer (more accurately, perhaps, serpent-slayer), although a century or so was to elapse before Ross Trench-Jellicoe observed on it a small number of graphs that appeared to be runes (pers. com.; cf. also Margeson 1983: 100; on the designation of this or these inscriptions as Andreas VI, see pp. 31–2, 113). In 1886 the fragment was taken into the church; subsequently it was put into various forms of shelter together with the other Andreas crosses before finally being set up inside the church (cf. the history of MM 99 Andreas I outlined on p. 89). Like two of its fellows it is now set in a cement base which makes measurement of the full height impossible.

MM 121 consists of a smallish piece of mudstone, measuring 68 cm (visible height) × 39.5 × 8. Kermode arrived at an almost identical height: 27 inches (= 69 cm or, more exactly, 68.6). Each face of the stone holds part of the shaft of a sculptured cross, on and to the sides of which are interlaces and, interwoven, figures from the Sigurðr story. No traces of a formal memorial inscription survive, but there are two graffiti, one of them clearly runic. The runes read:

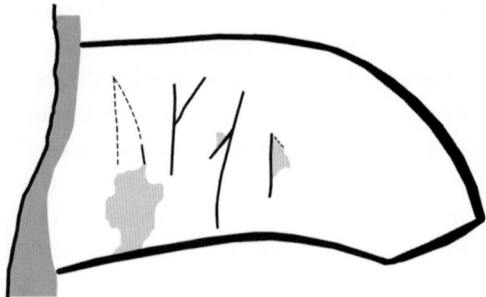

Fig. 8. MM 121 Andreas VI (drawing: Jonas Nordby).

 1 3
 ᚴ ᛆ *

k a *
 1 3

The inscription is placed along the neck of a horse (presumably Grani) that watches over the hero roasting Fáfnir's heart. Its total length is 11–12 mm; heights of the identifiable runes are 11 mm (r. 1), 17 mm (r. 2).

Before r. 1 a faint cut or two can be discerned, as of two verticals or, perhaps more accurately, a vertical and a long, curving line, but their import is so uncertain that we deem **k** to be the first character. Rune 3 has the appearance of ᛁ **l**, but is half the size of rr. 1–2, and could be an incomplete ᚾ **n**.

The only diagnostic form that can be clearly identified is ᛆ **a**.

The second graffito is to the right of the horse's head, next to the outer junction of the cross-ring and shaft of the monument. It consists of a curving line (not unlike the bow and tail of ᚱ **r**), followed by two shapes reminiscent of **i** and **k**. There is no certainty, however, that these are runes; indeed, some of the marks may not even have been deliberately carved. Accordingly, this graffito is omitted from further discussion.

Interpretation

It is difficult to make much of Andreas VI, which looks to be a very casual addition to the ornament on the stone. Given the position of the runes on the neck of the horse, it might be suggested that they represent an attempt to carve a form of the name *Grani* (cf. Margeson 1983: 100), but that is of course highly speculative.

MM 193 Andreas VII

Plates 25–6, Fig. 9

LITERATURE. Page 1992b: 6; Holman 1996: 109.

MM 193 was first reported by Page in 1992. According to his account the piece of stone was "found perhaps twenty years ago at Larivane Cottage, Andreas", where it "may have been reused as a gate post, and then again as building material". Holman's discussion of the piece and its inscription, based on Page's report and her own observations, is headed "Andreas VI", but VI has been altered in this edition to VII on the grounds that the designation Andreas VI is better given to the inscription of MM 121. That is in accordance with the principle of listing in order of find date established in Barnes (1992) and confirmed in Barnes and Page (2006: 22–3) – the inscription of MM 121 having been brought to scholarly attention earlier than that of MM 193 (cf. also pp. 31–2). MM 193 is currently in the keeping of the Manx Museum.

As it now survives, the Larivane Cottage find is but a small fragment, a trapezoidal piece of slate measuring 15 cm × 8 × 2. One face bears the lower half of a human figure with a sword at his belt, the other is undressed and rough; this would seem to be a bit of stone that has broken off from a larger piece, perhaps a substantial cross slab. A small length of one of the narrow edges survives, and on it can be seen five carved lines, more or less vertical, almost certainly the tops or bases of runes. The lines vary in height between 7 mm (r. 1; cf. below) and 15 (r. 2), and the distance from the first to the last is 11.5 cm. A single dot comes between two of the lines (the first and second or fourth and fifth), presumably a separation symbol or, more likely given its apparent height, a part thereof. In the absence of any distinguishing features such as branches, it is most natural to assume these incisions are the bases of runes (with the inscription running upwards – by far the most likely direction – and the human figure then upside-down in relation to the inscription – not unparalleled). Pursuing this assumption, we have:

```
 1         5
* ( : ) * * * *

* : * * * *
 1     5
```

Rune 2 slants a little, while rr. 3–4 curve slightly. Somewhere among these three lines could be the remains of ᚢ **u**, but that is very uncertain. Reading the grooves as rune tops gives no further insights.

Fig. 9. MM 193 Andreas VII (drawing: Jonas Nordby).

With so little to go on, all Andreas VII can provide is a further point on the Manx runic (and carved stone) distribution map.

Andreas VIII † (recorded in an early drawing)
Fig. 10

BL MS Add. 70484, Misc 17 (Wanley [*c.* 1700]), is a single leaf found among a collection of the seventeenth–eighteenth century scholar Humfrey Wanley's papers. It contains copies of three Manx runic inscriptions, each set out on a separate line. There is no statement about their authority. Two are of texts to be identified with certainty: first we have Kirk Michael V*a* (MM 132) and thereupon Andreas II*a* (MM 131). The third line contains another text from Andreas, but it is not immediately clear if it represents the extant Andreas IV (MM 113) in a more complete state than today, or some other memorial inscription, now lost. Both Kirk Michael V*a* and Andreas II*a* survive in good, readable condition, and here the copyist's, or more likely copyists', general accuracy can be assessed.

The version of Kirk Michael V*a* shows error only in details: omission of branches when representing **n** (rr. 10, 21) and **t** (r. 31) and of a dot at the centre of **h** (r. 19); **u** represented by two parallel verticals (r. 25 but not elsewhere); and the adding of a superfluous branch to **n** (r. 56).

The drawing of the runes of MM 131 Andreas II*a* is a more curious case, and seems to be by a different hand, or copied from the work of a different draughtsman. It presents rr. 1–39 (but omitting r. 13, which affects the numbering), then, following a pair of dots in vertical line, it begins again at r. 1 and (once more omitting r. 13) continues to r. 22, but no farther. The end of the text is not recorded. Nor is the drawing as precise as that of Kirk Michael V*a*, though they have some types of error in common. Branches are missed from the representations of **ã** (r. 2 both branches; r. 27, = 28 on the stone, the lower branch) and **n** (rr. 3, 10); and the dot at the centre of **h** (r. 8) is absent. The forms of **u** and **r** are not always precisely distinguished. Rune 29/30 (**a**) is given a second branch near its top, descending from the left, corresponding to a damaged patch on the surface of the stone. The branches of rr. 27/28, 35/36, 38/39 are placed much higher than they are in the inscription itself.

This summary gives us some idea of the degree of accuracy we may expect of the third drawing, which appears to be by, or to derive from, the same hand as that which copied Andreas IIa. Preceding the runes is a brief description:

> On the Edge of another stone in the same [Andreas] Churchyard, toward the South, is the following Inscription, somewhat defaced at the Top; as are also the Animals Engraven on the other parts of the same.

The drawing shows some sixty graphs divided by pairs of dots in vertical line into fourteen groups.

Taking plain verticals as **i** where the context clearly supports the identification, and distinguishing **u** from **r** according to whether the branch curves back at the base in the manner of ᛒ (= **r**) or not (= **u**), a preliminary reading might be:

[** ᚾ ᛏ ᛏ ᚼ : ' ᚾ ᚼ : ᛦ * R ** ᚼ ' : * ᛏ * : ' ** : * R ᚾ ' : Þ *** ᛏ : * ᛕ ᛁ I R : * ᚾ ᛕ ᚾ : ᛕ ᚾ ** ᚾ : ' I ᛏ * : * ᚾ : *** R : ᚾ ᛕ ** (:)]

[** u b a n : s u n : m * r ** n s : * a * : s ** : * r u s : þ **** a : * f t i r : * u f u : k u ** u : s i n * : * u : **** r : u f ** :]

Some of the groups are immediately identifiable, or at least deducible. The second (rr. 7–9) is clearly **sun** 'son', the sixth (rr. 23–6) likely to be **krus** 'cross', the eighth (rr. 32–6) **iftir** or perhaps **aftir** 'in memory of'. Patently the text was a version of the common Manx memorial formula. What is uncertain is whether the inscription was copied in its entirety or whether its ending ("somewhat defaced at the Top"), and possibly its beginning too, is lost. Following the pattern of other Manx texts, and assuming nothing essential is missing from the beginning, we can surmise that group 1 represents the name (complete or incomplete) of the monument's raiser, and group 3 (rr. 10–16) that of his father, preceded as it is by the **sun** of group 2 (minus the expected nom. -*r* ending), and ending as it does in **-s**, a common masculine genitive marker. Groups 4 and 5 (rr. 17–22) are then likely to represent the verb, apparently a form of *reisti* 'raised' despite the pair of separation points after r. 19. Runes 17 and 19 look to be forms of **r** and **i** respectively, each with an extraneous branch, while the two full-length verticals, rr. 21–2, could give **ti**. Group 7 (rr. 27–31) must then be acc. m. sg. of the demonstrative 'this', with r. 30 representing **n**, which means that the verticals rr. 28–9 stand for vowels, most likely **ai**. Group 9 (rr. 37–40), following what must be a form of the preposition *eptir* 'in memory of', gives the name of the deceased, and since group 10 (rr. 41–5) appears to be **kuinu** 'wife', with perhaps just the branch of **n** missing, we may assume the name is that of a female. This requires r. 49 to be **a** or **ã** (giving the reflexive possessive *sína* 'his [acc. f. sg.]'), more probably the latter given the closely similar form of r. 27 (**ã**) in the drawing of Andreas II*a* (= r. 28 of the actual inscription, cf. above).

What is likely to follow the text so far established? Possibly, on the analogy of MM 130 Kirk Michael III and MM 140 German II (Peel), a phrase defining the deceased's relationship to a member of her family. Thus rr. 50–55 could be a single word, ignoring the pair of points between rr. 51 and 52, as was suggested in the case of putative **rai:sti**. If r. 50 were reconstructed as **t** and graphs 52–4 as **tu**, taking the verticals 53, 54 as the vertical and branch of **u**, we have the word **tutur** 'daughter [acc. sg.]', which is certainly plausible. The final word would then be the father's/mother's name in the genitive. The whole text might thus be recreated:

NN sonr MMs reisti kross þenna eptir PP kvinnu sína, dóttur TT.

'NN son of MM put up this cross in memory of PP his wife, daughter of TT.'

This seems an eminently suitable restoration, but it is not therefore correct. The names present problems, for we cannot be sure if they are Scandinavian or Celtic. Runes 10–16 could suggest **martins**. *Marteinn* is certainly recorded in medieval Icelandic and Norwegian sources (Lind 1905–15: *s.n.*), and once, in all probability, on a late Viking-Age Swedish rune-stone (Sm 85, cf. Peterson 2007: *s.n.*). In a part-Celtic milieu a related form might occur earlier than elsewhere (cf. early Irish *Martan*, O'Brien 1973: 231; *Martain*, Stokes 1895: 234). There are, of course, other appropriate Celtic names not so far found in Scandinavian sources: as *Mercán*, *Mercón* (O'Brien 1973: 221). For rr. 37–40 Page (1980: 188) put forward **tufu**, which would be acc. sg. of the recorded though fairly rare *Tófa* (Lind 1905–15: *s.n.*; Peterson 2007: *s.n.*), and nothing more immediately obvious suggests itself. Runes 56–9 might have given **ufak/ufik** (cf. **uf∗ak** MM 112 Braddan I, **ufaik** MM 99 Andreas I, both accusative), *Ófeig*; but the lack of genitive ending then needs explaining. Either the inscription was incomplete, or was grammatically imprecise (cf. the omission of a probable genitive case marker in **smiþ**, MM 101 Kirk Michael II), or the

*Fig. 10. Andreas VIII †, recorded in the third line of BL MS Add. 70484, Misc 17 (the first line depicts Kirk Michael V*a*, the second Andreas II*a*; © British Library Board MS Add. 70484, Misc 17).*

draughtsman missed out the ending in error. For the representation of historical /æi/ by a single vowel rune in Manx texts, cf. the frequent form **risti** (*reisti*) 'put up' 'raised' (MM 126 Kirk Michael IV, MM 132 Kirk Michael V*a*, MM 135 Braddan IV, MM 136 Braddan III, MM 139 Marown) and the name **þurlibr** (*Þorleifr*, Braddan IV), though nowhere else in Man is /æi/ represented by **a** alone (cf., however, Peterson 2007: *s.n.*, for references to East Scandinavian runic spellings of *Ōfæigʀ* such as **ofahr, ufakʀ**). The name of the raiser of this memorial might well be Celtic, as, for instance, Irish *Dubán* (O'Brien 1973: 221; recorded in Scandinavian sources, cf. Lind 1905–15: *s.n. Dufan*) or possibly *Gobhán* (Stokes 1895: 368).

Finally there is the question of the relationship of the second Andreas inscription in the Wanley drawing with the now fragmentary MM 113 Andreas IV. In favour of identifying them as one and the same are (*a*) the desirability of applying Occam's razor and not multiplying lost rune-stones *præter necessitatem*, though there is no continuity of record from Wanley to 1886 when MM 113 was (re)found; (*b*) the apparent demonstrative form **þaina**, which does not otherwise appear in this exact form on Man, or indeed elsewhere. Against are (*c*) the form **aftir/iftir** whose final rune does not seem to coincide with the certain **ʀ** of Andreas IV; (*d*) the mention of "Animals Engraven on the other parts of the same" – there are no remaining signs of animals on

MM 113; (*e*) the length of the missing beginning of Andreas IV, estimated on the basis of what is left of the stone and its cross design (cf. p. 107): the suggested 10 cm (= *c.* 6 runes) at the start is nowhere near enough to have accommodated the 17 or so runes and 3 separators of the Wanley drawing. Of these five points (*a*) is less an argument, more a desideratum; (*b*) is quite suggestive, though there is one clear and one probable other case in the Manx corpus where /e/ or /æ/ is written **ai**, and one where apparent /e:/ is thus rendered (MM 106 Ballaugh **ai(f)tir**, MM 123 Kirk Michael VIII **ft(ir)**, both for *eptir*, MM 127 Jurby **raiti**, for *rétti*; cf. also the name element **mail-**, ON *Mel-*, in MM 101 Kirk Michael II and, seemingly, MM 175 Maughold V); (*c*) depends on the accuracy of the Wanley drawing (though nowhere else in the depictions of the three inscriptions is a half-length rune like ı converted into a full-size character with distinguishing branches or bows); the problem with (*d*) is the worn and battered state of the surface of MM 113, which may not permit us to make a sound judgement here; (*e*) is crucial: even if – despite its being identified as on a single "Edge" – the inscription the Wanley draughtsman was copying (conflated by him into a single continuous sequence) was spread over both the narrow edges, there still does not seem to be enough space on the remaining edge of MM 113 for the beginning of the Wanley text. The overwhelming probability is therefore that the inscription "On the Edge of another stone in the same [Andreas] Churchyard" is not to be equated with Andreas IV, but represents a now lost memorial text, Andreas VIII †.

A transcription of the suggested text into a "local" form may be hazarded as:

NN son MMs ræisti kross þennā æftir PP kvinnu sínā, dóttur TT.

MM 106 Ballaugh [ba'laf]

Plates 27–31, Fig. 11

LITERATURE: Marquardt 1961: 61–2. Kinnebrook 1841: 11 and fig. 6; Cumming 1857: 17 and fig. 2; Paterson 1863: following 18; Cumming 1868a: facing 23, no. 10, and 30; Kermode 1882: 94–5; Vigfusson and Savage 1887: 11–12; Kermode 1887b: 151; Vigfusson 1887: 168; Taylor 1887: 185; Bugge 1899: 238; Kermode 1907: 155–8; Brate 1907: 24; Olsen 1954: 189–90; Sanness Johnsen 1968: 225–6; Page 1983: 140; Holman 1996: 110–12.

The Ballaugh stone is first certainly recorded by Kinnebrook "in Ballaugh old Church-yard, on the south side of the Church". However, Feltham (1798:

188), writing of Ballaugh, reports the existence of "a stone pillar in the shape of a cross, with a cross cut thereon in relief [...] without the church-yard on a mount", though he makes no mention of any inscription. There is also an unattributed newspaper cutting in one of Kermode's unnumbered notebooks in the Manx Museum which speaks of "an ancient Cross of the 11th or 12th century" that had once stood "on a mound outside the old Churchyard [of Ballaugh]", but had been moved into it. Since no other early cross is known from this church or its environs it is very probable that both accounts refer to MM 106. Ballaugh Old Church is one of Bishop Wilson's remodellings, dated 1717, but it stands on "an ancient site likely to have been occupied by an early Keeill" (*The Manx Archæological Survey* 1911: 13).

Cumming (1857) confirms the Kinnebrook find spot "in the old churchyard of Ballaugh". His reproductions give an excellent impression of the monument, and include the inscription and part of the stone's base. Cumming took the trouble to have "the cross dug up prior to taking the cast [cf. pp. 51–2], and was thus enabled to obtain the lower portion, which had previously been buried deep in the earth". Certainly "buried deep in the earth" is how Kinnebrook had depicted the stone. The lower part seems to have been reinterred following Cumming's examination. It is thus it appears in a photograph in Paterson (1863), while Vigfusson (1887) reports that he found the cross "half sunk into the earth – the first letters below the turf, untouched, for long years past. A labourer's spade [...] soon dug it out, and we laid it flat on the ground." The first half dozen runes of the text seem to be better preserved than the later ones, which may serve to confirm that they were long protected below the earth's surface. The stone remained in the churchyard until about 1890 when it was moved inside the church (Kermode 1907: 155), where it still stands, set in the floor.

The Ballaugh inscription is carved on a slab of dark grey mudstone, measuring *c.* 114 cm (visible height) × 52 (base) – 46.5 (cross arms) × *c.* 7.5. Kermode (1907: 155) gives the height as 54 inches (= 137 cm). Kinnebrook saw the stone as only "two feet eight inches high" (= 81 cm), which shows how deeply it was interred. On both faces are carved relief crosses, and the upper part of the stone was shaped to follow roughly their outline. On the uninscribed face the cross itself is filled with interlace, with a background of varied interlaces to the right of the shaft and above the head; and to its left is a key pattern. The runic side has a circle-headed cross, again filled with interlace and with interlace to its right. To the left of the shaft the runes run from base to head and continue into the lower left quadrant of the head, implying perhaps that the inscription was not carefully planned in advance.

Kinnebrook drew the non-runic face of the standing cross but did not note the runes on the other side. If we are to believe Cumming's depiction, part of the text was in better condition than it is now after several decades of further weathering have affected its incisions. Yet his drawing shows palpable errors in the first two words, and it may well be that some of what he depicts derives from wishful thinking. Cumming says disarmingly: "The inscription is tolerably perfect [...] The fourth and fifth words are somewhat indistinct". Vigfusson and Savage give a rather different reading, which the complex slightly later description by Kermode (1887b) in the main confirms. Kermode's account reports much of what can now be seen, though perhaps with slightly more detail. Surprisingly, Taylor disagreed with these 1887 readings, returning to Cumming's text. Otherwise the Vigfusson and Savage-Kermode version has been generally accepted up to the present (Bugge, Brate, Olsen, Sanness Johnsen, Holman), though occasional non-essential details are questioned. In view of the various uncertainties there needs to be a detailed account of what can still be seen. We begin, as elsewhere, with a transrunification and transliteration.

ãulaibr:liutulbsunr:r**s****rs:þ*na:ai(f)tir:**(*)b:su(ns)in

Neither rendering indicates the difficulties involved in reading this inscription. The stone surface has suffered a good deal from weathering, with parts flaked away so that sections of its lettering are faint and sometimes ambiguous. The main part of the text, which runs from the base of the cross to its head (rr. 1–40), is 50 cm long. The lower edge of the runes here is defined by the incised line that shapes the shaft of the cross, though verticals sometimes overcut it slightly. There are upper framing lines too: one runs vertically above rr. 1–8, but is superseded (from about r. 7) by a line (some of it lost through damage) which swings down and then gradually slopes inwards as the stone becomes slimmer towards the cross head. Graph tops approach these upper lines but seldom reach them. Thus the runes of this section vary in height from 103 mm (r. 9 **i**) to 63 mm (r. 32 **a**). Rune 8 **l** is unusually small relative to those that follow it, 82 mm, apparently avoiding a rough patch of the surface above. Rune 1 has the unusual form ᚭ. This and the other opening graphs are quite well preserved (also true of the three points in vertical line that follow r. 7), but thereafter several tops are worn or weathered, as

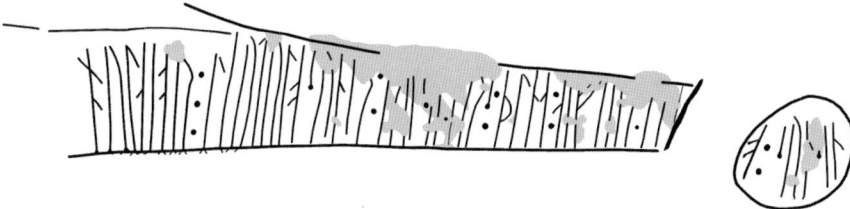

Fig. 11. MM 106 Ballaugh (drawing: Jonas Nordby).

rr. 12, 16, 18; and in the area rr. 19–27 tops are lost altogether through damage. Though there is no great problem in recognising rr. 19, 26, 27 from what survives, it would be speculative to offer a transrunification or transliteration of rr. 20–25, except r. 22 ⁱ, where most of the outline of the graph can be seen and the surface below is undamaged enough to allow only for a half-length vertical. Identifications here have depended in part on early drawings (of which some at least must be suspect), in part on context, and in part on what remains on the stone. Still visible are two verticals, placed close together (damaged in places and missing their tops – rr. 20–21), most of the left side of an ⁱ (r. 22), and the lower halves of three verticals (rr. 23–5). These runes have been read **aistik** by Cumming (1857, though note his slightly more tentative fig. 10 in 1868a), by Bugge, Brate, Kermode (1907), Olsen and Sanness Johnsen, not all of them even signalling difficulties in identifying individual graphs. Holman records problems with the sequence, though she regards the reading **raisti:krs** as "easily reconstructed". All the above but Brate and Holman (in her schematic drawing of the runes) have the usual separation symbol, two points in vertical line, after r. 24; two dots can certainly be seen here, but they are very shallow and it is unclear whether they belong to the inscription. Vigfusson and Savage – more wary than some – had RA- -US for the sequence rr. 19–27. On this Kermode (1887b) commented: "As for the blank space following the RA of the third word, I can plainly discern I and the dot of S, and the stems of TI K; the US should be RS, the R being as distinct as that in RAISTI." From this it is clear that what can be seen here now is much the same as in 1887, though it is impossible to confirm the branch that would convert the vertical r. 20 into **a**. Rune 27 ⁱ has a dot below, and another to its right; presumably these constitute a separator: perhaps the carver first wrote **kr:**, then, realising his error, converted the upper of the two dots into the base of ⁱ, adding a further dot to the right to make up the pair. Rune 29 is a puzzle. The context requires **a** or **ã** or possibly **i**, but what can be identified is a vertical with an upper branch as of **l** (but with no corresponding lower branch, which would give ⌐, a rare graph-type of ⌐). Below the centre of this vertical and to its left is a worn or damaged patch that could conceal the branch of **a**, though that would then be very low and the graph would stand perilously close to the preceding one. It seems likely that this is a form carved in error, with perhaps an attempt at correction. Kermode (1887b), Olsen and Holman report the problem; others miss it (though Taylor, 1887, has "[ ]" here, indicating inability to identify anything distinctive), and the account of Kermode (1907) appears to deny it (he reads A). Rune 34 is a vertical with a single clear branch to the right, and remains of a second, upper branch above. The top of r. 35 is badly weathered, but the end of a **t**-branch is traceable. Most of the top of r. 37 is gone, but the graph is identifiable as **r**. After this can be seen a lone point, quite low down; there was presumably another above it, now lost, to form the separation symbol : (used elsewhere, though not after r. 7, where there are three points). There follow two verticals, lost at their tops, and the upper part of a possible third, rr. 38–40; rr. 38 and 39 have traditionally been taken as **u**, though they do not lean towards one another discernibly and stand quite far apart. Rune 40 is a somewhat uncertain vertical with no branch or bow surviving; it is quite short, extending only as far down as the outer edge of the ring that encircles the head of the relief cross. Early drawings define the doubts here. Though Cumming (1857) confidently renders rr. 38–41 ULB, his picture suggests that he could not identify r. 40 with any certainty. Kermode (1887b) expresses himself with studied ambiguity about this part of the inscription. Later writers who deal with the matter conscientiously indicate that r. 40 = **l** is questionable. All that now can be seen for sure after r. 37 is a point and two verticals, followed by a hollowed gap in which there seem to be traces of a further vertical.

Details of the continuation of the inscription (in the lower left quadrant of the cross head) are also hard to define surely, for this sequence too is quite badly weathered. It is *c*. 9 cm long, and individual runes vary in height from 56 mm (r. 41 **b**) to 75 mm (r. 43 **u**). Rune 41 and the two dots of the separation symbol that follow it are clear. The rest is somewhat less well preserved, though there can be no doubt about the identification of rr. 42–3 and 47. The centre of r. 44 has weathered away, but parts of its branch remain. No separation symbol is visible after this graph, nor indeed does there seem to be space for one. Here we agree with Vigfusson and Savage, Kermode (1907), Olsen, Sanness Johnsen and Holman against some early readers. Of r. 45 only the dot at what is surely the base of **l** survives, so this character is identified largely by context. Following r. 45, almost the whole length of a vertical can be made out, on neither side of which is there really room for a branch: doubtless **i**. Sanness Johnsen managed to find a doubled **i** here, apparently following the suggestion in Kermode (1907), "in the final word are two scores which look almost like a narrow u", but there is scarcely space, and we were unable to trace the second score (cf., however, the spelling **siin** on MM 138 Braddan II).

The state of the stone surface makes it hard to determine some of the separation dots with certainty. After r. 7 there are undoubtedly three in vertical line; after rr. 18, 31, 41 clearly two. Only one is now visible after r. 37 but that is probably the effect of wear on the stone surface higher up. (On the dot below r. 27 and the one following it, see above.) It is conceivable that separation dots have some rhetorical function in this inscription. The unusual three after the first word perhaps stress the importance of the stone's sponsor. And the aberrant form of the initial **ã** of this name may make a similar point (cf. the ↑ of the opening name **tolfin** in the E 3 Carlisle A – now Carlisle I A – graffito which otherwise uses "short-twig" forms: Barnes and Page 2006: 291; Barnes 2010), though it could have an altogether different explanation (see below). The lack of a separator in the sequence rr. 42–7 (as read here) suggests that the two words were conceived by the carver as a grammatical unit.

Diagnostic rune forms are **n** ᚼ, **a** ᚭ, **s** ᛁ, **t** ᛐ, **b** ᛓ. Rune 1, ᚠ, is at this period probably best considered a graph-type of ᚠ **ã** (cf. below and pp. 69–70).

Interpretation

It is convenient to accept as correct, in general if not in detail, the values that have over the years been supplied to rr. 20–25. The greater part of the inscription can then readily be turned into an acceptable normalised text:

Óleifr Ljótólfssonr reisti kross þenna eptir NN son sinn.

'Óleifr Ljótólfr's son put up this cross in memory of NN his son.'

We must accept that the son's name is no longer readable with any certainty. Traditionally it has been taken as (acc. sg.) **ulb** *Ulf*, but the fragments visible are not entirely consistent with that. Only the last graph of the word, **b**, is unambiguous. Certainly the carver uses that rune for the voiced spirant [β], as rr. 6, 14 (cf. pp. 76–7). However, it is possible to suggest alternative personal names that could fit the surviving but indistinct incisions of rr. 38–40: as *Eilif* in the spelling **ilib**, *Leif* in the spelling **laib**, or perhaps *Kalf* **kalb**.

The name *Óleifr* and its runic spelling deserve some consideration. *Óleifr* is a variant form of *Óláfr*, *Áleifr*, like the latter seemingly derived from an etymon **anulaiƀaz* in which the stress lay on the second element, hence the preservation of the diphthong. This form of the name appears at some point to have become confused with one in which the stress originally lay on the first element, and the initial vowel thus underwent *u*-mutation, nasalisation and lengthening, becoming [ɔ̃:], and ultimately [o:] (Janzén 1948: 107–9). The rendering here of this initial vowel as ᛅᚾ suggests an attempt on the part of the carver to denote [ɔ̃:]. He may have reasoned thus: since ᛅᚾ is regularly used for [ɔ], ᛅᚾ would be a way of denoting its nasalised and lengthened counterpart, with ᛅ marking nasality, and perhaps also length, given that the initial sound of the fourth rune's designation at this time is likely to have been [ã:] or [ɔ̃:] (cf. **ãumuta** for *Ómunda* < ?*anumundan on DR 155; Nielsen 1988).

An alternative interpretation is that **ãulaibr** represents not *Óleifr* but *Eyleifr* (which would likely have been pronounced [øylæiβr] by at least some in tenth-century Man), its first element *Ey-* the reflex of **awiō* or *auja* (cf. Peterson 2007: 267–8). But while **ãu** is a possible way of rendering [øy-] (Williams 1990: 115–16), there is no certain example of the name *Eyleifr* to be found anywhere.

Against the background of these speculations, the appearance of the graph-type ᛅ raises an interesting question. Could it be a forerunner of an apparent medieval Norwegian grapheme denoting now [ø(:)] now [ɔ(:)] – based on ᚴ, but in which one of the branches is extended to cross the vertical (e.g. ᚴ̄)? If the Ballaugh inscription is to be dated to the tenth century, it would be early indeed for such an innovation, but it perhaps finds its place beside the dotted runes of the Manx corpus (see further pp. 61–2).

The spellings ***rs** (doubtless a damaged **krs**) for *kross* 'cross' and **ai(f)tir** for *eptir* 'in memory of' have both exact and partial parallels on the Manx stones. The omission of **u** in what most Manx carvers spell **krus** recurs on MM 118 Bride, and may thus constitute deliberate abbreviation of a common word (cf. also **þna** for *þenna* in MM 102 Kirk Michael I and MM 126 Kirk Michael IV), but it could simply be error. The carver of MM 123 Kirk Michael VIII, like his Ballaugh colleague, seems originally to have spelt *eptir* **aiftir**, while the writer of MM 113 Andreas IV appears to have rendered *þenna* 'this' **þaina**; in all three cases the spelling **ai** is likely to denote a monophthong, [e] or [æ] (cf. further under Andreas IV and MM 136 Braddan III).

In the light of various of the matters deliberated above, a transcription closer to presumed tenth-century Manx Norse might be:

Ǫ́læiƀr Ljótolƀssonr ræisti kross þennā æftir NN son sinn.

MM 159 Balleigh [ba'lai] †

Plate 32, Fig. 12

LITERATURE. Marquardt 1961: 62. Kermode 1929: 358 (fig. 4, no. 4), 360; Bruce and Cubbon 1930: 290, 294–5, 298–9; Olsen 1954: 190; Holman 1996: 112–13.

MM 159 was discovered in 1928 during excavation of a mound known as Cronk yn How on the quarterland of Balleigh in the parish of Lezayre (Bruce and Cubbon 1930). The excavation revealed evidence of an extended period of human habitation; also of Christian burials, implying the existence of an associated keill. However, MM 159 seems to come not from a cemetery but from the foundations of a twelfth-century building apparently put up on the site of an earlier keill and burial ground. Disturbance of the site during construction may have led to the incorporation of stones from the burial ground into the new building. This is described by the excavators as an "oratory-chapel, with associated burials" (Bruce and Cubbon 1930: 297), but Page (1980: 192) wonders "if the foundations were identified as a chapel because a rune-stone (assumed to be a grave-stone) was found in them". He argues that "the other [incised] stones from this early Christian burial place [the cemetery assumed to have preceded the twelfth- century building] are much earlier – by several centuries – than the Balleigh rune-stone", and thinks "there is at least the possibility that the foundations were of a later secular building, and that the runic fragment was brought as building stone from somewhere quite different". Trench-Jellicoe, however, is of the opinion that the other stones "could just as well be Viking-Age, in fact I suspect the designs on them indicate they are" (pers. com.). MM 159 was at some point (perhaps not long after discovery) placed in Lezayre parish church, where it was examined and photographed by Trench-Jellicoe in the 1970s (cf. Plate 32, Manx National Heritage ref. MNH PG/1459 - MC159). Subsequently it was removed, apparently stolen, from the church, and its whereabouts are currently unknown (Holman 1996). Fortunately, the Manx Museum has a cast showing the inscribed and decorated face, and Trench-Jellicoe's photographs together with a rubbing he made provide clear images of the original.

The Balleigh inscription is found on the small surviving fragment of a fine-grained mudstone slab, c. 23 cm long × 6 wide × 4 thick (these and all following measurements derive from Trench-Jellicoe's examination of the original unless otherwise stated). According to Trench-Jellicoe, the top of the piece is chiselled into a rounded shape, but on the evidence of photographs, rubbing and cast we were unable to confirm this. One face appears to have been crudely decorated with the outline of a cross. To the right of what has been

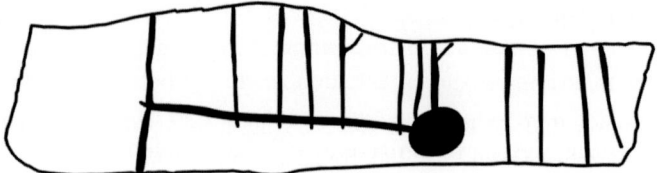

Fig. 12. MM 159 Balleigh † (drawing: Jonas Nordby).

taken to be the cross shaft, and at right-angles to it, runs the remains of a runic inscription some 15 cm long. The ?bases (cf. below) of what appear to be eleven verticals, 35–40 mm in height, can be seen. The sixth, because of its position and the unusually short distance to the adjacent verticals is judged to be part of the cross design and is therefore discounted in the following description. This is a somewhat arbitrary decision, but seems to be supported by the apparent branch or bow connecting with the seventh vertical (r. 6), which suggest this is the remains of a rune (cf., though, Kermode 1929: fig. 4, no. 4). The verticals that are bordered by the edge of the cross shaft (1–5) overcut it (the edge does not continue into the assumed cross arm). All ?top parts are lost with the breaking away of the material beyond. Provided the assumption about the location of the inscription in the overall design is correct, the runes run down the slab, intrude into the right cross arm, and are then lost at the present base of the stone shortly before the lower border of the arm is reached.

No transrunification is possible. The transliteration, discounting the sixth "vertical" as a rune, can only be:

$$[\underset{1}{*}\ \underset{\ }{*}\ \underset{\ }{*}\ \underset{\ }{*}\ \underset{5}{*}\ \underset{\ }{*}\ \underset{\ }{*}\ \underset{\ }{*}\ \underset{\ }{*}\ \underset{10}{*}\,[\,]$$

Gaps between verticals vary considerably in width, the one between rr. 1 and 2 (15–16 mm on the cast) being greater than those that separate rr. 2 and 3 and 3 and 4; the largest gaps occur between rr. 4 and 5 and 6 and 7 (19 and 28 mm respectively on the cast). Rune 3 leans back slightly towards r. 2, as does r. 10 towards r. 9, and it is conceivable that in both cases we have the remains of **u**. Alternatively rr. 9–10 might just preserve the vertical and tail of **r**. Runes 4 and 6 have what appears to be the remnant of a branch, or perhaps the lower part of a bow, extending upwards to their right. Other than these faint indications, no distinguishing features can be observed.

So little survives of this inscription that an interpretation is out of the question. Going by other Manx runic inscriptions one would imagine it began with a personal name. A couple that could fit with what can be seen, assuming longish branches on what would then be the third rune, are **tufi** *Tófi*, or **tuki** *Tóki* (both relatively well attested, in the Viking Age in Denmark in particular), but what might have followed is wholly unclear. It is noteworthy, if our and Kermode's (1929: fig. 4, no. 4) overall reconstruction is correct, that the runes run not only downwards, but down the face of the stone, an arrangement otherwise undocumented in Man.

MM 112 Braddan I
Plates 33–8, Fig. 13

LITERATURE. Marquardt 1961: 62–3. Feltham 1861: 197, 269–70; Cumming 1868a: facing 23, no. 11, and 30–31; Cumming 1868b: 13–14; Cumming 1868c: facing 12; Vigfusson and Savage 1887: 11; Kermode 1887b: 151; Bugge 1899: 239–40; Kermode 1907: 163–4; Brate 1907: 24–5; Olsen 1954: 190; Sanness Johnsen 1968: 226–7; Page 1983: 140; Holman 1996: 113–15.

MM 112 seems to have been discovered in 1859. In the second edition of *Feltham's Tour through the Isle of Man* (1861), the editor, R. Airey, adds the following note to an explanation of why Feltham failed to "take" any inscriptions in Braddan churchyard: "An interesting 'Runic Cross' was discovered two years since by some workmen engaged in making some alteration. It, with some others, is now placed upon a mound in the middle of the Churchyard." Since all the other rune-inscribed stones from Braddan were either known well before 1861 or found only much later, it is clear that the one "discovered two years since" must be MM 112. Paterson (1863: facing 38) has a photograph showing MM 112 on a mound accompanied by MM 135 Braddan IV and MM 136 Braddan III, the same arrangement as is shown in the engraving in Jewitt (1884: 97). Cumming (1868b; initially published 1866) records that MM 112 "formed a door-step in the church of Kirk Braddan. It is now placed in the centre of the churchyard, on a mound, along with the two so-called *dragon* crosses." The article makes clear that MM 112 was a post-1857 discovery (i.e. subsequent to the publication of Cumming 1857). Both the size of the slab and the condition of one of its surfaces fit the suggestion that it once acted as a doorstep to the church. An unattributed photograph held by the Victoria and Albert Museum, dated (by hand) 1900 (National Photographic Record and Survey, Sir Benjamin Stone, Kirk Braddon *sic*), shows MM 112, 135 and 136 in what appears to be the same position as in Paterson's 1863 picture (towards the centre of the south side of Braddan Old Kirk churchyard, going by the later image; see also Plate 33, Manx National

Fig. 13. MM 112 Braddan I (drawing: Jonas Nordby).

Heritage ref. PG/8794 - MC112-135-136). Kermode too (1907: 163, 205) reports the three in Braddan churchyard, MM 135 and 136 more specifically "on the mound". In 1907 (The Manx Museum and Ancient Monuments Trustees 1908: 7) MM 112 and its two fellows – together with MM 138 Braddan II – were moved into the church, where they all stand today, midway in the building, set in concrete bases.

The Braddan I runes are carved on one of the faces of a slab of light-coloured sandstone (non-local, possibly of lowland Scottish origin, perhaps left by melting ice), measuring c. 124 cm (visible height) × 43.5 × c. 9. Kermode (1907) gives the height as 60 inches (= 152 cm, presumably measured when the cross was moved into the church in 1907, notwithstanding that he records MM 112 as still in the churchyard, cf. above). The top of the slab is broken away. The non-runic side is much worn, though Kermode identified on it traces of a cross (still just visible today), broken off at the top. The runic face has a circle-headed relief cross whose shaft is decorated with ring chain ornament. To its left is an interlace pattern, to its right, cut between the raised band of the relief cross and the outer edge of the stone, is the inscription. It runs upwards from the cross base, and reads:

× þu(r)stain:raisti:krus:þan(ã):ift:uf∗ak:sun:
k(r)inais

The inscription is 97 cm in length measured from the initial saltire cross. Rune height varies slightly, as fits the space available: 88–98 mm. The opening runes are badly worn though mostly identifiable. The top halves of rr. 1–3 can be made out, and it is clear enough that rr. 1–2 were þu. Rune 3 is less well preserved, but what survives is consistent with **r**, which some have thought to see here. The lower part of r. 4's vertical is damaged, but an indentation can be observed where we would expect a dot (as in the other examples of **s** in this inscription).The branch of r. 10 is very faint; indeed, Holman depicts the graph as a plain vertical. Only one branch of r. 22 is preserved, but it is placed higher than that of the immediately preceding **n**; where a probable lower branch may once have stood, the surface is abraded. Rune 28 has a depression to the left looking like the branch of **a**, but this seems to be damage; there may well once have been a carved line here, but no clear trace of it now remains. Many of the features that must once have distinguished r. 35 are lost, and it is hard to tell whether this is ᚱ or ᚢ; there are indications of a slight indentation suggestive of the neck of ᚱ in the oblique line descending to the right from the top of the vertical – and while a reading **r** gives a possible Irish personal name, **u** creates problems of interpretation (see below). Between rr. 37 and 40 the spacing becomes somewhat wider. Since the inscription ends with r. 40, the carver may have wanted to distribute the graphs so as to cover the remaining surface.

Diagnostic rune forms are ᚾ **n**, ᛆ **a**, ᛁ **s**, ᛐ **t**, and possibly ᚨ **ã**.

Interpretation

The general sense is clear enough:

Þorsteinn reisti kross þenna eptir Ófeig son K-s.

'Þorsteinn put up this cross in memory of Ófeigr son of C-.'

The main problem is to identify the names. For the raiser some early readers put forward very strange forms, as the improbable [MA]LFIAAC (Vigfusson and Savage) or [MA]LFEAAC (Kermode 1887b), or the hybrid **þurfiaak** (Bugge). Prior to these Cumming (1868a) had offered the more sensible THURKETIL, but it hardly fits with what survives. Brate suggested **þurstain**, which has been commonly accepted and corresponds with what can now be seen of the runes.

The name of the man commemorated is taken to be *Ófeigr*, though the representation of the /æi/ diphthong as *a then needs comment. There seems to be no parallel in the Manx corpus, **ai** being the common spelling of /æi/ (though **i** also occurs); and on MM 99 Andreas I we have **ufaik**, which presumably gives the same name. Runes 28–9 look clearly enough cut, and the only question is whether r. 28 is to be taken as **i** or **a**. If the carver wrote **ufiak** we might be inclined to suspect transposition of **i** and **a**. If, on the other hand, he wrote **ufaak** we could compare with forms of the name spelt with a single **a** in East Scandinavian (especially Swedish) inscriptions from the Viking Age; conceivably the Braddan I form is a variant of the **ofahr**, **ufakʀ**, etc. found there (Peterson 2007: *s.n. Ōfæigʀ*), with doubled vowel as in **siin** for usual **sin** in MM 138 Braddan II.

The third name presents somewhat greater difficulties. Cumming (1868a) read KLINAIS, Vigfusson and Savage have CRINAAS, Bugge **krinaas**. Brate has **krinais**, as does Olsen, though with some uncertainty about r. 35, of which he says, while transliterating (**r**), "ᚾ **u** is possible, but not ᛚ **l**". Holman disagrees, saying the graph "looks like an l-rune to me". As noted above, **r** and **u** are both conceivable (hardly **l**), but **r** is perhaps slightly more likely (as earlier scholars seem to have agreed). A reading **krinais** also lends itself more readily to interpretation than **kuinais**. The name that emerges has commonly been linked to an Irish *Crínán*, and the form on Braddan I explained as a hybrid genitive: Irish *Crínáin* + Norse -*s* – either, reading **krinais**, with the non-marking of /n/ before dental /s/ (Olsen 1909: 16; cf. Williams 1994), or, reading **krinans** (speculatively, though there is space for a branch between rr. 39 and 40), with close adherence to the Irish pronunciation [-aːɲ] for -*áin* (Marstrander 1937: 244). In fact, it is hard to determine precisely what Irish name might underlie the runic representation. O'Brien (1973: 221) lists *Crínán* as a diminutive (without indication of its meaning or the extent to which it occurs), while *DIL s.v. crínna* 'aged' 'prudent' 'experienced' cites one usage as a masculine personal name. It is probably unwise to go further than noting these occurrences.

Olsen (1909: 7–20) contends, and Marstrander (1937: 243–8) denies, that the phrase **sun:k(r)inais** 'son of C-' reflects Irish word-order. This question is applicable to several of the Manx runic inscriptions, and is dealt with in ch. 7 'Language' (pp. 83–4).

A transcription of Braddan I more in keeping with assumed local pronunciation might be:

Þorstæinn ræisti kross þānnā æft Ófæig son K-s.

MM 138 Braddan II
Plates 39–40, Fig. 14

LITERATURE. Marquardt 1961: 63–4. Kinnebrook 1841: 14 and fig. 25; Munch 1850: 280–81; Cumming 1857: 24 and fig. 12; Kneale [*c.* 1860]: 61, no. 3; Cumming 1868a: facing 23, no. 12, and 31–2; Vigfusson and Savage 1887: 18–19; Taylor 1887: 185; Bugge 1899: 240–41; Kermode 1907: 207–8; Brate 1907: 25–9; Olsen 1954: 191; Sanness Johnsen 1968: 227–8; Page 1983: 140; Holman 1996: 115–17.

MM 138 appears to have been recorded first by Kinnebrook, who simply notes that it was "in Douglas Museum" and "found in the parish of Braddan", though he provides no authority for the latter statement (cf., however, Train 1845: 2, 32–3, who indicates the object was in Braddan churchyard in 1839). Munch is silent about provenance, but, like Kinnebrook, gives the location of the stone as "Museet i Douglas" 'the museum in Douglas', presumably the [J.R.] Wallace Museum in St George Street. By Cumming's time it was "in the Distington [Cumberland, now Cumbria] Museum", to where the Wallace Museum was transferred over the period *c.* 1842–1850 (from contemporary newspaper accounts it seems the move was gradual). Cumming (1857; cf. also 1868a) reported that he believed the stone "was taken from the wall at Kirk Michael" but Kermode (1907) rejected this as a misunderstanding, accepting the Braddan provenance. The miscellaneous collection of curiosities in the Distington Museum was sold off in the late 1890s (again, apparently a gradual process), and it was presumably then that MM 138 returned to the Isle of Man (Kermode 1907: ix). Certainly Kermode (1907) records it as "in Castle Rushen" (cf. also that it features as item 106 in his 1905 catalogue of the Manx Museum, Castle Rushen, collection). In 1907 it was taken into Braddan Old Kirk, accompanying MM 112 Braddan I, MM 136 Braddan III and MM 135 Braddan IV, which in that year were brought in from the churchyard (The Manx Museum and Ancient Monuments Trustees 1908: 7; cf. also pp. 127–8). The stone is currently placed midway in the building, set in a block of cement (the cement extending 1 cm or more up from the present base on both sides).

The Braddan II runes are carved on a fragment of grey mudstone, measuring *c.* 44 cm (height) × 39 (maximum width) × 6–8 (Kermode's height and width measurements are, oddly enough, smaller: 15½ inches × 9 = 39.5 cm × 23; for the depth he has 3¼ inches, which is a little over 8 cm; cf. Holman 1996, who suggests a mix-up with a different fragment of sculptured stone). As now set up, MM 138 is fairly clearly at right-angles to what must have been its original orientation, so the height given here is measured horizontally and the width vertically. The original slab had a sculptured cross on each face, decorated with different designs of interlace. On both sides part of the cross head remains; rather more on the runic side, which also preserves the very top of the shaft – enough to show that the text ran up the face along the shaft's centre line. The message overran, however, and had to be completed in the space above the left arm of the cross. Holman, who describes the inscription as running horizontally, seems to have been misled by the way the stone is currently oriented in the church (see Fig. 14). Manx runic inscriptions are not normally set horizontally, nor rune-stone texts in

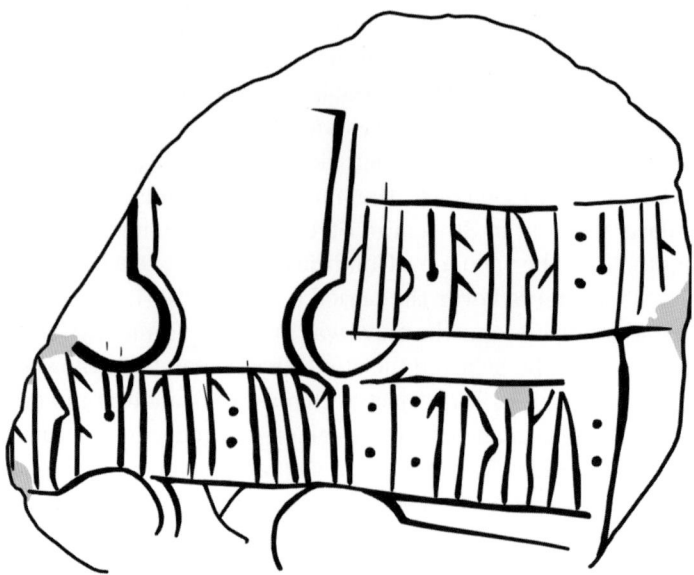

Fig. 14. MM 138 Braddan II (drawing: Jonas Nordby).

general; and what remains of the design strongly supports the reconstruction suggested here (see Plates 39-40). The main sequence of runes is 37.5 cm long, measured to the separator after r. 20; the overrun is *c.* 20 cm, measured from branch to branch. What survives of the inscription reads:

](n) r ã s k i t i l : u i l t i : i : t r i k u : | a i þ s ã a r a : s i i n

The graphs are cut between framing lines, all except rr. 1–6 where the design of the cross prevents this. In the main runes touch both top and bottom frames, although r. 13, **t**, ends some way short of the top line, again to fit in with the decoration. Rune height varies between 64 (r. 31 **i**) and 93 mm (r. 2 **r**). The graphs are firmly and cleanly carved, apparently in a back-and-forth movement, judging by the odd overcut at both top and base. Of r. 1 only the lower half remains: ᚼ **h** is theoretically possible, but there is no sign of an upper right-hand branch (any branches to the left would have been lost in the break), furthermore this graph-type occurs otherwise in Man solely in the Maughold IV*a* inscription, there in company with ᛅ **ã**, ᛏ, ᛐ, ᛂ **e**; ᚿ **n** must be judged much more likely. The final three runes of the word **siin** are somewhat more thinly cut than the rest. The separators are made up of almost perfectly rounded dots (as opposed, for example, to those of Braddan III, which are triangular).

Diagnostic rune forms are ᚨ ã, ᚾ n, ᛅ a, ᛁ s, ᛏ t.

Interpretation

The text is a subsidiary one, presumably intended to complement a now lost memorial formula. It is almost certainly to be expanded and normalised:

> *En Hrossketill vélti í tryggu eiðsvara sinn.*
>
> 'And/But Hrossketill betrayed the trust of a man to whom he was bound by oath.'

Such additional texts, beginning with adversative *en* 'and/but' are common enough on runic monuments; cf. on Man MM 99 Andreas I, and the implications of the incomplete MM 136 Braddan III, MM 107 German I (St John's) *a*, MM 127 Jurby. In the case of Braddan II the likelihood is that the cross was erected in memory of a man slain by Hrossketill. A probable parallel is U 954, which states: *?Þau ?ØyrikR frændr ræi[st]u s[tæin æfti]R Hælga, broður sinn. En Sassurr drap hann ok [gærði] niðingsverk, svæik felaga sinn. Guð hialp and hans* '?ØyrikR and the other kinsfolk put up a stone in memory of Hælgi their brother. But Sassurr slew him and committed a villainous act, betrayed his companion. God help his spirit'. (On the Viking-Age context of inscriptions alleging treachery and betrayal, see Jesch 2001: 254–65.)

Some uncertainty surrounds the sequence **triku**. It is a reasonable assumption that we have here a word related to the adjective *tryggr* 'faithful', the verb *tryggva/tryggja* 'secure' 'make trusty', and the noun *tryggð* 'good faith' (which is found in the collocation *svíkja í tryggð* 'betray under trust', not far removed from Braddan II's *vélti í tryggu*). The use of **i** for historical /y/ may indicate delabialisation, or it could be that **i** stands for /y/, but neither interpretation is unproblematic (cf. pp. 74–5). In its Braddan context the word should be dative, seemingly singular but according to some commentators plural. Vigfusson and Savage quietly supply a consonant ending: TRIICU[M]. Bugge accepts the word as a spelling of "*tryggu*, Dativ til et Hunkjønsord *trygg (= got. *triggwa*), som forudsættes af den i norske Love forekommende Flertalsform *tryggvar*" '*tryggu*, dative of a feminine *trygg (= Gothic *triggwa*), implied by the plural form *tryggvar* which occurs in the Norwegian laws'. In the course of a long discussion Brate determines that a final **m** has been omitted from **triku,** which he defines as *tryggum,* dat. pl. of *tryggvar.* Olsen suspends judgement on the point, while Sanness Johnsen and Holman ignore the question altogether. Certainly the examples referred to by Bugge and others confirm a plural form *tryggvar,* but the contexts in which the word is found have to do with the establishment of legal agreements rather than betrayal. Nor is there is any particular reason to think a plural -*m* ending has been omitted – certainly not deliberately since the carver found he had enough space at the line end to include a separation symbol. Noreen (1923: 263) lists a singular feminine noun *trygg* with a regular (if somewhat rare) dative in -*u*, but this entry is based on the Braddan II occurrence; the formation is plausible enough, however, as Bugge recognised: the singular of the documented plural *tryggvar* would have been *trygg,* with a possible dative in -*u*. Whatever the precise explanation of **triku,** the general sense of the inscription seems clear.

The form **aiþsãara** (= *eiðsvara*) invites comment because of its use of **ã** for what is presumably the semi-vowel [w]. The usage is unusual but not unparalleled: see, for example, **soïrþ** on IR 1, the ?eleventh-century Greenmount strap-end (= *sverð* 'sword', with **o** transliterating the fourth rune of the *fuþark* in this early medieval inscription, cf. p. 66), **soa, oar, koalt** (= *svá* 'so', *var* 'was', *kveld* 'evening') on N 178, a (?twelfth-century) metal door fitting from Røindal, Telemark (for further examples and discussion, cf. Williams 1990: 119–22). This is a question of identification, as perhaps in the case of **i** for /y/ above. To some rune writers the semi-vowel [w] must have seemed closer to /o/ than /u/, just as there were those who wrote **ï** rather than **i** for [j], cf. **fïal** (= *fiall* 'fell'), Ög 81, **hïalbi** (= *hialpi* 'help'), Sm 10 (further examples in Lagman 1990: 75; cf. also the discussion on pp. 73–4).

The repetition of the vowel in **siin** is highly unusual. Clear Viking-Age parallels are hard to find: [**faaþi**] ?[fa:ði], ?[fa:aði] 'made' (DR 192) depends on a drawing and the phonetic form underlying the spelling is uncertain; both **þuraaʀ** ?*Þorgæiʀʀ* (Sö 74), and **asaaiʀ** ?*Asgæiʀʀ* (U 775) represent names that are difficult to interpret; on MM 112 Braddan I's **uf*ak,** see pp. 129–30. Just possibly, **siin** is to be compared with U 59's **sïin,** which could have been a way of writing [sen:] (cf. Lagman 1990: 56–7), incorporating both the most common spelling (**sin**) and one that indicated more precisely the pronunciation of the vowel (**sïn**). Double "insurance" spellings of this kind seem a plausible explanation for at least some of the occurrences of **rʀ** or **ʀr** for /r/ or /ʀ/ (Larsson 2002: 40–43). However, since neither r. 30 nor r. 31 is dotted and there is no evidence the carver of Braddan II knew of dotted runes, this is something of a long shot (see further pp. 77–8).

In the light of the foregoing discussion, a transcription that reflects local pronunciation might be:

En Rosskætill vélti í triggu æiðsvara sinn.

On the (probable) loss of initial /h/ in the name *Hrossketill*, see p. 82.

MM 136 Braddan III
Plates 33, 41–4, Figs 15–16

LITERATURE. Marquardt 1961: 64–5. Kinnebrook 1841: 14 and fig. 23; Anon. 1855; Cumming [*c.* 1855]: fols 84r and 108r; Cumming 1857: 30–32 and fig. 23; Kneale [*c.* 1860]: 61, no. 2; Cumming 1868a: facing 23, no. 3, and 26–7; Vigfusson and Savage 1887: 16; Kermode 1887b: 151; Bugge 1899: 238; Kermode 1907: 205–7; Brate 1907: 29; Olsen 1954: 191–3; Sanness Johnsen 1968: 228–9; Page 1980: 187; Page 1983: 140; Holman 1996: 117–19.

MM 136 served as a lintel in Braddan church tower (Braddan Old Kirk), placed above the internal doorway into the loft over the gallery, and is recorded as such in Kinnebrook. Only one of its surfaces was then visible, and that not the rune-inscribed one. By the time of Cumming's 1857 engraving the slab had been removed from the tower and its runes recognised. The discovery of the rune-inscribed edge is described in *The Illustrated London News* (8 xii 1855: 685), which reports that the slab "was removed from its place [over the doorway] under the superintendence of an English gentleman who had been travelling about the island". From other sources this gentleman is known to have been the writer George Borrow (Cumming 1857: 30; cf. also Page 1980), and it was he who arranged for MM 136 to be set up in the churchyard next to MM 135 "which stands nearly opposite the door of Kirk Braddan" (*Illustrated London News* 1855; further details under MM 112 Braddan I, pp. 127–8). When Kermode compiled his 1907 account MM 136 seems still to have been in the churchyard. In 1907 it and its three fellow Braddan runic crosses were moved into the church (cf. The Manx Museum and Ancient Monuments Trustees 1908: 7), where they stand today, midway in the building, set in concrete bases.

MM 136 is carved on a substantial slab of grey mudstone, measuring *c.* 88 cm (visible height) × 16–30 × *c.* 9. Kermode (1907) gives the height as 48 inches (= 122 cm; see p. 128). The top is broken away. What remains is the lower part of a standing cross, tapering from the base. One face has interlace

Fig. 15. MM 136 Braddan III (drawing: Jonas Nordby).

dragons, the other a pair of elaborate interlace ornaments. A step pattern decorates one of the edges of the slab, the other has the runes, which run from base upwards between incised framing lines. The top section of the surviving inscription has suffered severe damage in modern times (apparently between Cumming's 1866/1868a and Vigfusson and Savage's 1887 accounts), removing the upper parts of rr. 22–36 and all of rr. 37–47, but an early cast (IC7 in the Museum of Scotland, Edinburgh; see Plate 44), rubbings and drawings enable us to reconstruct much of what was once there. It is, however, impossible to determine how many graphs have been lost after r. 47, so the final part of the inscription can be a subject of speculation only. What has, or had, survived reads (with runes supplied from the cast and early accounts in square brackets):

utr:risti:krus:þãnã:aft:frã[k]a:[f](aþ)[ursin]:[in]
:(þ)[urbiaurn:s(u)**[ ]

The length of the inscription (rr. 1–47; measurement taken from the Edinburgh cast) is 67 cm. Before r. 1 is a faint vertical line, perhaps signalling the opening of the text, or possibly this was a rune that was abandoned; rr. 1–3 would thus seem to present the full form of the raiser's name, and there is no need to supply any alternative, such as *Gautr* (as Kermode 1887b implies, but cf. Kermode 1907). The top of r. 23 is damaged, but there is possibly a trace of the start of the lowest part of the branch, and this rune is clear on the IC7 cast (and is given as ᚠ by Cumming 1857/1868a and Kneale [*c.* 1860]). Almost all the distinguishing features of rr. 25–9 and 31–6 are now lost, and of rr. 30, 37–47 nothing is visible at all; only part of the branch of r. 26 and the lower part of the bows of rr. 27, 35 can be discerned, and what might be the tail of **r** in r. 29 (also the lower points of what are clearly separators between

Fig. 16. MM 136 Braddan III, one of Cumming's c. 1855 rubbings (fol. 108r; reproduced by kind permission of the Bodleian Library, University of Oxford, MS Top. Man a 1).

rr. 32, 33 and 34, 35; cf. the following). Most of what is missing can be restored from earlier reproductions (notably Cumming's rubbings [c. 1855] in Bodleian MS Top. Man a 1, and the IC7 cast; see Fig. 16 and Plate 44). The very top of r. 45 had been lost as early as Cumming's c. 1855 and 1857 depictions; from his printed drawing there appears to be no doubt about the identification as **u**, but the rubbings here are rather less clear (though the cast seems to support the drawing). For rr. 46, 47 the cast shows for certain only the bases of two verticals. The rubbings in Top. Man a 1 show nothing but the base of a vertical for r. 46, while the drawings in this manuscript give or hint at the branch of **n**, also shown clearly in Cumming (1857), though the top of the graph is consistently depicted as lost. For r. 47 the fol. 108r rubbing and the drawings of Top. Man a 1, as well as the drawing in Cumming (1857), have what appear to be the bases of two verticals (just one is certainly visible on the cast). Kneale [c. 1860] gives a confident **nr** for rr. 46–7, but in the light of Cumming's representations, this is likely to be reconstruction. The separators in this inscription, two points in vertical line, are triangular in shape. Rune height varies between 42 (r. 1 **u**) and 55 mm (r. 13 **þ**).

Diagnostic rune forms are ᚬ **ã**, ᚾ **n**, ᛅ **a**, ᛌ **s**, ᛏ **t**, [ᛓ] **b**.

Interpretation

The general sense of what survives on the stone and in early representations is clear enough:

Oddr reisti kross þenna eptir Frakka fǫður sinn, en Þorbjǫrn ?sonr...

'Oddr put up this cross in memory of Frakki his father, but Þorbjǫrn ?son...'

What followed the third name was possibly a patronymic or appositional phrase (*sonr NNs* 'son of NN', or, unlikely, *sonr hans* 'his son'), provided rr. 44–6/7 really do give a form of the word 'son'; and presumably a statement about Þorbjǫrn's contribution – perhaps 'carved these runes' as in MM 107 German I (St John's) *a*, MM 142 Maughold IV*a* or 'made [the monument]' as in MM 99 Andreas I (*en Gautr gerði, sonr Bjarnar frá ?Kolli*), MM 101 Kirk Michael II. Or there could perhaps have been a second and distinctive comment, as apparently survives (without context) on the fragmentary MM 138 Braddan II.

Of the name forms only **frã[k]a** requires discussion (on the use of ã in the Manx inscriptions, cf. pp. 73–4). Are we to read it as a spelling for the accusative of the recorded, though apparently very rare and possibly Danish, *Franki* 'the Frank' (Knudsen and Kristensen 1936–64: 1, *s.n.*; Ekwall 1936: *s.n. Frankby*), with **ã[k]** denoting [ã(ŋ)k] (Williams 1994)? Or should we take it as *Frak(k)a* (nom. *Frak(k)i*) 'the bold' (< **frank-*), also rare (Lind 1905–15: *s.n. Frakki*; Knudsen and Kristensen 1936–64: 2, *s.n. Frak*; Peterson 2007: *s.n. Frakki*; further in Dodgson 1972: 287)? There is some discussion of the possibilities in Fellows-Jensen (1983: 50). Suffice it to say that the basic form of the name, [frã(ŋ)ka], is clear enough, even if the etymology is not.

The idea that there might be a Danish or at least East Norse flavour to Braddan III is perhaps bolstered by the spellings **risti** and **[f](aþ)[ur]**. The former could denote [reːsti] with East Norse monophthongisation /æi/ > /eː/, the latter [faður] with unmutated root vowel (West Norse [fɔður], though cf. N 59, N 271 both with **faþur**, and also further evidence of wanting *u*-mutation in Norwegian runic inscriptions, *NIyR* 5: 292). There are, however, counter-considerations. The diphthong /æi/ appears sometimes to be rendered **i** in the West (cf. **risti:stin** 'put up [this] stone' N 244–5 Helland II and III, further **risti:krus** 'put up [this] cross' MM 135 Braddan IV, MM 126 Kirk Michael IV, MM 132 Kirk Michael V*a*, MM 139 Marown, all four of which show West Norse features), while conversely, expected /e(ː)/, /æ/ may appear as **ai** (cf. **hailki, kaitil** for the personal names *Helgi, Ketil* (acc.) N 228 Tu, and on Man *inter alia* **þ(a)ina** for *þenna* 'this [acc. m. sg.]' MM 113 Andreas IV, **raiti** for presumed *rétti* 'put up' MM 127 Jurby), all of which suggests some vacillation in the denotation of /æi/, /e(ː)/, /æ/. Against **[f](aþ)[ur]** we have **(þ)[urbiaurn]**, which would seem to denote a pronunciation [þorbjɔrn], although that is a form that also occurs in East Scandinavia (Peterson 2007: *s.n. Þōrbiǫrn*).

Whatever the explanation of **risti**, it is very unlikely that it renders the 3rd sg. past of *rista* 'carve': the collocation *rista stein* 'carve the stone' is rare (cf. Palm 1992: 216, note 76; also the discussion in Källström 2007: 85–8).

Given the above considerations, a transcription that reflects the supposed speech of the carver is hard to achieve in every detail. We suggest:

Oddr ræisti kross þānnā æft Frānka/Frākka fǫður sinn, en Þorbjǫrn ?sonr...

MM 135 Braddan IV

Plates 33, 45–9, Figs 17, 36–7

LITERATURE. Marquardt 1961: 65–7. Camden/Gibson 1722: 1459–60; Camden/Gough 1789: 3, 704; Thorkelin [1789]; Oswald 1822: 504 and pl. XVII, B. nos 1–2; Jones [*c*. 1834–47]: 24; Kinnebrook 1841: 13 and fig. 21; Hibbert-Ware *et al.* [*c*. 1848]: 130; Munch 1850: 278; Cumming 1857: 29 and fig. 22; Kneale [*c*. 1860]: 61, no. 1; Cumming 1868a: facing 23, no. 4, and 27; Bugge 1899: 235–6; Kermode 1907: 203–5; Brate 1907: 29; Olsen 1954: 193; Sanness Johnsen 1968: 229–30; Page 1983: 140; Holman 1996: 119–22; Page 2005: 216–20.

MM 135 is the earliest of the Braddan memorials to be recorded, in the Gibson (1722) and Gough (1789) revisions of Camden's *Britannia* (cf. p. 48), where the depictions are simply labelled "Upon a Stone-Cross at *Kirk-braddan*" and "On the edge of a stone cross at *Kirk bradden*" respectively. In each case all that is shown is the inscribed narrow edge of this stone, and it appears intact and with its runes clearly visible. By the time of Oswald (1822) the cross had been damaged, one of its cross arms broken away, and the shaft shattered in two and bound together with metal clamps which obscured a central sequence of the text. Intermediate between Gough and Oswald is the 1789 Thorkelin drawing. This gives a rough representation of the whole stone, without any break recorded, but at rr. 33–7 there was clearly a problem of reading, which might have arisen from such damage (p. 55; also Page 2005). Oswald's drawing shows the cross standing upright in a circular stone base. Kinnebrook pictures MM 135 broken, but fixed with a single clamp, standing together with other, non-runic, stones "in Braddan Church Yard", and the same layout is implied by a rough sketch in Jones [*c*. 1834–47]. Jewitt (1884: 97) also shows the cross standing upright in the churchyard, but now on a mound and in the company of MM 112 and 136 (further details under MM 112 Braddan I, pp. 127–8). Kermode (1907: 205) reports MM 135 still on a mound in the churchyard (under his entry on MM 136 Braddan III, Kermode no. 109; but cf. below). In 1907 (see p. 128) it and its three fellow Braddan runic crosses were moved into the church (Braddan Old Kirk), where they stand today, midway in the building, set in concrete bases.

MM 135 is carved out of a slab of grey mudstone. Kermode (1907) describes the material as "a fine blue slate, probably from Spanish Head". The stone measures *c*. 148 cm (visible height) × 15–24 (width) × 14.5 (depth). Because of the complex shape of the object these figures can only give a general indication of size. Kermode (1907) records the height as 84 inches (= 213 cm), of which 27 inches (69 cm) is "a tongue-shaped prolongation" that

Fig. 17. MM 135 Braddan IV (drawing: Jonas Nordby).

supported the cross when it was originally set up (one imagines he examined and measured MM 135 on the occasion it was moved into the church, notwithstanding the fact that he records it as still in the churchyard). The stone is shaped as a cross shaft with pierced circled head. The shaft has interlaced beasts on both faces and one edge. The other edge has the runes, running from base to top between raised cable lines. Damage to the cross (cf. above) cuts across the inscription two-thirds of the way up, though without seriously affecting legibility. Otherwise the runes are clearly and well preserved. They read:

þurlibr:nhaki:risti:krus:þãnã:aft:fiak:sun(:)sin:(b)ruþur:sun:habrs×

The inscription is 87.5 cm long (91 if the saltire cross at the end is included). Rune height varies (as does the width of the inscribed edge) between 5 (r. 50 **b**) and 8.8 cm (r. 22 **þ**). Rune 1 begins well above the cross base so there is nothing missing before it. The upper dot of the separation symbol after r. 28 is lost. The break across the stone affects rr. 34, 35. Of r. 34 more than enough of the vertical and branch survives to confirm a reading **u**. Of r. 35 there remains a branch, which clearly supports the **n**-rendering of Gibson and Gough. After this there is a tiny triangular indentation that may be the remnant of a punctuation mark (the upper one of two points). Of r. 36 **s** only the dot is clear, but with a weak trace of a continuation upwards. The tops of rr. 37–39 are abraded, but this does not affect the reading – except of r. 39 whose upper branch can no longer be made out, though the identification is clear enough from the context. Gibson had no difficulty in reporting ᚭ here and Gough agreed. Thorkelin, however, reproduced a form ᚮ. Later writers have tended to confirm the uncertainty. In general graphs are carefully and professionally cut with a sharp blade. Page saw clear signs that they were formally laid out in advance, but we are unable to confirm this.

Rune 51 is rather roughly scratched in, and Page suggests this may have been added after the carver "got out of step with the first lay-out" or alternatively could be an original outline not completed (1981: 135; 2005: 219–20). Olsen, on the other hand, claims the rune was "undoubtedly [...] omitted and inserted later", a suggestion taken up by Holman. Runes 50–52 do look a little cramped, although without the **r**, the space between **b** and **s** would be unusually big for this inscription. All in all, Olsen's view is probably to be supported, and the putative (original) gap between **b** and **s** explained as the result of the carver's increasing the distance between graphs to fill the available space at the end of his inscription.

Following the runes, and seemingly by the same hand (judging from the similarity of the cut), is a large saltire cross. Thereafter comes a crudely carved group of symbols, 7.5 cm in length, probably by a different hand (see Plate 49). These have traditionally been read as roman IHSVS, a sequence the markings in part resemble. The saltire cross comes at the end of the shaft while the (apparent) letters proceed round the underside of the cross circle. Munch seems to have been the first to try to get to grips with this inscription: "nogle Træk [...] som synes at skulle forestille de latinske Bogstaver JHSUS, ɔ: *Jesus*" 'some grooves [...] that appear to represent the latin letters JHSUS, i.e. *Jesus*'. No alternative has so far been suggested.

Diagnostic rune forms are ᚽ **ã**, ᚼ **h**, ᚻ **n**, ᛆ **a**, ᛁ **s**, ᛏ **t**, ᛓ **b**.

Interpretation

There is no difficulty about interpreting this inscription. It clearly records:

Þorleifr hnakki reisti kross þenna eptir Fjakk son sinn, bróðurson Hafrs.

'Þorleifr neck put up this cross in memory of Fiacc his son, Hafr's nephew.'

The nickname *hnakki* 'nape of the neck' is recorded, though infrequently, in Scandinavia as a name form or byname (Bugge 1899: 235–6; Peterson 2007: *s.n. Hnakki*). The spelling **nhaki** with **nh-** rather than **hn-** can be compared with, e.g., **rhuulfʀ** for *Hroulfʀ* on the early Viking-Age Helnæs stone (DR 190), and perhaps with **ruhalts** for *Hroalds* on the equally early Snoldelev stone (DR 248). Such forms have sometimes been taken to suggest uncertainty about the writing of initial consonant clusters beginning with /h-/ (Brøndum-Nielsen 1957: 309–10; *DR*: 787). Possibly the /h-/ had been lost in the carver's speech; he recalled that the name was written with **h**, but was unsure precisely where to put it (cf. Braddan II's **rãskitil** *Hrossketill*, Maughold IVe's **lifilt** *Hlífhildi*, and, most probably, Kirk Michael IV's **rumu...** ?*Hrómund*, all with historical /h-/ unmarked). On the other hand, the spelling **rhoAl(t)R** on the ?seventh-century Vatn stone (KJ 68) – far too early for loss of initial /h-/ – suggests that when rendering /hl-/, /hn-/, /hr-/, rune carvers might place the **h** before or after the other consonant in the cluster.

Hafr 'billy-goat' occurs as a personal name and, less commonly, a byname. Up until the thirteenth century it is associated principally with Iceland. A genitive form **habs**, if that was what was originally carved (cf. above), could exemplify the "three consonant rule" whereby clusters of three or more consonants tend to be simplified in Scandinavian languages. The insertion of **r** would then be a later correction, either by the carver himself or someone else.

Fjakk, unlike *Þorleifr* and *Hafr*, is Irish. It almost certainly reflects *Fiacc* (O'Brien 1962: 635–6; Ó Riain 1985: 289), seemingly a hypocoristic form of *fiach* 'raven' 'warrior'. O'Brien (1973: 232) lists *Fiacc* among the "commonest names".

On the monographic spelling in presumed *Þorleifr* and *reisti* 'put up' 'erected', see the discussion under the interpretation of MM 136 Braddan III, and p. 73.

In the light of the above, a transcription in keeping with local speech might be:

Þorlæiþr hnākki ræisti kross þānnā æft Fjakk son sinn, bróðurson Haþrs.

It is possible, however, that *hnākki* should be given as *nākki*.

MM 176 Braddan V

Plate 50, Fig. 18

LITERATURE. Cubbon 1966b: 27–8; Sanness Johnsen 1968: 230–31; Holman 1996: 122–3.

This small fragment of Manx mudstone-siltstone was found in 1965 by Egil Bakka, a Norwegian archaeologist, in a fall of stones from the north-west wall of the churchyard of Braddan Old Kirk. It is currently held by the Manx Museum. The piece is of irregular, roughly triangular, shape and precise measurements are thus difficult to give. Approximate maximums are 24.5 cm × 12.5 × 2.5.

Parts of two lines of runes survive, one short and one longer, at right-angles to each other. There is no clear indication as to the order in which they are to be read, but assuming the inscription runs from left to right it makes sense to start with the former and assume rune bases face inwards,

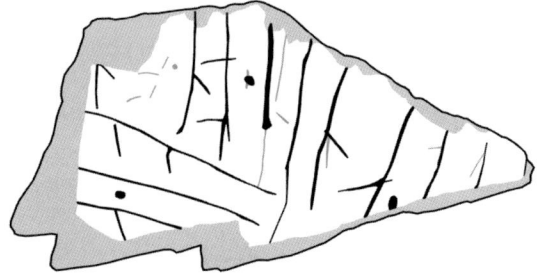

Fig. 18. MM 176 Braddan V (drawing: Jonas Nordby).

as the forms in general suggest. The short line, of which *c.* 5 cm survive, has three incomplete runes; the base of the first and the tops of all three are gone. The longer line is *c.* 18 cm, broken away at both ends; the tops of some of the runes are missing (perhaps not those of rr. 7–12) and the bases of the last three. Casual scratches and pitting of the surface make identification of many characters difficult, and transrunifications and transliterations are offered with some reservation. It is disturbing (but hardly rewarding) to compare the readings below with those Holman and Cubbon give. Since there is unlikely to be a convincing interpretation of these scraps of runes, Braddan V serves chiefly as an additional distribution point on a map of Manx inscriptions. It does, though, give a tentative indication of the graph-types used, which appear to be of the "short-twig" variety. The inscription can be read:

```
      1         5        10    13
] * · | ⟨ | | * ⊦ ⟨ · ⊥ | ⊦ ⟨ · * * * [

] * : i ( ã ) | | * n ( ã ) : s i n a : * * * [
  1           5           10        13
```

Rune 1 is broken away top and bottom; an ascending left branch meets what remains of the vertical slightly over half-way up: assuming the character originally to have been about the same length as the following two, this should be the remains of ⟨ (see r. 3). Rune 2 is a vertical without signs of any distinguishing feature; its top is missing however. Rune 3 is ⟨, in the Manx inscriptions mostly **b**, but occasionally **ã**; phonotactically a vowel is more plausible since if r. 6 too is **b** it gives the unlikely cluster /nb/. Rune 4 consists of the lower part of a vertical with a descending right branch just about connecting with its present top; depending on the original length this could be ⊦ or ⊩, probably the former going by the height of the branches on rr. 5 and 9. There follows a considerable space in which pitting and various gashes can be seen, but nothing that is certainly carved. Rune 6 appears to be ⟨ with almost horizontal branches (cf. the commentary on r. 3 above). What seems like a single, but substantial, separation point follows. Rune 7 looks to be ᛁ, with a line proceeding down from the dot as if from a slip of the tool (or perhaps the carver cut a full-length vertical in error and then compensated by deepening the upper part). Rune 8 is a plain vertical that reaches well below the bases of other graphs on this line – possibly the result of a further slip of the tool, or an attempt to provide a lower framing line for rr. 1–3 (conceivably also for characters that preceded them). Runes 9, 10 seem a clear **na**, and these are followed by what appears from its height to be a single separation symbol. Runes 11–12 are nothing more than the tops of two verticals. Rune 13 is the remnant of a vertical located on the very edge of the stone.

Diagnostic rune forms are ᚬ **ã**, or perhaps **b**, ᚾ **n**, ᚭ **a**, ᛁ **s**.

Interpretation

It is difficult to offer any interpretation of this fragmentary inscription, though rr. 7–10 may well contain a rendering of the reflexive possessive 'his' 'her' 'their' (most probably acc. f. sg. or perhaps m. pl. *sína*; formally possible, but highly unlikely, is gen. pl. *sinna*).

The graphs are cut fairly crudely, leading Cubbon to comment: "The general roughness of the whole piece suggests a fragment broken from a trial piece rather than an inscription from a cross-slab." Cubbon does, however, find a certain similarity of layout between Braddan V and II, and points out that the stones bearing these two inscriptions (MM 176 and 138) are "geologically similar". He denies, however, that Braddan V could be a missing part of Braddan II because

> the new fragment is only about half the thickness, will not fit into the pattern of the incomplete cross unless a completely new layout is followed on the missing portion, the runes are much cruder, and roughly chipped single spacing-dots occur in contrast to fairly well-formed pairs of spacing-dots on the Hrosketil stone.

Holman concurs, but reasons:

> as all of the stone's edges show fracture damage and the back of it is rough and unshapen, it is possible that this [the fragment] may have flaked off the surface of a larger monument.

We may speculate about Braddan V's original purpose, but too little remains of the stone on which it was carved for firm conclusions to be drawn. It is hard to see the similarity of layout Cubbon observed between Braddan V and II, and the geological similarity of the stones on which they are found does not appear to be particularly striking. Dave Quirk (pers. com.) defines the material of Braddan V as "banded mudstone-siltstone-fine grained sandstone typical of Port Erin", that of Braddan II as "mudstone, ?typical of Round Table", and notes yet further differences between the two.

MM 200 Braddan VI
Plate 51, Fig. 19

LITERATURE. Page 1992b; Holman 1996: 123–4.

This fragment was discovered in 1991 during restoration work at Braddan Old Kirk. It was being used to prop up a floor beam underneath the communion table. The piece is currently held by the Manx Museum. The rune-inscribed slab to which it once belonged has split horizontally, causing a roughly triangular section to break off the inscription-bearing edge. The resulting fragment is irregular in shape: maximum length *c.* 32.5 cm, width *c.* 22, depth (= height of rune-inscribed surface) 5.5 cm. The piece has also laminated; it has been stuck together again, but there is a crack running along most of its length, and at one end the lamination has led to complete loss of half the surface. All that remains of the inscription are the mid- to upper parts of what appear to be fifteen runes. These read:

]∗∗(ᛏR)∗(ᚲᛏ)R(:)ᚴIRᚦI(:)ᚾ∗[

]∗∗(ar)∗(ka)r:kirþi:u∗[

The length of the surviving sequence is *c.* 29.5 cm. The runes are cleanly cut, presumably with a knife, which created crisp, v-shaped grooves. From what remains it would seem that rune height was *c.* 70 mm, though of the best preserved graphs only about half of the original length survives (cf. above). Runes 1, 2 and 5 are now parts of verticals only. Rune 3 has the remains of a branch descending from the left, suggesting ᛏ **a** (cf. p. 154). Rune 4 is made up of two lines not now joining, but at such an angle to one another as

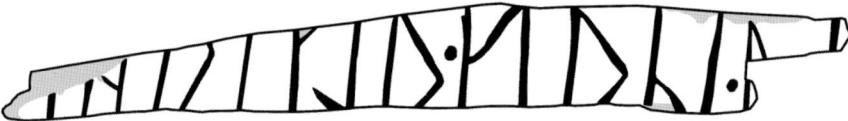

Fig. 19. MM 200 Braddan VI (drawing: Jonas Nordby).

to imply the lower part of the bow of **r** (hardly of ᛒ, which is not otherwise found on Man, cf. p. 69; in addition the apparent bow seems to stretch too far down to be the upper one of two). Rune 6 has the beginnings of a branch that would form **k**. Rune 7 is a vertical with a branch cutting into or across it, as ᚾ (which would agree with the shape of r. 3) or conceivably "long-branch" ᚿ. Runes 8, 11 are clearly the upper halves of **r**, r. 9 the upper half of **k**, and r. 12 that of **þ**, while rr. 10, 13 are parts of plain verticals, which can be identified, to some extent from context, as **i**. Between rr. 8 and 9 is a dot, clearly a separation symbol, and with its high placement probably the upper one of a pair in vertical line. A similar dot, but slightly lower down, is found between rr. 13 and 14. From here on the inscription is affected by the lamination of the fragment (cf. above). Rune 14 is more thinly cut and somewhat shallower than the other graphs; with the sharp angle of its truncated branch it appears to be the upper part of ᚢ (rather than of ᛚ), though the branch is then a little straighter than to be expected. Some 35 mm beyond is what seems to be the very top of a vertical line, of uncertain import. If this is the remains of a runic graph, it may in its complete form perhaps have had a branch to the left, though even then the distance from r. 14 is unusually large. For the sake of convenience this final mark is counted as a rune in the transliteration.

There are no diagnostic forms, save possible ᚾ **n** or ᚿ **a**.

Interpretation

If the reading of rr. 9–13 is correct, we would seem to have the verb form *gerði* 'made', with the implication that the preceding rune group, divided from the verb by a separation symbol, could conceal a personal name ending in -*r*, possibly -*kárr* (cf. Petersen 2007: *s.n.*). A patronymic in -*sonr* 'son' seems unlikely: what remains of r. 6 can hardly be reconciled with ᚠ or ᚯ for /o/, and ᚢ is out of the question. In support of this general interpretation it may be noted that **kir[þ]i/kirþi** occurs in makers' signatures in the Andreas I, Kirk Michael II and Maughold V inscriptions. Further than that it would be perilous to go.

MM 118 Bride

Plates 52–6, Fig. 20

LITERATURE. Marquardt 1961: 67. Kermode 1884: 151–2; Vigfusson and Savage 1887: 8–9; Kermode 1887b: 151; Bugge 1899: 240; Kermode 1907: 169–70; Brate 1907: 29–30; Olsen 1954: 193–4; Sanness Johnsen 1968: 231–2; Page 1983: 140; Holman 1996: 125–6.

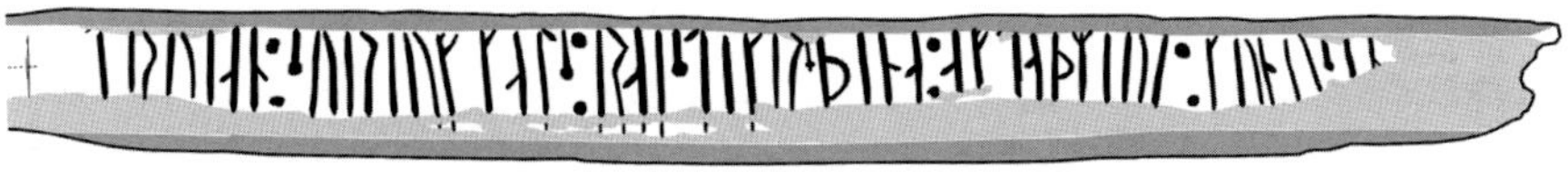

Fig. 20. MM 118 Bride (drawing: Jonas Nordby).

There is no detailed find report for MM 118. It turned up at Bride parish church when the remains of the old building were levelled in about 1869 (Kermode 1907: 169). From drawings that survive, the predecessor of the present church (completed in the 1870s) was a medieval structure of common Manx design, barn-like with a small western bell turret. The fragmentary runestone and several other carved pieces were found in its walls. The runestone was set up in the churchyard where it remained, partly sheltered, until 1981, when the Manx Museum had it brought indoors and put upright on a wooden stand near the south wall at the west end of the church, along with other, non-runic, monuments.

The Bride inscription is carved on a substantial slab of laminated mudstone measuring *c.* 107 cm (visible height) × 37 × *c.* 8. Kermode (1907) gives the height as 44 inches (= 112 cm). The stone's top is lost, and all that remains of what were presumably sculptured crosses on the two faces are their shafts, filled with ring-chain and interlace decoration. Interlace and animal ornament cover the areas to either side of each shaft. One of the narrow edges of the stone is blank. The runes run up the other edge, occupying its full breadth. The surviving text reads:

t r u i a n : s u r * u f k a l s : r a i s t i k r s þ i n a : a f t a þ m i u *
: k u n u s * (n) [

The length of the remaining inscription is *c.* 61 cm. There has been wear or weathering of one face of the stone, which has damaged some rune tops and caused loss of distinguishing branches. Here and there, and particularly towards the end of the text, rune bases may also be lost by lamination. Where tops and bases survive, there are no indications of framing lines above or below. Because of the raggedness of the surface runes vary in height: perhaps from 35 mm (r. 34 **þ**) to 53 (r. 19 **i**) – although some of the irregularity stems from damage that post-dates the carving of the inscription. Nearly all graphs were precisely cut with a sharp tool, seemingly first delineated firmly but thinly, then opened out into v-shaped grooves. Some separation points are deeply chiselled. Despite the initial layout, a number of "verticals" slope markedly, particularly towards the end of the inscription, where also the runes are more casually carved and in places more crowded.

Rune 1 begins *c.* 7 cm above the base-line of the sculptured crosses on the front and back of the slab. Before it, but very faint, there appears to be a cross. It is scratched lightly on a damaged patch of the surface, not firmly cut in the same way as the rest of the inscription. In the transrunification and transliteration it is ignored. Rune 1 has a clear vertical. It has traditionally been read as **t**, and indeed the very tip of a left-hand branch seems just visible, suggesting ↿; yet the space between the verticals of rr. 1 and 2 is considerably wider than would be expected if r. 1 had no right-hand branch (compare the gaps between rr. 10, 11 – see below – rr. 21, 22 **ti**, and rr. 32, 33 **ta**). Unfortunately damage has obliterated all carving there might once have been in the relevant area, but it is quite possible r. 1 was ↑, even though this implies the use of an occasional "long-branch" form in an otherwise "short-twig" inscription. A parallel would be the initial graph of the personal name **tolfin** in E 3 Carlisle A (now Carlisle I A following the discovery of a second Carlisle runic inscription; cf. Barnes 2010). The base and top of rr. 2 and 3 are lost but the identities are not in question. Of r. 10 only a vertical survives, but given the name that is almost certainly recorded here, the character is likely to have been **t**. The lower branch of r. 12, **f**, is clear; the upper is indicated by a slight bifurcation at the present top of the vertical; the context also confirms **f**. Rune 25, ↾, is very thin and faint, and is squeezed between rr. 24 and 26 as though the carver (or someone else) were seeking to supply a graph which had been accidentally omitted. There is no way of dating such an alteration/addition (if that is what it is). The lower of the two separation points after r. 29 coincides with damage to the surface. The tops of rr. 31, 32 have lost some of their distinguishing features through the damage to the slab's edge. Rune 31 has a clear lower branch and a tiny remnant of an upper fellow, certainly **f**. Rune 32 is a vertical with a damaged patch at its top; a short cut can be made out that is surely what is left of the tip of the branch of ↿, a reading supported by the context. Rune 38 is a vertical with no sign of branch or bow, though judging by the **u** that immediately precedes it, enough of the top is missing to have removed any branch that may once have been there. After r. 38 are two shallow dots in more or less vertical line. The graphs from r. 39 onwards are thinner than the earlier ones, and more clumsily laid out (conceivably they were later additions, or for some reason were never broadened and deepened). Both top and bottom of the edge here are in a poor state. The vertical of r. 39, **k**, is missing just above the point where the branch takes off, and vertical and branch of both rr. 40 and 42 no longer meet. Of r. 44 there can be seen only the fragment of a vertical. Rune 45 is similar, but with what seems to be the beginning of a descending right branch as of ᚠ. After r. 45 the stone breaks away, with no indication of what, if anything, may have followed.

Many of the uncertainties identified in the foregoing are admitted in the earliest records. Vigfusson and Savage concur about the difficulty of reading rr. 1, 32, and 38 (suggesting **t** for r. 1, "c", i.e. **k**, for r. 32, and **l** for r. 38). Kermode (1887b) agrees about r. 1, expresses some doubt about the identification of r. 32 as "c" and seems to prefer **t**, and further notes that he read r. 38 as **i** (a simple vertical). The drawing in Kermode (1907) shows tentative branches on rr. 1, 10 (both ↑), verticals only at rr. 32, 38; and a right descending branch on the attenuated vertical of r. 45. Brate signals rr. 1, 10, 31–2, 35, 38, 44–5 as seriously damaged, although in his discussion he suggests that the branch of r. 10 ought to be visible, had it ever been carved. Olsen's only additional comments of significance are: to note an apparent branch on r. 22 (giving ↑), but this is certainly surface damage; to observe that **l**, **k** or **t** are all possible identifications of r. 38; and to declare that no branch was visible to him on the vertical of r. 45. Holman's account stresses the uncertainties of many of the identifications suggested, and this must be kept in mind in any attempt to interpret the inscription.

Diagnostic rune forms are ᚠ **n**, ᚬ **a**, ᛁ **s**, ↑, and perhaps ↑ (r. 1), **t**, ᛉ **m**.

Interpretation

The general sense of the inscription is clear enough:

Drúan sonr Dufgals reisti kross þenna eptir NN konu sína.

'Drúan son of Dubgall put up this cross in memory of his wife NN.'

It is possible further text followed *konu sína* 'his wife'. A few details call for discussion.

Whether the omission of graphs in **sur**, **krs** is intentional or in error is hard to tell. The impression that r. 25, **s**, was added as an afterthought speaks in favour of error. However, MM 106 Ballaugh too has the spelling ∗**rs** (clearly originally **krs**), which might suggest this was an acceptable abbreviation in Man. Against that, though, is the possibility the Ballaugh carver may also to start with have omitted the final **s** of the word, implying carelessness (p. 124). Neither **sur** nor **krs** seem to be documented elsewhere, though *sonr* appears in a wide variety of forms in Scandinavia (cf., e.g., Peterson 2006: *s.v. sunʀ/ sunn*). If the /o/ in *sonr* was nasalised in the speech of the Bride carver, as is eminently likely, he may have deemed it unnecessary to denote /n/ separately, though in Viking-Age inscriptions such omission of nasals occurs otherwise only before homorganic consonants (see Williams 1994; cf., however, **mãʀ** *mannʀ* on KJ 101 Eggja).

The three personal names in the inscription are all of Celtic origin. Underlying **truian** would appear to be Irish *Drúan* (of uncertain meaning), attested in early Old Irish as *Drón* (Ó Riain 1985: 282, who lists manuscript variants with *Tr-*; O'Brien 1962: 597); possibly preserved in the place-name *Glentruan*, Kirk Bride (Broderick 1994–2005: indexes *s.n.*). The runic form **ufkals* is almost certainly a rendering of Old Irish *Dubgall* ['duβɣal:] 'black stranger' (O'Brien 1962: 600; and cf. MM 130 Kirk Michael III), with the addition of a Scandinavian genitive -**s** inflection (and concomitant shortening of [l:]). What remains of the third name has been expanded as **aþmiul** or, far less plausibly, **kaþmiul** (with r. 32 read as **k**, cf. above). The former might be a scandinavianised version of Old Irish *Admall* ['aðµal:] (cf. *DIL*: *s.v.* 1 *admall* 'slow witted', used as the name of a drinking-horn, but not apparently attested as a personal name). If so, the vocalism of the second syllable could reflect Middle Irish reduction of unstressed [a] to [ə], but precisely what Norse pronunciation underlies the spelling **miu*** can only be a matter for speculation.

It has been claimed that the word-order *Drúan sonr Dufgals* as opposed to the more usual Scandinavian *Drúan Dufgalssonr* manifests Irish influence (e.g. Olsen 1954: 225–8). While it is true that 'X son/daughter of Y' is standard patronymic usage in the insular Celtic languages, parallels can be found in Scandinavian runic inscriptions and Old Norse writings more generally. A distinction needs to be made, however, between true patro-/metronymics on the one hand and appositional phrases on the other, the latter simply supplying additional information about a person, as **muþiʀ:alriks:tutiʀ:urms** '[who was] mother of Alrikʀ, daughter of Ormʀ' in the Ramsund rock inscription (Sö 101). In the case of the Bride text there is nothing to suggest supplementary information is being offered about Drúan, as seems generally to be true where the order 'X son/daughter of Y' is encountered in Scandinavia. And it is perhaps also worth noting that the Isle of Man and adjacent areas of England have many place-names reflecting Celtic word-order, e.g. Kirkbride found side-by-side with Bridekirk. The deployment of the separation marks in: **truian:sur*ufkals:** seems neither to support nor undermine the patronymic interpretation, in spite of Olsen's claim to the contrary (1954: 227). He argues that the punctuation of the inscription "is adjusted to the phrase-rhythm", and that "the accentuation is thus exactly as in the corresponding

Irish personal-designation, with *mac* coming between the son's name and that of his father." It looks, however, more as though the separation marks divide the inscription into syntactic phrases (subject : ?patronymic : verb phrase : preposition phrase : appositional phrase). We might thus expect the assumed patronymic to have been divided from what immediately precedes and follows whether it was given in the form **surtufkals** or **tufkals(s)ur**.

Apart from this one possible example of Irish influence on the word-order, the grammar of the inscription (and seemingly the phonology too) appears to be wholly Scandinavian – notwithstanding the names of all involved are Celtic.

A transcription of the Bride text in keeping with assumed local speech patterns would differ in various details from the one given above:

Drúān sonr Duþgals ræisti kross þennā æft NN konu sínā.

MM 107 German I (St John's) *a–b*

Plates 57–62, Figs. 21–2

LITERATURE. Marquardt 1961: 68–9. Cumming 1857: 19 and fig. 5; Kneale [*c*. 1860]: 61, no. 5; Cumming 1868a: facing 23, no. 6, and 27–8; Vigfusson and Savage 1887: 18; Kermode 1892: 14, 44–5; Bugge 1899: 240; Kermode 1907: 159–60; Brate 1907: 32; Olsen 1954: 199–200; Sanness Johnsen 1968: 233–4; Page 1981: 134; Page 1983: 139–40; Holman 1996: 127–8.

German I*a*

Cumming (1857) reports that MM 107 was found "in the old church of St John the Baptist in Kirk German, when it was pulled down A.D. 1850". The old church was put up at the beginning of the 1700s and replaced an earlier structure (Harrison 1871: 50, who, pp. 78–80, gives the date of demolition as 1847, which seems to be correct). Cumming adds of the stone: "It is now erected in the churchyard [of the new, replacement building, the Royal Chapel – or, more properly, the Parish Church of St John the Baptist] in the angle between the tower and south porch." From this site it was removed, to stand within the porch, where Kermode (1892: 14) recorded it. There it stays, on the left as one enters, close up to the wall and set in the concrete floor. A *c*. 11–16 cm gap between stone and wall permits examination of what may be termed the stone's reverse face, which shows no trace of carving whatsoever.

The German I inscriptions are placed on a slab of dark grey mudstone,

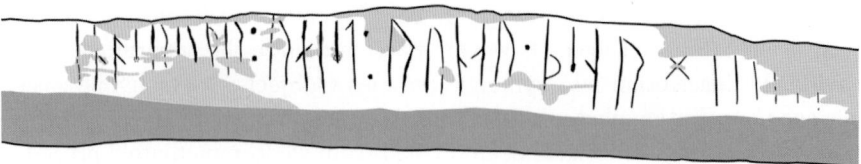

Fig. 21. MM 107 German I (St John's) a (drawing: Jonas Nordby).

measuring *c.* 114 cm (visible height) × 34–39 × 11–13. Kermode (1907) gives the height as 53 inches (= 135 cm). Only the lower portion of the slab remains; the upper section is broken away, and the extant surface suffers from general weathering and flaking. The (readily) visible face has what was presumably the shaft of a sculptured cross, with ring chain ornament set between plain borders. One of the narrow edges (on the right as the stone is now viewed) has traces of an incised line pattern. The other bears the inscription German I*a*. Some commentators have thought to see traces of a framing line above the runes, but this seems to be a natural furrow in the stone. The bases of several graphs are lost. The inscription reads:

```
      1      5        10       15       20       25    28
    ]ikf'RNÞR:R4I'1:RNF4R(:)Þ'4R×****(**)[
    ]inãsruþr:raist:runar:þsar×****(**)[
      1      5        10       15       20       25    28
```

Length extending from r. 1 to the last clear vertical fragment (r. 26) is a little over 69 cm. Rune heights are hard to measure precisely because of the damage many have suffered, but on the evidence of the reasonably well preserved rr. 14–18 the tallest were in the region of 70–80 mm. Before the present r. 1 there is a space of *c.* 27 cm down to the floor (measured from the base of the graph), in which nothing certain can be observed. Rune 1 is lightly scratched in compared with the rest of the inscription. Runes 4–8 are weathered and abraded in varying degrees. In addition the surface below them appears to have been damaged before they were written, so they are rather shorter than the other runes, perhaps 50 mm or less. All are readily identifiable, however, even r. 7, although it is in part very faint. The top half of its vertical can be seen easily enough, and with sympathetic lighting most of the bow can be traced, though this is not shown in the illustrations of Cumming (1857) or Kneale. Vigfusson and Savage report:

> The only doubtful letter in the word Osruth is þ, but we distinctly saw traces of the right hand curve of the letter, the slate however having peeled away, leaving a depression within the curve.

Bugge thought r. 7 doubtful too, but from Kermode (1907) and Brate onwards a reading þ has been accepted more or less without reservation, which indeed seems justified. There is a minor ambiguity affecting r. 10. At first glance it looks like ᛏ, but was almost certainly intended as ᛆ. Olsen appears to have been the first to observe

> a tiny incision to the right of the stem, but separate therefrom, which makes the rune look somewhat similar to ᛏ. That incision ought perhaps to be regarded as accidental and meaningless. Or, can it be that the carver had begun to carve the branch of a ᚭ a […] but later decided in favour of the usual rune ᛆ?

Sanness Johnsen made no comment. Holman, on the other hand, noted Olsen's observation and remarked that the "incision to the right of the main stem" was "in fact a separate cut and probably an error" – which accords with our observations. However the lines here are to be analysed, this graph was surely intended as **a**. Between rr. 13 and 14 the surface is severely damaged; the lower of two separation points can be clearly seen, the upper one is only partially preserved. Conversely, the upper of what were almost certainly two separation points between rr. 18 and 19 is clear, but it is hard to find traces of its lower fellow. Rune 21 has the unusual form ᛆ.

Beyond the saltire cross that appears to form the end of the only extant sentence of this inscription, there was further text. The remains of four faint verticals are visible and there are hints of two more, but none shows any distinguishing features.

The incisions that form the graphs are thin but cleanly cut, though they give a somewhat "amateur" impression. Page thought to see traces of marking lines and considered some of the graphs to have been carved out lightly in advance, but we were unable to confirm this.

Diagnostic rune forms are ᚭ **ã**, ᚦ **n**, ᛆ (rr. 10, 17) ᛆ (r. 21) **a**, ᛁ (rr. 4, 20) ᛁ (r. 12) **s**, ᛏ **t**.

Interpretation

The text is clearly part of a subsidiary statement, in all likelihood complementing a memorial formula:

En Ásrøðr reist rúnar þessar.

'And/But Ásrøðr carved these runes.'

There follows what may be the opening, now unreadable, of some further sentiment. How all this fitted into the design of cross and presumed commemorative inscription is impossible to tell, given the fragmentary nature of the stone. Olsen comments on the existing text: "This has been an addition to the real inscription (now lost), and put below it on the stone." Kermode (1907) describes it as "an afterthought". Thus can perhaps be explained the form **þsar**, from which the vowel rune of the first syllable is missing. The implications of the idea that a text recording the names of commissioner and deceased came above the existing inscription need pondering. Kermode seems to envisage that such a text would have run upwards, but why, one wonders, should the carver have begun his main inscription so high? There is, in fact, nothing in the few remnants of graphs visible above the saltire cross that would preclude a text that ran downwards. Granted, this would be unusual for Man (and western Scandinavia in general), but not unexampled (cf. MM 128 Andreas III).

Worthy of comment is the occurrence in German I*a* of ᚭ, a rare graph-type of **a**. In the Manx inscriptions **a** is usually ᚭ, though MM 101 Kirk Michael II has two examples of ᚠ in the name forms **mail:brikti** and **kaut**. The ᚠ graph-type is associated with the early Viking Age, while the only other certain examples of ᚭ **a** to our knowledge occur in IR 11 from Fishamble Street, Dublin (archaeologically dated to the mid-eleventh century), DR 101 (1100–1150) – both *fuþark* inscriptions – and U 780, an eleventh-century memorial stone (cf. also, however, two possible occurrences in MM 200 Braddan VI). Yet ᚭ is not an unexpected variant: it incorporates the essential features of **a**, vertical + oblique, mid-height branch, and there is little danger of its being confused with any other rune (unless it could be thought a graph-type of **n**, cf. ᚠ **n**, also found in IR 11).

The spelling **āsruþr** has been normalised by most commentators as *Ásrøðr*. The only other West Scandinavian example of this name appears to be from *Landnámabók*, and is cited by Bugge. He derives it from *Ásfrøðr*. Lind too identified the *Landnámabók* scribal manifestations *Asroðr*, *Asʀaudr* as instances of the man's name *Ásrøðr* (1905–15: *s.n. Ásrøðr*). The West Norse form is almost certainly a reflex of *Ansufreðuʀ (Lagman 1990: 86) as, too, seem to be Runic Swedish *Æstrøðr* (Peterson 2007: *s.n. Āsrøðr/Æstrøðr*) and Old Danish *Asfrith*; cf. further the Anglo-Scandinavian variants *Asfrið*, *Asferð*, *Asforth*, etc. (Björkman 1910: 10–11).

A transcription of the German I*a* inscription in keeping with assumed local speech patterns cannot differ greatly from the one given above:

En Ásrøðr ræist rúnār þessar.

Fig. 22. MM 107 German I (St John's) b (drawing: Jonas Nordby).

German I*b*

On the upper right-hand side of the decorated face of MM 107, close to its edge and outside the band delimiting the ornamentation, are found some further runes, running upwards. This appears to be a graffito, 11.5–13.5 (or even 17.5) cm in length, depending on how many of the faint lines are included. Maximum height of the graphs is 20 mm. Those that are certainly or presumably runic read:

(ᛘ)∗ᚱᛁᛁᛁᚱ'ᚿ∗∗

(m)∗riiirsu∗∗

Rune 1, of which only the very top survives, is most plausibly read as **m**. There follows a 12 mm gap in which there may once have been a runic graph. Rune 2 is the top of a vertical. Rune 3 has lost its base but is clearly **r**. Runes 4–6 are three verticals without distinguishing feature (rr. 4–5, at least, minus their bases). Runes 10–11 (some way beyond r. 9) appear to be the top halves of two verticals. Following r. 11 three slanting cuts and yet further marks can be made out, but it is uncertain whether these have anything to do with the inscription.

Diagnostic rune forms are ' **s**, ᛘ **m**.

Page surmised that this graffito represented an attempt to copy part of the main inscription (1983: 139), but it does not bear much similarity to what survives of the formal text. Indeed, it is hard to extract any sense from it at all. Possibly there was simply an attempt to imitate certain of the runes by someone with little or no grasp of the sense of the main inscription.

MM 140 German II (Peel)
Plates 63–7, Fig. 23

LITERATURE. Marquardt 1961: 69. Petit 1846: 58; Cumming 1857: 33–4 and fig. 27; Kneale [c. 1860]: 61, no. 6; Cumming 1868a: facing 23, no. 16, and 32–3; Bugge 1899: 242–3; Kermode 1907: 209; Brate 1907: 32; Olsen 1954: 200; Sanness Johnsen 1968: 248; Page 1983: 140; Holman 1996: 128–30.

MM 140 has had an adventurous existence, if the various reports of it are to be believed. It seems to make its first appearance in Petit (1846), who places it "among the rough stonework which blocks up one of the arches of the nave" of the ruined cathedral of St German on Patricksholm, Peel. Cumming (1857) gives the same location. Kneale ([c. 1860]: 171) reported the monument in "the southern wall of the nave of the Cathedral", which is repeated in various forms in contemporary guidebooks. Mayhew (1881: 54) has it in the south transept of the cathedral. Kermode (1907) is more precise: "This stone was built into the east wall of the north transept of Peel Cathedral some thirty years ago." It stayed there until 1906 when it was removed to a temporary museum on the site (Kermode 1907). The stone is now in the Manx Museum.

The German II runes are carved on a slab of greyish mudstone, measuring c. 69 cm × 33 × 7–10 (which figures accord closely with those given in Kermode 1907). No visible ornament remains; indeed, the stone appears totally undressed save for the edge along, up or down which the inscription runs. It reads:

]u·᛫þᚠᚾ'ᛏ·ᛏᛈ1ᛏR·ᛏ'RIÞI·ᛈᚾᚠᚾ'Iᚠᛁ·᛫ᚾ᛫ᚾR:ᚾ1(')
᛫᛫R᛫᛫(:')᛫...[

]us:þïnsï:ïftïr:asriþi:kunusina:᛫u᛫ur:ut(s)
᛫᛫r᛫᛫(:s)᛫...[

The length of the inscription, rr. 1–34, is 47.5 cm. There follows a section, extending for c. 4.5 cm, in which nothing runic can be traced, and indeed where no runes appear to have been carved (marked by a gap in the transrunification and transliteration). Thereafter is a worn and damaged patch with a confusing row of incisions, c. 11 cm long. Rune tops are not well preserved, so the heights of the graphs are approximate: c. 3.5–4.2 cm. There are no signs

Fig. 23 MM 140 German II (Peel) (drawing: Jonas Nordby).

of framing lines. How much is lost before the present r. 1, and how much after the final surviving incision, cannot be determined. Of r. 1 only the upper half survives in its entirety, though the right side of the branch can be traced for its full length, and the identification as **u** is certain. Rune 4 has a sharp cut, slightly skewed, towards the centre of its vertical, which makes clear it is to be read as **ï** rather than **i**. The same applies to rr. 7, 8, 11. The top of r. 21 is damaged, but there is no problem of identification. On the other hand, the complete loss of the tops of rr. 26–9 raises questions about their common rendering as **a:tut**. The branch of r. 26 comes rather high up, so much so that minus its top the graph resembles **t**; had the relevant line been placed lower, however, it might have collided with the **n**-branch of r. 25, so **a** seems to be the rune the carver intended. Enough remains of r. 28 for its identification as **u**, and that, in the context, suggests rr. 27, 29 were **t**; however, nothing of a **t**-branch can now be seen for sure on either. Rune 34 is the very top of a vertical, immediately below which there is great damage; farther down the surface is preserved, but without signs of carving (save what may be a layout line for a half- to two-thirds length vertical), which strongly suggests that what can be seen here is the remains of ' **s**. Runes 35, 36 are no more than the tops of verticals; damage has obliterated all traces of further carving. Rune 37, though incomplete at its top, is a clear **r**. Rune 38 is a vertical which does not extend as far up as those of rr. 37, 39–40. The latter two graphs appear to be **l** and ', though there is no context to support this identification (r. 39 could be ᚠ if the putative vertical top and branch are deliberately carved rather than the result of damage). There are a number of pock marks in this area, of which two quite prominent ones between rr. 39 and 40 may well be what is left of a separator. Rune 41 is either ᛅ or ᚾ; between a half and two-thirds of its upper part are missing. After a small space following r. 41 can perhaps be made out the remains of two or three verticals, but nothing here is certain.

Many of the characteristics just described are recorded, inconsistently, in the earlier reports. Cumming (1857) draws the dotted form ᛏ for r. 8, but not elsewhere (in his 1868 representation rr. 4 and 8 are both ᛁ). Brate reads "**þensi · ifter**" for rr. 3–12, but notes the difficulty here, quoting a fresh examination by Kermode which revealed to him that "dessa prickar icke äro bredare än stafven men utgöra små hål, borrade midt uti densamma" 'these dots [in rr. 4 and 11] are no broader than the vertical, but constitute small bore-holes at its centre'. Olsen gives ᛁ without comment for rr. 4, 7, 8, 11, as does Holman. Sanness Johnsen also reads **e** in these cases. For rr. 27–9 Cumming (1857) shows two clear ᛁs and an incomplete, but certain, ᚾ; nevertheless he observes: "The first two (or three?) letters of 'dutur' are imperfect, and they may be either 'dot' or 'mu'." Bugge is unsure whether r. 26 is **a** or **ą**, but transliterates rr. 27–9 **tut** without further ado. Brate has [**tu**]**t** for rr. 27–9 and Olsen (**tut**), while Sanness Johnsen underpoints the three letters. For rr. 26, 27, 29 Holman shows plain verticals. After r. 33 Brate adds a character not otherwise certainly deciphered, for he reads **uts**, without comment. Olsen and Sanness Johnsen follow more cautiously, suggesting **ut**[**s**] and **ut**(**s**) respectively. Holman gives simply ᚾᛁ.

Diagnostic rune forms are ᚼ **n**, ᛆ **a**, ᛁ **s**, ᛁ **t**, ᚼ **ī**.

Interpretation

This fragmentary inscription should almost certainly be supplied with the opening *NN reisti kr-*, which is common to most of the Manx memorials (there may of course have been more than this). It is also eminently likely, as Brate, Olsen and Sanness Johnsen assert or surmise, that an **s** followed r. 33 (cf. the account above). With these additions, and accepting rr. 26–9 as **a:tut**, the principal text of the inscription would say:

[*NN reisti*] *kross þenna eptir Ástríði konu sína, dóttur Odds.*

'[NN put up] this cross in memory of Ástríðr his wife, daughter of Oddr.'

What statement might have followed the memorial formula is wholly unclear. The possibilities are many, and no guess can sensibly be hazarded on the basis of the little that can still be seen.

Olsen notes the use of ᚼ, and of ᛆ for "nasal *a*", suggesting that they "may indicate that this is a memorial from a later date than the great majority of the Manx crosses". Holman draws attention to the form of the demonstrative pronoun 'this'. Accusative masculine *þennsi* is not otherwise found on Man, and is rare in West Scandinavian tradition, occurring only on the Vang and Kuli stones (N 84, 449), the lost Tangerhaug cross (N 237), and the Iona cross slab (SC 14). Of the Manx inscriptions German II alone has this word ending in *-si* rather than *-a*, and *þenna, þanna* (with related forms) are also the norm in the West Scandinavian world. Examples of *þennsi, þannsi* (and other variants in *-si*) do, however, abound in Denmark and Sweden (cf. Massengale 1972: especially 385–7). Holman concludes: "This spelling and the e-runes [the four instances of ᛐ] combine to suggest that the inscription was carved by someone who spoke an East rather than West Scandinavian dialect." We have two suggestions here: that German II is a late inscription in the Manx context, and that it was made by an East Scandinavian carver. Neither of these propositions is unproblematic. Dotted runes seem to make their first appearance in Denmark towards the end of the tenth century, but they are also found in different parts of the British Isles at what are, or may be, quite early dates. IR 12 Fishamble Street, Dublin, archaeologically dated to *c*. 1000, for example, sports a clear ᚼ, while MM 130, which on art-historical grounds should belong among the earliest of the Manx crosses, exhibits in its inscription, Kirk Michael III, multiple examples of ᛐ and two of ᚼ (cf. pp. 176–7). It has even been proposed that runic dotting first arose among Scandinavians in the British Isles (Page and Hagland 1998: 68–9; for a rebuttal see Knirk 2010, but cf. further pp. 61–2). The use of ᛐ for historical /ã:/, i.e. a vowel in which nasality was (once) distinctive, does perhaps point to the eleventh rather than the tenth century (though the marking of nasality in Viking-Age inscriptions, even early ones, is by no means consistent, cf. Williams 1990: 38); however, the regular rendering of /o(:)/ by **u** (cf. **kunu** for *konu*, and, presumably, *u*ur for *dóttur*,]**us** for *kross* and **ut**(**s**) for *Odds*) is indicative of a date not much later than *c*. 1020 (cf. Spurkland 1995: 4–10, but note also the reservation he expresses on p. 13). As for the linguistic affiliation of the carver, there is no certainty that dotting (in its early manifestations) is an exclusively East Scandinavian runic practice; and the several occurrences of the form *pennsi* in Western tradition should make one wary of identifying this as an East Scandinavian dialect marker – we know too little about local speech variation in the tenth and eleventh centuries to be able to make such pronouncements with confidence. It is nevertheless true that the appearance of ᛐ and *pennsi* in one and the same inscription renders German II somewhat unusual in the Manx corpus (MM 130 Kirk Michael III apart, ᛐ is documented otherwise only in MM 142 Maughold IV*a* and MM 141 Onchan *e*).

The use of ᛐ to represent the final unstressed vowel of *pennsi* and *eftir* also deserves comment. Since this rune occurs in the stressed syllable of *pennsi*, it is clear that for the German II carver it could denote an intermediate, front, unrounded vowel, [e] or possibly [æ] (as is generally the case). The spellings **þïnsï** and **ïftïr** – quite unusual in Viking-Age runic inscriptions (though cf., e.g., **ïftïr** in Kirk Michael III, **þinï** 'this [acc. m.]' in SC 10 Inchmarnock) – could thus indicate a tendency to lower historical /i/ in unstressed position. The spelling **asriþi**, however, suggests we are not dealing with a general lowering – and there is no indication of a parallel development /u/ >

/o/ (though it could be the carver had no way of denoting /o/ as distinct from /u/, cf. above). One might in these circumstances wonder whether **þïnsï** and **ïftïr** offer evidence of the workings of vowel harmony (chiefly a Norwegian and eastern Danish phenomenon), whereby the quality of an unstressed vowel, as it appears in writing at least, is regulated by the quality of its preceding stressed counterpart. However, although according to the common rules of vowel harmony *-e* follows [e], as probably in *þennse*, after root [æ], as (historically, at least) in /æftir/, the vowel normally to be expected is *-i* (Hagland 2013: 619–21). Another conceivable cause of the appearance of **ï** in the end syllables of **þïnsï** and **ïftïr** is the phenomenon known as vowel balance. In affected dialects (chiefly types of medieval and later Swedish) the quality of an unstressed vowel is regulated by the quantity of the preceding syllable (long syllables causing lowering, cf. Haugen 1976: 207, 260–61; for possible runic examples, see Lagman 1990: 76–7; Williams 1990: 109–10). Against this, however, stands **asriþi** (unless the /i:/ of the second syllable is assumed to have been shortened), as well as the fact that unstressed /u/ seems unaffected. In truth the spellings **þïnsï** and **ïftïr** could reflect anything from a local dialect development (perhaps simply the *onset* of a general weakening of unstressed endings, or at least of unstressed /i/) to a carver who was happy to dot **i** for other than phonetic reasons. He might, for example, have felt it looked neater to have one and the same vowel rune within each word. There is really no way of knowing what motivated the use of **ï** in the second syllable of pronoun and preposition, and we should be wary of drawing firm conclusions on the basis of two ambiguous attestations.

The uncertainties revealed by the preceding discussion make clear that the details of any proposed Manx transcription must be taken with a large grain of salt. One might suggest:

[*NN ræisti*] *kross þennse æfter Ásríði konu sína, dóttur Odds.*

MM 127 Jurby

Plates 68–71, Figs 24–6

LITERATURE. Marquardt 1961: 69–70. Cumming 1857: 23 and fig. 11; Kneale [*c.* 1860]: 61, no. 12; Cumming 1868a: facing 23, no. 8, and 29–30; Jewitt 1884: 105; Vigfusson and Savage 1887: 14–15; Kermode 1907: 187–9; Brate 1907: 32–3; Marstrander 1930a; Olsen 1954: 200–201; Sanness Johnsen 1968: 234–5; Page 1983: 140; Holman 1996: 130–33.

The Jurby cross fragment was first recorded by Cumming (1857), "in the garden of the Vicarage at Jurby". Jewitt reported it "at Jurby church"; Vigfusson and Savage "in the church"; Kermode (1907) "in Jurby churchyard". Marstrander (1930a: 370) found it "stillet op i en nisje i nordre yttervegg av kirken" 'set up in a niche in the outer north wall of the church'. Sanness Johnsen described it as placed "i våpenhuset" 'in the porch', a structure that dates from the 1940s. That is where it is now, fixed upright in a concrete base, and so near the west wall of the porch that examination of its inscription is rendered cumbersome. Holman speculates that the Jurby cross originally stood on an early church site in the parish, but of that there is no firm evidence.

With all this (apparent) shifting about it is not surprising that the stone's condition has deteriorated since it was first recorded. Indeed, it is likely that it was moved after Cumming's early drawings ([c. 1855]: fol. 29r, given here as Fig. 25; 1857: fig. 11, given as Fig. 26) but before Robert Paterson's photograph of 1862 (Plate 70, Manx National Heritage ref. MNH PG/13721 - MC 127B). This last is reproduced by Marstrander, who notes that part of the left side and with it part of the outer line of the inscription must have been lost between 1857 and 1862 (1930a: 374). Now the stone is even more fragmentary than it was in 1862, and the outer line has completely gone. This further damage had already occurred when Vigfusson and Savage reported their reading in 1887 (though it is not noted in Jewitt's rendering of the text, which is probably derivative however).

The Jurby inscription is carved on a slab of grey mudstone, measuring c. 72.5 cm (visible height) × 36–40.5 × 8. Kermode gives the height as 30 inches (= 76 cm). What remains is part of an elaborate cross slab, with detailed carvings on both faces. Each has a relief cross, decorated with interlace patterns. Figures are carved beside the tops of both crosses, one confidently defined as illustrating the horn-blowing god Heimdallr rousing his colleagues to fight the battle at Ragnarǫk (see, e.g., Kermode 1907: 188; but also Margeson 1983: 96; cf. Plates 68, 70, Manx National Heritage ref. for Plate 68 MNH PG/1421 - MC 127A). The runes run alongside the left border of the cross shaft on the face that carries the horn-blower (the side turned to the west wall). Such is the damage this edge of the slab has suffered over the years that early drawings and photographs now constitute primary sources. Cumming (1857) shows two lines of runes, separated by a framing line, running "up and down the left-hand side of the face" (cf. Fig. 26; in the drawing in Cumming [c. 1855]: fol. 29r – Fig. 25 – the runes are marginally clearer, but differ in one or two small matters of detail). Paterson's photograph also records two lines of graphs and the central framing line. At this stage the

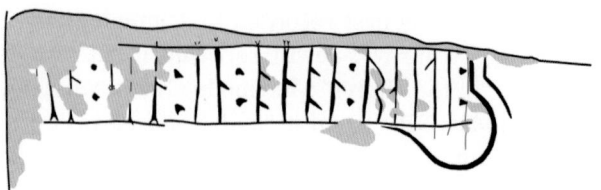

Fig. 24. MM 127 Jurby (drawing: Jonas Nordby).

runes were already severely weathered. The two sequences ran *boustrophedon*, with rune tops touching the line. The outer sequence of runes, as noted above, is now completely lost. The distance between the framing line (which survives) and the left edge of the cross shaft is *c.* 58 mm. Between them runs the remaining text, upwards from the cross base. It reads:

]*ⁿ:s i n:i n:ã n ã n:r a i t i:

Though the stone is much worn, good lighting allows us to distinguish fairly confidently between carved and accidental marks. Before the first identifiable graph, r. 2, can be seen a slightly curving vertical line; preceding this the surface is completely covered by cement. Runes 3 and 4 are weak, but clearly recognisable as **si**, the **s** seemingly terminating in a dot, though it is hard to be sure. Surface damage affects the right-hand side of r. 8, but there is little doubt about the reading. The branch of r. 13 can at first glance appear to cross the vertical, but breakage to the right is undoubtedly what creates this impression. Total length from r. 1 to the final separator is 32 cm. The graphs are quite cleanly cut, though here and there, most notably at the tops of rr. 6–9, there are examples of double-cutting; there is also occasional overcutting of the central framing line and the edge of the cross shaft.

Earlier reproductions of this text (of which the opening sequence is lost) are fairly, but not entirely, clear. Cumming's drawings (see Figs 25 and 26), for example, begin with something suggestive of **r**, followed by **u:sun:in:ãnãn:rasti:** (which he reads, 1857: "….RU : SUN : IN : ONON : RASTI :"). His later (1868a) version is much the same, save for its verb which is now amended to **raiti**. On the Paterson photograph the runes or parts of runes that "trær tydelig frem" 'stand out distinctly' are, says Marstrander (1930a: 374), **un:sin:in:ãnãn:raiti** (but, as transrunified, his r. 4, **i**, is a plain vertical that does not extend all the way down, r. 5, **n**, a full-length vertical and nothing more, and r. 15, **t**, something between ᛏ and ᛐ). Other older photographs of Jurby we have seen, as well

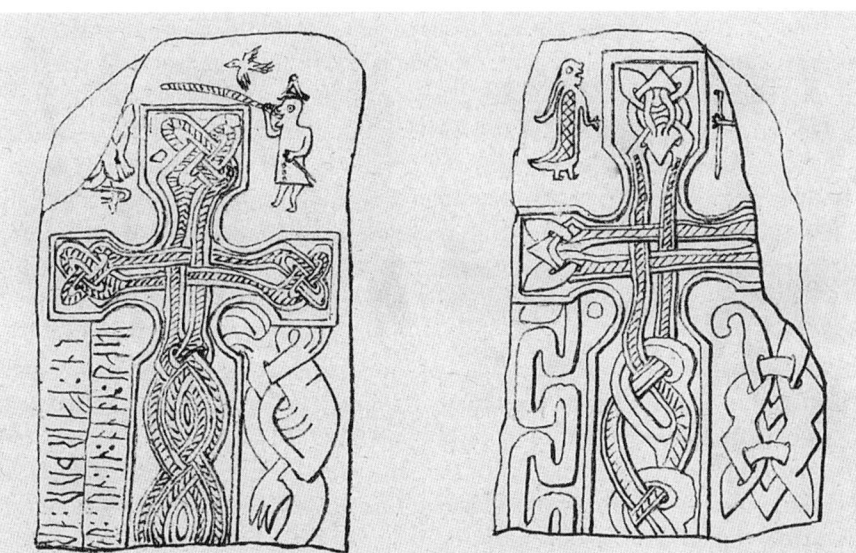

Fig. 25. MM 127 Jurby, Cumming's c. 1855 drawings (fol. 29r; reproduced by kind permission of the Bodleian Library, University of Oxford, MS Top. Man a 1).

as a cast (in the Manx Museum), tend to confirm rr. 1–2 as **un**. The slightly curving vertical line that can still be observed before the **n** would appear to represent the branch of **u**; cement now covers the surface where the vertical of **u** may be supposed to lie (cf. above).

For the now lost line of runes Cumming ([*c.* 1855]: fol. 29r = Fig. 25; 1857 = Fig. 26) shows, as far as can be judged:

| ✻ ✻ : f a i r þ u r : b r [
 1   5   10

Rune 1 is the top half of a vertical with, at its base, what is perhaps a branch descending to the right ([*c.* 1855]: fol. 29r; no branch clearly discernible 1857). Rune 2 is either ᛄ ([*c.* 1855]: fol. 29r), or ᛏ **t** with a very lightly drawn branch placed quite low down (1857). The graph transliterated **b** here is of the form ᛄ (but ᛄ in Cumming [*c.* 1855]: fol. 29r;): theoretically this could represent **ã** (but contrast ᚨ **ã** in the inner line of runes). Cumming (1868a) has:

a f t : f ✻ i r þ u r : b (r u) ...

which is a curious rendering, ignoring as it does the break after the third (here faintly delineated) **r** and offering no indication of where on the stone the material following this **r** is to be found. The series of dots that comes after the final **u** (a character also faintly delineated) presumably signifies the remains of further runes, some 8 to 10 to judge from the number of the dots and the space they take up. The fifth graph in this representation is ↑, a rune of uncertain identity.

On the evidence of a cast made for Cumming, Kermode (1907) claimed to see "[IFT] FAIRThUR : BR..", admitting the possibility of AFT for the "badly worn" first word; which would seem to confirm the general sense of Cumming's various attempts. However, the Paterson photograph, as read by Marstrander (1930a: 374), gives the rather different

| * * * : a f t i r þ u r b (r) [

(transliterated here chiefly on the basis of the Norwegian scholar's trans-runification; the asterisks represent a sequence of evenly spaced vertical lines, the first short, as ', the second longer, and the third approaching full length). This reading, though with the final graph treated as a mere vertical (or simply uncertain), has been followed generally since, as in Olsen, Sanness Johnsen, though Holman goes through the various possibilities without coming down in favour of any particular one. In our view Marstrander's reading accords best with what can be seen on the Paterson photograph.

In a postscript to his 1930a article, Marstrander makes the surprising claim that Kermode had in reality never seen the cast of the Jurby inscription he several times refers to in his 1907 work. We are, however, dealing here with second- or third-hand information. According to Marstrander, the man who discovered the Paterson photograph, W. Cubbon of the "National Manx Museum", had asserted in letters to him (a) that there was no Jurby cast "i Castle Rushen" 'in Castle Rushen', and, more significantly, (b) that Kermode had stated to him that he had never seen such a cast and had based his text of the inscription on Cumming, though he had "sterke tvil" 'grave doubts' about the correctness of Cumming's "transkripsjon" 'transcription'. The likelihood that Kermode would express himself as he does in 1907 if he had not seen a cast appears remote, and it is perhaps to be assumed that the passing of the years had clouded his memory. There is, though, the alternative or additional possibility that Marstrander, keen as he appears to be to establish the primacy of the Paterson photograph, over-interpreted what Cubbon had told him.

Diagnostic rune forms are ᚨ ã, ᚾ n, ᛆ a, ' or ' s, ᛏ t, [ᛒ] b.

Interpretation

The sense to be made of the remnants of the Jurby inscription depends greatly on which reading is followed. In the absence of a cast showing the outer line of runes, the 1862 photograph, although not clear in every detail, seems the most reliable source for this part of the inscription. Even though

Fig. 26. MM 127 Jurby, Cumming's 1857 drawings (1857: fig. 11).

Cumming and Kermode agree in all essentials, it is likely they have misread a couple of runes: **t:fairþur:br...** can easily conceal **aftirþurbr...**; separators apart (which can easily be mistaken on so worn a surface) it only takes confusion of ᚠ and ᛁ, which may happen if the branch is placed rather higher up than usual on ᚠ and rather lower down on ᛁ, as appears to be the case here. On the basis of the preserved segment of text and the evidence of early photographs, together with Cumming's drawings and his and Kermode's (seemingly in part faulty) readings, we then appear to have:

...*son sinn, en annan rétti NN/hann eptir ?Þorbrand*...

'...his/her/their son, but NN/he set up another in memory of ?Þorbrand ...'

The name Þorbrandr is Marstrander's suggestion, and certainly seems the most plausible expansion. The three evenly spaced vertical lines preceding **aftir** are taken either as the remains of a personal name or as the pronoun *hann* 'he' (cf. above and Marstrander 1930a: 374–5). It has been assumed that the lost, main part of the inscription announced that a person or (much less likely) persons had set up a cross in memory of a deceased relative (cf. the account in Kermode 1907). The surviving text then begins with the information that the deceased was the raiser's or raisers' son. Quite possibly, some explanation of ?Þorbrandr's relationship with raiser or deceased (or with putative NN) followed his name. Parallels to a general interpretation along such lines are, it turns out, hard to find. Sö 35 begins: *Let IngigæiRR/ Ingigærðr annan ræisa stæin at syni sina* 'IngigæiRR/Ingigærðr had another stone set up in memory of his/her sons', but this inscription is found on what appears to be the second of a pair of memorial stones, and the text complements that of Sö 34, which begins with a memorial formula of more standard type. The *annan...stæin* of Sö 35 thus refers to the stone on which the inscription itself stands, whereas in the case of Jurby the presumption (possibly incorrect) has been that a different stone or cross is meant. However this may be, it is far likelier that **ānān** gives the acc. m. sg. of *annarr* '(an)other' than that it conceals a personal name (Anundr/Ǫnundr or the improbable "Onon") as assumed by many of the early commentators.

The use of **raiti** (= *rétti* 'put upright' 'raised') to denote the erecting of a cross is unparalleled in the Manx corpus (Cumming's 1857 reading RASTI appears out of the question); the usual verb in such circumstances is *reisa* 'put up' 'raise'. However, *rétta* occurs commonly enough in the more northerly Swedish rune-stone areas in this sense (though hardly at all elsewhere in Scandinavia). While historical [e] or [æ] can appear as **ai** in Man (cf. MM 113 Andreas IV, MM 106 Ballaugh), Jurby provides the only conceivable example of a digraphic rendering of historical [e:], a usage that seems rare elsewhere too. Of course, it is possible that **raiti** was intended as **raisti**, and that the carver simply forgot the **s** (cf. U 79 where **raitu** is almost certainly in error for **raistu**). Acceptance of this idea would nullify the considerations just advanced, but the evidence is insufficient to decide one way or the other.

A text of the Jurby inscription transcribed in accordance with assumed local pronunciation cannot differ greatly from the West Norse normalisation above:

...*son sinn, en ānnān rétti NN/hānn æftir ?Þorbrānd*...

MM 102 Kirk Michael I
Plates 72–4, Fig. 27

LITERATURE. Marquardt 1961: 73–4. Kinnebrook 1841: 11 and fig. 5 (together with other Kirk Michael fragments); Cumming 1857: 18–19 and fig. 4; Vigfusson and Savage 1887: 14; Kermode 1887b: 151; Kermode 1892: 22, 47; Kermode 1907: 153–4; Olsen 1954: 208; Sanness Johnsen 1968: 239; Page 1983: 140; Holman 1996: 133–4.

Kinnebrook seems to have been the first to record MM 102, one of four fragments "on Michael Church-wall". It is perhaps among others this piece he was referring to when he wrote that (1841: 9):

Within the last few months two very richly carved crosses, one if not both, with Runic inscriptions upon them, were broken in pieces to form a part of Kirk Michael Church wall, upon the top of which, the fragments may be seen imbedded in mortar.

Kinnebrook places MM 102 on the north side of the church gate. It was probably still there when inspected by Cumming, although he is less specific about the location: "This fragment of a fine cross […] is on the churchyard wall of Kirk Michael." By 1892 it was under cover "within the Church tower" (Kermode 1892: 22). Cubbon (1964: 214) reports that the Kirk Michael cross slabs were brought for protection beneath the church's lych-gate in 1907. In 1963 they were reordered within the church for greater security and visibility. MM 102 now stands with its fellow crosses and cross fragments in the north transept, set in a concrete block (together with MM 130 Kirk Michael III and MM 129 Kirk Michael VI).

Kirk Michael I is carved on a fragment of dark grey mudstone, measuring $c.$ 106 cm (visible height) × 29 × 7.5. Kermode (1907) gives the height as 51 inches (= 130 cm). The fragment is irregular in form, and measurements can only be approximate. What survives is a small part of a formal memorial stone, with, on each face of the slab, the remains of a central sculptured cross shaft and side panels, with interlace and key pattern decoration (see Plates 72, 73, Manx National Heritage ref. for Plate 72 MNH PG/13721 - MC102A). The runes run upwards along the left side of the (badly worn) shaft on one of the faces, but only small parts of the text survive in readable form. The whole of the extant inscribed section is $c.$ 22.5 cm long, but much of this consists of fragmentary graphs only. No framing lines are visible, and original rune height is hard to assess, seemingly at least 45 mm. What can be made out reads:

]********ˡ:þh⊣:⊣ʞ****(:)*[

]********s:þna:af****:*[

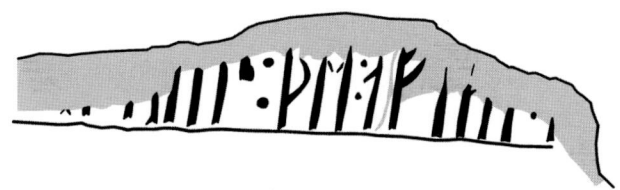

Fig. 27. MM 102 Kirk Michael I (drawing: Jonas Nordby).

The runes are in general boldly carved, all the grooves except the branches of rr. 10 and 11 having been deepened and widened. Neither of these two branches, which seem to have been pressed into a rather confined space, connects with its vertical; nor does the top of r. 9's bow. Runes 1–7 are the bases of what appear to be verticals; the upper parts are lost through damage, most drastically at the beginning so the grooves increase in height as they progress. A largish gap separates rr. 2 and 3. Rune 8 consists of a sizeable elongated dot at about mid height, clearly the remains of ᛁ. Before r. 13 there is a wavy line of a different character from the runes – possibly a bungled, and subsequently abandoned, attempt at a vertical. Following r. 13 are four verticals decreasing in height (likewise through damage), the second with what might be the remains of an ascending right branch or a bow. After r. 17 comes a point that is presumably the lower one of a double word separation symbol. Beyond this can be traced the very base of a vertical.

Diagnostic rune forms are ᚼ **n**, ᛆ **a**, ᛁ **s**.

Interpretation

A normalised text of Kirk Michael I can go no further than:

   ...[kross] þenna eptir...

   '...this [cross] in memory of...'

As early as 1857 Cumming had reached the same general conclusion, reading and interpreting the inscription "'CRUS : THNA : AFTIR,' i.e. '*This cross to*,' the names having altogether disappeared". That has been the common understanding of the text since (save for the erroneous reading PAN for rr. 9–11, as for example in Vigfusson and Savage). In the sequence **þna** the carver must (for whatever reason, cf. p. 78) have omitted the expected vowel rune between **þ** and **n**; it is unlikely he confused the **n** and **a** since all other Manx runic inscriptions that employ a deictic pronoun in conjunction with *kross* have *þenna* (*þennsi* etc.) 'this', never *þann* 'that'. The five bases immediately preceding r. 8 **s** could certainly be the remains of **kru** (the spacing fully supports such a reading) and there is room for a word separation symbol before that. And the four lines after **f** could have supported **tir**. It is true that *ept*, the shorter form of the preposition 'after' 'in memory of', is almost as common on Man as the longer *eptir*, but what remains of the inscription after r. 13, bar perhaps the putative branch or bow on r. 15, speaks in favour of the latter – not least the separation point after the four lines. We thus seem to have the remains of a memorial formula of common type: *NN reisti kross þenna* *eptir MM* 'NN put up this cross in memory of MM', though that is of course conjecture. And more may well have been said than this bare minimum.

So little is left of the text, that no useful purpose would be served by offering a "Manx transcription" as is done for many of the other inscriptions.

MM 101 Kirk Michael II

Plates 75–81, Figs 28–30

LITERATURE. Marquardt 1961: 74–6. Kinnebrook 1841: 10 and fig. 3; Munch 1850: 274–6; Cumming 1857: 15–17 and fig. 1; Vigfusson and Savage 1887: 9–10; Kermode 1887b: 151; Taylor 1887: 185; Kermode 1892: 47–9; Bugge 1899: 232–4; Kermode 1907: 149–53; Brate 1907: 82–4; Marstrander 1937: 248–56; Olsen 1954: 208–15; Alfvegren 1959: 221–6; Sanness Johnsen 1968: 239–41; Page 1983: 136, 140; Holman 1996: 134–7.

MM 101 appears to have been recorded first by Kinnebrook. He reported it "on Michael Church-wall [...] on the south side of the Church-gate". According to Cumming, it had not been there for long. He writes:

> This cross owes its preservation [...] to the circumstance of its having been built into the old church of St. Michael, from which it was removed and placed in its present position not more than thirty years ago.

In the light of this remark, it is possible MM 101 is identical with the object brought to the attention of the antiquarian Alexander Seton in the 1820s – well before the appearance of Kinnebrook's work. Seton mentions a "Runsten" 'rune-stone' "inuti Kirk-Michael Kyrka, (insatt vid ett fenster)" 'in Kirk Michael church (built in by a window)', which he was, however, unable to see in person (cf. Selling 1945: 127, who has no hesitation in identifying the reported artefact with MM 101, although it could as well have been MM 130 Kirk Michael III, perhaps even some other Kirk Michael rune-stone). Subsequent to Kinnebrook's and Cumming's accounts, the monument seems to have remained on the wall (Kermode 1907: 149) until moved for protection under Kirk Michael's lych-gate in 1907, where it stayed until taken into the church for greater security and visibility in 1963 (Cubbon 1964: 214). MM 101 now stands with its fellow crosses and cross fragments in the north transept, set in a concrete block.

Kirk Michael II is carved on a substantial slab of dark grey mudstone, measuring *c.* 127 cm (visible height) × 42.5 × 9. Kermode records the height as 72 inches (= 183 cm). The two faces of the slab have similar designs,

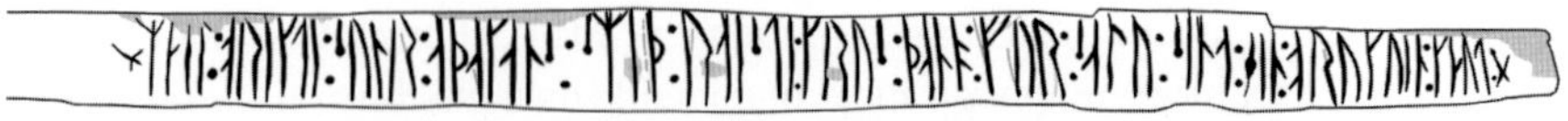

Fig. 28. MM 101 Kirk Michael II, rr. 1–64 (drawing: Jonas Nordby).

sculptured shafted crosses with circled heads and interlace. The text runs up one of the narrow edges, then continues on the face to the left of this edge, first in the right then in the left quadrant above the cross head. Since the text proceeds in an upward direction in both cases, the bases of the runes in the right quadrant turn outwards, those in the left inwards. The runes read:

1 5 10 15 20 25 30 35
× ᛘ ᚿ ᛁ ᛚ : ᛓ ᚱ ᛁ ᚴ ᛐ ᛁ : ᛌ ᚢ ᚿ ᚱ : ᛆ ᚦ ᛆ ᚴ ᛆ ᚿ ᛌ : ᛌ ᛘ ᛁ ᚦ : ᚱ ᛆ ᛁ ᛌ ᛐ ᛁ : ᚴ ᚱ ᚢ ᛌ :

40 45 50 55 60 65
ᚦ ᛆ ᚿ ᚭ : ᚠ ᚢ ᚱ : ᛌ ᛆ ᛚ ᚢ : ᛌ ᛁ ᚿ ᛆ : ᛌ ᛁ ᚿ : ᛓ ᚱ ᚢ ᚴ ᚢ ᛁ ᚿ : ᚴ ᚿ ᚢ ᛐ : × | ᚴ ᛁ ᚱ ᚦ ᛁ

70 75 80 84
: ᚦ ᛆ ᚿ ᚭ : ᛆ ᚢ ᚴ | ᛆ ᛚ ᛆ : ᛁ ᛘ ᛆ ᚢ ᚿ ×

×**mail:brikti:sunr:aþakans:smiþ:raisti:krus:þanã:**
1 5 10 15 20 25 30 35

fur:salu:sina:sin:brukuin:kaut:×|kirþi:þanã:auk|
40 45 50 55 60 65 70 75

ala:imaun×
80 84

The lengths of the three sections of the inscription (including the saltire crosses) are 106 and 17 cm (both the shorter sequences) respectively. There are no framing lines on the edge of the stone and heights of runes there vary between 5 and 7 cm. Rune heights in the quadrants differ considerably according to the space available. In the right quadrant r. 65 **k** is 2.7 cm, r. 73 **ã** 8.0; in the left r. 77 **a** is 3.6 cm, r. 82 **a** 8.8. The graphs seem to have been carved, or at least opened out, from their bases upwards, for there are a number of double-cuts, overcuts and incorrect lineations towards their tops, as rr. 23, 26, 40, 41, 45, 46, 68, 83. Occasional indications of the same at their bases suggest that, sometimes at least, the cutting implement was moved both up and down. The general effect is bold but rather crude. There seems to be the odd late addition, as in the double-dot separation symbol between rr. 31 and 32, whose verticals are rather too close together for neatness.

Diagnostic rune forms are ᚭ **ã**, ᚿ **n**, ᛆ and (rr. 2, 62) ᚿ **a**, ᛌ **s**, ᛐ **t**, ᛓ **b**, ᛘ **m**.

Fig. 29. MM 101 Kirk Michael II, rr. 65–76 (drawing: Jonas Nordby).   *Fig. 30. MM 101 Kirk Michael II, rr. 77–84 (drawing: Jonas Nordby).*

Interpretation

A normalisation and translation of Kirk Michael II in its entirety cannot be given since rr. 51–60 have yet to be satisfactorily interpreted. Most of the inscription is, however, relatively clear, and almost certainly says:

Melbrigdi sonr Aðakans smiðs reisti kross þenna fyr sálu sína... Gautr gerði þenna ok alla í Mǫn.

'Máel-Brigti son of Áedacán the smith put up this cross for his soul... Gautr made this one and all in Man.'

The text throws up both grammatical and semantic problems. There may well be some Irish input since the first two personal names recorded are of Irish origin: *Máel-Brigti* 'devotee of Brigit' (cf. Kirk Michael III, p. 180; Maughold V, p. 224) and *Áedacán*, a diminutive or hypocoristic form of *Áed* 'fire' (O'Brien 1973: 219, 221, 226; Uhlich 1993: 145). The third name, *Gautr*, is Norse, but lacks in Kirk Michael II the expected nominative ending (contrast **kautr** on MM 99 Andreas I). That raises the question of the syntactic function and morphological case of **smiþ** 'smith' (rr. 22–5). Is the word to be taken in apposition to **mail:brikti** ('Máel-Brigti the smith, son of Áedacán'), when it would, like **kaut**, be without its nominative -*r*, or to **aþakans**, in which case it lacks genitive -*s* or -*ar*? Medieval Scandinavian word-order patterns make the latter far more probable, but the former is not inconceivable (cf. *DR*: 873–4), and an inscription with aberrant morphology may of course also exhibit abnormal word-order. A further factor to be considered is that final -*r* seems in general to be more prone to loss than final -*s*.

The major semantic difficulty arises from the sequence rr. 51–60, and this has not yet been solved, despite the ingenuity of some suggestions (cf. Olsen 1954: 209–15; Holman 1996: 136). Indeed, there is dispute over how many words this sequence represents. Is the group **in** (rr. 59–60) a separate word (*en* 'and/but') opening a new sentence (as in the other signed *Gautr* inscription, MM 99 Andreas I, and apparently also in the two fragmentary texts MM 127 Jurby, MM 136 Braddan III, and the presumably fragmentary MM 107 German I (St John's) *a* and MM 138 Braddan II)? Or does it give the ending of a word **brukuin**, as the distribution of the separation symbols (quite regular in this inscription) might imply? And what of **sin**? Do these three runes represent a separate word or the first element of a compound?

The interpretations have been many and varied. Munch (1850: 275) claimed not to be able to read rr. 51–60 precisely, and so felt unable to give a translation, though later (1860: xxii) he suggested – for the full phrase *fyr sálu sína* **sin:brukuin** – *pro anima sua (peccatrice)* 'for his (sinful) soul', surmising that SIN BRVCVIN might be a "complete miswriting of SINTVCRI or SVNTVCRI (syndugri)" (notwithstanding the clash between acc. *sálu sína* and dat. *syndugri*). Vigfusson and Savage converted rr. 54–60 to "BURG-VIN = BORG-VIN, surety-friend" ("His surety-friend Gout worked this (cross)…" – grammatically highly improbable if rr. 51–3 **sin** are to be taken as the reflexive possessive *sinn* 'his' 'her' 'its' 'their', and cast in a subject modifier role), while admitting the compound did not, to their knowledge, occur elsewhere. Kermode (1887b) accepted the George Stephens interpretation (1866–1901: 2, 598) in which BRUKUIN is taken to be BROOK-WIN, a leaseholder or bailiff (slight support for the specific analysis of **brukuin** could perhaps be found in Fritzner 1883–1972: IV, *s.v. brúka*, glossed, *inter alia, forvalte* 'manage' 'oversee', but Stephens's overall interpretation suffers from the same grammatical problem as that of Vigfusson and Savage, namely that reflexive possessive *sinn* can hardly modify the subject). Bugge (1899) rejected such assaults on the Norse language, as well as the thought that rr. 51–60 might conceal a compound adjective *syndbrugginn* 'born in sin' or 'sullied by sin' (modifying the subject **kaut**). Instead he put forward the abbreviation (**auk:**)**sin**(**ar**)**:bru**(**þur**)**kuin**(**u**), giving a text meaning '[for his soul] and that of his brother's wife'. Who could have been expected to interpret this, he does not say. Brate argues that **sin:bruku** is a compound consisting of *syn*(*d*) 'sin' and a form of *vrangr* 'wrong' 'evil' (with **b** denoting a "v-ljud" '*v*-sound', which implies very early coalescence of historical [w] and [ß] in Man). This putative adjective, he thinks, modifies **salu**, and records that the cross was erected by one with a wicked soul (presumably in the hope of obtaining mercy thereby). Marstander (1937: 251–4) suggests a word **syndbruggvinn* "opsatt på å *bruggva synd*" 'intent on committing sin', notwithstanding the absence of *v* in any part of the relevant verb (past part. *brugginn*, inf. *brugga* or *bryggja*) – as well as the lack of grammatical agreement with **salu**, which the putative *syndbruggvin* supposedly modifies. In a long discussion of rr. 51–60, Olsen offers the creative idea that the group **sin:bruku** was an attempt at *synd-borgnu*, which he takes to be "accus. sing. fem. 'definite'" (modifying **salu**), but with **n** accidentally omitted and metathesis [or] > [ro]. He translates the word as 'saved' or 'freed from sin', but admits it is not recorded elsewhere. Much of Olsen's argument depends on an assumed precision of syntax and phrasing within the inscription, but one ought, perhaps, to be sceptical about this (as several of Olsen's predecessors seem to have been, going by the interpretations they offer, at least). How grammatically accurate was the wording displayed in the Manx runic inscriptions, particularly those that imply a mixture of Celtic and Norse communities?

Sanness Johnsen discusses briefly all these attempts to resolve the riddle and concludes that none is very convincing. She nevertheless thinks the sequence likely to contain some word meaning 'sinful'. Holman tends to agree. A point worth considering here, however, is that /y(:)/ is generally rendered by **u** in runic writing, only very rarely by **i**, though MM138 Braddan II has **i:triku**, commonly interpreted as *í tryggu(m)* 'in a situation of trust'(cf. pp. 74–5, where the possibility of delabialisation [y] > [i] is also mooted). The lack of indication of the final consonant in *synd* is unexpected, too, at least from a wider Scandinavian perspective. Parallels to the omission of a dental stop symbol after **n** do exist, but seem largely to be medieval. On the other hand, there is a tendency in Scandinavian languages to drop a consonant in clusters of more than two, and this could well have applied if **sin:bruku** or **sin:brukuin** was indeed a compound .

The final clause of the inscription, **auk|ala:imaun**, has traditionally been understood to mean *ok [hann gerði] alla í Mǫn* 'and [he made] all in Man' with *alla* paralleling *þenna* 'this [one]' as object of *gerði*. Holman, concerned that there were sculptured crosses by other carvers earlier than or contemporary with Kirk Michael II, and apparently unwilling to countenance exaggeration in Gautr's claim, puts forward the idea that **ala** "may be a form of the Norse male personal name Áli", either genitive ('Gautr made this cross and [that of] Áli in Man') or "an erroneous nominative form", indicating that Áli was also involved in the production of the Kirk Michael II cross. These suggested interpretations must be judged improbable: the sentence *Gautr gerði þenna ok Ála í Mǫn* 'Gautr made this one and Áli's in Man' is unlikely Old Norse, even if (which Holman does not suggest) Áli was commonly known as *Áli í Mǫn* 'Áli in Man' (though in that case 'Gautr made this one and Áli in Man [did too]' is conceivable – accepting Holman's suggestion that **ala** is "an erroneous nominative form"). Returning to the traditional, and eminently plausible, understanding of **ala**, we may note that Gautr's claim is to have made this particular cross and all in Man. He does not say specifically that he carved the runes.

The two different realisations of **a**: ᚭ and ᚬ, deserve brief comment. There may have been a deliberate intention to differentiate here. The older form, ᚭ, appears in the two major names of the text, those of the sponsor and the sculptor; the second, ᚬ, in all other cases. Is the use of ᚭ intended to highlight the names? There is a possible parallel in E 3 Carlisle A (now Carlisle I A, cf. Barnes 2010), which uses two forms of **t**: ↑ for the name of the carver (also the first word of the inscription) and ↑ otherwise (Barnes and Page 2006: 291; cf. also MM 118 Bride, which may possibly have exhibited the same phenomenon).

Taking the relevant parts of the foregoing into account, the following Manx transcription of the text may be suggested:

Melbrigdi sonr Aðakāns smið ræisti kross þānnā fyr sálu sínā... Gaut gærði þānnā auk alla í Mǫn.

MM 130 Kirk Michael III

Plates 82–92, Figs 31–3, 37

LITERATURE: Marquardt 1961: 76–8. Camden/Gibson 1722: 1457–8; Camden/Gough 1789: 3, 704; Kinnebrook 1841: 11 and fig. 4; Munch 1850: 278–9 (incorrectly ascribing line 2 of the inscription to Onchan); Cumming 1857: 34–5 and figs 28–9; Dodds 1865; Vigfusson and Savage 1887: 5–8; Kermode 1887b: 150–51; Taylor 1887: 185; Bugge 1899: 243–4; Kermode 1907: 195–9; Brate 1907: 84–5; Olsen 1954: 215–17; Sanness Johnsen 1968: 249; Page 1983: 137–8, 140; Holman 1996: 137–41.

Kirk Michael III is among the "Four Runick Inscriptions in the Isle of Man" reported in Edmund Gibson's revision of William Camden's *Britannia* (1722: 1457–60). MM 130 is there described as "laid for a Lintel over a Window in *Kirk-Michael* Church", and indeed the drawing (Gibson no. I) shows two angles of the stone face obscured by the window's sides. Gough's reissue of *Britannia* illustrates the same stone, together with the three others from the 1722 edition, this time set formally as though standing in the earth (but with no more of the inscription visible than in Camden/Gibson 1722). These pictures are said to be "exact representations", although in fact they are less precise in detail than Gibson's (see Figs 32, 37).

MM 130 has had an interrupted and at times uncertain history. When Oswald produced his accounts and drawings of the Manx rune-stones, it was "said to be built into the wall of the church of Kirkmichael" (Anon. 1822: 493), although apparently it could not at that point be located. *The Illustrated Guide* (1836: 99) speaks of its being in the churchyard. The old church was demolished to make way for a new one opened in 1835, and it was presumably then that MM 130 was relieved of its duty as a lintel and put outdoors. Certainly when Kinnebrook illustrated the stone in 1841 (Kinnebrook: fig. 4) it was outside, "on Michael Church-wall […] upon the north side of the gateway". Its inscription he recorded in a separate drawing, but only the last two-thirds or so of the first line (see the transrunification and transliteration below), implying thereby that its opening, and also the second line, were inaccessible (see the undated Manx National Heritage photograph, ref. MNH PG/14709 – MC130A, reproduced as Plate 83, which shows the stone set into the top of the wall). Cumming (1857: 34–5, fig. 28, reproduced here as part of Fig. 33) made a curious attempt at depicting the inscription (admitting that "a part of it is now buried in the wall"). Effectively he showed only the first line (though see below), and that oddly and inaccurately set out (and without framing lines), rounding the lower edge of the stone face before running up the right side; or, as he put it, reading "downwards, horizontally, and upwards". The other line of the text he added in a separate drawing (1857: fig. 29), reporting it "formerly at Kirk Michael, now lost" (also reproduced as part of Fig. 33). The stone itself stood, asserted Cumming, "on the north side of the churchyard gate". Dodds (1865: 3) saw it there too, adding that "the inscription is nearly perfect, though a portion of it is buried in the wall". So it was when Vigfusson and Savage inspected the site in 1886,

> erect on the top of the churchyard wall, the lower end for two feet completely immured in the masonry, leaving only the last word of the shorter legend and nearly two-thirds of the larger one, visible above the coping of the wall (1887: 7).

From all this we may deduce that Cumming's version of the runes was based quite heavily on conjecture, supported by earlier drawings. He could see the topmost word, **ilan**, of the second line, but interpreted it as the opening of the first. This word he read ᚾᛁᛅᛚ **nial**, perhaps incorporating elements from both ᛁᛚᛅᚾ **ilan** and ᛘᛅᛚ **mal**, or, as surmised by Vigfusson and Savage (see below), reading **ilan** "*backwards – nali*" and "changing the position of the *i*". The first line he could read from, say, r. 20 onwards, and most of what preceded it (available in earlier reproductions) he thought ran horizontally across the stone base. To add a final point, there survives an undated photo-

Fig. 31. MM 130 Kirk Michael III (drawing: Jonas Nordby).

graph showing the stone set against the churchyard wall but with both parts of the inscription easily visible (Plate 84, Manx National Heritage ref. MNH PG/14706 - MC130B). Either the cross had been repositioned or more likely that part of the wall excavated and rebuilt (presumably in 1886, as recounted by Vigfusson and Savage 1887: 8). Brate (1907: 84) reported parts of the texts again hidden: rr. 1–19 in the first line, rr. 72–93 in the second. Yet Kermode (1907: 195), though he recorded the stone as even then "on the wall, north side of the churchyard gates", showed the complete text.

The Kirk Michael cross slabs were brought for protection under the church's lych-gate in 1907, and in 1963 reordered within the church itself for greater security and visibility (Cubbon 1964: 214). MM 130 now stands with its fellow crosses and cross fragments in the north transept, set atop a concrete block together with MM 102 Kirk Michael I and MM 129 Kirk Michael VI, and held in place by metal supports.

Kirk Michael III is carved on a substantial slab of dark grey mudstone, measuring 178.5 cm × 43.5 × 12 (base) – 6 (top). Kermode (1907) gives the height as 69½ inches (= 177 cm). Its layout is unusual for Man in that the runic inscription stands alone on one face of the stone, arranged in two separate lines running upwards. This face was either deliberately left undecorated or earlier carvings were completely cut away to allow for the inscription, which is then secondary (cf. pp. 58–9). In addition to the runes, each face bears an ogam graffito: on the decorated side, bottom right, the complete ogam alphabet (the *Beith-Luis-Nin*), and on the runic side, to the left of the closing part of line 1 (roughly opposite rr. 42–58), an inscription of uncertain import. The decorated face of the stone has a sculptured ring-headed cross with elaborate interlace, and figures, human and animal, to both sides of the shaft. The runes read:

ᛘᚨᛚ:ᛚᚢᛘᚴᚢᚾ:ᚱᚨᛁᛋᛏᛁ:ᚴᚱᚢᛋ:ᚦᛁᚾᚨ:ᛁᚠᛏᛁᚱ:ᛘᚨᛚ:ᛘᚢᚱᚢ:
ᚠᚢᛋᛏᚱᚨ:ᛋᛁᚾᛁ:ᛏᚨᛏᚨᚱᛏᚢᚠᚴᚨᛚᛋ:ᚴᚨᚾᚨ:ᛁᛋ:ᚨᚦᛁᛋᛚ:ᚨᛏᛁ+|

mal:lümkun:raisti:krus:þïna:ïftïr:mal:murü:
1   5   10   15   20   25   30   35
fustra:sinï:tãtãrtufkals:kãna:is:aþisl:ati+|
40   45   50   55   60   65   70
]ïtra:ïs:laifa:fustra:kuþan:þan:sãn:ilan×
75   80   85   90   95   100 103

Existing lengths of the two lines are 1: 163 cm, 2: 59 cm (measured to the end of the cross in each case). Both are cut between irregularly set framing lines probably distorted by the inadequately dressed quality of the surface. The first line of runes follows the right-hand edge of the face, its lower frame largely lost at that edge (in fact only definitely visible near the very top). The upper frame does not run parallel to the lower, so rune height varies from 9.5 cm (r. 4 **l**) to 13 (r. 40 **r**, including the overcut at the top). The second line lies some distance both from the first and from the left-hand edge of the stone. Here the frames vary between 7.4 and 8.1 cm apart. The upper one continues well beyond the end of the text. In general the runes are weathered but quite well preserved, save, in the first line, for the very bases of some here and there; for the centres of most of rr. 44–58 (which has caused a difficulty of identification, as reported below); and for occasional branches.

The runes were carved with a sharp tool, probably a knife, those towards the opening bolder and more spacious than later ones. The tops of a number of graphs are overcut (e.g. rr. 12, 21, 22, 57, 100) and/or (slightly) double-cut (e.g. rr. 9, 10, 22, 95), suggesting, at least in part, a base-to-top direction of carving. There is also occasional overcutting at joins, notably in r. 85 **s** where the left part of the vertical is prolonged almost to the top framing line. And joins may sometimes be incomplete, as at the top of r. 90 **u**. The branch of r. 60 **n** is set low down on its vertical, to avoid clashing with the branches of r. 59, which suggests rather casual planning of the inscription. Dots for word separation seem to have been punched with the point of a knife and then made circular by turning the knife on its axis. Indentations similar to such dots can be observed here and there at the ends of branches (as those of r. 3 **l**, r. 9 **n**, r. 14 **t**, r. 99 **n**). This is sometimes helpful to the modern reader, for the indentations may remain where the branch they adorned has weathered away, as in rr. 44 **n**, 49 **ã** (but not r. 55 **a**, only the very bottom of whose crossing branch can be discerned in an area of damage). Earlier runologists may not have noted these marks or not have grasped their significance. Indeed,

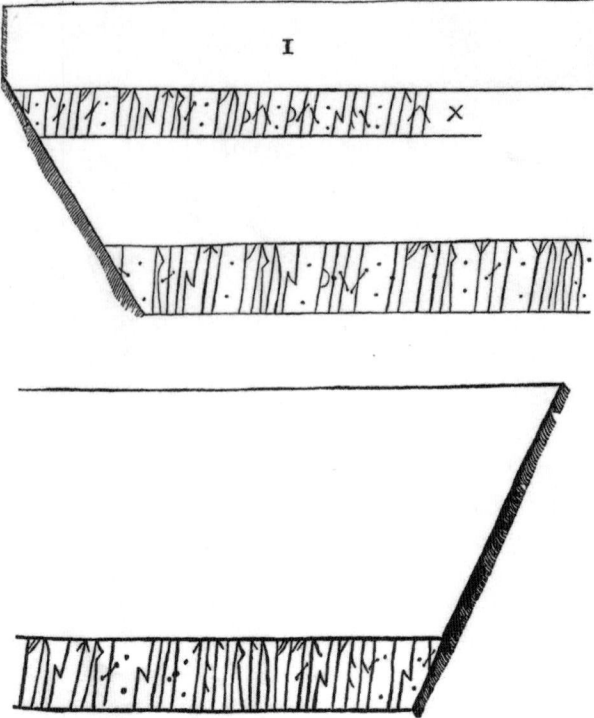

Fig. 32. MM 130 Kirk Michael III as portrayed in Gibson's 1722 revision of Camden's Britannia (pp. 1457–8).

r. 49 has traditionally been read as **i** rather than **ã** (giving **tãtir**, the usual nominative form). Two more observations should be made on dots in this inscription. (1) No separation marks are visible between **tãtãr** and **tufkals** (rr. 50 and 51), nor did the earliest recorders of this inscription, Gibson and Gough, portray any. However, there is a formidable series of runic scholars, from Munch (1860: facing xxi) to Olsen and Sanness Johnsen (but not Holman), who reported them. (2) There are two occurrences of dotted **u**, in rr. 5, 35. That on r. 5 has not generally been noted (though – for what it is worth – this part of the inscription was long hidden). Gibson recorded the dot of r. 35, and it has been sporadically observed since, for instance by Brate (who dismisses it as unintentional) and Olsen (who considers it "not carved"). Both these marks appear deliberate, even if their significance is hard to gauge. (In contrast, a dot that Olsen represents after r. 80, though certainly there, seems shallower than others of its kind, and so is probably accidental.)

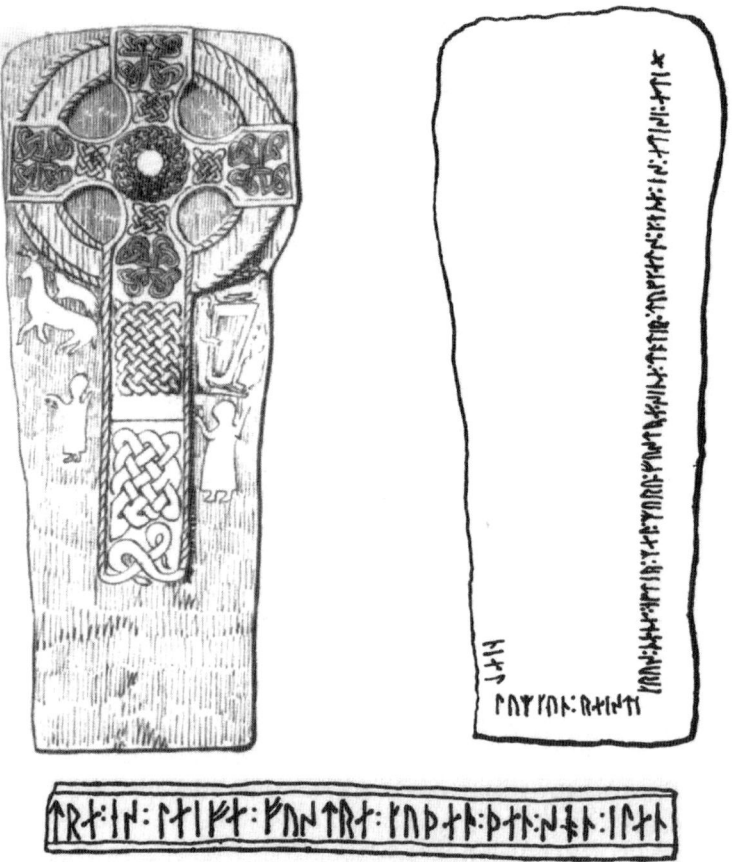

Fig. 33. MM 130 Kirk Michael III, Cumming's 1857 drawings (1857: figs 28–9).

The first line conceivably and the second certainly are missing something at their openings. Rune 1 is very close to the current base of the slab (and the bottom of its vertical is lost), making it unclear whether anything preceded what can now be seen. Judging from the sense of the inscription, however, there is unlikely to have been additional text here. Only the lower half of r. 72 survives, though the dot is clear and identification not in doubt. From the context it seems virtually certain this rune was originally preceded by a **b**. Since both lines end with a cross it is possible that both began with one.

Diagnostic rune forms are ᚨ ã, ᛏ n, ᛏ a, ᛋ s, ᛏ t, ᛉ m, ᚢ ü, ᛏ ï.

Interpretation

The grammar of this inscription does not always conform to what we expect of Old Norse, which makes it difficult to supply a definitive normalisation and translation of the inscription. Most likely is:

> *Mellomkun reisti kross þenna eptir Melmýru fóstru sína, dóttur Dufgals, konu er Aðísl átti. Betra er leifa fóstra góðan en son illan.*

> 'Máel-Lomchon put up this cross in memory of his foster-mother Máel-Muire, Dubgall's daughter, the woman whom Aðísl was married to. It is better to leave a good foster-son than a bad son.'

The raiser of the cross seems to have had an Irish compound name, *Máel-Lomchon*. As a first element, OIr *Máel-* 'devotee' is common, forming mostly masculine names, though with a few notable exceptions (O'Brien 1973: 229). The second element appears to be the genitive of the sparsely attested name *Lomchú* (Best and Lawlor 1931: 6). The sequence **mal:murü** apparently gives a Norse oblique form of *Máel-Muire*, a feminine personal name 'devotee of Mary' (O'Brien 1973: 230), with **fustra:sinï** in apposition to it, despite its unconventional inflectional endings (see below). The group **tātārtufkals:kāna** presumably also stands in apposition to **mal:murü**, the nominative form **kāna** notwithstanding (on the name *Dubgall*, see MM 118 Bride, p. 150). Thereafter the text becomes more straightforward, and the implication of its second statement that the memorial was put up by a foster-son for a foster-parent helps us interpret the uncertain grammar of the first.

If **fustra:sinï** (rr. 36–45) means 'his foster-mother', as the name *Máel-Muire* and the sense of the second line of text together suggest, the standard Old Norse, to agree in case (acc., governed by *eptir* 'in memory of'), would be *fóstru sína*. In terms of inflectional morphology *fóstra* can be nom. f. sg. (= 'foster-mother' 'foster-daughter'), oblique m. sg. (of *fóstri* 'foster-father' 'foster-son'), or (out of the question in the present context) acc. m. pl. (or gen. pl. of either the masculine or feminine word), but admission of any of these would introduce yet greater confusion into this text. As for the reflexive possessive **sinï**, it might be a way of writing dat. f. sg. *sinni*, but that would suggest a quite radical breakdown of the inflectional system. Distant parallels are **þinï** ('this', for standard *þenna*, acc. m. sg.) on SC 10 the Inchmarnock cross from Strathclyde, and **sini** (reflexive) in Sö 338, where we would expect acc. m. pl. *sína*. However, it is unclear what, if any, significance either spelling has for our understanding of Kirk Michael III's **sinï**. All three examples seem to indicate weakening of final [-A] (to [-æ]?), but that vowel (as also non-final unstressed [A]) is otherwise preserved intact in Kirk Michael III.

The inscription does, however, appear to offer evidence of the weakening of unstressed [i] in **ïftïr**, which perhaps lends some support to the idea that **sinï** might indeed be the dat. f. sg. form *sinni*. (On the possible weakening of unstressed vowels in the Manx inscriptions and the likely vowel sounds denoted by **ï**, see further pp. 76, 159–60.) The grammatical uncertainty continues with **kãna** 'woman', which syntactically should be accusative, one would think, agreeing with **mal:müru**, **fustra** 'foster-mother' and **tãtãr** 'daughter', but which in form is nominative singular. Here we may perhaps surmise that in defining the woman commemorated the writer switched in his mind from the construction with *eptir* + accusative to one in which *kona* was the subject complement ('And she was the woman whom…'). Fairly clearly there is aberrant grammar at various points in the text, either error or the use of a demotic set of inflections, perhaps very regional in nature. The fact that three of the four people recorded on the stone have Celtic names, may go some way to account for this irregularity.

There are also inconsistencies of runic usage on the stone. For the mid-rounded vowel /o(:)/ the carver sometimes put **u** (**krus**, **fustra**, **kuþan**, rendering *kross*, *fóstra*, *góðan*), sometimes ᚫ, the graph here transliterated **ã** (**tãtãr**, **kãna**, **sãn**, representing *dóttur*, *kona*, *son*). Though ᛁ **ï** had been introduced into his runic inventory (**þïna**, **ïftïr**, **sinï**, **|ïtra**, **ïs**), he does not employ it consistently: contrast **ïs** 'is' (rr. 76–7) with **is** 'whom' (rr. 62–3). On the dotted form ᚢ **ü** and the sounds it may denote in this inscription and otherwise, see pp. 61, 75–6.

The only residual point for discussion is the use of *þan* rather than the normal *en* for the correlative clause-introducer 'than' – and its implications. In the western Scandinavian world *þan* is not certainly documented in this function; there is a rare occurrence in a Danish runic text (Olsen 1954: 216–17; *DR*: 726, *s.v. þan*); in Swedish inscriptions it is not infrequent (Bugge 1899: 244; Peterson 2006: *s.v. þæn*). The form might be thought to accord quite well with the "long-branch" graph-types of this inscription (otherwise rare in Man), which are ubiquitous in Viking-Age Denmark and eleventh-century Sweden. However, "long-branch" runes also occur in Viking-Age Norway, and Swedish influence, at least, seems unlikely if Kirk Michael III is, as suggested by the Borre art style of its decorated face, from the early or mid-900s – for at that time "short-twig" runes were the norm in Sweden. However, artwork and inscription of MM 130 may not be contemporary: it would certainly be unexpected to find dotted runes or use of ᚫ for /o(:)/ in the first half of the tenth century (see further pp. 58–9).

In the light of the preceding discussion, a transcription more in conformity with the linguistic testimony of the inscription might be:

Mellomkun ræisti kross þenna æfter Melmýru fóstra sínæ, dóttur Duðgals, kona es Aðísl átti. Betra es læiba fóstra góðan þan son illan.

MM 126 Kirk Michael IV
Plates 93–7, Fig. 34

LITERATURE. Marquardt 1961: 78–9. Kinnebrook 1841: 11 and fig. 5 (together with other Kirk Michael fragments); Cumming 1857: 18 and fig. 3; Kneale [*c.* 1860]: 61, no. 9; Cumming 1868a: facing 23, no. 14, and 32; Vigfusson and Savage 1887: 13–14; Kermode 1887b: 151; Kermode 1892: 23–4, 51; Kermode 1907: 189–90; Brate 1907: 85; Olsen 1954: 217; Sanness Johnsen 1968: 242; Page 1983: 140; Holman 1996: 141–3.

Kinnebrook appears to have been the first to record MM 126. He reported it among three fragments (which he thought belonged to the same monument, but one is clearly MM 129 Kirk Michael VI) "on Michael Church-wall […] upon the south side of the gate" (cf. the account of Kirk Michael I's discovery, pp. 166–7, with the quotation from Kinnebrook 1841: 9). Cumming (1857) confirms the site and fragmentary state of preservation. By 1887, according to Vigfusson and Savage, the two pieces which make up MM 126 were in the church porch (perhaps the situation illustrated in Plate 95, reproduced from Manx National Heritage photograph MNH PG/13721 – MC126C); by 1892 they were "within the [church] tower" (Kermode 1892: 23). Cubbon (1964: 214) relates that in 1907 the collection of cross slabs at Kirk Michael was brought for protection beneath the church's lych-gate. In 1963 they were reordered within the church for greater security and visibility. MM 126, its two pieces crudely cemented together, now stands with its fellow crosses and cross fragments in the north transept, mounted in a wooden frame and set on a low concrete pillar.

Kirk Michael IV is carved into dark grey mudstone. As now preserved and displayed, the remnants of the original slab measure *c.* 101 cm × 39 × *c.* 5.5 (the breadth of the top fragment, though, is only 34.5). Kermode (1907) estimated the height "setting the two pieces in their relative position one with another" as 38½ inches (= 98 cm). Top and base of the stone are completely lost. Each face had a sculptured cross (small parts of the circled cross heads survive). Their shafts are filled with interlace. There is further extensive carving on both faces: on the one we find additional interlace patterns; on the other depictions of animals and humans, including what has been interpreted as a Christ figure (Margeson 1983: 99, 105). The runes run up one of the narrow edges of the stone, which is badly worn (the other edge

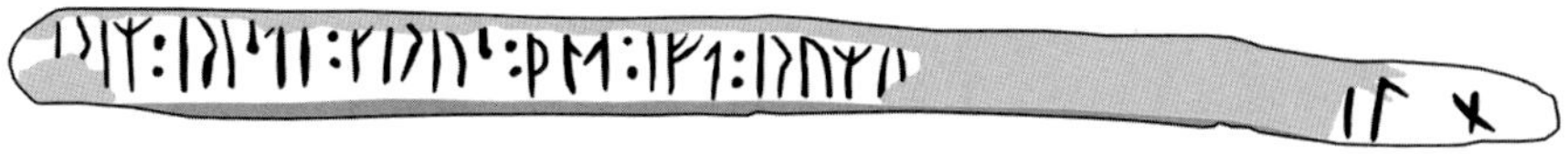

Fig. 34. MM 126 Kirk Michael IV (drawing: Jonas Nordby).

is lost through damage). No traces of framing lines can be seen, and exact heights of runes are difficult to determine (a rough estimate is 39–32 mm decreasing as the inscription proceeds upwards). What remains of the text reads:

1 5 10 15 20 24
]ᚱᛁᛘ:ᚱᛁᛌᛐᛁ:ᚴᚱᚢᛌ:ᚦᚿᛆ:ᛁᚠᛐ:ᚱᚢᛘᚢ...∗ᛚ

]**rim:risti:krus:þna:ift:rumu...∗l**
1 5 10 15 20 24

The sequence rr. 1–22 is *c.* 46 cm long. Thereafter is a gap where the two pieces of the slab have been joined together. Vigfusson and Savage, Kermode (1907), and Olsen all suggest space for about thirteen runes. As currently reconstructed, the stone indicates *c.* 24.5 cm missing here. What survives of the text thereafter is the suggestion of a vertical, then a character that appears to be an ᛚ with slight damage at its top. After that is a 25 mm gap followed by two crossing lines which some have taken as a saltire cross; however, it is unclear that this mark has anything to do with the inscription. There is no trace of further writing.

Nothing can be seen before r. 1, though Cumming (1857; 1868a) showed a vertical there. Kneale has a clear ᚴ. Kermode (1887b) observed that "a portion of the K can be traced" and in 1892 he read, without reservation, the name KRIM (= *Grím*). In his 1907 work he noted that the letters of this name were quite distinct "except for the K, which, however, shows the character-stroke". Nobody seems to have reported the "character-stroke" certainly thereafter, and it can no longer (2016) be made out. Cumming (1857; 1868a), Kneale, and Kermode (1892) read a clear **n** immediately after r. 22, but by the time of Kermode's 1907 work this rune seems no longer to have been visible (Brate, however, claimed he could see "ett stycke af öfre stafven" 'a bit of the upper [part of the] vertical' – probably to be identified with the mark that appears in the relevant spot in Plate 95, cf. above). In later accounts where this rune is included, it is placed in square brackets, presumably to indicate that it is supplied from earlier representations. We were unable to identify any trace of the character.

Diagnostic rune forms are ᚿ **n**, ᛆ **a**, ᛌ **s**, ᛐ **t**, ᛘ **m**.

Interpretation

The general sense of the inscription is clear enough, though details are uncertain:

-grímr/Grímr reisti kross þenna eptir Hrómund.

'-grímr/Grímr put up this cross in memory of Hrómundr.'

That **krim** was what immediately preceded **risti** is highly likely. That suggests either the personal name *Grímr* or a compound with *-grímr* as the second element (e.g. *Þorgrímr*), in either case lacking the usual nominative singular ending (though it is perhaps worth noting that the following word begins with *r-*; cf. p. 225). It is also possible to propose a name for the person in whose memory the cross was put up. Olsen observes: "Vigfusson was of opinion that here [i.e. following r. 22] have stood: [**nt: bruþur: sun: s]in**", a reference to Vigfusson and Savage's treatment of the inscription. For the relevant section he himself gives "**rumu[nt—s]in**", and Sanness Johnsen the identical "r u m u [n t . . s] i n", but neither explains how they arrived at these extended readings (their **in**, though, is fairly clearly derived from rr. 23–4). If we base our interpretation solely on what can now be seen, ON *Hrómund* (acc.) seems indeed to be the only name that fits. The initial /h-/ would then not be marked, but was probably lost in Manx Norse by the time the inscription was carved, as it ultimately came to be in the clusters /hl-/, /hn-/, /hr-/ in all forms of Scandinavian except Icelandic. Support for this notion comes from MM 138 Braddan II, which almost certainly has **rãskitil** for ON *Hrossketill*, and MM 142 Maughold IV*e* with, apparently, **lifilt** for *Hlífhild(i)* (cf. also Maughold IV*a* 2); perhaps further from **nhaki** (MM 135 Braddan IV), a spelling that could be taken to suggest that the opening of the byname *hnakki* 'neck' gave the writer trouble (cf. pp. 141–2).

In **þna** a vowel rune is missing between **þ** and **n**, possibly an error by the carver (but thus also in MM 102 Kirk Michael I; and cf. p. 78). It is uncertain whether the spelling **risti** denotes [reːsti] or [ræisti]. Monographic spelling of diphthongs is a phenomenon known from Norwegian inscriptions (cf. p. 138). On the other hand, there is nothing in the graph-types, orthography or language of Kirk Michael IV to identify it positively as West Scandinavian (though the layout with the runes running up one of the narrow edges is strongly suggestive), and in the East monophthongisation /ei/ > /eː/ began in the mid- to late Viking Age.

In the light of these considerations it is not easy to achieve a transcription that might reflect the forms underlying the runic orthography. With considerable reservation we suggest:

-grím/Grím ræisti kross ?þanna/?þenna æft Rómund.

MM 132 Kirk Michael V*a–b*
Plates 98–107, Figs 35–8

LITERATURE. Marquardt 1961: 79–81. Wanley [*c*. 1700]; Camden/Gibson 1722: 1459–60; Camden/Gough 1789: 3, 704; Thorkelin [1789]; Anon. 1822: 491–2 and pl. XVI, no. 2; Oswald 1822: 505 and pls XVII–XVIII, D. nos 1–3; Kinnebrook 1841: 10 and fig. 1; Hibbert-Ware *et al*. [*c*. 1848]: 128; Munch 1850: 277–8; Cumming 1857: 24–5 and fig. 13; Vigfusson and Savage 1887: 12–13; Kermode 1887b: 151; Bugge 1899: 235; Kermode 1907: 199–202; Brate 1907: 85–6; Olsen 1954: 217–18; Sanness Johnsen 1968: 243–4; Page 1981: 133; Page 1983: 140; Holman 1996: 143–6.

Kirk Michael V*a*

Kirk Michael V*a* is among the "Four Runick Inscriptions in the Isle of Man" reported in Edmund Gibson's revision of William Camden's *Britannia* (1722: 1457–60). The monument bearing it is described simply as "a Stone-Cross at *Kirk-Michael*" (Gibson no. II), though elsewhere the text, on the authority of Thomas Wilson, Bishop of Sodor and Man from 1697 to 1755, places it as standing "in the High-way, near the Church of St. *Michael*" (Gibson 1722: 1455). A drawing in Humphrey Wanley's papers (Wanley [*c*. 1700]; see p. 49 and Fig. 10, line 1) puts it "at the West End of S*t*. Michael's Church [...] near the Church-yard". Gough's reissue of *Britannia* illustrates the same stone, together with the three others from the 1722 edition, this time set formally, as though standing in the earth. These pictures are said to be "exact representations", though in fact they are less precise in detail than Gibson's (see Figs 36–7).

In contrast to MM 130 Kirk Michael III, MM 132 has had an uneventful modern history. In notes on his journey to the Isle of Man in 1789, Grímur Jónsson Thorkelin recorded a rune-inscribed cross "in Kirk Michael on the outside of the Church yard", and made two sketches of its inscription: clearly Kirk Michael V*a* (Thorkelin [1789]). His rough attempt at drawing the decoration on the two faces of the stone shows that he had first-hand knowledge of it, and was not relying for the runes on Wilson, whose authority he quotes. Woods (1811: 162) observed the cross "opposite the entrance of the church

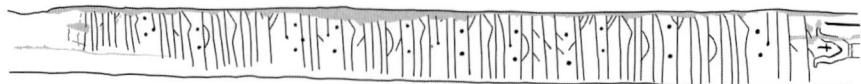

*Fig. 35. MM 132 Kirk Michael V*a *(drawing: Jonas Nordby).*

yard [...] forming the center of a horse-block". Anon. (1822, quoting from a letter written by H.R. Oswald in 1817) reported the stone "at the gate of the church"; Oswald himself places it "in front of the church-yard gate", and his plates XVII and XVIII depict it set in what would appear to be a horse block. Kinnebrook locates the "pillar" more precisely "on the roadside, in the middle of the village, near the northern corner of the Church-yard"; Cumming "in front of the churchyard gates". By the time of Kermode's *Manx Crosses* it was "set on the horse block in front of the church gates [...] where it was placed when the present entrance was made, about 1850" (1907: 199; but cf. Woods and Oswald above). What must be this location is shown on some early photographs (e.g. MNH PG/13721 - MC132B-C, reproduced as Plate 100). The continuity of description here, although differing on points of detail, makes clear that we need give no credence to late eighteenth- and nineteenth-century tales of a completely different primary site for this stone (Page 1980: 191–2).

The Kirk Michael cross slabs were brought for protection under the church's lych-gate in 1907, and in 1963 reordered within the church for greater security and visibility (Cubbon 1964: 214). MM 132 now stands with its fellow crosses and cross fragments in the north transept, set in the floor.

Kirk Michael V*a* runs up one of the narrow edges of a substantial slab of dark grey mudstone, measuring *c*. 228 cm (visible height) × 53 × 16. Kermode (1907: 199) gives the height as "eighty-eight inches above the surface" (= 224 cm), while Cubbon (1964: 215) records "an overall height, as revealed in the move [i.e. before the stone was fixed in its current position], of exactly eleven feet (= 335 cm); whether some of the base was removed before mounting is unknown, but the stone is tall and heavy and a substantial section may be in the floor to lend support. This is the most elaborate extant runic memorial in Man. Both faces have sculptured low-relief shafted crosses, with circled heads and interlace ornament. On one face (Kermode's A; 1907: 199–200) the cross has two dragons below it, and to both sides of its shaft are ring-headed crosses, circles and animal ornament. The other face (Kermode's B) has, above its cross head, a stag and a bird, while to the two sides of the cross shaft are beasts, including horse and rider. The non-runic narrow edge of the stone is covered with sculptured interlace. Text *a*, the formal runic inscription, reads:

iual∗ir:sunr:þurulfs:hins:rauþa:risti:krus:þãnã
:aft:friþu:muþur:sinã

From r. 1 to the end of the lower branch of r. 57 is 149.5 cm. Earlier representations of this text often show it beginning and ending with a cross. Immediately before r. 1 there are various faint scratches, vertical and horizontal, but they seem too weak and casual to be part of the inscription. Before them again is a short vertical line of uncertain import: unlike the putative cross, this line has the depth and breadth of some of the runic grooves and might therefore be a mark indicating the beginning of the text, or perhaps an abandoned attempt at the first graph. There is a very clear cross at the end of the inscription, but that is certainly to be viewed vertically and connected with the incised figure of a man above it, who holds a shield and spear. Below r. 1 there is at present visible some 56 cm of stone. A faint runic graffito can be made out for part of its length, and this continues under rr. 1–8 (see text *b* below). With the space preceding the inscription and the male figure immediately following it, we can be sure that no part of text *a* has been lost at either end.

The graphs are for the most part deeply and evenly cut, though rr. 1–7 are somewhat more tentative. Dots seem to have been made by rotating the carving implement. Most of the runes fill the whole edge (there are no framing lines), giving a maximum height of *c.* 14 cm (e.g. r. 52 **u**); but the earlier graphs, rr. 1–7, are noticeably smaller, *c.* 8 cm, for their bases run along a natural break in the surface. Rune tops are sometimes lost, but it is only in the case of r. 5 that this causes a problem of identification. The graph can appear to have two branches, as of ᚠ **f**, but what seems to be the lower one shows no evidence of having been cut and is almost certainly surface damage; unless a branch has been lost at the top, we have ᚴ **k**. Brate and Olsen discuss the pros and cons of an **f** versus **k** reading, Brate without coming down in favour of the one or the other, Olsen preferring **f**. Rune 4 ᚱ has most of its branch missing, but the end survives. The same is true of r. 31 ᛏ (here in addition the space to the left suggests the presence of a carved line of some sort). Rune 1 has caused difficulty in the past. The earliest drawings show a simple vertical (presumably **i**), and that is all that can be seen today; there is no trace of a branch (or indeed of a dot that would convert the rune to **h**,

188

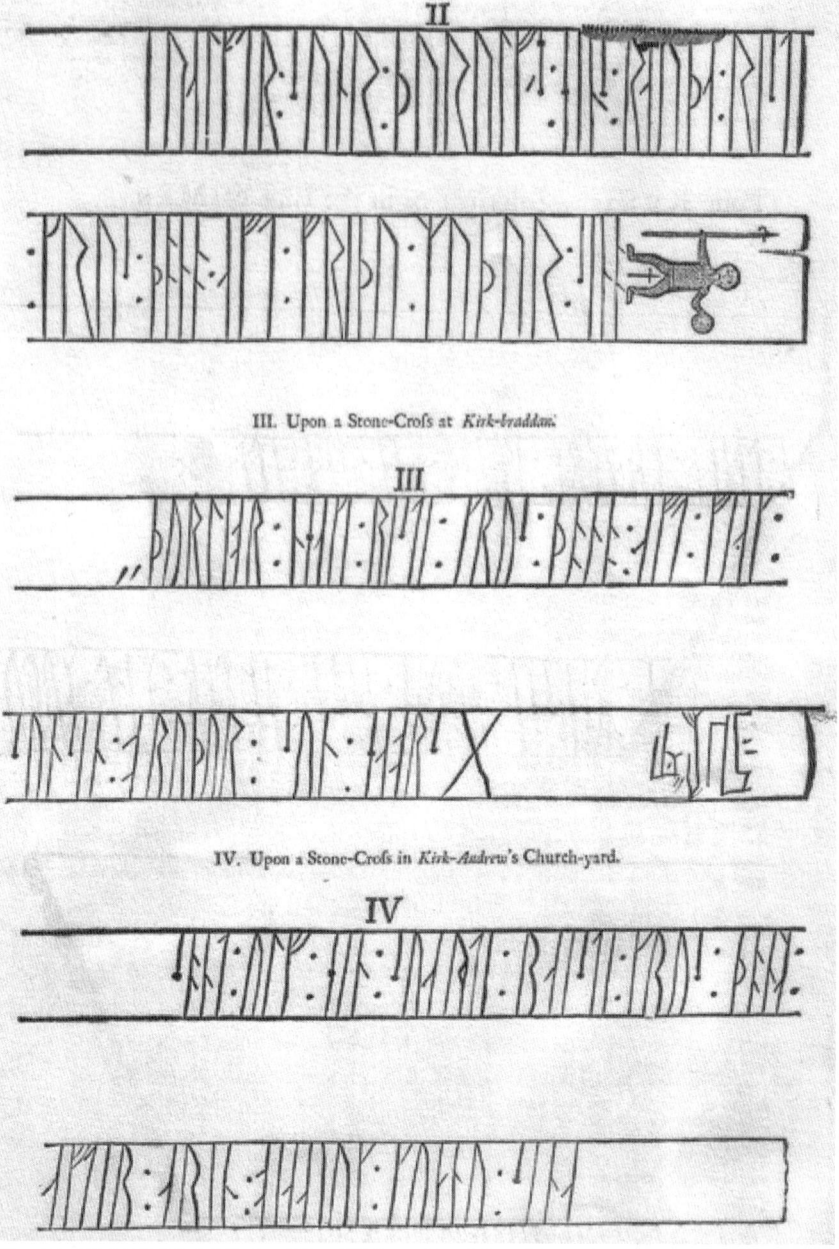

Fig. 36. MM 132 Kirk Michael Va, MM 135 Braddan IV, and MM 131 Andreas IIa as portrayed in Gibson's 1722 revision of Camden's Britannia *(pp. 1459–60).*

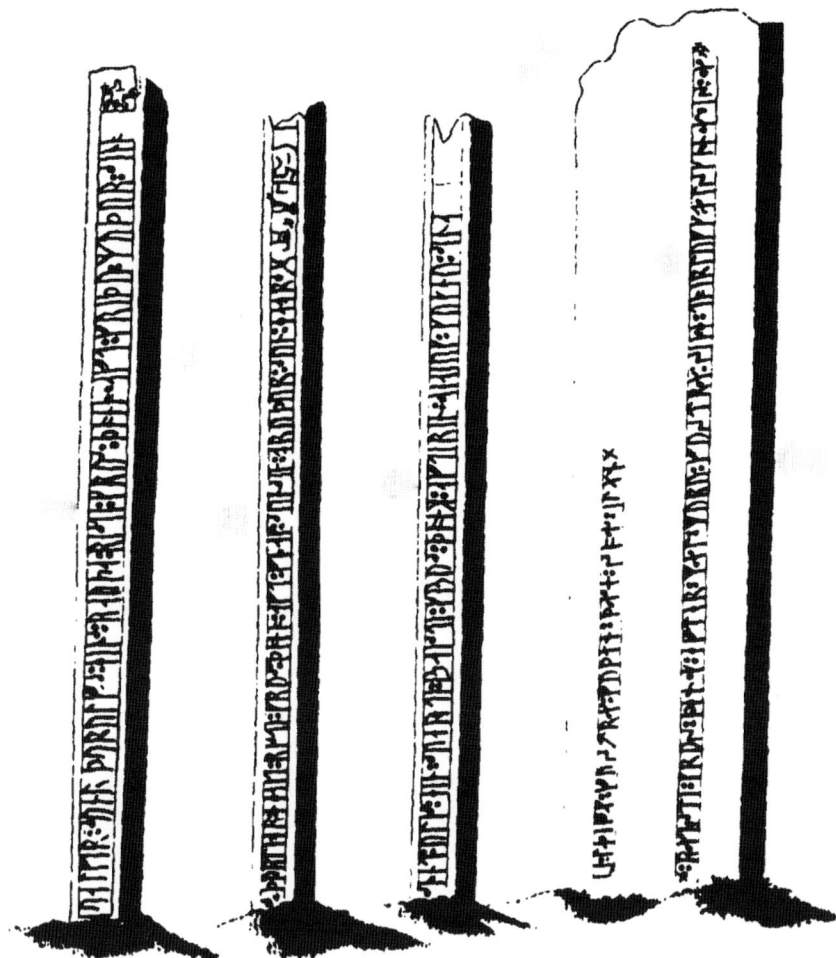

Fig. 37. MM 132 Kirk Michael Va, MM 135 Braddan IV, MM 131 Andreas IIa, and MM 130 Kirk Michael III as portrayed in Gough's 1789 revision of Camden's Britannia.

but the surface is abraded in the relevant area). However, Munch proposes **a** as an alternative and Vigfusson and Savage read A without comment. Olsen rejects the idea: "R. 1 cannot be read as ᛅ **a**". Rune 3, on the other hand, has commonly been taken as **a**, but here Brate suggests and Olsen prefers ᛒ **b**, "as I think the trace of a lower branch can certainly be made out". There is indeed something faintly like a lower branch, though it is almost certainly a damaged patch of the surface. Rune 29 appears to be dotted, but the dot is placed to the right of the vertical and does not seem to be part of the inscription; ᛁ ī can hardly have been intended since this would be indistinguishable from the ᛡ h of r. 19. The early recorders, Gibson, Gough, Thorkelin, have no problems with any of the rune forms in these sections of the inscription, reading **iualfir** for rr. 1–7 and **risti** for rr. 28–32 (save for Thorkelin's second sketch, which depicts both r. 5 and r. 31 as branchless). The Wanley drawing ([c. 1700]) omits a number of branches, preferring simple verticals, so its representations **iuaifir, risii**, have little significance.

Diagnostic rune forms are ᚨ ã, ᚼ h, ᚿ n, ᛆ a, ᛌ s, ᛐ t, ᛘ m.

Interpretation

The general sense of the inscription is clear enough:

NN sonr Þórólfs hins rauða reisti kross þenna eptir Fríðu móður sína.

'NN son of Þórólfr the red put up this cross in memory of his mother Fríða.'

The only problem is to identify the first word, undoubtedly a personal name. The reading **iualfir** implies one not otherwise recorded, traditionally normalised as *Jóalfr* (Munch, Bugge, Sanness Johnsen; listed in Lind 1905–15: *s.n. Ióálfr*). Both elements of the suggested name, *Jó-* and *-alfr*, are common enough in Norse sources (and cf. Peterson 2003 on the many hapax compound names in Scandinavian Viking-Age inscriptions). Brate objected (i) that this interpretation leaves r. 6 **i** unexplained, (ii) that by analogy with other Manx spellings, one might expect **b** rather than **f** in the second element (denoting [ß]). His first objection is reasonable enough, but it is unclear what force the second has. In this very inscription we find **þurulfs** 'of Þórólfr', and other Manx stones exhibit spellings such as **sãnt:ulf** 'Sǫndulfr' (MM 131 Andreas IIa), **laifa** 'leave' (MM 130 Kirk Michael III; see further pp. 76–7). Brate's own suggestion for rr. 2–7, *Valgeirr*, an otherwise unrecorded name, but a not implausible one, requires r. 1 to be a "gränslinje" 'bordering mark' (i.e. a vertical line marking the beginning of the inscription), and r. 5 to be ᚴ **k** (which latter is eminently possible, cf. above). Vigfusson and Savage, reading r. 1 as **a**, proposed a form of *Óláfr* for the raiser's name (AULAFIR – later retracted, cf. Kermode 1907: 201; cf. also Munch's suggested *Aualfir*). Olsen was unwilling to commit himself, commenting only: "*Jóalfr* [...] is very uncertain". If, for the sake of argument, we were to interpret rr. 1–7 as *Jóalfr*, we would have to assume either that r. 6 **i** denotes an epenthetic vowel, or, unlikely, that **-al∗ir** represents an otherwise undocumented *ia*-stem derivative of *alfr*. Although there do not seem to be further examples of epenthetic vowels in the Manx corpus, the appearance of one, especially in connection with [r], should not surprise us – even at so early a date. What appear to be such vowels are denoted sporadically throughout the Viking Age (e.g. **uesteʀ**, **tauþeʀ** Ög 68, ON *vestr* 'west', *dauðr* 'dead'; **ualtiʀ** U 942, ON *valdr* 'ruler'; and, less strictly comparable, **boroþur** N 260, ON *bróðr* 'brother': all fairly certainly eleventh-century and all probably with [r] following the relevant vowel despite the **ʀ** spellings in the Swedish examples; cf. Larsson 2002: 53–4). Having considered the evidence, however, we find the reading and interpretation of rr. 1–7 too uncertain for us to come down in favour of any particular name or name form.

On the monographic spelling of the root vowel in **risti**, see the discussion of MM 136 Braddan III and MM 126 Kirk Michael IV.

A transcription of Kirk Michael V*a* closer to the spoken forms to be deduced from the inscription might be:

NN sonr Þórólfs hins rauða ræisti kross þānnā æft Fríðu móður sínā.

Kirk Michael V*b*

On the lowest part of the inscribed edge there is a natural break along its surface (cf. above). Underneath this, and extending at least as far as below r. 8 of text *a*, a line of runes, some 36 cm long, is faintly, indeed tentatively and crudely, scratched. The runes decrease in height from *c*. 5 cm near the beginning to *c*. 2 cm at r. 18 **þ**, and become even slightly shorter towards the end. This carving presumably postdates the main text of Kirk Michael V, but there is no way of determining by how long; or indeed whether it was invested with any meaning, though the repeated occurrence of what may have been intended as a separation symbol suggests a possible division into words. With considerable reservation, we read:

¹ ∗ (ꜰ R ꜰ) ˧ ∗ R ∗ (') þ (R) ᴎ ∗ (') ˧ ᴎ (') ꞁ ᛁ þ (' ꜰ) ᛁ ᴎ (') R ᛁ ∗ ∗ (ᴎ)

s ∗ (k r k) t ∗ r ∗ (:) þ (r) u ∗ (:) a u (:) l i þ (: k) i u (:) r i ∗ ∗ (u)

The first graph looks to be ¹, followed by what appears to be the lower half of a vertical (r. 2) and perhaps the group **krk** (rr. 3–5). After a smallish gap comes ˧ (r. 6), succeeded (after another gap) by an undulating vertical, an **r**, and a further undulating vertical (rr. 7–9). This is followed by yet another gap

Fig. 38. MM 132 Kirk Michael Vb (drawing: Jonas Nordby).

in which a short vertical line can be seen, possibly a separation symbol, and then apparently **þ** (although the character in some ways resembles a roman 'p'), a possible **r**, a **u**, and thereafter an assortment of verticals obliterated in the middle (counted here as a single rune, giving rr. 10–13). In the space that follows, there are short vertical and oblique lines, one or more of which might have been intended as a separator. Next is **au** (rr. 14–15), then perhaps a separator, once again in the shape of a short oblique line. Thereafter comes **liþ** (rr. 16–18). We then have a possible separator and **k** (r. 19). Thereupon is **iu**(:) **ri** (rr. 20–23), with rr. 21 and 22 perhaps divided by a separator. The inscription concludes with two verticals that lack obvious distinguishing features (rr. 24–5), followed by two short lines that might be the remains of **u** (r. 26).

Kermode (1907: 202) recorded the line with the comment: "it seems to begin ɪᴍᴜ, and higher up one recognises Thᴜʀ." It is not possible to confirm this on the basis of what can be seen now (2016).

Diagnostic rune forms are ᚨ **a**, ᛁ **s**, ᛐ **t**.

No linguistic sense is to be extracted from this inscription. One could surmise that the writer copied individual runes and groups such as **kr**, **au**, **ri** from Kirk Michael V*a*, the formal text that runs above and beyond the graffito.

MM 129 Kirk Michael VI

Plates 108–10, Fig. 39

LITERATURE. Marquardt 1961: 81–2. Kinnebrook 1841: 11 and fig. 5 (together with other Kirk Michael fragments); Cumming 1857: 20–21 and fig. 8; Vigfusson and Savage 1887: 13; Taylor 1887: 185; Kermode 1892: 24, 52–3; Kermode 1907: 190–92; Brate 1907: 86; Olsen 1954: 218; Sanness Johnsen 1968: 244; Page 1983: 140; Holman 1996: 146–7.

MM 129 seems first to have been recorded by Kinnebrook. He reported it among three fragments "on Michael Church-wall […] upon the south side of the gate" (see the accounts of MM 102 Kirk Michael I, MM 126 Kirk Michael IV). Cumming confirms the general find spot, but notes: "This fragment is at present in the Vestry of Kirk Michael." By 1887, according to Vigfusson

Fig. 39. MM 129 Kirk Michael VI (drawing: Jonas Nordby).

and Savage, MM 129 was within the church porch, while Kermode (1892: 24) locates it "in Church tower". In 1907 it was brought for protection beneath the church's lych-gate, together with other Kirk Michael crosses and cross fragments, and then in 1963 accompanied the others into the church, where they were all placed for greater security and visibility (Cubbon 1964: 214). MM 129 now stands in the north transept, set on a concrete pedestal fixed atop the block that holds MM 102 Kirk Michael I and MM 130 Kirk Michael III.

Kirk Michael VI is found on a fragment of dark grey mudstone, measuring *c.* 47 cm (visible height) × 45 × 9. Kermode's measurements (1907) differ only marginally: 18½ inches × 17½ × 3 (= 47 cm × 44 × 8). No more than the uppermost part of an elaborately decorated slab remains, the faces preserving arms and top of carved circle-headed crosses decorated with interlace; there are also on the one side a Christ figure (Margeson 1983: 105), what appears to be an angel, and a cock, and on the other a serpent-like animal and a man attacked by a bird. The runes run up one of the narrow edges of the slab. The first surviving graph is roughly level with the lower line of the cross arms, so it is likely that an extensive section of text has been lost before it. The runes occupy more or less the full width of edge (*c.* 7.5 cm), without framing lines. What is left of the text reads:

](k)rims:ins:suarta×

The length of the preserved sequence (from the remains of r. 1 to the end of the saltire cross) is 30 cm. Some tops and bases of verticals are lost, making the heights of the affected graphs impossible to define precisely. Runes 4 and 10, which seem to be complete, are 6.4 and 6.9 cm respectively. The upper part of the inscription-bearing edge of the slab has a ragged gash above rr. 13–14, which, at 5.0 and 4.2 cm high, look to have been cut subsequent to this damage. Other, less prominent, gashes are found near the top edge of the inscription. A thin line, reminiscent of a 1-branch, stands above r. 13 1 (colliding with the bow of r. 12 **r**), and three thin upright lines are found above r. 14 4, as if in extension of its vertical, but it is unclear whether these marks represent a half-hearted attempt to bring rr. 13–14 up to full height, or are mere casual scratches. Of r. 1 only a branch remains. Cumming's published drawing shows a complete ᚴ here, though his rubbing (Cumming [c. 1855]: fol. 15r) indicates no more than can be seen today. Vigfusson and Savage omit the rune from their transliteration, but Taylor asserts that "the first rune of Grim's name [...] is visible on the cast". Kermode (1907) records the graph as certain, though damaged in its lower part. Brate says that only "kännestrecket" 'the distinguishing stroke' of the character can be found, and Olsen confirms this. Their observations coincide with what can now be seen, though Holman, like Vigfusson and Savage, omits the rune altogether. The strong likelihood is that r. 1 was **k**, but not enough of the graph is visible to confirm this absolutely.

Diagnostic rune forms are ᚾ **n**, ᛅ **a**, ᛁ **s**, ᛏ **t**, ᛘ **m**.

Interpretation

What survives is, from its present position on the stone, the end of what could have been quite a lengthy inscription. Interpreting r. 1 as **k**, we have:

...-gríms/Gríms ins svarta.

'...of -grímr/Grímr the black.'

It is impossible to know whether rr. 1–5 gave a complete name, or only the second element of a compound: cf. here MM 126 Kirk Michael IV where the same difficulty arises. Coming at the end of the text, the genitive phrase *-gríms/Gríms ins svarta* presumably followed a kinship noun that defined the relationship of the person commemorated in the inscription to -grímr/Grímr, as, e.g., MM 135 Braddan IV: *Þorleifr hnakki reisti kross þenna eptir Fjakk son sinn, bróðurson Hafrs* 'Þorleifr neck put up this cross in memory of Fiacc his son, Hafr's nephew'.

A "Manx transcription" of this fragmentary inscription would not differ from the normalisation given above.

MM 110 Kirk Michael VII

Plates 111–14, Fig. 40

LITERATURE. Marquardt 1961: 82. Kermode 1905: 16; Kermode 1907: 162–3; Olsen 1954: 218–19; Sanness Johnsen 1968: 244–5; Holman 1996: 147–8.

MM 110 was spotted in 1899 when a "Mr. Royston" (Kermode 1907) who was taking casts of some of the Kirk Michael crosses noticed that a well-known tombstone decorated with a skull and crossbones and bearing the date 1699 was in fact a reused fragment of a memorial cross. What is generally assumed to have been its base (see below) had been reshaped into the rounded head of a seventeenth-century gravestone. The stone was immediately removed from its grave, and was then presumably taken somewhere in the vicinity for safe-keeping (the church porch? the church tower? – cf. MM 126 Kirk Michael IV, MM 129 Kirk Michael VI). In 1907 it joined the other Kirk Michael crosses and cross fragments under the lych-gate, where it remained until 1963 when the whole collection was moved into the church (Cubbon 1964: 214; see the accounts of Kirk Michael I–VI). It now stands in the north transept, set in the floor.

Kirk Michael VII is found on the remains of a slab of grey mudstone, measuring *c.* 78 cm (visible height) × 36.5 × 8. Kermode (1907) gives the height as 35 inches (= 89 cm). One face of the fragment shows traces of a cross shaft and interlace patterns, the other a hint of interlace only (although Kermode, 1907, notes "the lower end of the shaft of a cross" on both faces). Any account of the runes must acknowledge the generally worn state of the surface, which renders identifications difficult. Measurements are similarly uncertain. The seventeenth-century reshaping of the monument left but a small section of the inscription surviving. It is placed on one of the narrow edges, and going by other Manx rune-stones with this type of layout presumably originally ran upwards (as the stone is currently oriented, with the 1699 head uppermost, the inscription runs down the edge). The graphs are *c.* 5 cm tall. Before the remaining runes the stone has been cut away towards the rounded top of the new gravestone; after them is a small portion of the surface with indecipherable marks on it.

What can be made out is:

```
          1      5        10
 ](* * *) * * R Þ Ո R (:) * * [

 ](* * *) * * r þ u r (:) * * [
   1      5        10
```

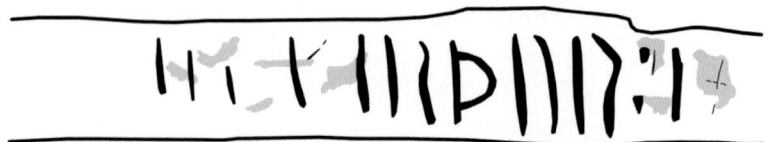

Fig. 40. MM 110 Kirk Michael VII (drawing: Jonas Nordby).

The eleven characters (if characters they all are) occupy 24 cm, and there is no way of calculating what has been lost. What we take to be rr. 1–3 are the remains of three vertical lines standing on an abraded and uneven surface. Runes 4 and 5 are more prominent. Rune 4 is a vertical with what might be a very thin branch, as of ᚠ. Rune 5 is likewise a vertical; it may once have had an ascending left branch at about mid height (as of ᚾ or ᛏ), but surface damage has obliterated all traces of carving here. Runes 6–9 are clearly enough **rþur**. After r. 9 **r** there are various marks, some of which appear to be part of the inscription. First are two indentations that could very well represent a separation symbol (:), then two vertical lines, the first very short, the second longer and slightly curved (counted as separate characters but conceivably the remains of **u**). Finally there is what can at first glance appear to be the outline of ᛏ; its grooves are, however, much thinner and shallower than those of rr. 1–11, and it is unlikely to represent a continuation of the text.

Kermode's account is rather different (1907: 163):

> All that can now be deciphered is the word RUNER, Runes, preceded by the stem-line of another, and indications of several more characters [...] The two characters which I read N E are, unfortunately, much worn about the middle, but I can detect the stroke in one and the dot of the other.

Olsen followed Kermode, but preferred to read (from a cast) **runar** largely because the *-ar* ending was the one he expected at the early date he attributed to the cross. The Kermode/Olsen readings can in no way be confirmed, though looking at the graphs in certain kinds of lighting (both on the original and on a cast held by the Manx Museum) one can see how the two scholars might have arrived at them.

Interpretation

So little is left of this inscription that interpretation can only be guesswork. Perhaps, since the preserved runes seem likely to represent an early part of the text, we have here the remains of a personal name (a compound with second element *-þórr*?). Or conceivably rr. 4–8 give *gerðu* 'made', 3rd pl. past tense of *gera*, although that sits uneasily with the immediately following **r**(:). If we ignore the possible separator and assume r. 9 **r** to represent the beginning of a fresh word, one wonders what that word might have been: in the Manx inscriptions otherwise the object of *gera* is *kross* (almost certainly in Andreas I, implied in Kirk Michael II) or **lik+tinn** (Maughold V), clearly also a memorial of some kind. Possibly rr. 4–9 conceal a noun of kin, perhaps *bróður* 'brother' or *móður* 'mother' – in the accusative after some form of the preposition *eptir* 'in memory of' – but then with aberrant spelling. Of course, both this and the *gerðu* suggestion presuppose space for a good length of text before the preserved sequence, and that is perhaps unlikely given the way the monument has been reshaped (cf. above). With so little to go on, it would be fruitless to speculate further about meaning; nor is it possible to supply a normalised text.

MM 123 Kirk Michael VIII

Plates 115–18, Fig. 41

LITERATURE. Marquardt 1961: 82. Kermode 1912: 74–6; Kermode 1925: 341–2; Olsen 1954: 219; Sanness Johnsen 1968: 245; Page 1983: 141; Holman 1996: 148–50.

MM 123, a small fragment, was discovered in 1911 in a garden adjoining the parish churchyard of Kirk Michael. It was set up under the church's lych-gate together with the other Kirk Michael crosses and cross fragments (Kermode 1912: 74–5). In 1963 the whole collection was reordered within the church for greater security and visibility (Cubbon 1964: 214; see the accounts of Kirk Michael I–VI). The piece is now fixed to the northern wall in the north transept.

Kirk Michael VIII is found on the remnant of a dark grey mudstone slab, measuring *c*. 39 cm × 25.5 × 5 (Kermode's figures differ marginally, but that is hardly surprising given the very irregular shape of what survives). The stone has split along a lamination, which has taken off the outer layer of the surface that now faces the wall. The runes are placed on one of the narrow edges, but only their upper parts are left. The surviving face has the remains of a sculptured cross shaft with, to its right, what seems to be a female figure holding a staff, and below it a tethered horse. Interpretations have been given to these images, but they are quite uncertain (Margeson 1983: 96). What can be made of the runes reads:

Fig. 41. MM 123 Kirk Michael VIII (drawing: Jonas Nordby).

```
     1          5           10              15
] * * * * ( : ) * * ⌶ ↑ ( I R : ) ¥ ⋂ * ( : ) * * [

] * * * * : * * f t ( i r ) : m u * : * * [
  1       5       10          15
```

Beginning and end of the inscription are lost. Surviving graphs extend for some 27.5 cm and have a maximum height of 32 mm. Runes 14–15 seem to be slightly shorter than those preceding them, possibly due to damage to the surface above, which almost certainly predates the carving. Several of the characters are only the top parts of vertical lines, which cannot be identified. Runes 1–4 are such, fairly roughly cut (but also damaged) and with a rather wider space between rr. 3 and 4, which might suggest one or more branches lost there. What follows is almost certainly the dot of a separation symbol (the top one of two or more), and thereafter two verticals, rr. 5, 6, quite close together, though there would have been space for a left-hand branch on r. 5. Runes 7, 8 are top parts only, but clearly identifiable. Runes 9, 10 are likely to be the tops of **ir**, given their shape and the context, but not enough of either can be seen for certain identification. Then comes a dot that is presumably the higher of two (hardly three since it is placed relatively low down). Runes 11, 12 clearly indicate **mu**. What follows is the upper half of a vertical with, seemingly, the trace of a descending right-hand branch (as of ↾) at the point where the lower part of the narrow edge is broken away (as Holman also observed). Thereafter is a further dot, quite low down, to be interpreted in the same way as the one following r. 10. Rune 14 is the top part of either **u** or **r**; what remains looks more like r. 12 **u** than r. 10 (**r**). Rune 15 is part of the top of a vertical, with what in some lights can appear to be the trace of a branch as of ⋂ or ℟, or possibly ↾.

Diagnostic rune forms are ↑ **t**, ¥ **m**.

Interpretation

Any interpretation must be speculative, considering the state of this text. It is natural to assume, as previous scholars have done, that rr. 5–10 represent some form of the preposition *eptir* – from what survives most likely **aiftir**, as almost certainly on MM 106 Ballaugh. So:

...*eptir*...

'...in memory of...'

This suggests a (basic) sense for the whole original inscription something like 'NN put up this cross in memory of MM'. Runes 1–4 should then supply a form of the acc. m. sg. demonstrative *þenna* 'this'. The problem here is with r. 1, which hardly seems to have the space to its right to accommodate the bow of **þ** (though Kermode supplies one, rather squeezed in: cf. 1912: 74, fig. 17; 1925: 341, fig. 2). Conceivably the spelling here was **þaina** as apparently in MM 113 Andreas IV, in which case **þ** would have been located on a part of the stone that is now broken off. Runes 3, 4 could certainly have been **na**, particularly if the branches were at slightly different heights. Following *eptir* one would expect either a personal name or an indication of kinship. To supply the former Olsen suggests that rr. 11–13 are "perhaps **mun**, *Munn*, accus. of the man's name *Munnr* (otherwise unknown)", quoting the "eke-name" *munnr* 'mouth' for which he refers to four parallels (cf. Lind 1920-21: *s.n.*). This is repeated in Sanness Johnsen and Holman. If that is the correct interpretation, the **u** or **r** (r. 14) following the separation symbol would be likely to denote the initial sound of a kinship term, of which only *ver* (acc.) 'man' 'husband' seems possible, attested in a dozen or so Viking-Age inscriptions. Sanness Johnsen offers, as an alternative, the documented personal name (acc.) *Munulf* (cf. Peterson 2007: *s.n.*); and indeed, the putative branch at the top of r. 15 (cf. above) might just be that of ᛚ. For a kinship noun (rather than a personal name) to follow *eptir* some rendering of *móður* 'mother' (acc.) could be suggested (cf. MM 132 Kirk Michael V*a*'s **muþur**). The problem then is that, though rr. 11–13 might conceivably be the remnant of **muþ** (with the apparent trace of a descending right branch in r. 13 in fact the very top of a bow), and r. 14 is a plausible **u**, yet there is a separation symbol between rr. 13 and 14. To maintain this interpretation we thus have to accept that the reading was **muþ:ur** (cf. the possible **tu:tur** in Andreas VIII ✝). On balance, a separation symbol after *Mun-* is more convincing than after *móð-* (cf. MM 131 Andreas II*a*'s **sānt:ulf, arin:biaurk**).

To sum up: the remains of the inscription may render ... *þenna eptir Munn ver/Munulf*... '...this [cross] in memory of Munnr [her] husband/Munulfr...', but other possibilities cannot be excluded.

With several doubts attaching to the reading and the lack of any certain text, no purpose would be served by offering a "Manx transcription" of Kirk Michael VIII.

MM 139 Marown
Plates 119–20, Fig. 42

LITERATURE: Marquardt 1961: 70. Jenkinson 1874: 37; Kermode, 1884: 151; Vigfusson and Savage 1887: 15; Kermode 1892: 11, 42, listed under Braddan; Kermode 1907: 208–9; Brate 1907: 33; Olsen 1954: 201; Sanness Johnsen 1968: 235; Page 1983: 141; Holman 1996: 150–51.

Jenkinson reported the finding of this stone:

> [...] at the Rhyne farm [...] we were shown the ground where existed the chapel and graveyard, which had been completely razed, and not a stone left to mark the spot. After searching some little time, we found lying loose on the wall, in the stackyard, a broken slate slab, with Runic characters as legible as when first made.

Jenkinson appears to have done the preparatory work on his guide book sometime in the period 1872–4, so the discovery can presumably be attributed to one of those years. That is slightly, but not impossibly, at variance with Kermode's statement (1884: 151): "I am informed by Mr Kneale that this slab [MM 139] was brought to him about seven years ago [shortly after the finding, so Kneale might interpret it, cf. Jenkinson 1874: 37]". For safe keeping the stone was taken to the Government Offices at Castle Rushen. In Kermode (1907) it is still described as "in Castle Rushen", which at that time housed the local museum. At some point thereafter the slab was set up in the ruined chapel of St Trinian (NGR SC 317803), pegged to the internal wall of its east end, where it still stands, open to the elements. Why a derelict chapel was thought a suitable place to preserve MM 139 is unclear, but the fact that both find spot and chapel are in the parish of Marown may have been a factor, coupled with the widespread association of rune-stones with ecclesiastical sites. The positioning of the stone tight up against a wall means its rear face cannot be examined, but Kermode (1884: 151) describes it as plain, and (1907) even more specifically as having "no appearance of workmanship" and being "not even surface-dressed".

In its present condition the slab is a piece of unworked mudstone of irregular shape, c. 52.5 × 26.5 × 7 cm (Kermode's 1907 measurements are almost identical). It is broken away at the top, as the truncated inscription shows, and probably at the base too. The runes run upwards and centrally on the face of the slab, without framing lines. (This description is based on the current orientation, which may not be the original.) It is assumed that a representation of a cross in one form or another once occupied a missing

Fig. 42. MM 139 Marown (drawing: Jonas Nordby).

part of the stone, and that is certainly what the surviving text implies. It reads:

þurbiaurn:risti:krus:þ(ã)*[

The length of what remains of the inscription is some 27.5 cm. The lack of framing lines affects the layout and tidiness of the graphs. Rune height varies a good deal; representative values are 50 mm (r. 1 **þ**), 42 mm (r. 6 **a**), 57 mm (r. 15 **k**). Otherwise the characters are firmly and neatly cut, as by an expert rune carver. Some of the verticals continue below their bases in attenuated lines, which suggests there may have been a light setting out before the final cutting. A few graphs show minor damage from weathering. Only a single branch of r. 4 survives for certain, but it is clear enough that it is the upper of an original pair. Its lower fellow appears to be lost through damage, though with the eye of faith it is perhaps possible to trace parts of its outline. Weathering is also observable in rr. 8 and 16, but nowhere near enough to hinder identification. The base of r. 12 is damaged, resulting in uncertainty about whether or not the character is dotted. There are perhaps hints of an indentation, and since the inscription's other example of **s** ends in a clear dot, we assume that to have been the case with r. 12 as well. The tops of rr. 19, 20 are lost. This presents no difficulty in the case of r. 19 for the remains of its bow are clear; but of r. 20 all that survives is part of the vertical and a branch sloping down to the right, placed rather lower than that of r. 9. It is uncertain whether this is a form of **n** or of **ã**, though the combination of shape and context strongly suggests the latter. Rune 21 is only the lower fragment of a vertical, the remainder of the character lost beyond the stone's broken edge. Brate, who had not seen the original, claimed to read **þn(a)** on the basis of a plaster cast in Castle Rushen. Sanness Johnsen has **þa** followed by an uncertain **n**. Word separation is by pairs of triangular-shaped points in vertical line.

Diagnostic rune forms are ᚾ **n**, ᚭ **a**, ᛁ **s**, ᛏ **t**, ᛒ **b**, and perhaps ᚭ **ã**.

Interpretation

There is no serious problem of interpretation. What is left of the inscription says:

> Þorbjǫrn reisti kross þenna...

'Þorbjǫrn put up this cross...'

There is no direct evidence to help us determine whether MM 139 was a memorial cross or not, so the stone's precise purpose cannot be deduced. On the monographic spelling of the root vowel in **risti**, see the interpretations of MM 136 Braddan III and MM 126 Kirk Michael IV.

Earlier scholars sought to make a connection between the Marown carving and the MM 136 Braddan III, MM 135 Braddan IV and MM 132 Kirk Michael V crosses (e.g. Olsen 1954: 220–21), claiming that one and the same rune carver and artist was responsible for all four (no account was, of course, taken of the Kirk Michael V*b* graffito). The identification, artwork aside, is based on two considerations. First, the likelihood that the Þorbjǫrn mentioned on the incomplete Braddan III was proclaiming himself cross maker or rune carver coupled with the fact that, according to early representations (confirmed by an extant cast), he writes his name there exactly as in the Marown inscription; second, the "orthography" of the verb **risti** 'put up', the pronoun **þãnã** 'this', and the preposition **aft** 'in memory of'. Only in this Þorbjǫrn's work, it is maintained, are the forms **risti**, **þãnã** and **aft** found together, though individually **risti** and **aft** may occur in other Manx inscriptions. That, it must be said, is a rather tenuous connection, and as far as Marown goes all we have is **þurbiaurn** and **risti**, neither spelling unusual enough to form the basis of an identification. In other respects the MM 139 slab is quite unlike the MM 136, 135 and 132 crosses. The latter three are highly ornamented, while MM 139 has no visible decoration at all; and it has its inscription placed centrally on a broad face, whereas on MM 136, 135 and 132 the runes run up a narrow edge. Holman suggests that if the identification of MM 139 with MM 136 and 135 is correct "it affords an interesting example of a rune-carver raising his own cross". The implications of this remark are not wholly clear. Patently a certain Þorbjǫrn was involved in the erection of MM 139, but the reasons for his involvement cannot be known unless the relevant missing part of the slab one day comes to light (cf. above).

A "Manx transcription" of the Marown text can only differ in a couple of details from the Old West Norse version given above:

Þorbjǫrn ræisti kross þãnnã...

MM 145 Maughold I
Plates 121–3, Fig. 43

LITERATURE. Marquardt 1961: 71–2. Kermode 1902a: 632–3; Kermode 1907: 213–14; Brate 1907: 77–8; Marstrander 1930b: 385–6; Megaw 1950: 173; Olsen 1954: 202; Sanness Johnsen 1968: 235–6; Page 1983: 141; Page 1992a: 134–7; Holman 1996: 151–2.

MM 145 came to light in 1900 during repairs to Maughold parish church where it seems to have been reused as building stone (Kermode 1902a: 629, 632; 1907: 213). In 1906 a shelter was built in the churchyard to house the crosses associated with the parish (Kermode 1907: 216, fig. 58). MM 145 was moved into it in the same year, and remains there in the right-hand corner affixed to the back wall.

Maughold I is carved on an irregular piece of grey mudstone, broken on all sides, c. 34 cm high × 34.5 broad × c. 4.5 thick (Kermode's 1907 figures are approximately similar). With the artefact tight up against the wall, thickness is hard to measure precisely. This position also partially conceals one of the broad faces: while the top part is visible (with difficulty) the lower is completely hidden. Kermode (1907) noted that this side had a rough (and from his words clearly uncarved) surface. The stone's inscribed face has no decoration, nor indeed any obvious sign of having been dressed. There are two lines of runes, here designated *a* and *b* because of their different content but with the graphs numbered consecutively. Immediately below them as the stone is now oriented are carved the first two groups (*aicmí*) of the ogam alphabet (the *Beith-Luis-Nin*, see McManus 1991) <b l f s n h d t c q>. While there is space before the <b>, <q> occurs at a broken edge, with the implication that the inscription may once have continued. Since ogam normally runs vertically, it may be, on the (uncertain) assumption that one individual

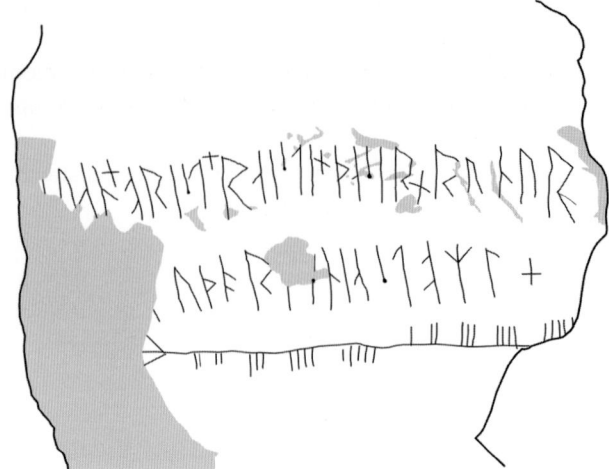

Fig. 43. MM 145 Maughold I (drawing: Jonas Nordby).

was responsible for all the writing on MM 145, that the runes were intended to be displayed rising from base to top (cf. MM 144 Maughold II by the same runic hand, whose inscription may have been planned with this orientation in mind). The runes read:

a

]∗u a n + b r i s t + r a i s t i + þ a s i r + r u n u r

b

]∗u þ ã r ∗ h n i a s t b m l +

The first graph of each text comes at the edge of an area of damage that has removed the surface beyond – in both cases a fragment of a vertical is all that survives. The missing characters, clearly **i** in *a* (cf. below and MM 144 Maughold II) and **f** in *b*, can be supplied from context, but also with reference to the distance to the following graph. Preceding the runes of either or both lines there could once have been a cross. Some have identified the remains of a cross at the broken edge following r. 25 **r**, but we were unable to confirm any carving here. Theoretically, there might have been further writing following on from r. 25 (cf. that the ogam inscription is possibly incomplete), though nothing more is needed for the sense. In the light of the damage at the beginning of each text, line lengths cannot be measured precisely; commencing with the remains of r. 1 and extending to the bow of r. 25 **r**, *a* is *c*. 30.5 cm, and *b*, starting at the remains of r. 26 and including the cross at the end, 22.5. Rune height varies a good deal: r. 9 (**t**) is 2.9 cm, r. 25 (**r**) 4.4; r. 28 (**þ**) is 2.7 cm, r. 38 (**b**) 3.7.

The graphs are roughly and unskilfully carved, without framing lines. The crosses between rr. 4 and 5, 9 and 10 are placed markedly high up, that between rr. 20 and 21 unusually low down. An old abrasion partially distorts the forms of rr. 17–19, but they are certainly read. Of r. 31 only the lower half of a vertical survives. The top half of r. 32 is also damaged, but for the most part discernible, and a clear central dot can be seen, to give ᛡ for **h**.

Diagnostic rune forms are ᚨ **ã**, ᛡ **h**, ᚾ **n**, ᛅ **a**, ᛋ **s**, ᛏ **t**, ᛒ **b**, ᛘ **m**.

Interpretation

The language of line *a* is somewhat distant from Old Norse as we generally encounter it. In normalised Old West Norse it would run:

> *Jóan prestr reisti þessar rúnar.*
>
> 'Jóan the priest ?put up these runes.'

The title **brist** 'priest' lacks the usual nominative *-r* ending, ON *prestr*. It is unlikely the closing **r** of this word is to be sought in the initial **r** of **raisti** (though the practice, where an identical rune is required, of marking the ending of one word and the beginning of the next with a single graph is well documented in runic writing): **brist** and **raisti** are divided by a separation mark, and in Maughold II the same Jóan (cf. below) again employs **brist** as a nominative, notwithstanding the following word there is *í* 'in'.

The verb form **raisti** normally represents the third person singular past tense of *reisa* '[to] put up' '[to] raise'. There is perhaps confusion here between the two past tense forms *reist* (from *rísta*) and *risti* (from *rista*), both meaning 'carved', or possibly Jóan was influenced by the *reisti kross* 'put up (a) cross' of so many Manx runic texts (see below).

The Old Norse word for 'runes' is commonly *rúnar*, although forms can be found with other vowels in the ending. Syntactically, we would assume **runur**, presumably a feminine plural, to be in the accusative (as the object of **raisti**), yet the demonstrative **þasir**, which should agree with it, sports the nominative masculine plural *-ir* ending in place of expected accusative feminine *-ar*.

The word-order is also slightly unusual, *rúnar þessar* being the normal way of writing 'these runes', at least in Viking-Age inscriptions.

Most of the aberrations identified are not without parallel. Nom. *-r*, for example, is lacking in at least four other Manx inscriptions (MM 131 Andreas IIa, MM 101 Kirk Michael II, MM 126 Kirk Michael IV, MM 141 Onchan *e*). And what are presumably monophthongs can have digraphic spellings, as, for example, **ai(f)tir** (MM 106 Ballaugh) for *eptir* 'in memory of', **raiti** (MM 127 Jurby) for presumed *rétti* 'put up' (and cf. the common rendering of /ɔ/ by **au**), though digraphic representations of /i(:)/ (which would make **raisti** a recognisable spelling of *risti*) do not otherwise appear to be documented, in Man or elsewhere. The phrase *reisti rúnar* does occur on U 897, however, where it seems intended to mean 'carved runes'. Parallels to acc. pl. **runur** can be found in the odd medieval inscription: once in the Swedish province of Västergötland (Vg Fv1992;172), once in Närke (Nä 20), while DR 222 from Zealand has **runu** (immediately followed by **ra͡þi** and thus perhaps to be read **runura͡þi** *runur. Raði* '…runes. Let him read…'). Nevertheless: the appearance of so many unexpected forms in a short, everyday sentence, as here in Maughold I, does call for comment. The content of MM 144 Maughold II, in *opinione communis* by the same *Jóan prestr* as Maughold I, shows that that inscription can hardly antedate the mid-twelfth century, and is probably to be placed in the thirteenth (cf. p. 210). Maughold I must thus be of roughly similar age, much later than the bulk of the Manx corpus, conventionally dated to *c.* 925–1020. We may surmise that after some three hundred years of intimate language contact (assuming the Norse settlement in Man to have begun late in the second half of the ninth century) the Scandinavian idiom or idioms of the island had undergone considerable change, which could explain Jóan's unorthodox Old Norse. However, the rune forms he employs are those found on the majority of the Manx crosses. There is no sign in his usage of the developments that had been taking place in runic writing since the end of the tenth century. In Scandinavia we might expect a rune carver working in the late 1100s or the 1200s to write ᛁᚭᛅᚿ or ᛁᚮᛅᚿ **ioan**, ᛒᚱᛁᛋᛏ **brïst**, if not ᛒᚱᛁᛋᛏ **brïst**, ᚱᛅᛁᛋᛏᛁ **ræisti**. The discrepancy between likely date and language on the one hand and rune forms and orthography on the other led Page (1992a: 135–6) to propose that Jóan's purpose in carving his inscriptions was antiquarian, and that he was "a man not well acquainted with runes, and perhaps not even with the Norse language". Certainly Maughold I seems to have no other *raison d'être* than to record the *fuþark* and the fact that Jóan 'carved runes'. If the ogam inscription that follows is also his, which it may be, the impression of a person with an interest in ancient alphabets is strengthened.

Given the uncertain nature of the language, and the possibility that Jóan was "not well acquainted" with Norse, it is difficult to suggest a Manx transcription of line *a*. Adhering to the carver's orthography, we might suggest:

Jóan prest ræisti þassir rúnur.

Line *b* presents an almost complete sixteen-character *fuþark*. The final rune may have been forgotten, or perhaps the carver did not know it. The sixteenth rune is only evidenced once in the surviving Manx corpus, and then in the early to mid-Viking Age form ᛁ (cf. MM 113 Andreas IV). The fifteen graph-types presented are those found on the bulk of the Manx crosses (as in line *a*).

MM 144 Maughold II

Plates 124–30, Fig. 44

LITERATURE. Marquardt 1961: 72–3. Harrison 1890; Kermode 1892: 19, 47; Bugge 1899: 241–2; Kermode 1902b: 193; Kermode 1907: 212–13; Brate 1907: 78–81; Megaw 1950: 173; Olsen 1954: 202–5; Sanness Johnsen 1968: 236–7; Page 1992a: 134–7; Holman 1996: 152–4.

The discovery of MM 144 was reported in early 1890 (Harrison 1890). It was found the year before lying on the bank of a stream at the upper end of the Cornaa valley (Kermode 1907). Local tradition connected the stone with the chapel Keeill Woirrey (Harrison 1890), more than six kilometres from Maughold parish church (NGR SC 433895). Yet its inscription clearly links to MM 145 Maughold I, a warning not to ascribe too much significance either to find place or local traditions. The slab is not a gravestone, and when discovered was being used as a flat surface on which to set down pails and tubs. To begin with it was kept in the Masonic rooms in Ramsey (Kermode 1892: 19). However, in 1906 it was taken into the cross shelter in Maughold churchyard (Kermode 1907: x, 212, 216, fig. 58), where it remains today, fixed to the back wall near the right-hand corner (the south-west side of the shelter). The positioning means that one surface of the slab is hidden, but there is nowhere any suggestion that face bore carvings.

Maughold II is incised into an irregular-shaped, largely unworked piece of mudstone, measuring *c*. 69.5 cm × 29.5 × 5 (almost the exact equivalent of Kermode's 1907 figures). It is not possible to determine which way up the stone was intended to stand, if stand it ever did. The runes may have run

Fig. 44. MM 144 Maughold II (drawing: Jonas Nordby).

vertically, as would be usual for Manx texts (and cf. the large space below the inscription – for fixing the stone in the ground?). However, they could have been placed horizontally across the stone surface (which is how they appear the way the stone is currently oriented), although this is an arrangement not otherwise certainly attested in Man (though cf. MM 175 Maughold V), and distinctly uncommon on raised rune-stones in general. There are two lines of runes, very roughly cut and set out. It is hard to identify clearly some of the incisions, and this must be kept in mind in reading the following trans-runification, transliteration and description. We proceed from the left/upper line to the right/lower (and treat the two as semi-discrete entities, which their content seems to warrant).

+krisþ:malaki:ãkbaþrik:aþanman:
:∗∗nal:sauþar:iuan:brist:ikurnaþal:

Line 1 is 34 cm long, measured from the initial cross to the punctuation mark following r. 26, and runs up/across the face at a point slightly to the left of/above its centre. As well as being crudely cut, the graphs are often affected by striations of the rock face, with the effect that tops or bases are unclear. This makes it hard to give more than a general indication of height: r. 1 **k** is *c*. 5.5–6 cm, r. 12 **ã** is 3. At some distance before the initial cross are three lines; the first two look as if they were deliberately carved and have the appearance of the vertical and branch of the top of **k**. Olsen comments (1954: 203): "A little way to the left of r. 1 there may be seen incised the angle of the ᚴ **k** rune, certainly an ill-fated attempt to begin the inscription there." He could be right, but the carving here is much lighter than in the inscription that follows, and may be a later addition, or, if contemporary, by a different hand. The separators in this line all consist of two dots, but they can be placed high, low or mid-line, and are not always set fully vertically (in relation to the runes). There is an incision ascending from the left to meet the top of r. 5, suggesting the bind t͡þ; it is unusually short for a branch, however, and may well be a carving error. The left branch of r. 6 ᛘ **m** is very weak, and the graph can at first glance resemble ᚴ **k**. Rune 11 has what seems to be a branch descending to its right, giving the appearance of ᚼ; however, this incision is shallower than the vertical and is judged a carving error. The two dots that complete the line are set almost horizontally. Above this punctuation mark is a Y-shaped figure, taken by some as a cross; it does not, however, appear to be deliberately carved.

Line 2 is *c.* 41.5 cm long, measured from the punctuation mark at the beginning to the one at the end, its base running along the right-hand/lower edge of the stone. Rune height varies between 3.5 cm (r. 40 **a**) and 4.5 (r. 36 **a**). The text opens with a triangle of dots. Then follow two "verticals" sloping towards one another but with no prospect of meeting at their tops, so that a reading **u** (as has been given) seems impossible. What these two lines were intended to denote remains unclear: the first could be **i**, and the second conceivably **s** (although the graph is then placed rather lower down than one would expect and lacks the terminating dot of other examples of **s** in this inscription). Runes 29–30 are damaged at their bases but can be identified with considerable certainty. Rune 32 carries the very slight indication of a dot. Between rr. 35 and 36 is a mark reminiscent of the single point used throughout this line as a separator, but it is quite shallow, and there is some surface damage in the area; in the transrunification and transliteration the mark is ignored. Rune 37 is partially obliterated, but **r** is the only possible reading of what remains on the stone. Scattered through these two sequences of runes are faint lines and dots, some of which Olsen suggests may be intended, although they have more the appearance of accidental scratches and marks.

Diagnostic rune forms are ᚬ **ã**, ᚾ **n**, ᛆ **a**, ᛌ **s**, ᛐ **t**, ᛓ **b**, ᛘ **m**.

Interpretation

No satisfactory explanation has been found for the opening of line 2, though it has been the subject of much and varied guesswork (cf., e.g., Olsen 1954: 204; Holman 1996: 153–4). The edited text and translation therefore appear with a lacuna.

Kristr, Malaki ok Patrekr, Adamnán. …sauðar-Jóan prestr í Kvernárdal.

'Christ, Malachy and Patrick, Adamnan. …sheep-Jóan the priest in Kvernárdalr [Cornaa valley].'

What can be understood is simple enough in content. We have four holy names, Christ, Malachy, Patrick and Adamnan. Significant is the second of these, *Malachy*, provided, as seems almost certain, it refers to the Malachy who became Bishop of Armagh in 1132, died in 1148 and was canonised in 1199 (Holweck 1924: *s.n.*), for this would seem to provide a *terminus post quem* for Maughold II, well after the Viking Age and most likely after 1199. Line 2 presents problems: its damaged and hence uncertain opening makes it hard to see whether 'Jóan the priest in Cornaa valley' is linked in any way with the names in line 1. Runes 32–37 are traditionally taken to give *sauðar*, gen. sg. of *sauðr* 'sheep', which would seem to indicate a byname or epithet, 'sheep-Jóan' (cf., with plural first element, *sauða-Gísli* 'sheep-Gísli', *sauða-Ulfr* 'sheep-Ulfr', Lind 1920–21: *s.n.*). That suggests the uncertain point after r. 35 should be ignored, and indeed there seems every reason to do so (cf. above). Marstrander (1932: 142) claims that the *sauðar-* of this inscription "betegner Ión som hyrden over den kristne flokk i Cornadal" 'designates Ión as the shepherd of the Christian flock in Cornadal', but that is a highly debatable assertion. It may be noted that the saga texts in which *sauða-Gísli* and *sauða-Ulfr* appear give no indication that either was a cleric.

As in Maughold I, *prestr* 'priest' lacks its normal nominative *-r* ending. That is also true of *Kristr*. On the other hand, *dalr* 'valley' could in Old Norse have a dative with or without *-i* ending, so **ikurnaþal** 'in Kvernárdalr [dat.]' cannot be said to exhibit aberrant grammar. How far the non-Scandinavian Malachy, Patrick and Adamnan might be expected to sport Norse inflections in late twelfth- or thirteenth-century Man is unclear, but given the lack of *-r* in *prestr* and *Kristr*, it is no surprise that the three saints' names are without obvious grammatical marker.

The spelling of **aþanman** must reflect either confusion or error on the part of a carver trying to render Middle Irish [ˈaðəμnaːn], or metathesis /mn/ > /nm/ in his pronunciation.

The use of **þ** for historical [d] and in **krisþ** for historical archiphoneme /t/-/d/ is striking (**brist** for *prest* provides the only exception to this tendency, unless r. 5 really is to be read t͡þ, with the bind indicating both the traditional and novel spelling). Some have seen in it evidence for the influence of Gaelic pronunciation on Norse (cf. Marstrander 1932: 142–3; Olsen 1954: 204), but **þ** for [d], at least, can be found in Scandinavia, sporadically in the Viking Age, more commonly in the medieval period (cf., e.g., Gs 7 **þrukn**∗**þi** for *drunknaði* 'drowned [3rd sg. past]', U 539 **iklanþs** *Ænglands* 'England [gen. sg.]', and the medieval N 312 **lerþal** 'Lerdal [Sogn]'). What in any particular case might have encouraged a rune carver to use **þ** to denote what was presumably a plosive is unclear; perhaps [d] may on occasion have been conceived as a variant of [ð], whose written representation was **þ** (cf. Fridell 2010; see further p. 77).

Marstrander (1932: 143) identified Gaelic influence not only in the **þ** spelling of **kurnaþal** but also, and more particularly, in the vocalism of the initial syllable (as suggested by the runic rendering). Assuming (almost certainly correctly) that the Norse name of the valley was Kvernárdalr 'Millstream Valley' (if not Kvernar- or Kvernadalr 'Valley of the Mill/Mills'), he argued with some justification that a development *kvern* > *korn* was unlikely in any Scandinavian dialect of the thirteenth century. On the other hand, it could be readily explained with reference to Middle Irish, he affirmed – a language in which the cluster [kw] did not occur.

In contrast to his archaising orthography in Maughold I, Jóan in this inscription makes a concession to modernity, representing the /o/ of *ok* by ᚮ rather than ᚢ (cf. pp. 73–4). In **kurnaþal**, however, assumed /o/ is rendered ᚢ, as commonly in the Manx inscriptions.

A transcription reflecting more closely the language forms possibly familiar to the carver might be:

Krist, Malaki ok Padrig, Aðamnán. ...sauðar-Jóan prest í Kornadal.

MM 133 Maughold III
Plates 131–2, Fig. 45

LITERATURE. Marquardt 1961: 73. Kermode 1884: 151; Jewitt 1884: 109; Kermode 1892: 21, 47; Kermode 1907: 202; Olsen 1954: 205; Holman 1996: 155–6.

There are varying accounts of the discovery of MM 133. According to Kermode (1884) a ticket accompanying the piece stated: "June, 1869. – A fragment of a runic stone found by the Rev W. Stainton Moses, near the Hibernian Hotel, Maughold, in 1868". Jewitt (1884), however, claims the stone was taken from an ancient burial place in Ballagilley (NGR SC 457914) in 1868. Kermode (1907) confirms Jewitt's find place but not his date: MM 133, according to this account, was discovered in 1869 at "Ballagilley [...] the site of an old

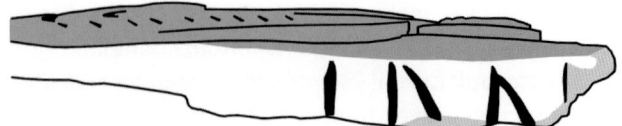

Fig. 45. MM 133 Maughold III (drawing: Jonas Nordby).

Keeil and burial-ground off the high-road to Douglas, about two miles from Ramsey". "1869" might be an error (induced by "June, 1869"? – cf. above) since the two earlier sources agree on 1868, and according to the *Oxford Dictionary of National Biography* (Rigg 1894), Stainton Moses moved from his parish in Maughold to Douglas that year. The references to the Hibernian Hotel and Ballagilley are in fact likely to be to the same place, for Ballagilley is but 300 metres or so from the hotel. Whatever the precise spot, the area where MM 133 was found is some 3–4 kilometres from Maughold churchyard, so it is hazardous to connect it too closely with the church. It is further possible that the attribution to an old keeill and burial-ground site was motivated by the belief that cross slabs generally came from churches, chapels or burial grounds. Page (1980: 193) suggests the stone could be "simply a roadside cross, for Ballagilley stands on one of the roads from Ramsey to Laxey". MM 133 was placed "in the museum at Castle Rushen" (Kermode 1907), but was at some point moved into the cross shelter erected in Maughold churchyard in 1906, where it currently resides, fixed to the right wall (close to the inner corner).

The fragment consists of a tiny, irregular piece of grey mudstone, laminated so that only one face remains, together with part of a narrow edge. Measurements must therefore be imprecise: *c.* 18.5 cm × 16 × 2.5 (height and breadth given in Kermode 1907 are both slightly greater). The surviving face has the head of a boar carved in relief, while the edge has the remnant of a runic inscription. No rune can be certainly identified, however. We read:

* * * (*) [
1   4

The remains of the graphs are *c.* 1.5–1.8 cm high. They comprise the top of a vertical and two further tops suggestive of ᚢ **u** or ᚱ **r** (theoretically possible is also ᛒ **b**); r. 3 has, however, a somewhat straighter branch, which could just indicate ᛁ **l**. The break thereafter may coincide with the top of a further vertical, but that is very uncertain. Before r. 1 there is 5 cm of uncarved surface, suggesting that the preserved fragments represent the start of a word or even of the inscription. If r. 1 were **i**, r. 2 **u** and r. 3 **r**, they could give *Jór-*, the first element of several personal names (cf., e.g., Peterson 2007: *s.n.*). Clearly no transrunification or persuasive interpretation can be offered, and this fragment is mainly of importance as supplying another find spot for a rune-stone (and decorated stone), albeit a slightly uncertain one. The carving is deep and well executed, and the piece may indeed once have formed part of a "large and handsome monument", as Olsen remarks.

MM 142 Maughold IV*a–f*
Plates 133–43, Figs 46–51

LITERATURE. Marquardt 1961: 73. Kermode 1916: 55–62; Kermode 1925; Olsen 1954: 205–8; Page 1981: 133–4; Page 1983: 137, 141; Holman 1996: 156–9.

MM 142 was discovered (in 1913 according to Kermode, cf. Meeting 1913) "when excavating at the north keeill in Maughold Churchyard" (Kermode 1916: 55). There, according to this scholar's later, more detailed, account (1925: 333):

> a lintel grave was found, at the east end of which was an upright slab, buried beneath the rubbish of the ruined walls [of the keill …] This was broken at both ends, and some modern cuts and scribblings on it showed that it had been previously disturbed.

Kermode's wording here and elsewhere (e.g. 1916: 55–6) makes clear the slab was not in its original position when found. It was subsequently placed within the purpose-built cross shelter in Maughold churchyard, set in concrete on a stone pillar at the right-hand end of the building.

The Maughold IV inscriptions are carved on a piece of light grey mudstone, measuring 69 cm (visible height) × 30.5 × 9. Kermode (1916: 56) gives the height as "about 30 inches" (= 76 cm). Each face has the remains of a sculptured cross, its shaft decorated with a step pattern. There are a good many runic sequences (as the lettering *a–f* makes clear), a number of them clearly not part of the original plan. What from the bold outline of its runes and the sense of its message appears to be the principal text is found on both faces (here referred to as A and B for convenience) spread across three different locations. These we designate Maughold IV*a* 1, 2 and 3.

Inscription *a* 1 runs upwards on face A, the bases of the runes set along the left side of the shaft of its cross. There is no upper framing line. Inscription *a* 2 is a fragment only, a line of three graphs running up the right edge of the same face, tops inward, above the incised figure of what has been described as "a rather elaborate medieval ship" (Wilson 1970–71: 15; but cf. p. 47 in this volume). On face B inscription *a* 3 runs upwards to the right of its cross shaft, tops touching the shaft but with no lower framing line.

On face A we find further texts, designated (based on their placement and beginning with the lowest) Maughold IV*b–e*. Inscription *b* is set quite far down, close to the right edge of the face; its runes run upwards, bases outwards. Inscription *c* is placed slightly higher, to the right of the cross shaft; it too runs upwards, tops approaching the border of the shaft. Inscription *d* begins yet higher up, but still on the lower part of the face; it is situated about half-way between the cross shaft and the edge of the stone and also runs upwards, bases outwards. Inscription *e* is placed within the carving of the ship, to the left of its mast, and runs upwards like the others. Maughold IV*f* is to be found on face B; it runs upwards, squeezed in between the (patently) earlier inscription Maughold IV*a* 3 and the edge, the tops of its runes sometimes colliding with the former. Face A has various designs and scratches over and above those mentioned here, but none approximate closely enough to runes to qualify for inclusion in this account. Maughold IV thus consists of eight separate pieces of runic writing, which read as follows:

On face A:

a 1

hiþin : siti : krus : þinã : aftir : tutur : sinã [

a 2

li (f) [

On face B:

a 3

arni : risti : runar : þisar (×)

On face A again:

b

```
 1       5
ᛚᚨᚾᛁᛦ
```

l a n i r
1   5

c

```
     1     5
... * * * þ * * * ...

... * * * þ * * * ...
     1     5
```

d

```
1       5
ᛁᛁᚴᚢᚦᛦ
```

s i k u þ r
1   5

e

```
1       5
ᛚᛁᚠᛁᛚᛏ
```

l i f i l t
1   5

On face B again:

f

```
 1        5         10        15        20  23
ᛅᚱ*ᛁ(:)ᚱᛁ'ᛏᛁ:ᚱᚢᚾᛅᚱᚢᚾᛅᚱ(ᚦᛁ)ᛁᛅᚱ
```

a r * i (:) r i s t i : r u n a r u n a r (þ i) s a r
1   5   10   15   20 23

Inscription *a* 1 is 37.5 cm long (measured from the outer branches of r. 1), and rune heights vary from 2.5 cm (r. 11 **r**) to 3.5 cm (r. 22 **r**). The graphs, several of which are double-cut, seem to have been made with quite a sharp tool. Before r. 1 is a fairly wide space that could have held runes or an opening cross, but there are no signs of any. Rune 18, **a**, has previously been read as **i** but clearly has a rising branch on the left side. Rune 30 can appear to have a branch on

Fig. 46. MM 142 Maughold IVa 1 (drawing: Jonas Nordby).

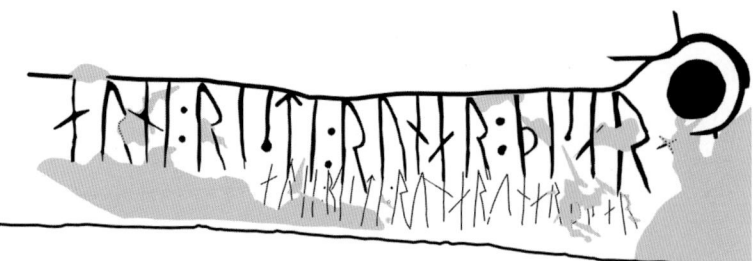

Fig. 47. MM 142 Maughold IVa 2 (drawing: Jonas Nordby).

Fig. 48. MM 142 Maughold IVa 3 and IVf (drawing: Jonas Nordby).

Fig. 49. MM 142 Maughold IVb (drawing: Jonas Nordby).

Fig. 50. MM 142 Maughold IVc and IVd (drawing: Jonas Nordby).

Fig. 51. MM 142 Maughold IVe (drawing: Jonas Nordby).

the right side only, but careful examination shows that it almost certainly crosses the vertical. The final rune, 31, runs into the broken top of the slab. The three verticals of inscription *a* 2 occupy 2.6 cm, and r. 1, **l**, is 3.4 cm tall. Of r. 3 only the top of a vertical remains wholly intact, although the left side of its line may be traced right down to the base. From the point where the fully preserved part of this graph starts, the beginning of an ascending right branch can just be discerned, conceivably the upper branch of **f**. Inscription *a* 3 is *c.* 32 cm in length. Its graphs vary somewhat in height, in general becoming a little smaller from r. 11 onwards: r. 8, **t**, is 4.3 cm high, r. 14, **r**, 4.0 cm. There is space before r. 1 for some sort of opening symbol, but no sign of one. The line appears to end with a saltire cross, but it is hard to disentangle runic carving, ornament and breakage here. Runes 3 and 16 have sustained damage to their middle section, but the readings **t**, **l** seem reasonably well assured.

Inscription *b* is 4.5 cm long, its runes *c.* 25–30 mm high. The graphs are very lightly scratched into the surface, and not easy to distinguish in all particulars from the casual gashes and pitting that mark the stone in this area. The reading seems secure, however. Rune 1 leans to the left and is rather shorter than the following graphs. Runes 4–5 are shallower than those that precede them.

The "runes" of inscription *c* are weaker than those of *b*. What are here designated rr. 1–7 measure 2 cm in length; r. 4, **þ**, is 4 mm wide and 2.4 cm high.

After some obscure incisions (that may or may not be part of the carving) the sequence identified here begins with three vertical lines, the first quite short, the second broken. The fourth graph is a quite clear þ (the reason for deeming this a runic inscription). There follow three verticals, the second and third curving to the right at their bases. Beyond can be seen a small gap, a much shorter vertical line (though part of it may well have been lost through damage), another, rather larger, gap, and then a small nick at vertical-top height and what might be the tops of two further verticals (the surface of the stone below has flaked off). Possibly the writing continued even farther, but anything that might once have been inscribed in this area is now so faint and uncertain one cannot be sure.

Inscription *d* – it too lightly scratched – is much more legible, and more clearly runic, than *c*. It nevertheless has a very informal appearance. It is 3.3 cm in length and runes vary in height from 2 cm (r. 2 **i**) to 3.2 (r. 6 **r**). There is no doubt about the reading and no indication the carver wrote more than the six graphs that can now be seen.

The runes of inscription *e* are somewhat bolder than those of *b–d*, but small and cramped. Just as *b–d* they look like a casual graffito, complete in itself. Length is 2.3 cm. Rune 1, **l**, is 1.2 cm tall, and r. 6, **t**, 2.1.

Inscription *f* is lightly incised. It is 14.9 cm in length, and the runes vary in height from 2.1 cm (r. 1 **a**) to 2.8 (r. 14 **r**). It was clearly added some time after the carving of the cross and the main inscription since its graphs have, to the best of the writer's ability, been fitted in between the runes above and the edge of the stone. For all that, the carving does not look very recent. It is perhaps worth mentioning that indications of it appear, albeit dimly, on Kermode's earliest drawing of the slab (1916: 57), a fact Page (1992a: 136) denies. A little way before r. 1 a short vertical line can be seen, reminiscent of ¹, but it appears unconnected with the inscription. Rune 2 clearly represents the graph-type ᚱ; it seems the carver, whose intention was surely to copy inscription *a* 3 (see below), was misled as to the shape of the graph by damage to r. 2 of the earlier text. Some have managed to detect a branch on r. 3, descending as of ᛏ or rising (perhaps the upper branch of ᚴ), but neither postulate can be confirmed. As with r. 2, it may be that the carver was slavishly following what he thought to see in inscription *a* 3 (where damage has all but obliterated the crossing branch of r. 3 ᛏ). However, it is worth noting that inscription *f*'s r. 7 – ¹ – contrasts with *a* 3's r. 7 – a clear ᛁ. Following r. 4 there seem to be two dots in vertical line; if intentional these must constitute a separator. Rune 5 is met at the point where bow and tail connect by an oblique gash descending from inscription *a* 3 above – possibly an overcut from *a* 3. The left side of r. 12's branch has an extensive overcut that runs through the preceding ᚾ. Runes 19 and 20 have suffered considerable damage, but what remains is suggestive of **þi**.

Diagnostic rune forms are *a* 1: ᚦ ã, ✱ h, ᛏ n, ᚭ a, ᛌ s, ᛐ t, ᛐ ï; *a* 3: ᛏ n, ᛏ a, ᛌ s, ᛐ t; *b*: ᛏ n, ᚭ a; *d*: ᛌ s; *e*: ᛐ t; *f*: ᚱ r, ᛏ n, ᛏ a, ' and ᛌ s, ᛐ t.

Interpretation

As it stands, inscription *a* 1 presents no difficulties of interpretation. It states: *Heðinn setti kross þenna eptir dóttur sína* 'Heðinn placed this cross in memory of his daughter.' However, the relationship between *a* 1 and *a* 2 is uncertain. It could be that *a* 2 represents what is left of some sort of completion of *a* 1. It would be natural to name the daughter, and while this word may of course have been lost from *a* 1 when the top of the stone was broken off, it is also possible, as Kermode (1925: 335) suggests, that "an arm of the cross came in the way" so that *a* 1's "last word [...] was cut parallel to it at the other side of the shaft". If he is right *a* 2 provides the opening of that name, its conclusion missing but perhaps to be supplied from text *e*, an apparent graffito that possibly copies or gives the name. Inscription *a* 3 fits in easily as the signature of the monument's rune carver (though whether in fact inscribed by the same hand as *a* 1 cannot be said for sure). In the light of all this, we can suggest for *a* 2 and *e* (combining them): *Hlífhildi* 'Hlífhildr', and, more readily, for *a* 3: *Arni risti rúnar þessar* 'Arni carved these runes'. Together with *a* 1 that gives a possible complete text:

> *Heðinn setti kross þenna eptir dóttur sína Hlífhildi. Arni risti rúnar þessar.*
>
> 'Heðinn placed this cross in memory of his daughter Hlífhildr. Arni carved these runes.'

It should be noted that a name *Hlífhildr* is otherwise unknown, though both of its elements are met with in a variety of names (cf. Peterson 2003: 583–7). If the above interpretation is correct, **lifilt** has lost its accusative case marker. Loss of case endings is a feature of certain of the Manx inscriptions (p. 83), but sporadic instances can also be found in Viking-Age and early medieval Scandinavia (cf., of particular relevance here, acc. **kunilt** *Gunnhild* in DR 394). It is of course far from certain that Maughold IV*e*'s **lifilt** forms the completion of Maughold IV*a* 1, or even if it does, that the carver would have been grammatically aware enough to put it in the accusative. S/he may simply have wanted to record the name in its basic form (devoid of inflectional ending).

Inscription *b* appears to consist of a single word. Judging by the two other casual single-word texts that can be clearly recognised on this stone, we could be dealing with a personal name (one of the most popular types of runic graffito). Certainly, no other option readily suggests itself. If we reckon with loss of /h/ before /l/ (as evidenced by **lifilt** in inscription *e*), and that **a** may represent [e] or [æ] (as, for example, in **aftir**, found in several Manx inscriptions including Maughold IV*a* 1), we might have a name *_Hlennir_, related to Old Norse *Hlenni* (Lind 1905–15: *s.n*). The postulated variant in *-ir* need not trouble us; quite a few Old Norse personal names alternate between the *-i* and *-ir* paradigm (cf. *Vm*: 74–5).

Too little of inscription *c* can be made out for any interpretation to be hazarded.

More assuredly than *b*, inscription *d* gives a personal name. Olsen (1954: 207) suggests *Sigurðr* or *Sigrøðr*, but the loss of medial /r/ is remarkable, unless **r** has been omitted in error (though as a parallel, cf. B640 **siguþrr**, from *c.* 1170). An alternative might be female *Sigunnr* or *Siggunnr* (cf. gen. **shunar** *Sigunnar* in U 503), with the common development [n:r] > [ðr].

Inscription *f* is almost certainly an attempt to copy *a* 3 (cf. above). It does not reproduce *a* 3 exactly, though. In place of **runar:þisar** 'these runes' we have the repetitious **runarunar** 'runes runes' followed, apparently, by **þisar**. Theoretically **runarunar** could conceal *rúnar Unar/Unnar* 'Unr's/Unnr's runes', with the sequence **unar** giving the genitive of either the (postulated) male name *Unr* or the female *Unnr* (Lind 1905–15: *s.n. Uni, Unnr*; Peterson 2007: *s.n. Unn, Unnr*). However, it is hard to find runic parallels to such a statement, and one wonders what situation might have given rise to it. Further: if the final word of this inscription is indeed **þisar** 'these', **runarunar** can hardly have been intended as 'Unr's/Unnr's runes'.

Though all these texts are simple enough in themselves, some (*a* 1 and 3 in particular) contain features worthy of comment. The use of the verb *setja* to describe the putting up of a memorial stone is not documented elsewhere on Man, where *reisa* is the usual word. However, *sætia* is common enough in Danish and Swedish memorial texts (Palm 1992: 206), and is occasional in Norway. Kermode (1925: 335–6) moots the possibility of influence from English usage, where in a few inscriptions (Great Urswick, Thornhill I and II; Page 1999: 149–52) *settan* occurs.

The weak past form *risti* 'carved' (inf. *rista*), encountered in Maughold IV*a* 3 and *f*, contrasts with strong *reist* (inf. *rísta*) in MM 107 German I (St John's) *a* and MM 141 Onchan *e*. The weak variant is rare in Norway and Denmark until the thirteenth century, but becomes common in Sweden from the eleventh onwards.

Certain graph-types occurring in some of the Maughold IV inscriptions differ from those found in the bulk of the Manx corpus. We have ✳ **h**, ✝ **n**, ✝ **a**, ↑ **t**, so-called "long-branch" variants, whereas generally rune carvers on the island seem to have opted for "short-twig" ⊦ **h**, ⊦ **n**, ⊦ **a**, ↑ **t** (and indeed ⊦ appears in Maughold IV*a* 1 side-by-side with long-branch types, while ⊦ and ⊦ are the sole diagnostic forms in *b*). The writer of inscription *a* 1 also uses ⊦ **ï**, otherwise attested in Man only in MM 140 German II (Peel), MM 130 Kirk Michael III and MM 141 Onchan *e*. On the other hand several of the Maughold IV texts exhibit short-twig ׀ or ׀ for **s**, as against Kirk Michael III's long-branch ℅ (a graph-type not encountered at all on MM 142).

It is hard to draw conclusions from these scraps of evidence. If Maughold IV*a* is from the early eleventh century, as many have supposed (e.g. Olsen 1954: 208), it might be argued that the appearance of *setti* and *risti* in company with long-branch graph-types points towards East Scandinavian tradition. However, use of *setja* to describe the putting up of a runic memorial is not unknown in Norway, nor even the employment of weak *rista* to signify the carving of runes, while inscriptions with a mixture of long-branch and short-twig forms are well attested both in Norway (cf., e.g., N 68), and the British Isles (e.g. IR 11, SC 14, 15). Page (1983: 137) describes the Maughold IV*a* inscriptions as "exotic in the Manx setting, suggesting perhaps Danish influence", though noting in the monument as a whole "a mixture of tradition and innovation". The graph-types, not least ⊦ **ï**, represent a break with tradition as represented by the bulk of the extant Manx corpus (pp. 68–70), but the use of the term *kross* to refer to the monument and the layout of the memorial text are firmly within the mainstream.

Maughold IV*b–f* could be from a somewhat or considerably later date than the main text. All of them look like additions, but it is impossible to tell when they might have been added. They display no features that could help in dating or provide any other determination of origin, unless it be the retained nom. sg. *-r* in the personal name **sikuþr** of inscription *d*. Since this ending is occasionally lost even in Viking-Age inscriptions on Man (p. 83), its retention might imply that **sikuþr**'s contribution to Maughold IV was made during or not long after the period in which Norse was a common language in the island. But there are many imponderables here; **sikuþr** might have had antiquarian interests and the knowledge to employ an inflectional ending that by his time had become archaic. According to what Page (1980: 191) calls "Kermode's slightly confused account" of the excavation of MM 142, it appears its use as a gravestone is likely to have been secondary: "Evidently it had been moved before, as it was broken at both ends and bore on each face cuts and scribblings which appear to be comparatively recent" (Kermode 1916: 55–6). The cross may thus originally have been free-standing, and the "cuts and scribblings", if these are to be equated with Maughold IV*b–f*, added at almost any time before the 1913 discovery. Uncertainties about linguistic affiliation and date(s) make attempts to give a Manx transcription of the texts a hazardous undertaking. With considerable reservation we suggest:

a 1–3 + e Heðinn sætti kross þennā æftir dóttur sínā, Lífild. Arni risti rúnār þessar.

b Lænnir.

d ?Sigurðr/?Sigrøðr/?Siguðr/?Sigguðr.

f Arni risti rúnar rúnar þessar.

MM 175 Maughold V

Plates 144–51, Fig. 52

LITERATURE. Cubbon 1966a: 23–6; Sanness Johnsen 1968: 238–9; Holman 1996: 159–61.

MM 175 was found in 1965 (Cubbon 1966a: 23). It had been reused as a floor slab in a cottage in Maughold village, but was "believed" (Cubbon 1966a: 24) to have been taken about sixty years earlier from Port Mooar beach or nearby, a kilometre or so south-west of Maughold parish church. The owner of the cottage had removed a number of slabs prior to putting in a new cement floor, and they were stacked in Maughold churchyard, where the vicar noticed that one of them bore faint scratches which he recognised as runes. The stone is now in the keeping of the Manx Museum, but a replica has for long stood in the churchyard cross shelter (p. 203; this replica had been removed when we visited in April 2015 and had not been replaced by September 2016).

Maughold V is carved on a roughly rectangular piece of thin bedded sandstone-mudstone, measuring 96 cm × 43 × 6.5. There are two lines of runes, and as the stone is portrayed by Cubbon and Sanness Johnsen these run horizontally across the face, near the top. This is perhaps how the inscription was designed to be read, for if the stone were oriented so that the runes ran vertically, some of them would be close to or in the ground (see further under *Interpretation* below). There are no framing lines, nor any decoration. The text reads:

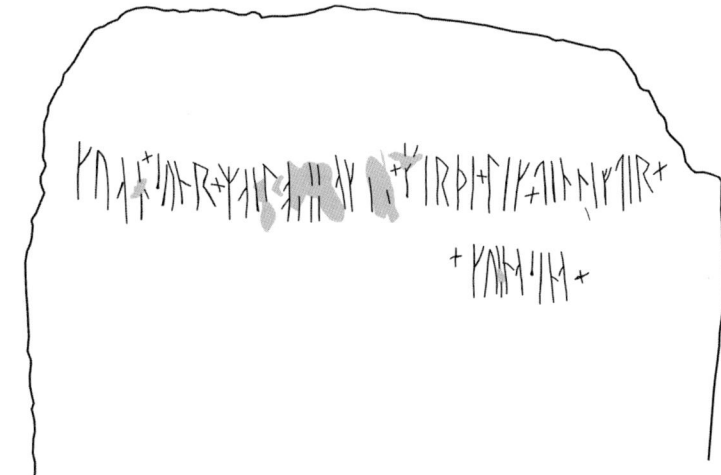

Fig. 52. MM 175 Maughold V (drawing: Jonas Nordby).

k u a n + s u n r + m a i l b ✳ ✳ ✳ a k ✳ ✳ + k i r þ i + l i k + t i n n i f t i r + |
+ k u i n a s i n a +

The runes consist of slim incisions, and differ considerably in size. For instance, r. 1, **k**, is 4 cm tall, while r. 6, **u**, is 2.8 cm. Both lines undulate slightly. The upper one occupies almost the full width of the surface and measures 35.3 cm across. Flaking has obscured a few graphs. Rune 14 is lost above the base of its vertical, and the middle parts of rr. 15, 16 are gone; of r. 19 only the lower half of the vertical remains and of r. 20 just the base. There are no remnants of branches or other distinguishing features on any of these characters. Runes 15 and 16 stand quite close together, while between rr. 16 and 17 is a space that looks larger than to be expected; the surface to the immediate right of r. 16 is cracked and uneven, and the carver may have decided to bypass it. Rune 13 could in theory be a graph-type of **ã**, but there is every reason to take it as **b**: historical [ã(:)] is not distinguished from [a(:)] otherwise in this inscription, and on the overwhelming majority of the Manx stones where it occurs ᛔ denotes [b] or [ß]. Rune 32 has by almost all been read as **n**, and that is certainly correct. Page (manuscript) noted that the branch of this rune was somewhat deeper than its vertical: he thought there might be accidental damage here, causing what had been intended as **i** to look like **n**. However, the groove in question bears all the marks of having been deliberately cut. The lower line of writing, which begins under r. 24, is 8.3 cm long (including the crosses at both ends), and though some incisions are faint, there is no doubt about the reading.

Diagnostic rune forms are ᛅ **n**, ᚭ **a**, ᛁ **s**, ᛏ **t**, ᛒ **b**, ᛘ **m**.

Interpretation

This inscription is clearly some kind of memorial, as the words **iftir+| +kuinasina** 'in memory of his wife' confirm. Much about it is obscure, however. The unreadable runes mean we cannot easily determine the name or names of the maker's parent (beyond the first element **mail-**). The sequence **lik+tinn**, though legible, has also proved hard to interpret. Only a partial attempt at a normalised text can therefore be made:

Kúan sonr Mel-…gerði…eptir kvinnu sína.

'Cúán son of Máel-…made…in memory of his wife.'

Cubbon, who based his interpretation on advice from Aslak Liestøl, is non-committal about the continuation of *Mel-*, though he does offer Liestøl's view that "after the father's name there would seem to be room for a short surname or nickname" (1966a: 24). Given the occurrence of **mail:brikti** in MM 101 Kirk Michael II and **malbriþa** on SC 2 the Hunterston brooch (cf. also *Melbrigda, Melbrikta, Melbrigbason*, etc. in *Orkneyinga saga*, Nordal 1913–16: 6–8, 161, 168–9), it is tempting to try to find a sequence reminiscent of **brikti/briþa** in some or all of rr. 13–20. The required characters are hard to square with what remains of this part of the inscription, however, even if we allow for the presence of "a short surname or nickname". Of names with first element *Máel-* and second beginning *b-* or *p- Máel-bennachtan*, or the variant *Máel-bennachtai*, 'devotee of grace' and *Máel-Pátraic* (all male) come closest (O'Brien 1962: 685, 692; 1973: 229). However, no likely Norse spellings of these compounds seem to accord entirely with what can now be seen. Runes 13–20 could just about have been **bainakti** or **bianakti**, and the former, at least, might have been a way of rendering *-bennachtai* (with digraphic spelling of [e] as in a number of Norse words in the Manx inscriptions, cf. p. 73), but this is an interpretation dependent on several assumptions.

Cubbon accepts, though in part misunderstands, Liestøl's attempt to explain **lik+tinn**. In a letter to Cubbon dated 23 vi 1965 (copy preserved in the Runic Archives, Oslo), Liestøl suggests it is a rendering of *leg þann* 'that grave' (or *leg þenna* 'this grave', which of the two is not entirely clear), with "hardening" of initial /θ/ in *þenna* to /t/, and the pronoun given masculine gender even though historically *leg* is a neuter noun. If the pronoun is indeed *þenna* 'this' (in the form *tenna*), then in addition r. 33 has to be read twice (and stand for /a/ – Cubbon, 1966a: 25, identifies on it a "light side-stroke"). The practice of using a single graph for the final sound of one word and the initial sound of the next (where both could be denoted by the same rune) is not certainly documented in Man (though cf. the graffito Maughold IV*f*). Moreover, it is associated particularly with Viking-Age inscriptions, and the notion that Maughold V is from the Viking Age sits ill with the spelling **nn** in putative *þann* or *þenna*: the doubling of consonant runes to mark length is by and large a medieval phenomenon in Scandinavia, usually ascribed to the influence of roman-alphabet writing. Cubbon translates the phrase 'this gravestone' (1966a: 24), although in his letter Liestøl explicitly states that *leg* means 'grave' 'tomb' "and the stone bearing this inscription would have been called legsteinn". Page (1983: 146) adds the consideration that a *leg* 'grave' "would not be in memory of anyone, rather it would contain someone". Holman wonders whether perhaps "**lik + tinn** may […] represent *legsteinn*, with the s-rune omitted, although this word is not found in other runic inscriptions" (1996: 160). She ignores the additional difficulty that the runic sequence would in fact have to represent acc. *legstein* (the object of *gerði*) notwithstanding the geminate **nn** suggests *-steinn*, the nominative form. However, given the problems thrown up by the interpretation *leg tenna* (or whatever), *legstein* (with **i** for /æi/ as **risti** for presumed /ræisti/ in, e.g., MM 135 Braddan IV or MM 126 Kirk Michael IV, **þurlibr** for presumed *Þorleifr* in Braddan IV) may be thought preferable, though it is in truth no more than an educated guess. An alternative guess (if one can accept the spelling **nn** for /n/) is that **lik+tinn** renders *líkstein* 'corpse stone' 'gravestone' (cf. Page 1998: 21). The word is not certainly documented, but is a plausible Scandinavian compound and has been thought to occur in the medieval G 65 where we find **giarþi:*ualis(t)ana** '?*gærði* [*t*]*va likstæina* '?made two gravestones'; cf. also the sequence in Ög 49 (likewise medieval) **iste(n)nlikaka** – interpreted, perhaps fancifully (and certainly with unusual word-order), *i stæin lik a ga[nga]* 'into the stone the corpse has to go'. The problem of the missing **s** remains, however (*steinn/stæinn* is one of the commonest words in Scandinavian runic texts, but in only a few cases does the word appear without its initial consonant). Just possibly – something of a long shot – **lik+tinn** gives *líktein 'corpse monument' (with second element as in *jartein* < *jarteikn* 'sign' 'proof' 'miracle'; cf. Peterson 1992: 92–3), in imitation of Anglo-Saxon *licbecun* with that meaning (as on the Crowle stone; Page 1999: 142).

Several scholars have drawn attention to the occurrence of **kuina**, which seems to be nominative, where we expect *kvinnu*, accusative, governed by the preposition *eptir*. Given the deviations from the grammatical norm found in several of the Manx inscriptions (cf. p. 83), the Maughold V form should occasion no great surprise. Nevertheless, Cubbon (1996a: 25) takes the "breakdown of both the cases and genders of the Old Norse language", together with other features of the carving (crosses as separation symbols, "scratched" rather than deeply carved runes, the absence of decoration), as evidence that the monument was made late, perhaps in the twelfth century "when the practice of erecting carved crosses on graves was passing out of fashion". He does, though, also entertain the idea that the general appearance of the stone might be because "Kuan simply could not afford to pay a sculptor to carve a handsome cross, or a rune master to cut an inscription for him".

There is really not much to go on that would help date Maughold V. The use of the verb *gera* 'make' to describe the production of a memorial occurs in both the Viking and Middle Ages. Had the stone been carved late, one might perhaps have expected to see one or more dotted runes (cf. pp. 58–9), though these are rarely used consistently in the early medieval period. *If* rr. 26–32/33 are to be interpreted *líkstein*, **líktein*, *leg þann*, or *leg þenna* (cf. above), there is evidence of what one would think to be post-Viking Age orthographical and linguistic developments (the geminate **nn**, [θ] > [t]), but these are highly uncertain postulates. And the word *líkstein*, were it accepted, would seem to belong in a medieval context. All one can say for sure is that MM 175 is a very different object from the raised crosses that carry most of the Manx runic inscriptions. It is unclear even whether the stone was designed to be raised up or laid on the ground. In the former case the text would almost certainly have been presented horizontally (cf. above), which in itself is most unusual, though perhaps replicated on Maughold I and II, both of which seem to be medieval products. This possible point of similarity, plus the fact that the separators in all three inscriptions are placed at wildly different heights, might tempt one to wonder whether the *Jóan prestr* who carved Maughold I and II could also have been responsible for Maughold V, but that is of course speculative in the extreme.

The "maker" of the monument, and his father (or mother), both bear Irish names. The sequence **kuan** renders *Cúán*, diminutive of *Cú* 'wolf' 'hound', a common personal name element (O'Brien 1973: 228). Although we do not have the name of Cúán's parent in full, its first element was clearly *Máel-* 'devotee', as in MM 101 Kirk Michael II **mail:brikti** and MM 130 Kirk Michael III **mal:lümkun, mal:murü** (cf. above). The commemorated wife's name is not mentioned, so we do not know whether it was Irish or Norse.

A Manx transcription of the text cannot differ greatly from the Old West Norse version given above:

Kúan sonr Mel-…gærði…æftir kvinna sína.

MM 141 Onchan *a–g*
Plates 152–9, Figs 53–7

LITERATURE. Marquardt 1961: 67–8. Kinnebrook 1841: 13 and fig. 19; Munch 1850: 279–80; Cumming 1857: 32–3 and fig. 26; Cumming 1868a: facing 23, no. 7, and 28–9; Vigfusson and Savage 1887: 16–18; Kermode 1892: 13, 43–4; Bugge 1899: 236–8; Kermode 1907: 209–12; Brate 1907: 30–32; Olsen 1954: 194–9; Sanness Johnsen 1968: 232–3; Page 1983: 141; Holman: 1996: 161–5.

Kinnebrook was the first to record the Onchan cross, one of two "in Mrs. Quane's garden in the village of Onchan". According to him it was already in a condition where the runes were hard to make out, and he depicted only one face of the stone (that bearing inscriptions *a–d*, see below). When Cumming came to report the cross (1857) it was still "in a garden at Kirk Conchan". He showed both faces, and the inscriptions "which are badly cut and spelt, and much worn". There are a number of similar references to the stone in nineteenth-century accounts, not all of them convincing as first-hand reports; but there is a general consensus that it remained outside, somewhere in Onchan, until 1892 when it was brought into the church (Kermode 1907: 209). It is now fixed to the west wall, to the left of the main entrance as you enter the building, and only the face carrying inscriptions *a–d* is visible. There is, however, an actual size photograph of the hidden face next to the stone; and the Manx Museum preserves a cast. Brate, Olsen and Holman all note that they were unable to examine this side of the monument. Nor, in the end, were we, since it was clear that removal from its mount risked damaging the artefact.

The Onchan inscriptions are carved on a slab of thin bedded sandstone-mudstone, measuring *c.* 111 cm × 48 × 5.5; the base and parts of the top are broken away, so only approximate measurements are possible (Kermode's

1907 figures do not differ greatly, though he gives the height as forty-five inches = 114 cm). Each face has an incised shafted cross with circled head; the shaft of the cross on the surface currently visible is considerably longer than that of its hidden counterpart. The inscriptions are scattered over both faces, and it is not obvious in what order they are to be taken, or how far different sequences of runes are to be linked together. Ordering and numbering must thus necessarily be somewhat arbitrary.

The visible face with the longer shaft has to the left of it and below the cross arm what appears to be a memorial inscription. It is set vertically and is carved *boustrophedon*: in the first line the tops of the runes, which run upwards, point towards the edge of the stone, in the second, which moves downwards, they touch the shaft of the cross; a single incised line divides the two. This is here taken as the main text and designated Onchan *a*. On the same face, running upwards along the right edge of the shaft, rune-tops touching it, is an inscription that may form a pendant to Onchan *a* insofar as it seems to offer a comment on what is presumably the earlier text. This is designated Onchan *b*. To the right of Onchan *b* and parallel with its lower part, also apparently running upwards, are four more runes or rune-like symbols that appear to comprise an independent inscription: Onchan *c*. A few further, faint, runes, observed by Jonas Nordby during examination on 24th March 2014, are located in the bottom left-hand corner of the cross shaft, close to the current (broken) edge of the slab: Onchan *d*. These characters run downwards, bases towards the edge. Since this inscription does not appear to have been noticed previously, the possibility exists that it is of recent origin. The earliest photograph clear and detailed enough to show it is from 1972. Overall, though, the incisions have a quite worn appearance (see below), which is suggestive of age (the text is also medieval in character, cf. under *Interpretation*).

The face with the shorter shaft – now turned towards the wall and unavailable for inspection (but see Plates 153, 154, the former reproduced from an early photograph, ref. MNH PG/14708 - MC141B) – bears two, quite possibly three, perhaps even four, inscriptions. Beginning left of the foot of the cross is the lowest (one or two) of them. The runes run downwards, bases towards the slab edge, and approach the bottom of the stone (as it now exists). There is a sequence of five runes divided from a further sequence of ten by a large gap. Sense-wise the two appear to belong together and they are accordingly designated Onchan *e*. Incised into the top of the shaft, moving down its left edge, bases outwards, is yet another sequence of runes: Onchan *f*. Running up from there, above the shaft, are three more runes, bases inwards. These may, or may not, belong with Onchan *f*, but since there are no compelling reasons to think the two connected, the inscription is treated as independent and designated Onchan *g*. Previous accounts of the Onchan inscriptions have read them in different order and numbered them differently. For comparison, Olsen's (1954) and Page's (1983) numbering is here set out: Onchan *a* = Olsen A and B, Page 1; Onchan *b* = Olsen C, Page 5; Onchan *c* = Olsen D, Page 6; Onchan *e* = Olsen G, Page 2; Onchan *f* = Olsen F, Page 4; Onchan *g* = Olsen E, Page 3.

Onchan *a–g* read as follows:

On the face with the longer cross shaft:

a

] * s u n r × r a i s t i × i f t * u * n (u) s i n a | m u r k i a l u × m [

b

× u k i k a t × a u k r a þ i k r * t

c

a͡l * * *

d

m a͡r ...

On the face with the shorter cross shaft:

e

þ u r i þ (×)   r a i s t × r u n ï *

f

1 5 8
×ᛁᛌᚢᚴᚱᛁᛌᛐ

×**isukrist**
1 5 8

g

1 3
ᚴᚱᚢ[

kru[
1 3

The first line of inscription *a* undulates somewhat, and its graphs are crudely cut, sloping at angles to one another. These features make precise measurement of length hard to record. Runes 1–23 occupy some 32–33 cm. Rune 5, **r**, is 7.4 cm high, r. 10, **t**, 4.7. Rune 1 consists of the lower part of a vertical with no trace of a branch. The tops of rr. 14–23 are broken away, and in a few cases identification must be chiefly or solely by context: r. 15 we would expect to be **k**, r. 17 **i**, and r. 19 **u**; in r. 15 there is perhaps a trace of the lowest part of the branch, but not enough can be made out for identification; r. 19 consists of two more or less vertical lines, truncated at the top, but the second line does appear to curve in slightly towards the first, making a shape compatible with **u**. Some have thought to see a cross after r. 23, but we cannot confirm this. The second line of the inscription is 25 cm long (measured outer branch to outer branch). It is for the most part more precisely cut than line 1, and the graph-tops align with the cross shaft. Rune 29, **a**, is 5.8 cm high, r. 26, **r**, perhaps 4.2. Rune 24 is missing almost entirely its vertical above the height of the branches. Rune 32 is set much lower down than its fellows; it may have been somewhat shorter than these, but damage to the bottom part of its vertical obscures the original length. Both beginning and end of this text are lost, and there is no way of determining how many runes either might once have contained.

Inscription *b* is *c*. 28.5 cm in length. Rune height varies from 2.4 (r. 1 **u**) to 4 cm (r. 9 **k**). The upper part of r. 4 is damaged, but the very base and, in sympathetic lighting, perhaps top of the branch can be discerned. Rune 9 may be a later insert, as Olsen remarked (1954: 195); it stands rather close to its neighbours, r. 8 **u** and r. 10 **r**, while r. 10 is about equidistant from r. 8 and r. 11 **a**. Between rr. 15 and 17 the surface of the stone has flaked off; only the tiny remnant of (what seems to be) a vertical top is now visible; **i** and **a** are

Fig. 53. MM 141 Onchan a *(drawing: Jonas Nordby).*

Fig. 54. MM 141 Onchan b and c *(drawing: Jonas Nordby).*

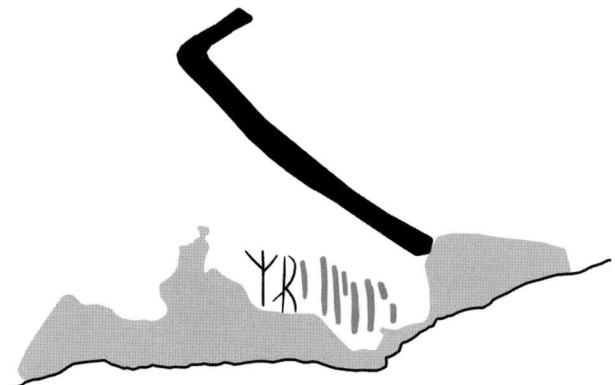

Fig. 55. MM 141 Onchan d *(drawing: Jonas Nordby).*

possible, as well as several other runes. Olsen noted a saltire cross after r. 17, but it is not identifiable now.

Inscription *c* is roughly 7 cm long, and the height of the characters varies between 25 mm (r. 2) and 58 mm (r. 3). An area of damage precedes the first symbol (reading upwards), but no sign of writing can be discerned here. The incisions that make up this inscription have been taken as runes, though readings have diverged so widely there must be doubt. If runes they are, the first is the bind **a͡l**. There follows a symbol that might be ✝ (see *Interpretation* below), but is perhaps more likely to be a slightly malformed saltire cross. Thereafter is a vertical with an unusually long branch leaving it about two-thirds of the way down, descending to the right: possibly a very misshapen ᚱ. Finally comes a backward sloping vertical of uncertain identity.

Runes 1–2 of inscription *d* measure 11 mm in length (branch to bow) and 12 mm in height. Total length of what seems originally to have been carved here is 28 mm. While rr. 1, 2 are quite clear, the marks that follow have the appearance of a series of faint verticals set close together; these might once have been legible runic characters, but are certainly no longer so.

Runes 1–5 of inscription *e* are some 7 cm long measured to the bow of r. 5 (9 cm to the end of the somewhat uncertain cross, which, if part of the inscription, is at the base of the runic line), while rr. 6–15 occupy *c*. 16.5 cm. The two groups are split from each other by a 6.5–7 cm gap, and are not aligned. There is a very lightly sketched **r** below the uncertain cross after r. 5. It is in line with rr. 6–15 but separated from these by several centimetres; perhaps an initial attempt to carve *reist*, which was then abandoned. Rune 1 (**þ**) is *c*. 6 cm high, the later characters rather smaller – r. 11 (**r**), the tallest, is *c*. 5.5 cm. The graphs are roughly cut and poorly spaced, and surface damage has rendered some of them hard to make out in detail. Of r. 15 there survives for sure only the lower part of a vertical. Following r. 15, some have identified a saltire cross, but we cannot confirm this.

Inscription *f* is 11.5 cm long measured from the initial cross, and graph height varies between 3.1 cm (r. 5 **r**) and 4 cm (r. 8 **t**). The runes are cut clearly and are in the main well preserved, though here and there is slight flaking of the surface, which affects details but creates no problems of reading. The top of r. 8 is damaged, but its form, ᛏ, can be confirmed with side lighting.

Inscription *g* is 4.5 cm in length, and r. 1, the tallest, is some 8 cm. Just possibly the dot of an ᛁ can be made out at the break following r. 3, but it is not clear enough for a rune to be recorded in the transrunification or transliteration. This looks a casually added text, faintly cut and with rather larger graphs than the other inscriptions.

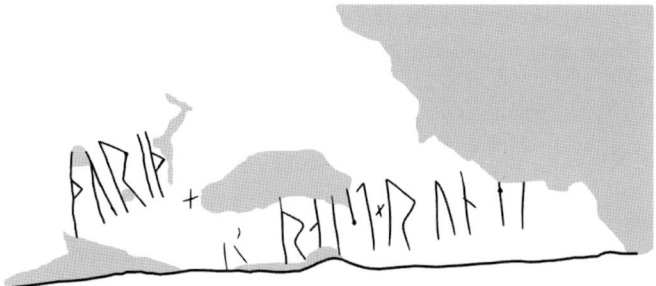

Fig. 56. MM 141 Onchan e *(drawing: Jonas Nordby).*

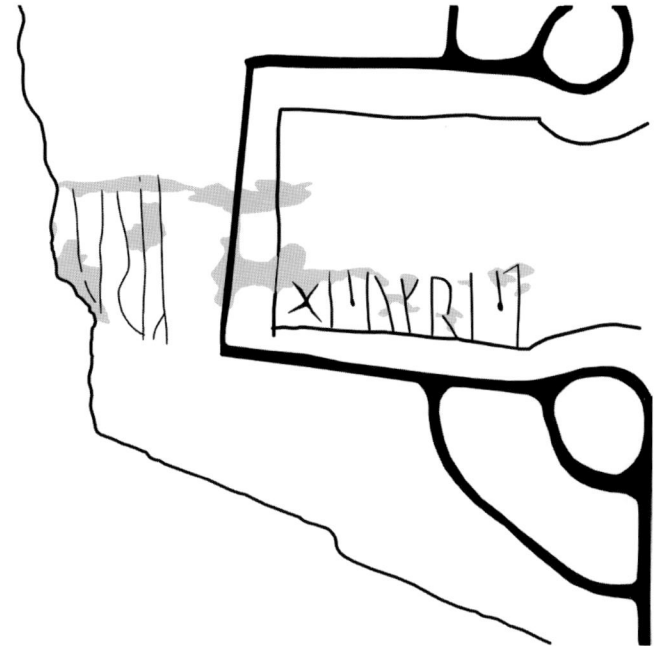

Fig. 57. MM 141 Onchan f *and* g *(drawing: Jonas Nordby).*

Diagnostic runes are *a*: ᚾ **n**, ᚭ **a**, ᛁ **s**, ᛏ **t**, ᛘ **m**; *b*: ᚭ **a**, ᛏ **t**; *c*: ᚭ **a** in the apparent bind ᛐ; *d*: ᚭ **a** in the bind ᛦ, ᛘ **m**; *e*: ᚾ **n**, ᚭ **a**, ᛁ **s**, ᛏ **t**, ᛁ **ï**; *f*: ᛁ **s**, ᛏ **t**.

Interpretation

Inscription *a* gives part of a memorial formula. Unlike the texts on other Manx crosses, however, it does not refer to the monument: no *kross* is mentioned. It may be surmised the text began with the name of the raiser and that in]∗**sunr** we have the remains of a patronymic, as **liutulbsunr** *Ljótólfssonr* 'Ljótólfr's son' in MM 106 Ballaugh. Thus:

[*NN*] *MM-sonr reisti eptir kvinnu sína Myrgjǫlu...*

'[NN] MM's son put [this] up in memory of his wife Muirgheal...'

How the inscription might have continued after r. 31 is less clear. Rune 32 **m** seems to be smaller than those that precede it, and is placed lower down, so conceivably it is part of a later addition, which would mean that the main text ended with the name of the woman commemorated. If, on the other hand, the text went on, it may have proclaimed the name of a son (or daughter) of Myrgjǫl (*móður PP-* 'the mother of PP'). Alternatively, there could have been a phrase describing one of her attributes.

Myrgjǫl is clearly of Celtic origin. The name corresponds to Old Irish *Muirgal*, later *Muirgheal, Muriel* (cf. Uhlich 1993: *s.n.*; Russell *et al.* 2007: *s.n.*). Nevertheless, it has been given a Norse accusative inflection (*-u*, as in a number of female names). A "Myrgjol, dóttir Gljómals Írakonungs" 'Myrgjol, daughter of the Irish king Gljómall' appears in *Landnámabók* (Jakob Benediktsson 1968: 138). The quality of the vowel in the second element of the scandinavianised form of the name is uncertain, but the runic spelling **murkialu** hardly suggests the [o] implied by Jakob Benediktsson: the possibilities here would seem to be either [ɔ] or [a], but it is hard to tell which (cf. p. 75).

Several attempts have been made to interpret inscription *b*. The most plausible, in that it is based on the text as it stands and expresses sentiments paralleled in other runic inscriptions, was given by Olsen (1954: 195–8):

Hygg ek at ok ræð ek rétt.

'I ponder on this and I interpret correctly.'

Understood thus, the text is a commentary on one or more of the other inscriptions on the stone: most likely on the memorial text, given the prominent placement of the two on the same face of the stone. A slight uncertainty affects the first word. Olsen, who saw here a piece of rough-and-ready verse, considered that the carver deliberately omitted the initial /h-/ of *hygg* in order to achieve alliteration with stressed *at*, "just as *ræð* alliterates with *rétt*" (1954: 197). This assumption seems hard to avoid if the interpretation is to stand. There is no evidence otherwise that /h-/ was lost before vowels in Manx Norse (although later in his account Olsen suggests there were "certain circles, where an initial *h* in Old Norse words was dropped", taking support for the idea from Scandinavian loans in Irish such as *abor* < *hábora* 'rowlock'). The phenomenon is, however, well documented in certain parts of the Scandinavian-speaking world (cf. Minugh 1985).

Inscription *c* was read by Olsen (1954: 198–9) ᚨᛚᛅ' **ālæns** (which assumes the medieval, effectively post-1100, distinction ᚨ **a** : ᛅ **æ**), and interpreted as *alleins* 'fully in agreement'. Page (1983) gives the reading a half-hearted blessing and Sanness Johnsen cites both reading and interpretation with apparent approbation. There are problems here, however. The runes, if runes they are, look most like ᚠ×ᛅ plus short sloping vertical, as reported above, while the adverb *alleins* seems to mean 'exactly the same' in the one quotation Olsen offers in support (cf. Fritzner 1886–1972: *s.v.*; *Dictionary of Old Norse Prose*: *s.v. einn*, num. card. B 1). With so much uncertainty attaching, Onchan *c* is best left uninterpreted.

Onchan *d*, judging by the many apparent parallels from medieval Scandinavia, is likely to have been an attempt to write the name *María*, either nom. *María* or perhaps gen. *Maríu*, as in *Maríu sonr* 'son of Mary' (from the three verticals immediately following r. 2, ᚱ, the eye of faith might just manage to reconstruct the remains of ᛁᚢ) – in that case conceivably a reference to the **isukrist** of inscription *f*, although this is located on the other side of the stone.

Onchan *e* looks straightforward enough:

Þúríðr reist rúnar.

'Þúríðr carved runes.'

The large gap between personal name and verb phrase makes it unclear whether the two belong together, though if they do not, *reist rúnar* has no subject. Conceivably Þúríðr first carved her name and later she or someone else added the comment about the activity in which she was engaged. Whether, assuming a single inscription, Onchan *e* is to be taken as an addition to the main *a* text, and thus names its carver, or whether it is a casual addition recording someone's presence or boasting of their runic skills, is impossible to determine. Given the placement on the opposite face from the main inscription, one of the latter two is perhaps more likely. In any event, it is of some interest that we here meet a female rune carver. Not many are attested, though they make occasional appearances (as in Maeshowe nos. 24, 32, and perhaps 30, cf. Barnes 1994: 186–90, 205–6, 209–10; also Larsson 2002: 74 with note 64). Two linguistic forms require comment: first, the personal name *Þúríðr*, which is without its nominative -*r* ending; second, the presumptively plural form **runï**⁎ 'runes', where the end vowel is written ᛅ **ï**, and may thus have been weakened to [æ], [e] or [ə]. Both phenomena are exemplified elsewhere in the Manx corpus. Nominative (masculine) -*r* is missing in the personal names **sãnt:ulf** (MM 131 Andreas IIa), **kaut** (MM 101 Kirk Michael II), **rim** (clearly a damaged **krim**, MM 126 Kirk Michael IV), while in **smiþ** 'smith' (Kirk Michael II), the female personal name **lifilt** (MM 142 Maughold IVe), and **kuinasina** 'his wife' (MM 175 Maughold V) other case endings seem to be lacking or are not in accordance with traditional Old Norse grammar (further pp. 83, 171). On the other hand, *ijō*-stem female names (as *Púríðr*) do not always appear with nom. -*r* in Scandinavia either (Peterson 1981: 56–63). Regarding possibly weakened end vowels, MM 140 German II (Peel) has acc. m. sg. **þïnsï** 'this' with final **ï** for expected **i**, and MM 130 Kirk Michael III **sinï** for probable acc. f. sg. *sína* 'his [reflexive possessive]' (though cf. pp. 180–81).

Inscription *f* clearly says 'Jesus Christ' (cf. the apparent IHSVS on MM 135 Braddan IV), but it is less certain in what language this is couched, or what morphological case was intended. Bugge (as part of a fanciful interpretation: 1899: 237–8) saw here a Norse genitive phrase, dependent on the *kross* he identified in inscription *g*. Olsen agreed. Both men note the form *Krist* for expected genitive *Krists*, Olsen putting it down to the fact that "Old Norse case-inflexions were no longer strictly observed in certain classes of the community". Going purely by the disposition of the runes on the stone one might consider the phrase **isukrist** independent of any of the other inscriptions, and thus nominative, even though the inflection neither of **isu** nor **krist** supports that interpretation. Bugge thought that **isu**, with initial **i**, reflected Irish influence. Olsen is more positive: "instead of *Jesus* the Irish form *Ísu* is used". 'Jesus Christ' in Early Middle Irish is indeed *Ísu Críst*, indeclinable but with expected lenition to *Chríst* [χri:st] in the vocative and genitive ("though examples of where that actually happens are vanishingly rare", Paul Russell pers. com.), so the whole phrase could be Irish rather than Norse, nominative or genitive. On the other hand, Scandinavian rune carvers seem to have had trouble with the name *Jesus* (cf. *NIyR* 6: 267, 270 *s.n. Jesus*), which is perhaps not surprising since [je] was a rare sound combination in medieval Scandinavian and until the advent of ᛂ for [e(:)] (as perhaps in Onchan *e*; certainly in other Manx inscriptions, e.g. MM 130 Kirk Michael III), or ᛂ for [æ(:)], a single ᛁ would have had to have served for both [j] and [e], or ᛁ been written twice, or some other rune used to denote [j] (all of which spellings are documented). Thus **isu** cannot be entirely discounted as a Norse form, though the lack of final -*s* perhaps speaks against it (at least, only in GR 13 do we seem to have a nominative form of the name without -*s*). Conceivably it is a Latin genitive borrowed into Norse, but then it is unclear how **krist** is to be construed. The possibilities are many, and we can really say no more than that a form of Christ's name was intended, either in the nominative or genitive case. With this degree of uncertainty, a normalised Old West Norse text of the inscription is clearly out of the question.

Inscription *g* is most likely to give the word *kross*, though that is not assured (cf. the transrunification and description above). Beyond **kru** the surface is broken away, and there could have been several additional runes, which had we had them would have altered totally our conception of this text. If all it said was *kross* 'cross', it may have belonged with inscription *f*, as already suggested. The possibility of a genitive interpretation of *f* offers mild encouragement to that thought; layout is by and large against it.

The dating of the Onchan cross and its inscriptions is no easier than the interpretation of some of its texts. Shetelig and Olsen claim the cross is Celtic and pre-dates the inscriptions (Shetelig 1925: 270; Olsen 1954: 194), but Page (1983: 145, note 7) records David Wilson's disagreement and contends that "the roughly carved decoration could [...] be by the same hand as some of the roughly cut characters". Whatever the relationship of cross and inscriptions, it is likely that Onchan *a*, the main, memorial, text, was incised before the others (though possibly not before Onchan *f* or *g*). Unfortunately Onchan *a* holds few clues to dating. Nor, for what it is worth, do Onchan *b–g*, although the occurrence of ᛁ **ï** in *e* would normally be considered to point to a period not much earlier than the year 1000, and probably a little or somewhat later (pp. 58–9). The design of the monument is different from that of other Manx crosses, and MM 141 might thus be thought later than these (hardly earlier), but of course not all cross makers will necessarily have followed mainstream fashion. One conclusion that can be drawn from the Onchan stone (as also from MM 142 Maughold IV) is that feelings of piety did not prevent people from adding prominent graffiti to cross slabs.

For such Onchan inscriptions as permit of an Old West Norse normalisation, versions can be offered reflecting more closely the assumed Manx pronunciation of the carvers:

a [NN] *MM-sonr ræisti æft kvinnu sína Murgjǫlu/Murgjalu...*

b Ygg ek at ok ræð ek rétt.

e Þúríð ræist rúner.

MM 42 Maughold AS I

Plates 160–62, Fig. 58

LITERATURE. Marquardt 1961: 70–71. Kermode 1902b: 185–6; Kermode 1907: 110–11; Brate 1907: 33–4; Page 1998: 10–11; Page 1999: 137–8.

MM 42 was found during extensive renovations made to Maughold parish church in 1900. According to Kermode (1907), the stone "formed the side of a grave near the north-west corner of the church, at a depth below the surface of about two feet [= 61 cm]". This he deemed a reuse, as it appeared evident to him that MM 42 had originally been an "upright headstone". In 1906 a shelter was built in the churchyard to house the crosses associated with the parish (Kermode 1907: 216, fig. 58). MM 42 is fixed to the back wall on the left side of the shelter, with its base set into a slate ledge.

Maughold AS I is carved on a slab of local fine grained sandstone, measuring 97 cm × 42 × 9. Kermode (1907) gives the height as 44 inches (= 112 cm). The top and the two narrow sides of the slab have been roughly cut, and the base too, from what can be seen, appears to be in an irregular state. Page (1999: 137) suggests this last is so the stone "would stick easily into the ground", which, if true, offers some support for the idea that it originally functioned as a headstone. As currently positioned, the slab is tight up against the wall of the cross shelter, so only one of the broad faces is visible. Kermode (1907) implies that the other side was uncarved. The visible face is much smoother than the edges of the stone, but does not appear to have been dressed. It is decorated with a pattern consisting of two concentric circles, c. 31 and 24 cm respectively in diameter, the inner one containing a cross pattée, the ends of its arms convex, coinciding with the circle. The arms are decorated with triquetras (all somewhat worn and the left one greatly damaged). Below this figure are three much smaller circles, quite faint, each containing a cross pattée similar in shape to the one above. In the band between the two circles of the main design, close to its apex, stands an inscription in Anglo-Saxon runes. It reads:

ᛒᛚᚪᚷᚳ∗ᛗᚩᚾ

blagc∗mon

Total length of the inscription is 9 cm, measured from vertical to end of branch. There is room for much more, but no indication of any further writing. However, the surface of the stone is broken away on the left-hand side

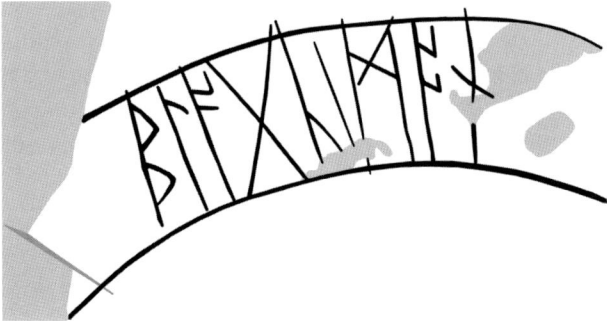

Fig. 58. MM 42 Maughold AS I (drawing: Jonas Nordby).

and something could conceivably have been lost here (though given the *c.* 3 cm of space before r. 1 this is perhaps unlikely). The runes fill the whole width of the band and have an average height of 3.7 cm. They are evenly carved, and well preserved. Only r. 6, if rune it is, presents a problem. It consists of a mildly left-leaning line, shallower than the grooves of the other graphs, and seemingly squeezed in between rr. 5 and 7. It may well be a cutting error, or perhaps an attempt at separating the two elements of the name that emerges (see below).

Interpretation

If the sixth graph is disregarded, the inscription is easily interpreted as the Old English personal name *Blacmon* (cf. PASE: *s.n. Blacman, Blæcmann, Blæcmon*). It is relatively well attested, although almost all the surviving examples are in eleventh-century sources. The unusual spelling **gc** (for the expected **c**) has been taken to indicate palatalisation of the final consonant of the first element of the name (Page 1999: 137), as in *ecg* 'edge', *hrycg* 'ridge' (with **gc** an alternative rendering of what might plausibly have been spelt **cg**). However, ᚪ denotes [a(:)], and it is unclear why there should be palatalisation following a non-palatal vowel. Yet forms of the name in *Blæc-* also exist (cf. above), and it seems different etyma (<*blaikaz, *blaikiz 'bright' 'shining'; <*blakaz 'black') may have become confused.

On the assumption the inscription is complete, it is reasonable to suppose MM 42 was set up to mark Blacmon's grave. Perhaps it was indeed a headstone, as originally suggested by Kermode. The grave need not necessarily have been connected to Maughold church itself; its churchyard contains the remains of four keeills.

The principal interest of this inscription lies in the fact that it is carved in Anglo-Saxon runes and records an Old English personal name. Although there is little direct evidence for the presence of Anglo-Saxons in Man, Maughold AS I (together with MM 43 Maughold AS II) might be thought to presuppose the existence of at least a small group. There is Blacmon himself, who judging by his name was probably English, and the rune carver, who was not only familiar with English runic writing but saw some purpose in recording Blacmon's name in English runes on what may well have been the headstone of a grave monument. Kermode considered (1907: 218) "there would be no object in having a memorial inscription which could not be deciphered or understood by contemporary residents", and this argument has perhaps some validity, although it is scarcely decisive. Possibly, as Page comments (1999: 29), MM 42, 43 Maughold AS I and II are to be connected with the English rune-stones from Northumbria. In detail, however, they do not resemble any of them. The Manx specimens are quite different in inscription and design from the lengthier memorial stones such as Great Urswick and (from the Northumbrian-Mercian border) Thornhill III. They show perhaps slightly greater similarity to the so-called "name-stones" of Lindisfarne, Hartlepool and Monkwearmouth but these are much smaller objects with a layout unlike that of Maughold AS I and II. Even if a link with Northumbrian rune-stone tradition could be substantiated, it does not appear it would help greatly in assigning a date to the two Manx stones. For the Northumbrian corpus as a whole Page offers (1999: 29) "a wide range of dates between the late seventh or early eighth centuries and the eleventh". Most of the Anglo-Saxon memorial stones, however, probably belong in the eighth and ninth centuries, and it is thus legitimate to wonder whether MM 42, 43 may not pre-date the Scandinavian runic crosses of Man by a good span of years.

MM 43 Maughold AS II

Plates 163–4, Fig. 59

LITERATURE. Marquardt 1961: 71. Meeting 1906: 50–51; Kermode 1907: 217–18; Brate 1907: 34; Page 1998: 10–11; Page 1999: 143–4.

MM 43 came to light in 1906. It was discovered by the vicar of Maughold in conversation with a builder who had been "working at a grave about twenty-two yards N.N.E. of the East gable of the church" (Kermode 1907: 217). MM 43 is now housed in Maughold's cross shelter (see MM 145 Maughold I), to the right of MM 42, with its base on a slate ledge.

Maughold AS II is carved on a slab of local fine grained muddy sandstone, measuring 55 cm × 29 × 5 (Kermode's measurements are roughly similar).

Fig. 59. MM 43 Maughold AS II (drawing: Jonas Nordby).

The stone is broken on all sides, and its edges are chipped, the latter apparently a result of the work undertaken in 1906 (Kermode 1907: 217). Neither face appears to have been dressed, though this cannot be confirmed absolutely since as currently positioned the stone is tight up against the wall of the cross shelter. However, according to Kermode the now hidden side "shows the natural bedding of the rock". The visible face bears the remains of a cross pattée, set inside two concentric circles in the manner of MM 42 Maughold AS I (p. 238). There are no traces of further designs. The runic legend is set more or less horizontally at the bottom of the lower cross arm, the bases of the runes above and touching the inner of the two circles (see Plate 163, reproduced from an early photograph, ref. MNH PG/1467 - MC43A).

The inscription reads:

]∗X M F (†)

]∗**g m o** (**n**)

Total length of the surviving text is *c.* 11 cm (cf. the description below). There is no sure sign of any additional writing, but large parts of the stone are broken away and much of the design has been lost. Kermode (1907: 217) detected the faint outlines of two fragmentary characters (interpreted AK) before r. 2, but all that can be seen in the area now is a short vertical line by the present edge of the stone, its base apparently lost in breakage, followed by one broken and uneven and two undulating vertical lines of indeterminable significance. It is unclear whether any of these marks are to be deemed runic, though the incision that forms the vertical line close to the edge looks not unlike those of rr. 2–5 and is therefore (with some reservation) designated

r. 1. One or at most two runes may have stood between rr. 1 and 2, but this is so uncertain it is not marked in the transrunification and transliteration. The runes differ in height: r. 3, the tallest, is 5 cm and r. 5, the shortest, 3.4. There are difficulties with the reading other than those just outlined. The lower branch of r. 4 crosses the vertical in what seems to be a slight overcut. A little above this mark but almost in line with it there is a short incision. Some have seen here a crossing branch, which has raised the question of whether a bind **o͡n** was intended (cf. Page 1998: 10–11). That idea gains perhaps a little in plausibility from the circumstances that r. 5 is shorter than its fellows and the branch that supposedly turns it into **n** very faint indeed. While it is possible that flaking of the surface has affected a weakly carved branch, it is also conceivable that what is here designated r. 5 may not have been a rune at all, but rather a punctuation line closing the text. Another possibility is that it was intended as a half-length **i**, a graph-type occasionally attested in Anglo-Saxon runic usage, both epigraphical and manuscript (Page 1999: 40). In her discussion of this sequence MacLeod (2002: 85) makes the point that the **o͡n** bind envisaged is "doubly ambiguous" because it requires a reverse reading (the **n** is farther to the left but is read after the **o**) and (a section of) the lower branch of **o** is "contained" in the **n**. Such "partly hidden" binds (with shared distinguishing features) are rare, MacLeod points out, though not unknown. But she finds very little certain evidence for the existence of the postulated **o͡n** elsewhere in Anglo-Saxon tradition (the only example appears to be on the worn Bewcastle cross), and wonders "why the carver of the similar Maughold I stone [...] did not make use of it". The likelihood must be that the reading of Maughold AS II presented above is the correct one.

Interpretation

Given the similarity between what remains of this inscription and rr. 4, 7–9 of Maughold AS I, as well as the strong resemblance of the two designs, it is tempting to think that we have here a second example of the personal name *Blacmon*, albeit with slightly different spelling (**blacgmon** or **blagmon** as opposed to Maughold AS I's **blagc∗mon**). That is a temptation to which those who have commented on the inscription have succumbed (Kermode 1907: 217; Brate 1907; Page 1999: 143–4), understandably enough, since it is unclear what alternative interpretation might be offered. Page, considering the possible reading **gmo͡ni** wonders whether there might be here "a dative/?instrumental following the preposition *æfter* ['in memory of']", or "the genitive of a Latinised form of the name, the complete text being *(crux) Blacgmoni* ['cross of Blacmon']" (1999: 144), but both suggestions are highly speculative, depending, as each does, on a reading that cannot be substantiated and a word that cannot be seen. And they do not alter the general impression that the same name and thus quite possibly the same man is involved. Previous commentators have in fact suggested there might be a stronger connection still between MM 42 Maughold AS I and MM 43 Maughold AS II – that the two stones could have formed part of a single monument. Perhaps one stood at either end of the postulated grave. There is, however, no evidence for the existence of this type of grave monument in Man at any period in which MM 42, 43 are likely to have been made. On the question of dating and the wider implications of the occurrence in Man of Anglo-Saxon runic inscriptions, see under Maughold AS I (p. 240).

Appendix. Cross-references to the principal naming and numbering systems applied to the Manx runic corpus

Brate-Olsen*	Manx Museum	Kermode (1907)
Andreas I	MM 99	73
Andreas II	MM 131	103
Andreas III	MM 128	102
Andreas IV	MM 113	87
Andreas V	MM 111	84
Andreas VI	MM 121	95
Andreas VII	MM 193	
Ballaugh	MM 106	77
Balleigh	MM 159	
Braddan I	MM 112	86
Braddan II	MM 138	110
Braddan III	MM 136	109
Braddan IV	MM 135	108
Braddan V	MM 176	
Braddan VI	MM 200	
Bride	MM 118	92
German I (St John's)	MM 107	81
German II (Peel)	MM 140	112
Jurby	MM 127	99
Kirk Michael I	MM 102	75
Kirk Michael II	MM 101	74
Kirk Michael III	MM 130	104
Kirk Michael IV	MM 126	100
Kirk Michael V	MM 132	105
Kirk Michael VI	MM 129	101
Kirk Michael VII	MM 110	85
Kirk Michael VIII	MM 123	
Marown	MM 139	111
Maughold I	MM 145	115
Maughold II	MM 144	114

Maughold III	MM 133	106
Maughold IV	MM 142	
Maughold V	MM 175	
Onchan	MM 141	113
Maughold AS I	MM 42	25
Maughold AS II	MM 43	117

Manx Museum	Brate-Olsen*	Kermode (1907)
MM 42	Maughold AS I	25
MM 43	Maughold AS II	117
MM 99	Andreas I	73
MM 101	Kirk Michael II	74
MM 102	Kirk Michael I	75
MM 106	Ballaugh	77
MM 107	German I	81
MM 110	Kirk Michael VII	85
MM 111	Andreas V	84
MM 112	Braddan I	86
MM 113	Andreas IV	87
MM 118	Bride	92
MM 121	Andreas VI	95
MM 123	Kirk Michael VIII	
MM 126	Kirk Michael IV	100
MM 127	Jurby	99
MM 128	Andreas III	102
MM 129	Kirk Michael VI	101
MM 130	Kirk Michael III	104
MM 131	Andreas II	103
MM 132	Kirk Michael V	105
MM 133	Maughold III	106
MM 135	Braddan IV	108
MM 136	Braddan III	109
MM 138	Braddan II	110
MM 139	Marown	111
MM 140	German II	112
MM 141	Onchan	113
MM 142	Maughold IV	
MM 144	Maughold II	114

MM 145	Maughold I	115
MM 159	Balleigh	
MM 175	Maughold V	
MM 176	Braddan V	
MM 193	Andreas VII	
MM 200	Braddan VI	

* See pp. 28, 31–2. Names have been modified to conform to the relevant place-names as given on current Ordnance Survey maps. Inscriptions not known to Brate or Olsen, or excluded from their accounts as outside the corpus (MM 42 Maughold AS I, MM 43 Maughold AS II), have been added. All such additions are named after the place with which the stone and its inscription(s) are associated (essentially maintaining the Brate-Olsen system), and their number in the sequence determined by the date of the inscription's discovery (see, e.g., Andreas VI, VII). Maughold AS I and II are listed after the Scandinavian inscriptions.

Abbreviations

acc.	accusative
accus.	accusative
anon.	anonymous
AS	Anglo-Saxon
dat.	dative
ed.	edited/editor
eds	editors
f.	feminine
fem.	feminine
Fig./fig.	figure
Figs/figs	figures
fol.	folio
fols	folios
gen.	genitive
ill.	illustration
ills	illustrations
inf.	infinitive
m.	masculine
MM	Manx Museum
MNH	Manx National Heritage
n.	neuter
NGR	National Grid Reference
nom.	nominative
OIr	Old Irish
ON	Old Norse
part.	participle
pers. com.	personal communication
Pl./pl.	plate
pl.	plural
Pls/pls	plates
r.	rune
ref.	reference
rev.	revised

rr.	runes
sg.	singular
sing.	singular
s.n.	*sub nomine*
s.v.	*sub verbo*
*	(preceding a linguistic example) non-attested, reconstructed form
†	(following the name and number of a Manx inscription) lost

Other abbreviations are explained or expanded in the bibliography, pp. 249–60. Capital 'F' in "Fig." or "Figs" and capital 'P' in "Pl." or "Pls" indicates a Figure or Plate published in this volume, lower case 'f' or 'p' a figure or plate in some other publication.

Bibliography

Alfvegren, L. 1959. 'Om de nordiska runinskrifterna på Isle of Man', *Arkiv för nordisk filologi* 74, 218–26.
Andersen, H. 1991. 'Dendrokronologisk datering af Mammengraven.' In Iversen 1991, 43–4.
Anon. 1822. 'Account of a stone with a runic inscription, presented to the Society by the late Sir Alexander Seton of Preston, and of some other inscriptions of the same kind in the Isle of Man', *Archaeologia Scotica: or Transactions of the Society of Antiquaries of Scotland* 2, 490–501 and plates XVI and XIX. (Based in part on material supplied by H.R. Oswald; cf. Oswald 1822.)
Anon. 1855. 'Ancient runic stone, recently found in the Isle of Man', *The Illustrated London News* 8 xii 1855, 685.
Anon. 1886. 'Kk. Andreas runic crosses: lecture by Mr P.M.C. Kermode', *Ramsey Courier* 20 xi 1886.
B + number = archaeological (pre-publication) number of runic inscription found at Bryggen, Bergen (cf. *NIyR* 6: 245–9).
Bailey, R.N. 1980. *Viking-Age Sculpture in Northern England*. London.
Bailey, R.N., and Cramp, R. 1988. *Cumberland and Westmorland and Lancashire North-of-the-Sands* (The British Academy Corpus of Anglo-Saxon Stone Sculpture 2). Oxford.
Barnes, M.P. 1994. *The Runic Inscriptions of Maeshowe, Orkney* (Runrön 8). Uppsala.
Barnes, M.P. 2010. 'A new runic inscription from Carlisle Cathedral', *Cumberland and Westmorland Antiquarian and Archaeological Society Newsletter* 64, 12.
Barnes, M.P. 2012. *Runes: a Handbook*. Woodbridge.
Barnes, M.P., and Hagland, J.R. 2010. 'Runic inscriptions and Viking-Age Ireland.' In: (J. Sheehan and D. Ó Corráin eds) *The Viking Age: Ireland and the West. Papers from the Proceedings of the Fifteenth Viking Congress, Cork, 18–27 August 2005*. Dublin, 11–18.
Barnes, M.P., Hagland, J.R., and Page, R.I. 1997. *The Runic Inscriptions of Viking Age Dublin* (National Museum of Ireland, Medieval Dublin Excavations 1962–81, Ser. B, vol. 5). Dublin.
Barnes, M.P., and Page, R.I. 2006. *The Scandinavian Runic Inscriptions of Britain* (Runrön 19). Uppsala.
Best, R.I., and Lawlor, H.J. (eds). 1931. *The Martyrology of Tallaght* (Henry Bradshaw Society vol. 68). London.
Björkman, E. 1910. *Nordische Personennamen in England in alt- und frühmittelenglischer Zeit: ein Beitrag zur englischen Namenkunde* (Studien zur englischen Philologie 37). Halle (Saale).

Black, G.F. 1889. 'Notice of two sculptured stones at Kirk Andreas, Isle of Man, one bearing an inscription in bind-runes; with notices of other bind-rune inscriptions', *Proceedings of the Society of Antiquaries of Scotland* 23 (= New Series vol. 11), 332–43.

Bo NIYR + number = Inscription from Bohuslän published in *NIyR* vol. 5; the number represents that given to the Bohuslän inscriptions in *NIyR*.

Brate, E. 1907. 'Runinskrifterna på ön Man', *Fornvännen* 2, 20–34, 77–95.

Broderick, G. 1994–2005. *Placenames of the Isle of Man* (7 vols). Tübingen.

Bruce, J.R., and Cubbon, W.C. 1930. 'Cronk yn How: an early Christian and Viking site, at Lezayre, Isle of Man', *Archaeologia Cambrensis* 85, 267–308.

Brøndum-Nielsen, J. 1957. *Gammeldansk Grammatik i sproghistorisk Fremstilling* 2 (2nd ed.). København.

Bugge, S. 1899. 'Nordiske Runeindskrifter og Billeder paa Mindesmærker paa Øen Man', *Aarbøger for Nordisk Oldkyndighed og Historie* 2. Række, 14. Bind, 229–62.

Camden, W. 1607. *Britannia, sive Florentissimorvm Regnorvm Angliæ, Scotiæ, Hiberniæ [...] Descriptio*. London. (See under Gibson, Gough.)

Cubbon, A.M. 1964. 'The repositioning of the Kirk Michael cross-slabs', *The Journal of the Manx Museum* 6, 214–16.

Cubbon, A.M. 1966a. 'Viking runes: outstanding new discovery at Maughold', *The Journal of the Manx Museum* 7, 23–6.

Cubbon, A.M. 1966b. 'Cross-slabs and related inscriptions found since 1939', *The Journal of the Manx Museum* 7, 26–8.

Cumming, J.G. [c. 1855]. Unpublished rubbings and drawings, Bodleian Library Oxford, MS Top. Man a 1.

Cumming, J.G. 1857. *The Runic and Other Monumental Remains of the Isle of Man*. London.

Cumming, J.G. 1868a. 'The runic inscriptions of the Isle of Man.' In: (J.G. Cumming ed.) *Antiquitates Manniæ* (The Manx Society vol. 15). London, 19–35. (Previously published in a slightly different version in *Archaeologia Cambrensis* 3rd Series, vol. 12, 1866, 251–60.)

Cumming, J.G. 1868b. 'On some more recently discovered Scandinavian crosses in the Isle of Man.' In: (J.G. Cumming ed.) *Antiquitates Manniæ* (The Manx Society vol. 15). London, 13–18. (Previously published in a slightly different version in *Archaeologia Cambrensis* 3rd Series, vol. 12, 1866, 460–65.)

Cumming, J.G. 1868c. 'On the ornamentation of the runic monuments in the Isle of Man.' In: (J.G. Cumming ed.) *Antiquitates Manniæ* (The Manx Society vol. 15). London, 1–12. (Previously published in a slightly different version in *Archaeologia Cambrensis* 3rd Series, vol. 12, 1866, 156–67.)

Dictionary of Old Norse Prose/Ordbog over det norrøne prosasprog (edited for the Arnamagnæan Commission). 1989 (in progress). Copenhagen. (Now on-line at: http://onp.ku.dk)

DIL = Quin, E.G., *et al.* (eds). 1913–76. (*Contributions to a) Dictionary of the Irish Language Based mainly on Old and Middle Irish Materials*. Dublin. (Revised and supplemented version on-line at: http://edil.qub.ac.uk/dictionary/search.php)

Dodds, G. 1865. 'Observations on an ancient slab which stands on the north side of the churchyard of Kirk Michael, in the Isle of Man', *The Gentleman's Magazine and Historical Review* vol. 1 (= New [3rd] Series, vol. 18), 3–15.

Dodgson, J.McN. 1972. *The Place-Names of Cheshire* 4 (English Place-Name Society 47). Cambridge.

DR = Jacobsen, L., and Moltke, E. 1941–2. *Danmarks runeindskrifter* (2 vols + index). København.

DR + number = inscription published in *DR* (*Danmarks runeindskrifter*).

Dryden, H. 1887. 'The Manx runic inscriptions', *The Academy* 31, 202–3, 221, 290.

E + number = inscription from England published in Barnes and Page 2006.

Edwards, N. 2013. *A Corpus of Early Medieval Inscribed Stones in Wales* 3: *North Wales*. Cardiff.

Ekwall, E. 1936. *The Concise Oxford Dictionary of English Place-Names*. Oxford.

Elmevik, L. 1992. 'Runsvenskt **ak** "och".' In: (L. Elmevik and L. Peterson eds) *Blandade runstudier* 1 (Runrön 6). Uppsala, 13–17.

Fell, C., *et al.* (eds). 1983. *The Viking Age in the Isle of Man: Select Papers from the Ninth Viking Congress, Isle of Man, 4–14 July 1981*. London.

Fellows-Jensen, G. 1983. 'Scandinavian settlement in the Isle of Man and north-west England: the place-name evidence.' In Fell *et al.* 1983, 37–52.

Feltham, J. 1798. *A Tour through the Island of Mann in 1797 and 1798…* . Bath. (2nd ed., *Feltham's Tour through the Isle of Man…*, 1861, ed. R. Airey, Douglas = The Manx Society vol. 6.)

Finnur Jónsson. 1913–16. *Lexicon Poeticum Antiquæ Linguæ Septentrionalis. Ordbog over det norsk-islandske skjaldesprog* (2nd ed.). København.

Fisher, I. 2001. *Early Medieval Sculpture in the West Highlands and Islands* (Royal Commission on the Ancient and Historical Monuments of Scotland and the Society of Antiquaries of Scotland Monograph Series 1). Edinburgh.

Freke, D. 2002. *Excavations on St Patrick's Isle, Peel, Isle of Man 1982-88: Prehistoric, Viking, Medieval and Later.* Liverpool.

Fridell, S. 2010. 'Den fonematiska statusen hos [ð] i fornsvenskan.' In: (E. Magnusson and L. Rogström eds) *Språkhistoria: hur och för vem?* (Studier i svensk språkhistoria 10 = Meijerbergs arkiv för svensk ordforskning 36). Göteborg, 119–25.

von Friesen, O. 1933. 'De svenska runinskrifterna.' In: (O. von Friesen ed.) *Runorna* (Nordisk kultur 6). Stockholm/Oslo/København, 145–248.

Fritzner, J. 1886–1972. *Ordbog over Det gamle norske Sprog* (3 vols + supplement ed. F. Hødnebø). Kristiania/Oslo/Bergen/Tromsø.

Fuglesang, S.H. 1980. *Some Aspects of the Ringerike Style: a Phase of 11th-Century Scandinavian Art*. Odense.

Fuglesang, S.H. 1991. 'The axehead from Mammen and the Mammen style.' In Iversen 1991, 83–107.

G = Jansson, S.B.F., *et al.* 1962 (in progress). *Gotlands runinskrifter* (2 vols, Sveriges runinskrifter 11–12; vol. 3 available on-line at: www.raa.se/kulturarvet/arkeologi-fornlamningar-och-fynd/runstenar/digitala-sveriges-runinskrifter/gotlands-runinskrifter-3/). Stockholm.

G + number = inscription published in *G* (*Gotlands runinskrifter*).
Gibson, E. (ed.). 1722. [*Camden's*] *Britannia: or a Chorographical Description of Great Britain and Ireland...* . London. (See under Camden.)
Goodall, J.A. 2004. 'Manx arms and seals revisited', *Proceedings of the Isle of Man Natural History and Antiquarian Society* 11:3, 441–52.
Gough, R. (ed.). 1789. [*Camden's*] *Britannia: or, a Chorographical Description of the Flourishing Kingdoms of England, Scotland, and Ireland...* (3 vols). London. (See under Camden.)
GR + number = inscription from Greenland included in *Samnordisk runtextdatabas*.
Graham-Campbell, J. 1995. *The Viking-Age Gold and Silver of Scotland (AD 850–1100)*. Edinburgh.
Graham-Campbell, J. 2011. *The Cuerdale Hoard and Related Viking-Age Silver and Gold from Britain and Ireland in the British Museum* (British Museum Research Publications 185). London.
Graham-Campbell, J. 2013. *Viking Art*. London.
Griffiths, D. 2010. *Vikings of the Irish Sea: Conflict and Assimilation AD 790–1050*. Stroud.
Gräslund, A.-S. 2002. *Runstensstudier*. Uppsala.
Gs = Jansson, S.B.F. 1981. *Gästriklands runinskrifter* (Sveriges runinskrifter 15:1). Stockholm.
Gs + number = inscription published in *Gs* (*Gästriklands runinskrifter*).
Hagland, J.R. 2013. 'Gammalislandsk og gammalnorsk språk.' In: (O.E. Haugen ed.) *Handbok i norrøn filologi* (2nd ed.). Bergen, 600–638.
Harrison, S.N. 1890. 'Note on an inscribed slab from Cabbal Keeil Woirey, Corna', *Yn Lioar Manninagh* 1:5, 140–41.
Harrison, W. 1871. *Records of the Tynwald and Saint John's Chapels in the Isle of Man* (The Manx Society vol. 19). Douglas.
Haugen, E. 1976. *The Scandinavian Languages: an Introduction to their History*. London.
Hibbert-Ware (also Hibbert), S., et al. [c. 1848]. Unpublished drawings, Manchester Public Library MS F. 091 H21.
Holman, K. 1996. *Scandinavian Runic Inscriptions in the British Isles: their Historical Context* (Senter for middelalderstudier, Skrifter 4). Trondheim.
Holman, K. 1998. 'The dating of Scandinavian runic inscriptions from the Isle of Man.' In: (A. Dybdahl and J.R. Hagland eds) *Innskrifter og datering/Dating Inscriptions* (Senter for middelalderstudier, Skrifter 8). Trondheim, 43–54.
Holweck, F.G. 1924. *A Biographical Dictionary of the Saints: with a General Introduction on Hagiology*. St Louis, MO/London.
IR + number = inscription published in Barnes, Hagland and Page 1997.
Iversen, M. (ed.). 1991. *Mammen: Grav, kunst og samfund i vikingetid* (Jysk Arkeologisk Selskabs Skrifter 28). Højbjerg.
Jakob Benediktsson. 1968. *Landnámabók* (Íslenzk fornrit I, 2 vols). Reykjavík.
Jakobsen, J. 1936. *The Place-Names of Shetland*. London and Copenhagen. (Reprinted 1993, Kirkwall.)
Jansson, S.B.F. 1976. *Runinskrifter i Sverige* (2nd ed.). Stockholm.

Janzén, A. 1948 (also dated 1947). 'De fornvästnordiska personnamnen.' In: (A. Janzén ed.) *Personnamn* (Nordisk kultur 7). Stockholm/Oslo/København, 22–186.
Jenkinson, H.I. 1874. *Jenkinson's Practical Guide to the Isle of Man*. London.
Jesch, J. 2001. *Ships and Men in the Late Viking Age: the Vocabulary of Runic Inscriptions and Skaldic Verse*. Woodbridge.
Jewitt, Ll. 1884. 'Passing notes on some of the sculptured stone crosses and other remains of past ages in the Isle of Man', *The Reliquary and Illustrated Archaeologist* 25, 97–112.
Jones, E. [c. 1834–47]. Unpublished drawings, Society of Antiquaries of London MS Capt. Edw. Jones, Sketches. Ireland II.
Kermode, P.M.C. 1884. 'The monumental crosses of Mann: with suggestions as to means to be adopted for their better preservation', *Transactions of the Isle of Man Natural History and Antiquarian Society* 1 (1879–84, published 1888), 148–57.
Kermode, P.M.C. 1887a. *Catalogue of the Manks Crosses with the Runic Inscriptions and Various Readings and Renderings Compared*. Ramsey/London.
Kermode, P.M.C. 1887b. 'The Manx runic inscriptions', *The Academy* 31, 150–52.
Kermode, P.M.C. 1892. *Catalogue of the Manks Crosses with the Runic Inscriptions and Various Readings and Renderings Compared* (2nd ed.). Ramsey/London/Edinburgh.
Kermode, P.M.C. 1902a. 'Sculptured and inscribed stones recently found at Kirk Maughold', *Yn Lioar Manninagh* 3:12, 629–33.
Kermode, P.M.C. 1902b. 'Some early Christian monuments recently discovered at Kirk Maughold, Isle of Man', *The Reliquary and Illustrated Archaeologist*, New Series 8, 182–93.
Kermode, P.M.C. (ed.). 1905. *Catalogue of the Manx Museum (Antiquities), Castle Rushen, 1905*. Douglas.
Kermode, P.M.C. 1907. *Manx Crosses: or the Inscribed and Sculptured Monuments of the Isle of Man from about the End of the Fifth to the Beginning of the Thirteenth Century*. London. (Reproduced 1994 with an introduction by D.M. Wilson, Balgavies.)
Kermode, P.M.C. 1912. 'Cross-slabs recently discovered in the Isle of Man', *Proceedings of the Society of Antiquaries of Scotland* 46 (= 4th Series vol. 10), 53–76. (Reprinted as Appendix B in the 1994 reproduction of Kermode 1907.)
Kermode, P.M.C. 1916. 'Further discoveries of cross-slabs in the Isle of Man', *Proceedings of the Society of Antiquaries of Scotland* 50 (= 5th Series vol. 2), 50–62. (Reprinted as Appendix C in the 1994 reproduction of Kermode 1907.)
Kermode, P.M.C. 1925. 'The Hedin cross, Maughold, Isle of Man', *Saga-Book of the Viking Society* 9:2, 333–42.
Kermode, P.M.C. 1929. 'More cross-slabs from the Isle of Man', *Proceedings of the Society of Antiquaries of Scotland* 63 (= 6th Series vol. 3), 354–60. (Reprinted as Appendix E in the 1994 reproduction of Kermode 1907.)
Kermode, P.M.C. Undated notebook XXIX, Manx Museum.
Kermode, R.W. 1882. 'Some antiquities connected with the parish of Ballaugh', *Trans-*

actions of the Isle of Man Natural History and Antiquarian Society 1 (1879–84, published 1888), 91–5.

Kinnebrook, W. 1841. *Etchings of the Runic Monuments in the Isle of Man, with Remarks*. London.

KJ + number = inscription published in Krause and Jankuhn 1966.

Kneale, W. [c. 1860]. *Kneale's Guide to the Isle of Man...*. Douglas.

Kneen, J.J. 1937. *The Personal Names of the Isle of Man*. London.

Knirk, J.E. 2010. 'Dotted runes: where did they come from?' In: (J. Sheehan and D. Ó Corráin eds) *The Viking Age: Ireland and the West. Papers from the Proceedings of the Fifteenth Viking Congress, Cork, 18–27 August 2005*. Dublin, 188–98.

Knudsen, G., and Kristensen, M. (in collaboration with R. Hornby). 1936–64. *Danmarks gamle Personnavne* 1–2 (*Fornavne + Tilnavne*; 4 vols). København.

Krause, W., and Jankuhn, H. 1966. *Die Runeninschriften im älteren Futhark* (Abhandlungen der Akademie der Wissenschaften in Göttingen, philologisch-historische Klasse, 3. Folge 65). Göttingen.

Källström, M. 2007. *Mästare och minnesmärken: studier kring vikingatida runristare och skriftmiljöer i Norden* (Stockholm Studies in Scandinavian Philology, New Series 43). Stockholm.

Lagman, S. 1990. *De stungna runorna: användning och ljudvärden i runsvenska steninskrifter* (Runrön 4). Uppsala.

Lang, J.T. 1988. *Viking-Age Decorated Wood: a Study of its Ornament and Style* (National Museum of Ireland, Medieval Dublin Excavations 1962–81, Ser. B, vol. 1). Dublin.

Larsson, P. 2002. *Yrrunan: användning och ljudvärde i nordiska runinskrifter* (Runrön 17). Uppsala.

Laughton, J.B. 1842. *A New Historical, Topographical, and Parochial Guide to the Isle of Mann*. Douglas.

Liestøl, A. 1969. Review of I. Sanness Johnsen, *Stuttruner i vikingtidens innskrifter*, 1968. *Norsk Tidsskrift for Sprogvidenskap* 23, 171–80.

Liestøl, A. 1983. 'An Iona rune stone and the world of Man and the Isles.' In Fell *et al.* 1983, 85–93.

Lind, E.H. 1905–15. *Norsk-isländska dopnamn ock fingerade namn från medeltiden*. Uppsala/Leipzig.

Lind, E.H. 1920–21. *Norsk-isländska personbinamn från medeltiden*. Uppsala.

MacLeod, M. 2000. 'The inscription on the Andreas V runic cross', *Scandinavica* 39, 207–15.

MacLeod, M. 2002. *Bind-Runes: an Investigation of Ligatures in Runic Epigraphy* (Runrön 15). Uppsala.

Margeson, S. 1983. 'On the iconography of the Manx crosses.' In Fell *et al.* 1983, 95–106.

Marquardt, H. 1961. *Bibliographie der Runeninschriften nach Fundorten 1. Die Runeninschriften der Britischen Inseln* (Abhandlungen der Akademie der Wissenschaften in Göttingen, philologisch-historische Klasse, 3. Folge 48). Göttingen.

Marstrander, C.J.S. 1915. *Bidrag til det norske sprogs historie i Irland* (Videnskapsselskapets Skrifter. II. Hist.-Filos. Klasse. 1915. No. 5). Kristiania.

Marstrander, C.J.S. 1930a. 'Jurbykorset (Isle of Man)', *Norsk Tidsskrift for Sprogvidenskap* 4, 370–77.
Marstrander, C.J.S. 1930b. 'Killaloekorset og de norske kolonier i Irland', *Norsk Tidsskrift for Sprogvidenskap* 4, 378–400.
Marstrander, C.J.S. 1932. 'Det norske landnåm på Man', *Norsk Tidsskrift for Sprogvidenskap* 6, 40–356.
Marstrander, C.J.S. 1937. 'Om sproget i de manske runeinnskrifter', *Norsk Tidsskrift for Sprogvidenskap* 8, 243–56.
Marstrander, C.J.S. 1938. 'Suderøyingen Gaut Bjørnson', *Norsk Tidsskrift for Sprogvidenskap* 10, 375–83.
Massengale, J. 1972. 'A test study in runic dialectology.' In: (E.S. Firchow *et al*. eds) *Studies for Einar Haugen Presented by Friends and Colleagues*. The Hague/Paris, 379–88.
Mayhew, S.M. 1881. 'Notes on the Isle of Man', *The Journal of the British Archaeological Association* 37, 47–55.
McManus, D. 1991. *A Guide to Ogam*. Maynooth.
Meeting 1906 = 'Meeting at Ramsey, December, 1906', *The Isle of Man Natural History and Antiquarian Society, Proceedings*, New Series 1:3 (1907), 49–51.
Meeting 1913 = 'Meeting at the Town Hall, Douglas, 4 December, 1913', *The Isle of Man Natural History and Antiquarian Society, Proceedings*, New Series 2:2 (1923), 56–7.
Megaw, B.R.S. 1950. 'The monastery of St. Maughold', *Isle of Man Natural History and Antiquarian Society, Proceedings*, New Series 5:2, 169–80.
Megaw, B.R.S. 1959–60. 'The ship seals of the Kings of Man', *The Journal of the Manx Museum* 6, 78–80.
Minugh, D. 1985. 'As old as the 'ills: variable loss of *h* in Swedish dialects', *NOWELE, North-Western European Language Evolution* 6, 23–43.
Moltke, E. 1985. *Runes and their Origin: Denmark and Elsewhere*. Copenhagen.
Moore, R.B. 1959. *Kirk Andreas, Skyll Andrea: Memoir*. Privately printed; unpaginated.
Munch, P.A. 1850. 'Rune-Indskrifter fra Öen Man og Syderöerne', *Annaler for Nordisk Oldkyndighed og Historie*, 273–87.
Munch, P.A. 1860. *Chronica Regvm Manniæ et Insvlarvm: The Chronicle of Man and the Sudreys, Edited from the Manuscript Codex in the British Museum and with Historical Notes*. Christiania.
N + number = inscription published in *NIyR* (*Norges innskrifter med de yngre runer*).
Nielsen, K.M. 1960. 'Til runedanskens ortografi', *Arkiv för nordisk filologi* 75, 1–78.
Nielsen, K.M. 1988. 'Runedansk akk. ạumutạ', *Studia anthroponymica Scandinavica* 6, 5–10.
NIyR = Olsen, M., *et al*. 1941 (in progress). *Norges innskrifter med de yngre runer* (6 vols). Oslo.
Nordal, S. 1913–16. *Orkneyinga saga* (Samfund til udgivelse af gammel nordisk litteratur 40). København.
Noreen, A. 1923. *Altnordische Grammatik* 1. *Altisländische und altnorwegische*

Grammatik... (Sammlung kurzer Grammatiken germanischer Dialekte 4, 4th ed.). Halle (Saale).
Nä = Jansson, S.B.F. 1975. *Närkes runinskrifter* (Sveriges runinskrifter 14:1). Stockholm.
Nä + number = inscription published in Nä (*Närkes runinskrifter*).
O'Brien, M.A. (ed.). 1962. *Corpus Genealogiarum Hiberniae* I. Dublin.
O'Brien, M.A. (ed. R. Baumgarten). 1973. 'Old Irish personal names', *Celtica* 10, 211–36.
Olsen, M. 1903. *Tre orknøske runeindskrifter* (Christiania Videnskabs-Selskabs Forhandlinger for 1903, no. 10). Christiania.
Olsen, M. 1909. *Om sproget i de manske runeindskrifter* (Christiania Videnskabs-Selskabs Forhandlinger for 1909, no. 1). Christiania.
Olsen, M. 1933. 'De norröne runeinnskrifter.' In: (O. von Friesen ed.) *Runorna* (Nordisk kultur 6). Stockholm/Oslo/København, 83–113.
Olsen, M. 1954. 'Runic inscriptions in Great Britain, Ireland and the Isle of Man.' In: (H. Shetelig ed.) *Viking Antiquities in Great Britain and Ireland* 6. Oslo, 151–233.
O'Meadhra, U. 1979. *Early Christian, Viking and Romanesque Art: Motif-Pieces from Ireland* (Theses and Papers in North-European Archaeology 7). Stockholm.
OR + number = inscription from Orkney published in Barnes and Page 2006.
Ó Riain, P. (ed.). 1985. *Corpus Genealogiarum Sanctorum Hiberniae*. Dublin.
Oswald, H.R. 1822. 'Notes of reference to the series of delineations of the runic and other ancient crosses found in the Isle of Man', *Archaeologia Scotica: or Transactions of the Society of Antiquaries of Scotland* 2, 502–8 and plates XVII and XVIII.
Page, R.I. 1980. 'Some thoughts on Manx runes', *Saga-Book of the Viking Society* 20:3, 179–99. (Reprinted in Page 1995, 207–24.)
Page, R.I. 1981. 'More thoughts on Manx runes', *Michigan Germanic Studies* 7 (= C. Thompson ed., *Proceedings of the First International Symposium on Runes and Runic Inscriptions*), 129–36.
Page, R.I. 1983. 'The Manx rune-stones.' In Fell *et al.* 1983, 133–46. (Reprinted in Page 1995, 225–44.)
Page, R.I. 1992a. 'Celtic and Norse on the Manx rune-stones.' In: (H.L.C. Tristram ed.) *Medialität und mittelalterliche insulare Literatur*. Tübingen, 131–47.
Page, R.I. 1992b. 'New runic fragment from the Isle of Man', *Nytt om runer* 7, 6.
Page, R.I. (ed. D. Parsons). 1995. *Runes and Runic Inscriptions: Collected Essays on Anglo-Saxon and Viking Runes*. Woodbridge.
Page, R.I. 1998. *A Traveller's Guide to the Manx Rune-Stones* (mimeographed for the Manx Runic Symposium, March 1998).
Page, R.I. 1999. *An Introduction to English Runes* (2nd ed.). Woodbridge.
Page, R.I. 2005. 'Seeing and observing.' In: (H.F. Nielsen ed.) *Papers on Scandinavian and Germanic Language and Culture Published in Honour of Michael Barnes on his Sixty-Fifth Birthday 28 June 2005* (= *NOWELE, North-Western European Language Evolution* 46/47). Odense, 211–25.

Page, R.I., and Hagland, J.R. 1998. 'Runica manuscripta and runic dating: the expansion of the younger fuþąrk.' In: (A. Dybdahl and J.R. Hagland eds) *Innskrifter og datering/Dating Inscriptions* (Senter for middelalderstudier, Skrifter 8). Trondheim, 55–71.

Palm, R. 1992. *Runor och regionalitet: studier av variation i de nordiska minnesinskrifterna* (Runrön 7). Uppsala.

PASE = *Prosopography of Anglo-Saxon England*. At: http://pase.ac.uk/index.html

Paterson, C., et al. 2014. *Shadows in the Sand: Excavation of a Viking-Age Cemetery at Cumwhitton, Cumbria*. Lancaster.

Paterson, R. 1863. *Manx Antiquities: or Remarks on the Present Condition of the Antiquarian Remains of the Isle of Man, especially those Situated around its Coast Line*. Cupar-Fife.

Peterson, L. 1981. *Kvinnonamnens böjning i fornsvenskan: de ursprungligen starkt böjda namnen* (Anthroponymica Suecana 8). Uppsala.

Peterson, L. 1992. 'Hogastenen på Orust.' In: (L. Elmevik and L. Peterson eds) *Blandade runstudier* 1 (Runrön 6). Uppsala, 81–111.

Peterson, L. 1996. '*Aft*/*æft*, *at* och *æftiʀ* på de nordiska runstenarna: regional variation eller vad?' In: (M. Reinhammar et al. eds) *Mål i sikte: studier i dialektologi tillägnade Lennart Elmevik*. Uppsala, 239–52.

Peterson, L. 2003. '*Arnnjótr, Dýrgeirr, Vígþorn* and others: a bouquet of rarities from the personal name flora of Viking Age Scandinavia.' In: (W. Heizmann and A. van Nahl eds) *Runica – Germanica – Mediaevalia* (Ergänzungsbände zum Reallexikon der Germanischen Altertumskunde 37). Berlin/New York, 581–94.

Peterson, L. 2006. *Svenskt runordsregister* (Runrön 2, 3rd ed.). At: http://uu.diva-portal.org/smash/get/diva2:437203/FULLTEXT01.pdf

Peterson, L. 2007. *Nordiskt runnamnslexikon* (5th ed.). Uppsala.

Petit, J.L. 1846. 'Ecclesiastical antiquities of the Isle of Man: cathedral of St. German, in Peel Castle', *The Archaeological Journal* 3, 49–58.

RCAHMS 1982 = *The Royal Commission on the Ancient and Historical Monuments of Scotland*, twenty-second report (Argyll 4: Iona) 1982. Edinburgh.

Richards, J.D. 2004. *Viking Age England* (2nd ed.). Stroud.

Rigg, J.M. 1894. 'Moses, William Stainton (1840–1892).' Rev. (with year of birth amended to 1839) H.C.G. Matthew. In: (H.C.G. Matthew and B. Harrison eds), *Oxford Dictionary of National Biography* 39 (2004). Oxford, 465.

Russell, P., with McClure, P., and Rollason, D. 2007. 'Commentary: A. Personal names: A.1 Celtic names.' In: (D. Rollason and L. Rollason eds) *The Durham Liber Vitae: London, British Library, MS Cotton Domitian A.VII* (3 vols). London, vol. 2, 35–43.

Rye, E. 2017. 'A new runic inscription from Sockburn Hall, County Durham: E 19 Sockburn', *Futhark* 8, 89–110.

Samnordisk runtextdatabas. At: http://www.nordiska.uu.se/forskn/samnord.htm

Sanness Johnsen, I. 1968. *Stuttruner i vikingtidens innskrifter*. Oslo.

Sawyer, B. 2000. *The Viking-Age Rune-Stones: Custom and Commemoration in Early Medieval Scandinavia*. Oxford.

SC + number = inscription from Scotland published in Barnes and Page 2006.

Schetelig, H. 1920. *Vestfoldskolen* (as vol. 3 of A.W. Brøgger, H.J. Falk and H. Schetelig eds, *Osebergfundet*). Kristiania.

Seip, D.A. 1930. 'Norske paralleller til de uregelmessige fleksjonsformer i manske og irske runeinnskrifter', *Norsk Tidsskrift for Sprogvidenskap* 4, 401–4.

Selling, D. 1945. *Alexander Seton (1768–1828) som fornforskare* (Kungl. Vitterhets Historie och Antikvitets Akademiens handlingar 59:3). Stockholm.

SH + number = inscription from Shetland published in Barnes and Page 2006.

Shetelig, H. 1925. 'Manx crosses – relating to Great Britain and Norway', *Saga-Book of the Viking Society* 9:2, 253–74.

Shetelig, H. 1954. 'The Norse style of ornamentation in the Viking settlements.' In: (H. Shetelig ed.) *Viking Antiquities in Great Britain and Ireland* 6. Oslo, 113–50.

Sm = Kinander, R. 1935–61. *Smålands runinskrifter* (Sveriges runinskrifter 4). Stockholm.

Sm + number = inscription published in *Sm* (*Smålands runinskrifter*).

Spurkland, T. 1995. 'Kriteriene for datering av norske runesteiner fra vikingtid og tidlig middelalder', *Maal og Minne* 1995, 1–14.

Stephens, G. 1866–1901. *The Old-Northern Runic Monuments of Scandinavia and England* (4 vols). London/København (Cheapinghaven etc.)/Lund.

Stewart, J. 1987. *Shetland Place-Names*. Lerwick.

Stokes, W. 1895. *The Martyrology of Gorman* (Henry Bradshaw Society vol. 9). London.

Stoklund, M., et al. (eds). 2006. *Runes and their Secrets: Studies in Runology.* Copenhagen.

Sö = Brate, E., and Wessén, E. 1924–36. *Södermanlands runinskrifter* (Sveriges runinskrifter 3). Stockholm.

Sö + number = inscription published in *Sö* (*Södermanlands runinskrifter*).

Taylor, I. 1886. 'The Manx runes', *The Manx Note Book* 2, 97–113.

Taylor, I. 1887. 'The Manx runic inscriptions', *The Academy* 31, 184–6.

The Illustrated Guide and Visitor's Companion through the Isle of Man (by a Resident). 1836. Douglas.

The Manx Archæological Survey, Third Report. 1911. (Published for the Isle of Man Natural History and Antiquarian Society.) Douglas.

The Manx Museum and Ancient Monuments Trustees. 1908. *Third Annual Report, Being for the Year Ended 31 December, 1907...* . Douglas.

The Manx Museum and National Trust. 1958. *Annual Report for the Year Ended 31st March, 1958*. Douglas.

Thorkelin, G. [1789]. Unpublished drawings, Rigsarkivet, Copenhagen: Privatarkiv no. 6431 (unpaginated notebooks entitled "Thorkelinske Noticer fra hans Ænglandsrejse").

Townley, R. 1791. *A Journal Kept in the Isle of Man...* (2 vols). Whitehaven.

Train, J. 1845. *An Historical and Statistical Account of the Isle of Man, from the Earliest Times to the Present Date...* (2 vols). Douglas.

U = Wessén, E., and Jansson, S.B.F. 1940–58. *Upplands runinskrifter* (4 vols, Sveriges runinskrifter 6–9). Stockholm.

U + number = inscription published in *U* (*Upplands runinskrifter*).

Uhlich, J. 1993. *Die Morphologie der komponierten Personennamen des Altirischen*. Bonn.

Vg = Jungner, H., and Svärdström, E. 1940–70. *Västergötlands runinskrifter* (Sveriges runinskrifter 5). Stockholm.

Vg + number = inscription published in *Vg* (*Västergötlands runinskrifter*).

Vg Fv + numbers = inscription from Västergötland published in *Fornvännen*; the numbers give the year of publication and page.

Vigfusson, G. 1887. 'The Manx runic inscriptions', *The Academy* 31, 131–2, 167–8.

Vigfusson, G., and Savage, E.B. 1887. 'The Manx runic inscriptions re-read', *The Manx Note Book* 3, 5–22.

Vm = Jansson, S.B.F. 1964. *Västmanlands runinskrifter* (Sveriges runinskrifter 13). Stockholm.

Wanley, H. [c. 1700]. Unpublished drawings of Manx inscriptions among Humfrey Wanley's papers in the British Library: BL MS Add. 70484, Misc. 17 (formerly BL Loan 29/259 from the Duke of Portland's collection).

Williams, H. 1990. *Åsrunan: användning och ljudvärde i runsvenska steninskrifter* (Runrön 3). Uppsala.

Williams, H. 1994. 'The non-representation of nasals before obstruents: spelling convention or phonetic analysis?' In: (J.E. Knirk ed.) *Proceedings of the Third International Symposium on Runes and Runic Inscriptions, Grindaheim, Norway, 8–12 August 1990* (Runrön 9). Uppsala, 217–22.

Wilson, D.M. 1970–71. 'Manx memorial stones of the Viking period', *Saga-Book of the Viking Society* 18:1–2, 1–18.

Wilson, D.M. 1983. 'The art of the Manx crosses of the Viking Age.' In Fell *et al*. 1983, 175–87.

Wilson, D.M. 1994. 'Philip Kermode and *Manx Crosses*: ninety years on' (introduction to the facsimile reprint of Kermode 1907). Balgavies, xiii–xx.

Wilson, D.M. 1995a. *Vikingatidens konst* (Signums svenska konsthistoria 2). Lund.

Wilson, D.M. 1995b. 'Scandinavian ornamental influence in the Irish Sea region in the Viking Age.' In: (T. Scott and P. Starkey eds) *The Middle Ages in the North-West*. Liverpool, 37–58.

Wilson, D.M. 2004. 'A ring from Greeba', *Proceedings of the Isle of Man Natural History and Antiquarian Society* 11:3, 437–9.

Wilson, D.M. 2008. *The Vikings in the Isle of Man*. Aarhus.

Wilson, D.M. 2009. 'Stylistic influences in early Manx sculpture.' In: (J. Graham-Campbell and M. Ryan eds) *Anglo-Saxon/Irish Relations before the Vikings* (Proceedings of the British Academy 157). London, 311–28.

Wilson, D.M. 2014a. 'The conversion of the Viking settlers in the Isle of Man.' In: (J. Garipzanov and R. Bonté eds) *Conversion and Identity in the Viking Age*. Turnhout, 117–39.

Wilson, D.M. 2014b. 'Conversion and Christian symbolism in the Isle of Man: evidence, origin and content', *Proceedings of the Isle of Man Natural History and Antiquarian Society* 12:4, 573–95.

Wilson, D.M., and Klindt-Jensen, O. 1966. *Viking Art*. London.

Wood, G.W. 1924. 'The earliest drawings of the runic crosses of the Isle of Man', *The*

Isle of Man Natural History and Antiquarian Society, Proceedings, New Series 2:3, 302–3.

Woods, G. 1811. *An Account of the Past and Present State of the Isle of Man*. London/ Edinburgh.

Worsaae, J.J.A. [c. 1850]. "Optegnelser især om nordiske Spor i Irland, Skotland, England og Frankrige, begyndte i Dublin i Januar 1847 og endt i Paris i Marts 1852" (notebook containing, *inter alia*, drawings of and observations on various Manx runic inscriptions; preserved in the National Museum of Denmark, Det Museumshistoriske Arkiv, Antikvarisk-Topografisk Arkiv og Bibliotek, Danmarks Middelalder og Renæssance).

Worsaae, J.J.A. 1851. *Minder om de Danske og Nordmændene i England, Skotland og Irland*. Kjöbenhavn.

Ög = Brate, E. 1911–18. *Östergötlands runinskrifter* (Sveriges runinskrifter 2). Stockholm.

Ög + number = inscription published in *Ög* (*Östergötlands runinskrifter*).

Plates

Acknowledgements

The Plates enumerated below are reproduced by kind permission of the following:

Sally Foster and Doug Simpson: 44
Judith Jesch: 1, 6, 14–16, 23, 27, 39–43, 45–6, 49, 58, 73, 82, 93–4, 98–9, 105, 110, 112, 133–5, 161
James Knirk: 121–32, 145–51, 162, 164
Manx National Heritage: 17, 21–2, 32–3, 68, 70, 72, 83–4, 95, 100, 153, 163
Jonas Nordby: 2–5, 7–13, 18–20, 24–6, 28–31, 34–8, 50–57, 59–67, 69, 71, 74–81, 85–92, 96–7, 101–4, 106–9, 111, 113–20, 136–44, 152, 154–60
Henrik Williams: 47–8

(It should be noted that Knirk and Nordby, who together provided most of the Plates for this edition, worked as a team, the one organising the lighting the other operating the camera.)

Plate 1. MM 99, Kermode's face A (photo: Judith Jesch).

Plate 2. MM 99 Andreas I (photo: Jonas Nordby).

Plate 3. MM 99 Andreas I, rr: 1–20 (photo: Jonas Nordby).

Plate 4. MM 99 Andreas I, rr: 18–39 (photo: Jonas Nordby).

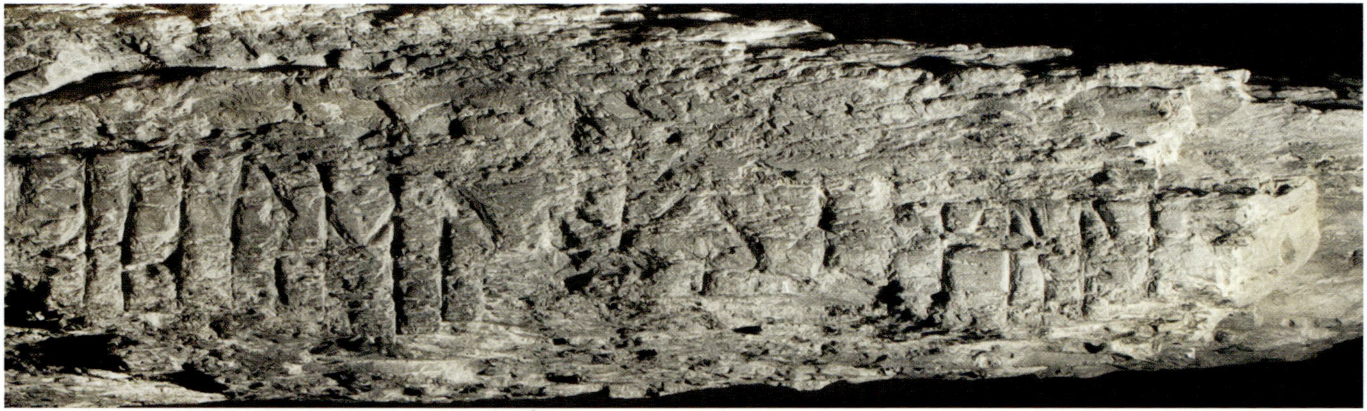

Plate 5. MM 99 Andreas I, rr. 37–50 (photo: Jonas Nordby).

Plate 6. MM 99 Andreas I, rr. 1–8 in detail (photo: Judith Jesch).

Plate 7. MM 131, Kermode's face A (photo: Jonas Nordby).

Plate 8. MM 131 Andreas IIa (photo: Jonas Nordby).

Plate 9. MM 131 Andreas IIα, rr. 1–19 (photo: Jonas Nordby).

Plate 10. MM 131 Andreas IIα, rr. 17–35 (photo: Jonas Nordby).

Plate 11. MM 131 Andreas IIa, rr. 35–54 (photo: Jonas Nordby).

Plate 12. MM 131 Andreas IIb (photo: Jonas Nordby).

Plate 13. MM 131 Andreas IIb, in detail (photo: Jonas Nordby).

Plate 14. MM 128, Kermode's face A (photo: Judith Jesch).

Plate 15. MM 128, Kermode's face B (photo: Judith Jesch).

Plate 16. MM 128 Andreas III (photo: Judith Jesch).

Plate 17. MM 128 Andreas III, before the lengthwise split (image courtesy of Manx National Heritage, ref. MNH PG/13721 - MC128C).

Plate 18. MM 113, Kermode's face B (photo: Jonas Nordby).

Plate 19. MM 113 Andreas IV (photo: Jonas Nordby).

Plate 20. MM 111 Andreas V, Kermode's face B with the inscription (photo: Jonas Nordby).

Plate 21. MM 111 Andreas V, before the breakage (image courtesy of Manx National Heritage, ref. MNH PG/13721 - MC111B).

Plate 22. MM 111 Andreas V, showing the broken end (image courtesy of Manx National Heritage, ref. MNH PG/5211-2 - MC111B).

Plate 23. MM 121, Kermode's face A (photo: Judith Jesch).

Plate 24. MM 121 Andreas VI (photo: Jonas Nordby).

Plate 25. MM 193 Andreas VII, decorated face and inscription (photo: Jonas Nordby).

Plate 26. MM 193 Andreas VII, with the assumed original orientation of the runes (photo: Jonas Nordby).

Plate 27. MM 106, Kermode's face A (photo: Judith Jesch).

Plate 28. MM 106 Ballaugh, Kermode's face B with the inscription (photo: Jonas Nordby).

Plate 29. MM 106 Ballaugh, rr. 1–41 (photo: Jonas Nordby).

Plate 30. MM 106 Ballaugh, rr. 16–40 (photo: Jonas Nordby).

Plate 31. MM 106 Ballaugh, rr. 41–7 (photo: Jonas Nordby).

Plate 32. MM 159 Balleigh † (image courtesy of Manx National Heritage, ref. MNH PG/1459 - MC159).

Plate 33. MM 112 Braddan I, MM 136 Braddan III, and MM 135 Braddan IV, situated on a mound on the south side of Braddan Old Kirk churchyard (image courtesy of Manx National Heritage, ref. MNH PG/8794 - MC112-135-136).

Plate 34. MM 112 Braddan I, Kermode's face B with the inscription (photo: Jonas Nordby).

Plate 35. MM 112 Braddan I, rr. 1–15 (photo: Jonas Nordby).

Plate 36. MM 112 Braddan I, rr. 13–27 (photo: Jonas Nordby).

Plate 38. MM 112 Braddan I, rr. 33–40 (photo: Jonas Nordby).

Plate 37. MM 112 Braddan I, rr. 26–33 (photo: Jonas Nordby).

Plate 39. MM 138, Kermode's face A, oriented as the stone must originally have stood (photo: Judith Jesch).

Plate 40. MM 138 Braddan II, Kermode's face B with the inscription, oriented as the stone must originally have stood (photo: Judith Jesch).

Plate 41. MM 136, Kermode's face A (photo: Judith Jesch).

Plate 42. MM 136, Kermode's face B (photo: Judith Jesch).

Plate 43. MM 136 Braddan III (photo: Judith Jesch).

Plate 44. Museum of Scotland cast IC7 of MM 136 Braddan III, showing rr. 1–47 (© Doug Simpson; the image was funded by the Henry Moore Foundation as part of *The Biography of a National Collection: the acquisition of casts of sculpture by the National Museum of Scotland* project led by Dr Sally Foster and Professor D.V. Clarke).

Plate 45. MM 135, Kermode's face B (photo: Judith Jesch).

Plate 46. MM 135 Braddan IV (photo: Judith Jesch).

Plate 47. MM 135 Braddan IV, rr. 1–19 (photo: Henrik Williams).

Plate 48. MM 135 Braddan IV, rr. 17–38 (photo: Henrik Williams).

Plate 49. MM 135 Braddan IV, rr. 37–52 and putative IHSVS (photo: Judith Jesch).

Plate 50. MM 176 Braddan V (photo: Jonas Nordby).

Plate 51. MM 200 Braddan VI (photo: Jonas Nordby).

Plate 52. MM 118, Kermode's face A (photo: Jonas Nordby).

Plate 53. MM 118, Kermode's face B (photo: Jonas Nordby).

Plate 54. MM 118 Bride (photo: Jonas Nordby).

Plate 55. MM 118 Bride, rr: 1–22 (photo: Jonas Nordby).

Plate 56. MM 118 Bride, rr: 21–45 (photo: Jonas Nordby).

Plate 57. MM 107, decorated face (photo: Jonas Nordby).

Plate 58. MM 107 German I (St John's) *a* (photo: Judith Jesch).

Plate 59. MM 107 German I (St John's) *a*, rr: 1–10 (photo: Jonas Nordby).

Plate 60. MM 107 German I (St John's) *a*, rr: 10–22 (photo: Jonas Nordby).

Plate 61. MM 107 German I (St John's) *a*, rr. 18–28 (photo: Jonas Nordby).

Plate 62. MM 107 German I (St John's) *b* (photo: Jonas Nordby).

Plate 63. MM 140 German II (Peel) (photo: Jonas Nordby).

Plate 64. MM 140 German II (Peel), rr. 1–18 (photo: Jonas Nordby).

Plate 65. MM 140 German II (Peel), rr. 13–30 (photo: Jonas Nordby).

Plate 66. MM 140 German II (Peel), rr. 27–41 (photo: Jonas Nordby).

Plate 67. MM 140 German II (Peel), rr. 35–41 in detail (photo: Jonas Nordby).

Plate 68. MM 127, Kermode's face A (image courtesy of Manx National Heritage, ref. MNH PG/1421 - MC127A).

Plate 69. MM 127 Jurby, Kermode's face B with the inscription (photo: Jonas Nordby).

Plate 70. MM 127 Jurby, Kermode's face B with the more fully preserved inscription in Robert Paterson's photograph of 1862 (image courtesy of Manx National Heritage, ref. MNH PG/13721 - MC127B).

Plate 71. MM 127 Jurby (photo: Jonas Nordby).

Plate 72. MM 102, Kermode's face A (image courtesy of Manx National Heritage, ref. MNH PG/13721 - MC102A).

Plate 73. MM 102 Kirk Michael I, Kermode's face B with the inscription (photo: Judith Jesch).

Plate 74. MM 102 Kirk Michael I (photo: Jonas Nordby).

Plate 75. MM 101, Kermode's face A (photo: Jonas Nordby).

Plate 76. MM 101 Kirk Michael II, Kermode's face B with rr. 65–84 visible at the top (photo: Jonas Nordby).

Plate 77. MM 101 Kirk Michael II, rr. 1–18 (photo: Jonas Nordby).

Plate 78. MM 101 Kirk Michael II, rr. 15–41 (photo: Jonas Nordby).

Plate 79. MM 101 Kirk Michael II, rr. 40–64 (photo: Jonas Nordby).

Plate 81. MM 101 Kirk Michael II, rr. 77–84 (photo: Jonas Nordby).

Plate 80. MM 101 Kirk Michael II, rr. 65–76 (photo: Jonas Nordby).

Plate 82. MM 130, Kermode's face A (photo: Judith Jesch).

Plate 83. MM 130 set into the top of the churchyard wall and showing Kermode's face A (image courtesy of Manx National Heritage, ref. MNH PG/14709 - MC130A).

Plate 84. MM 130 Kirk Michael III set against the churchyard wall and showing Kermode's face B with the inscription (image courtesy of Manx National Heritage, ref. MNH PG/14706 - MC130B).

Plate 85. MM 130 Kirk Michael III, rr. 1–17 (photo: Jonas Nordby).

Plate 86. MM 130 Kirk Michael III, rr. 13–30 (photo: Jonas Nordby).

Plate 87. MM 130 Kirk Michael III, rr. 24–47 (photo: Jonas Nordby).

Plate 88. MM 130 Kirk Michael III, rr. 36–61 (photo: Jonas Nordby).

Plate 89. MM 130 Kirk Michael III, rr: 51–71 (photo: Jonas Nordby).

Plate 90. MM 130 Kirk Michael III, rr: 72–96 (photo: Jonas Nordby).

Plate 91. MM 130 Kirk Michael III, rr. 85–103 (photo: Jonas Nordby).

Plate 92. MM 130, the ogam inscription on the runic face (photo: Jonas Nordby).

Plate 93. MM 126, Kermode's face A (photo: Judith Jesch).

Plate 94. MM 126, Kermode's face B (photo: Judith Jesch).

318

Plate 95. MM 126 Kirk Michael IV (image courtesy of Manx National Heritage, ref. MNH PG/13721 - MC126C).

Plate 96. MM 126 Kirk Michael IV, rr. 1–13 (photo: Jonas Nordby).

Plate 97. MM 126 Kirk Michael IV, rr. 12–22 (photo: Jonas Nordby).

Plate 98. MM 132, Kermode's face A (photo: Judith Jesch).

Plate 99. MM 132, Kermode's face B (photo: Judith Jesch).

Plate 100. MM 132 set on a horse block and showing Kermode's face B; right: Kirk Michael V from the same photograph (images courtesy of Manx National Heritage, ref. MNH PG/13721 - MC132B-C).

Plate 101. MM 132 Kirk Michael Va, rr. 1–14; preceding and below rr: 1–8 Kirk Michael Vb is visible (photo: Jonas Nordby).

Plate 102. MM 132 Kirk Michael Va, rr. 12–30 (photo: Jonas Nordby).

322

Plate 103. MM 132 Kirk Michael Va, rr. 25–43 (photo: Jonas Nordby).

Plate 104. MM 132 Kirk Michael Va, rr. 43–57 (photo: Jonas Nordby).

Plate 105. MM 132 Kirk Michael V*a*, rr. 52–7 and male figure above (photo: Judith Jesch).

Plate 106. MM 132 Kirk Michael Vb, rr. 1–13 (photo: Jonas Nordby).

Plate 107. MM 132 Kirk Michael Vb, rr. 12–26 (photo: Jonas Nordby).

Plate 108. MM 129, Kermode's face A (photo: Jonas Nordby).

Plate 109. MM 129, Kermode's face B (photo: Jonas Nordby).

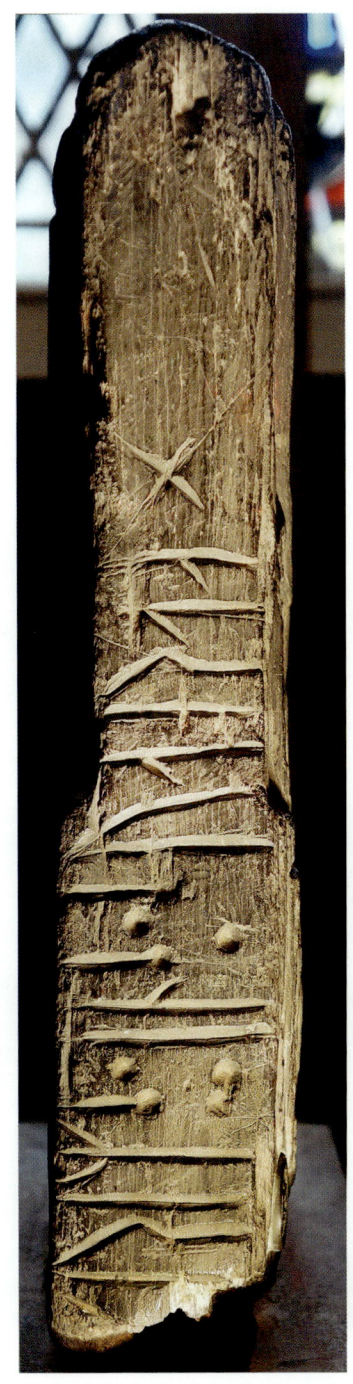

Plate 110. MM 129 Kirk Michael VI (photo: Judith Jesch).

Plate 111. MM 110, Kermode's face A (photo: Jonas Nordby).

Plate 112. MM 110, Kermode's face B (photo: Judith Jesch).

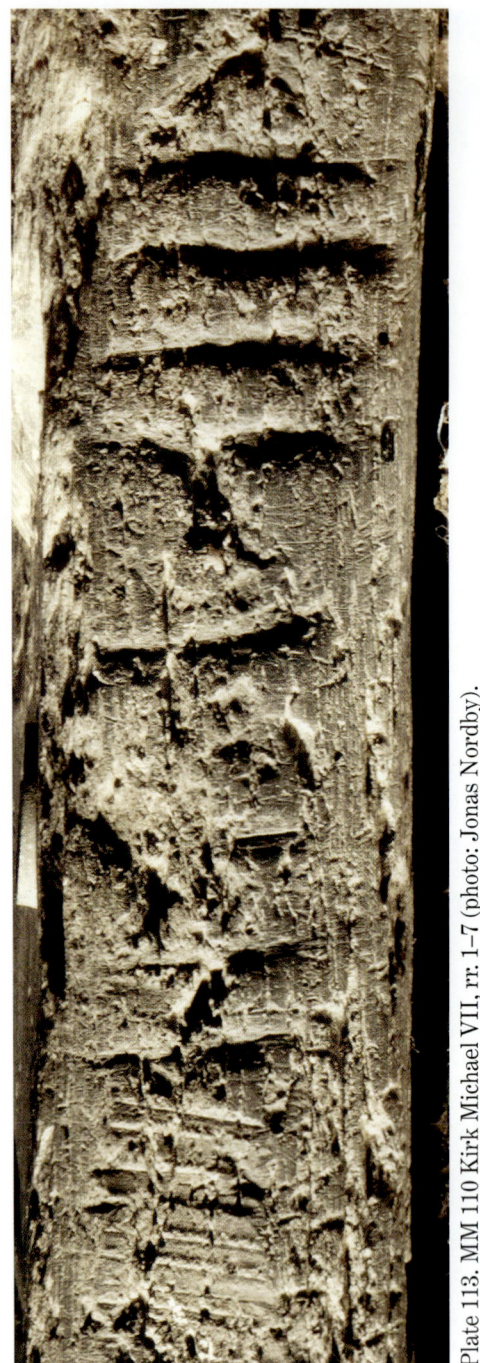

Plate 113. MM 110 Kirk Michael VII, rr. 1–7 (photo: Jonas Nordby).

Plate 114. MM 110 Kirk Michael VII, rr. 5–11 (photo: Jonas Nordby).

Plate 115. MM 123, the surviving face (photo: Jonas Nordby).

Plate 116. MM 123 Kirk Michael VIII (photo: Jonas Nordby).

332

Plate 117. MM 123 Kirk Michael VIII, rr: 1–7 in detail (photo: Jonas Nordby).

Plate 118. MM 123 Kirk Michael VIII, rr: 11–15 in detail (photo: Jonas Nordby).

Plate 119. MM 139 Marown, visible face with the inscription (photo: Jonas Nordby).

Plate 120. MM 139 Marown (photo: Jonas Nordby).

Plate 121. MM 145 Maughold I and the ogam inscription (photo: James Knirk).

Plate 122. MM 145 Maughold I (photo: James Knirk).

Plate 123. MM 145 Maughold I, rr. 30–36 in detail (photo: James Knirk).

336

Plate 124. MM 144 Maughold II, visible face with the inscription (photo: James Knirk).

337

Plate 125. MM 144 Maughold II, rr. 1–10 (photo: James Knirk).

Plate 126. MM 144 Maughold II, rr. 9–21 (photo: James Knirk).

Plate 127. MM 144 Maughold II, rr. 19–26 (photo: James Knirk).

Plate 128. MM 144 Maughold II, rr. 27–38 (photo: James Knirk).

Plate 129. MM 144 Maughold II, rr. 35–48 (photo: James Knirk).

Plate 130. MM 144 Maughold II, rr. 44–55 (photo: James Knirk).

339

Plate 131. MM 133, the surviving face (photo: James Knirk).

Plate 132. MM 133 Maughold III (photo: James Knirk).

Plate 133. MM 142 Maughold IV, "face A" with inscriptions IVa 1, IVa 2, and IVe visible (photo: Judith Jesch).

341

Plate 134. MM 142 Maughold IVa 1, rr. 1–18 (photo: Judith Jesch).

Plate 135. MM 142 Maughold IVa 1, rr. 17–31 (photo: Judith Jesch).

Plate 136. MM 142 Maughold IVa 2 (photo: Jonas Nordby).

Plate 137. MM 142 Maughold IV, "face B" with inscription IV*a* 3 and (faintly visible) IV*f* (photo: Jonas Nordby).

Plate 138. MM 142 Maughold IVa 3, rr. 1–12 with inscription IVf, rr. 1–11, below (photo: Jonas Nordby).

Plate 139. MM 142 Maughold IVa 3, rr. 7–19 with inscription IVf below (photo: Jonas Nordby).

Plate 140. MM 142 Maughold IVb (photo: Jonas Nordby).

Plate 141. MM 142 Maughold IVc and IVd with most of inscription IVb below (photo: Jonas Nordby).

Plate 142. MM 142 Maughold IVe (photo: Jonas Nordby).

Plate 143. MM 142 Maughold IVf (photo: Jonas Nordby).

Plate 144. MM 175 Maughold V (photo: Jonas Nordby).

Plate 145. MM 175 Maughold V, rr. 1–8 (photo: James Knirk).

Plate 146. MM 175 Maughold V, rr. 8–17 (photo: James Knirk).

Plate 147. MM 175 Maughold V, rr. 17–20 (photo: James Knirk).

Plate 148. MM 175 Maughold V, rr. 21–5 (photo: James Knirk).

Plate 149. MM 175 Maughold V, rr. 24–32 (photo: James Knirk).

Plate 150. MM 175 Maughold V, rr. 29–37 (photo: James Knirk).

Plate 151. MM 175 Maughold V, rr. 38–46 (photo: James Knirk).

Plate 152. MM 141 Onchan, Kermode's face A with Onchan *a*, *b*, and *c* (photo: Jonas Nordby).

Plate 153. MM 141 Onchan, Kermode's face B with Onchan *e, f*, and *g* (image courtesy of Manx National Heritage, ref. MNH PG/14708 - MC141B).

Plate 154. MM 141 Onchan, the photograph of Kermode's face B displayed in Kirk Onchan, showing Onchan *e, f,* and *g* (photo: Jonas Nordby).

Plate 155. MM 141 Onchan *a* (photo: Jonas Nordby).

354

Plate 156. MM 141 Onchan *b* (above) and *c* (below) (photo: Jonas Nordby).

Plate 157. MM 141 Onchan *d* (photo: Jonas Nordby).

Plate 158. MM 141 Onchan *e* on the photograph of Kermode's face B displayed in Kirk Onchan (photo: Jonas Nordby).

Plate 159. MM 141 Onchan *f* (right) and *g* (left, inverted in relation to *f*) on the photograph of Kermode's face B displayed in Kirk Onchan; below: Onchan *g*, rotated 180°, from the same photograph (photo: Jonas Nordby).

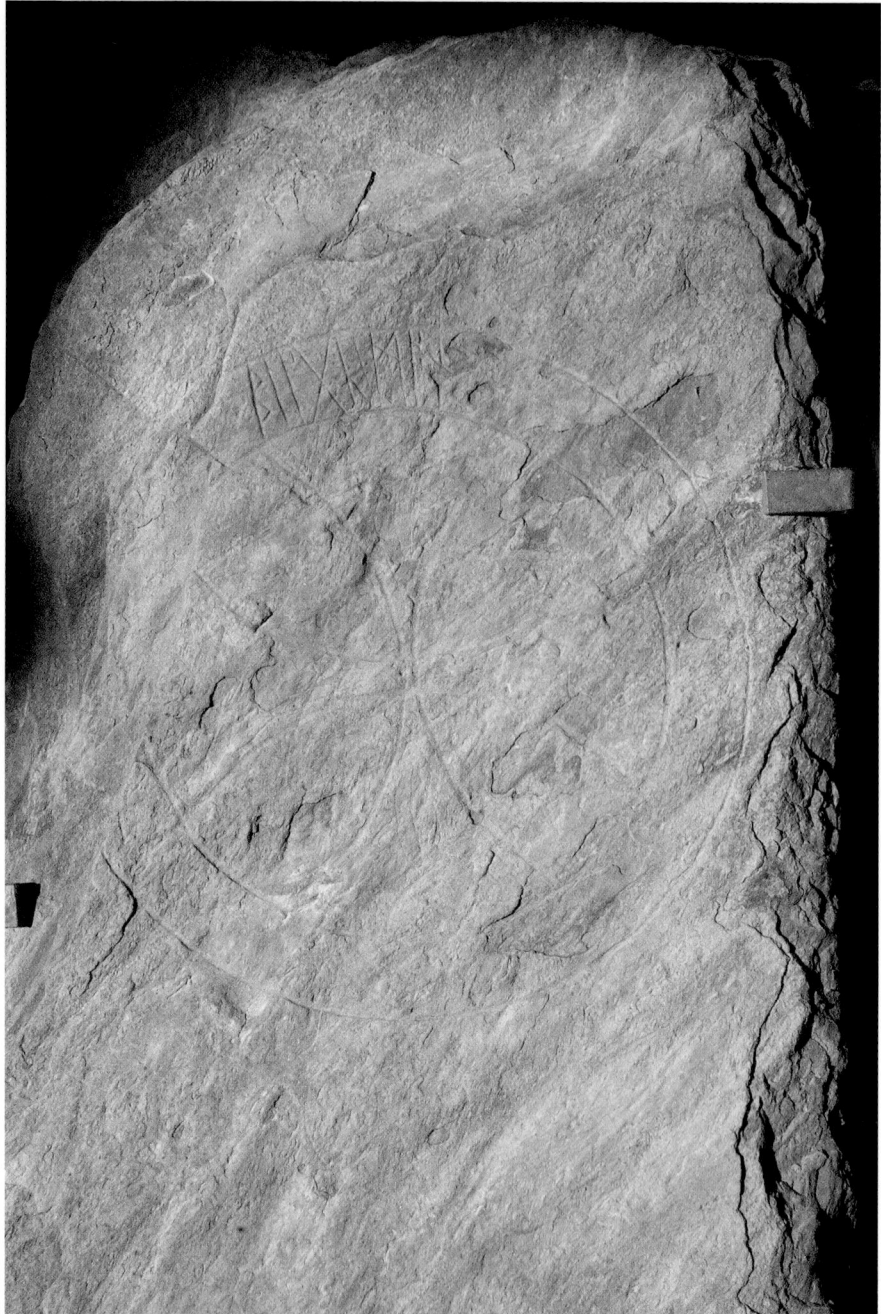

Plate 160. MM 42 Maughold AS I, the decorated face with design and inscription (photo: Jonas Nordby).

Plate 161. MM 42 Maughold AS I, main design and inscription (photo: Judith Jesch).

Plate 162. MM 42 Maughold AS I (photo: James Knirk).

Plate 164. MM 43 Maughold AS II (photo: James Knirk).

Plate 163. MM 43 Maughold AS II, the decorated face with design and inscription (image courtesy of Manx National Heritage, ref. MNH PG/1467 – MC43A).